From Mad Man
to Happy Farmer

From Mad Man
to Happy Farmer

Fifty-five Years of Sane, Sage Advice From a
Marketing Guru Still Crazy About the Ad Biz

HANK WASIAK

W. Brand Publishing
NASHVILLE, TENNESSEE

W. Brand Publishing
j.brand@wbrandpub.com
www.wbrandpub.com
Printed and bound in the United States of America.

Cover design by: Caroline Teagle
Photography by: Greg Lord

From Mad Man to Happy Farmer / Hank Wasiak – first edition

Available in Paperback, Kindle, and eBook formats.
Paperback ISBN 978-1-950385-48-5
eBook: 978-1-950385-49-2
Library of Congress Control Number: 2020921853

Dedication

This book is dedicated to:

My "greatest generation" mom and dad for their example and values instilled in me and my brother Ken and sister Ginny.

My wife Vicki for her love, support, and putting up with my antics and foibles for fifty-five years. For sticking with me through thick and thin and raising three great kids. I couldn't have done any of this without her.

My sons Brian, Gregg, and Jason for making me so proud of being their dad every day. Their creative talents are extraordinary—they get that from their mom. They're great guys and my best friends.

My grandson Lucas, an amazing young man whom I love to pieces. He makes me hopeful and joyful in knowing that the future is in his great hands.

In memory of:

My dear friend, business partner, and co-author Dr. Kathy Cramer and her life-changing gift of Asset-Based Thinking. She was and is my positivity muse.

Beyond a Book

An Interactive Journey

This book is an amalgam of a career memoir (my story), advice forum (Mad Man & Happy Farmer Wisdom) and marketing manual (Marketing Truisms & Tips). Decade by decade, it simultaneously chronicles the fifty-five-year evolution of my career and of the art and science of marketing communications.

From the outset, I wanted to design a more interactive reader experience. As such, the book has a companion resource website—madmanhappyfarmer.com— featuring videos, print ads, and other content featured in my stories so you're just one click or scan away from experiencing them in real time. You can find clickable links in the chapter footnotes and there are scannable QR codes for the website content at the end of each chapter. Have fun with them.

The website is a living and growing resource that includes addendum material that keeps the narrative flowing. Check back often and please reach out to me with any questions, ideas, or comments at hank@madmanhappyfarmer.com.

Thanks for reading my book and I look forward to hearing from you.

Hank Wasiak

www.madmanhappyfarmer.com

Mad Man to Happy Farmer Website

Table of Contents

Introduction

The ad game has been very, very good to me.

I've spent almost six decades living and loving advertising and marketing communications. Here are the four big reasons why I love the playing field as much today as I did when I first suited up in the mad-men era.

First, marketing is the rocket fuel that powers the engines of business today. The essence of marketing is the ability to move people to take action—from purchasing a product or service, to building communities of like-minded people, to saving lives, and everything in between. Marketing provides an awesome opportunity (and an even more profound responsibility) to create loyalists and build momentum.

Second, marketing is a magnificent mix of science, art, and common sense. The science requires you to think logically and rationally based on facts, circumstances, and data, to connect the dots and develop strategies. The art of marketing demands that you then switch gears entirely. The science-driven preparatory work becomes the guiding force and inspiration for the out-of-this-world creativity that brings a concept, a brand, or a campaign to life. The common-sense element cautions you to put aside your marketing jargon and speak directly to people on a human level. You need the right balance of all three to be effective. It's a symbiotic relationship.

Third, at its core, marketing is a people-driven business. That's become a bit of a cliché in business today, but in marketing it's a core truth. People and their understanding of others create the strategies, ideas, and tactics that inspire great marketing—not algorithms, formulas, machine learning, or artificial intelligence. Yes, all of those are important tools, but they are enablers not creators. In marketing, you can only be your best if you respect and enjoy working with a talented and eclectic mix of people with different skills. Ego is the enemy of great marketing. Leave it at home, be flexible, and expect the unexpected.

Fourth is change. Marketing holds an unfiltered mirror to society and culture and, as such, evolves with it. Being able to adopt and adapt to change has always been essential for success. It keeps you on your toes and in a constant learning loop.

Today feels like constant change on steroids. Digital transformation has brought about more change in the last decade than the last half century combined. The old playbooks are being shredded. It's exciting to be part of creating new ones.

Why I wrote this book

There's a great Sean Rowe song I listen to often called, "To Leave Something Behind." That's exactly what this book is all about: my leaving something behind by sharing my decades of life experiences, marketing wisdom, and Asset-Based Thinking advice. It is my time to give back and pay it forward.

But…who am I that I have something to give back?

I'm a grizzled and grateful ad guy that's been in the business for fifty-five years—from the go-go Mad Men era at the industry's biggest firms like, Benton & Bowles, Doyle Dane Bernbach, McCann Erickson and Ketchum, to today working with our award-winning digital agency in New York, Concept Farm. I spent seven years of that time on the client side running divisions of Brown-Forman, Norton Simon, and Charles of the Ritz. I've seen it all and done it all and am fortunate to have a rare, longitudinal perspective and insight into what makes for marketing success.

When I started my career in 1965, it was a watershed time with the advent of television and modern marketing practices. We are now well into the midst of another exciting watershed time in marketing: the digital transformation. I have a pretty firm grip on how to succeed in today's digital era and what the future of marketing communications holds. And guess what? The future that I see is fantastic.

After all these years I am even more passionate about the power of positivity in marketing as a force for good and progress. At the same time, I'm concerned that in today's digital world of 24/7 instant communication, short-term thinking, and even shorter attention spans, there is a serious risk of devaluing and devolving the core marketing fundamentals and personal values essential for success. I want to share my wisdom and experience to help next-generation leaders get it right and contribute to the brilliant, bright future that I see.

I want the next generation of business and marketing leaders to be as excited and inspired by the wonderful world of possibilities as I am. I'm in my seventies and I don't have thirty years to make the most of this future but they do. You do.

I hope this book will instill in you the same passion that I have for how far you (and marketing) can go.

Why you should read this book

I have an interesting story to tell for anyone considering a career in marketing and advertising. For you, this book will no doubt offer a unique take on a profession and career in which you just might spend the rest of your life. For others, it's an inside look at how a mad man survived and thrived in a business that is constantly changing. Enjoy the stories…I certainly enjoyed living them.

But just to get it all out up front: This book is not an old Mad Man longing for the good old days of marketing and advertising. Quite the contrary.

I believe the future of marketing is stronger and better than ever. Not because of the often-over-hyped deluge of data available to marketers, but rather for data's ability to help marketers better serve consumers, to enliven and liberate creativity, and to have an exponentially bigger positive impact.

Today, Walt Disney's quote, "If you can dream it, you can do it," is more than motivational encouragement. In marketing communications, it's a reality. And along with that reality comes the responsibility to harness that potential wisely. I provide some encouraging foresight (bolstered by my hindsight) on how to do that.

I share valuable lessons learned from past marketing campaigns I've been directly involved with, ones that resonate even more loudly today. I also offer a glimpse into content I've developed for my University of Southern California classes about current marketing campaigns and what makes them work (or not). Together, they provide valuable lessons you can take with you and apply throughout your career.

Last, I have a very powerful way of looking at my experiences that I believe is important to share. Later in my life, I had the good fortune to team up with Dr. Kathy Cramer, a celebrated psychologist and leadership expert at The Cramer Institute. Kathy pioneered Asset-Based Thinking (ABT), a mindset management process that shows you how to look at yourself and the world through the eyes of what is working, what strengths are present, and what the potentials are. It literally "changes the way you see everything," which, not at all coincidentally, was the title of the first book we co-authored.

Kathy and I co-authored three successful books based on Asset-Based Thinking principles. We were Madison Avenue meets Positive Psychology, an unlikely match made in heaven. I now look at everything through the ABT lens of what is working and possible instead of what is problematic and broken. And that's exactly the mindset I believe is needed in today's world of digital communications. Among other things, this book will show you how ABT has directed the course of my life for the better.

Previously, I mentioned that Sean Rowe song that I like. Here's my favorite lyric:

> *I can get through the wall if you give me a door.*
> *So, I can leave something behind.*

I hope this book can be a door that helps get you through the walls that you may encounter so you have the opportunity to leave your something behind.

A special shout-out

I've often thought about writing a book like this, but it took a nudge from one of my University of Southern California students to get me off my butt to do it. Izzy Sellon was working on a project for another class in which she had to interview a person about how and why they started their business career, write a brief report, and present it. I was delighted that she chose me.

We met after class for what was to be short discussion. I started at the beginning of my story and once I got rolling it was hard to stop. Izzy didn't want me to stop either. We spent over an hour discussing my experiences and choices and how it could help Izzy shape her career. I was energized by the process.

Izzy told me, "Wow this is a great story with valuable lessons. You should share it with the class." Then I thought, why not share with everyone? So, here we are. Thanks, Izzy.

Chapter 1:

Don't Let Where You Come From Dictate Where You Go

I sometimes think of my life in the context of Betty Smith's classic novel, *A Tree Grows In Brooklyn*. The roots of my tree are firmly planted in Brooklyn and from there grew into a bountiful tree of life with four main branches: Family, Career, Teaching, and Volunteering.[1] My story is about a middle-class, blue-collar kid from Brooklyn who messed up a lot yet managed to rise to the highest levels of the advertising and marketing world replete with three-martini lunches, first-class travel budgets, and expense accounts larger than my family's annual food budget growing up. It's about my almost six-decade career that started in the Mad Men era and is still going today. My story is full of twists and turns, interesting people and experiences, and fulfillment that I never imagined possible.

It just goes to show…where you come from doesn't dictate where you go or grow.

Prequel: Everyone's story has a beginning…here's mine.

I was born in Bay Ridge Brooklyn on July 5, 1943.

My dad Henry was the son of Polish immigrants (yes, I'm a Junior). He was a New York City fireman and worked on the side as a janitor in our apartment building for extra cash.

My mom Josephina Candida Sierra was the daughter of Cuban immigrants. She worked part-time as a sales clerk in a children's clothing store. My older brother Ken, younger sister Ginny, and I were always very well-dressed.

The five of us shared a two-bedroom, one-bathroom apartment in a three-story walk up—we definitely were a close family.

A product of the Catholic school system, I managed to survive eight years with Notre Dame nuns at St. Anselm's school (my knuckles still hurt) and four years with the Xaverian Brothers at Xaverian High School. Xaverian was a new, boys-only Catholic high school that required tuition payments. My parents really wanted me to go there so the deal was that I would get a job and contribute to the school cost—not a lot, just enough to ease their burden and teach me the value of work. And so at age fourteen, I took over my brother's job as a delivery/stock-boy at Christiansen's Norwegian delicatessen. It was my first exposure to real potato salad, lutefisk, and honest work. Mom and dad instilled in me the importance of a strong work ethic and my first job in that deli helped me realize that working hard was the way to get what I wanted.

---

1. My Life Tree https://bit.ly/BklynTree

Since then, I've always had a job working at something.

But I also messed up. A lot.

From an early age, I spent most of my time playing and growing up on the streets of Brooklyn; I just had to be home by sundown. As I got into my teenage years, that curfew evaporated and the streets, parks, local hang-outs, and pool halls became my second home.

I had a few different circles of teen friends but spent most of my time with the more adventurous and rebellious types—tough, rough-and-tumble guys, some of whom regularly got into serious trouble. We called ourselves The Rebels.

For me, it was more run-of-the-mill trouble making: pranks, fights, and pushing boundaries. But I'll never forget the time when a few friends thought it would fun to steal a car and I went along for the joy ride. We were caught by the police and brought to the 64th precinct station house, which happened to be right around the corner from my apartment. As we stood in front of the sergeant's desk, my father walked by the window and saw me. He was shocked. Fortunately, the owner of the car knew one of my friends and decided not to press charges.

We were off the hook with the justice system, but I faced the music at home, big time. Dad yelled a lot, mom cried, and I was put under house arrest for a month. My mother, who was very religious, personally escorted me to confession at St. Anslem's church. That had an impact. I began to realize that my actions had ripple effects and I've tried to remind myself of that as life progressed. You know, look—back *and* ahead—before you leap.

Despite that experience, a year later I made a potentially more serious mistake. I accepted a ride home from two friends in what I knew was a stolen car. Not smart. Fortunately, I resisted their urging to stay out and instead had them drop me home for dinner. I didn't want to repeat my past mistake and end up in front of that sergeant's desk—or in the confessional—again. About an hour after I was dropped off, they had a serious accident with the car, were apprehended, convicted, and served some jail time. That could have been me.

And so early on I learned the pitfalls and perils of being overly influenced and swayed by others. That saved me from making even bigger mistakes later on in both my personal and business life. Sure I valued the advice and input of others, but ultimately, I relied on my gut and instincts to make the right decisions for my life. For example, if I had followed advice I received about not switching jobs as quickly or how crazy I was to move our family to Manhattan in the 1970s, I would have missed out on some of the most rewarding experiences of my career. I learned to be selective and true to myself.

College or else

Despite being a kind of a wild, know-it-all misbehaving teen, I did pretty well in high school. Fortunately, Brother Merrick, my Latin teacher (yes, Latin) took a liking to me and gave me some frank talk and advice that I took. Brother M convinced me that I was on a precarious path and that I needed to go to college or I'd wind up in other less hospitable institutions. He knew I had the academic skills and gave me the push I needed to get on the right path. Brother Merrick also advised me not to go to a Catholic college. He said that after twelve years of having my education filtered through the same lens and being in classrooms with like-minded and like-looking people, it was time to get out of my comfort zone. I agreed.

Fordham and St. John's were the default Catholic college choices in New York City at that time so he steered me to a more secular education at Pace College in lower Manhattan. Pace was primarily a business school with an ethnic and religiously diverse student population. It was just the exposure I needed.

I graduated from Xaverian and started at Pace three months later as an ambivalent college freshman not at all sure of where I wanted this to lead. I lived at home, commuted to school on the NYC subway (about forty-five minutes), and, for me, campus life was non-existent. The tuition was $40 per credit; with 120 credits needed to graduate, that meant about $5,000 for my college degree. Again, I split the cost with my parents, landing an after-school job at the Home Insurance Company. Luckily, I was also able to make a little spending money shooting pool on Park Row, a skill well-honed in Brooklyn. I now see how having to contribute to both my high school and college tuition spurred me to do well and make the most of my education. Having some skin in the game is a great motivator.

When it came to selecting a major, I had no clue what to do. No one in my family circle had yet attended college or was in the business world, so I winged it. I went down the list of majors. The first was accounting...not for me. The Joseph Trimble real estate and accounting office was on the ground floor of our apartment building in Brooklyn and although the people who worked there were nice, they were much too serious and, to be honest, a bit boring.

Next was advertising. That sounded interesting. As a kid I spent a lot of time in front of our Dumont TV set and enjoyed watching the commercials. I can still sing the Pepsodent toothpaste jingle.

"You'll wonder where the yellow went when you brush your teeth with Pepsodent."

So I checked the advertising box. When you don't have resources or experience to lean on you just have to bet on your gut. Don't be afraid to guess. Sometimes a SWAG is all you have.[2] And it's essentially how I picked the career in which I would spend the rest of my life. Not very scientific. It just happened. And it worked.

There I was in 1961, eighteen years old, on the first stepping stone to the rest of my life.

---

2. Scientific Wild-Ass Guess

A foot in the door is your first step

At Pace I took a few marketing communications and research courses with excellent professors who made the material engaging and piqued my interest in the field. It was the first subject that really sparked my attention and imagination. I felt good about where I was headed but I was also impatient. I wanted to get on with things and prove myself in the real world. I took extra courses and graduated in three-and-a-half years. In January 1965, I became the first Xaverian High School college graduate. Thanks again Brother Merrick! For once, I made my impatience work for me.

I mentioned that I worked my way through college at the Home Insurance Company. That job did more than help pay for my college; it opened the door to the best decision I would make in my life.

Home Insurance hired college students to work afternoons and evenings in their policy discrepancy department. We basically reconciled paperwork errors—not very challenging, but no pressure and paid a decent hourly rate. There were about fifteen of us, all male, from different colleges in Manhattan.

Our department shared the floor with the secretarial pool, about forty young women. We were seated right outside the ladies' restroom. It doesn't take much imagination to see how that dynamic could play out. But we behaved, had some good-natured fun and back-and-forth banter and, eventually, after-work get-togethers with the ladies. The women even had fun nicknames for each of us. Later on, I found out mine was Babyface.

There was one secretary who caught my eye and then captured my heart: Vicki Pandullo. Vicki was a petite, pretty, confident, Italian girl from Staten Island. She had a friendly, disarming smile and never seemed to get frazzled. After getting to know each other at work, Vicki and I began dating. We got engaged on December 21, 1963, were married on February 6, 1965, and are still together. It was the best decision I ever made.

I was getting married one month after graduation and desperately needed a job. The professors at Pace often held up big consumer packaged goods companies as examples of best practices in marketing and great places to start a career. I was really keen on finding a position at a company like General Foods, Johnson & Johnson, or Procter and Gamble. I applied for marketing jobs at a number of client companies and a few of their ad agencies but at that time those types of companies were only hiring MBAs from Ivy League schools. A kid from Brooklyn with a Pace BBA degree really had no chance.

Fortunately, their rejections also opened up opportunities.

My resumé connected with someone at P&G and they referred me to Benton and Bowles (B&B) and Grey, both large, top-tier agencies that were flourishing in those Mad Men days. B&B's human resource (HR) person Kent Kroeber called me in for an interview. Remember his name for later. Kent hired me as media department trainee at a salary of $100 per week—big bucks for me! A great first job. I was offered another position at Grey for $80 a week and turned that one down.

Vicki and I celebrated our wedding and after a one-week honeymoon in the Poconos, I started working at B&B. It was February 1965. The media trainees sat in cubicles, put in long hours, and worked in rooms full of Nielsen, Arbitron, and SRDS books, printed reference books that contained thousands of pages of television, radio, and magazine audience data used to develop media plans and evaluate their effectiveness. There were no computers; we used calculators and slide rules and did analytics the old-fashioned way. We looked things up, copied numbers, and made spreadsheets by hand. It was very hands-on hard work—literally and figuratively—and I enjoyed it.

But it definitely wasn't all work and no play. Far from it. In those days, the big media companies like Time Inc. and the TV networks constantly wined and dined media people. We held the keys to the budgets. I dined and drank at some of the best restaurants in town and had too many three-martini lunches, evening parties, and boondoggles. I worked late, partied later, and was hooked on the industry. What can I say, it was it was the '60s. I felt pretty good about things.

Among my childhood Brooklyn friends and Xaverian classmates only Tom Prendergast, my best friend and fellow Rebel, went on to work in advertising. Tom had a successful career in the magazine publishing side of the business. We had many fun-filled Madison Avenue adventures, the majority of which are not fit for print. We stay in touch regularly and Tom told me to include him in the book or else. Promise fulfilled.[3]

Now at age twenty-one, the stage was set. A Bachelor of Business Administration Degree, married, and a good entry-level job, I was ready to start my family and career.

Mad Man Wisdom

- The past is just prologue. Don't make it an anchor that holds you back.
- Mistakes happen. Learn from them, don't repeat them.
- Family is your best asset. Love and lean on them always.
- Be open to advice—especially when you think you know it all.
- But also be selective and make your own decisions.
- Cultivate your work ethic early. Embed it in your DNA.
- Put skin in the game. Take on responsibilities and invest in yourself.

---

3. If you want to see how two Brooklyn punks looked at fourteen years old and later at sixty, click the link. You'll enjoy it. https://bit.ly/hankandtom

- Turn rejection into resolve. There are always other options.
- Be grateful and proud when you cross that first big career threshold.

Marketing Truisms and Tips

Is Marketing Really For You?

First, is a marketing or advertising career right for you? You won't know for sure until you're in the thick of it, but here's my short list of important personality traits you should have and the skills you'll need to develop. See how you stack up and if you're ready to make the commitment.

You should be a person who:
- Enjoys working with people
- Is a good listener
- Has imagination
- Respects and values creativity
- Can make decisions and be flexible
- Is resilient and can handle rejection
- Isn't afraid or intimidated by change
- Has common sense and a sense of humor

You should have and be developing your skills in:
- Communication (written and in person)
- Storytelling
- Persuasion
- Analytics and insight discovery capabilities
- Multi-tasking
- Signature presence (your personal brand)
- Tolerance and flexibility
- Humility

Chapter 1 Footnotes
Scan QR codes for direct links to footnote content.

1.1 A Tree Grows in Brooklyn

1.3 Hank & Tom Brooklyn Boys

Chapter 2:

Forget Perfection, Pursue Progress

I started my career with expectations of landing the perfect first job: a brand management trainee at a major packaged goods company. This was the dream job I'd heard about in my business school classes. But I didn't fully recognize the prerequisites needed for securing such a position. When that reality sunk in, I switched to a next-best progress mindset. I accepted that perfection does not exist—especially in a first job out of college—I let go of my expectations and pushed ahead.

My reality was a media position at Benton & Bowles—more than good enough to get me started on my path, but a number-four ranking on my perfect job scale. First was brand management, second was any client marketing job, third was agency account management, and next was media. Luckily, my progress mindset kept me focused, realistic, and restless. And as I pursued progress instead of perfection more doors swung open and different, unexpected opportunities arose.

My media experience helped me secure my first account executive position at B&B. Pushing for new business extra work connected me to the agency chairman, Ted Steele, and brought my assignment to the Avis pitch team. One move led to another and five years later I had progressed to where I *wanted* to be, even though that was not where I had *expected* to be. I had expected to be on the client side as a brand manager and I wound up on the agency side working with client brand managers. And that was just fine. It was the best of both worlds and I loved it.

It just goes to show…it's not about perfection, it's about progress.

Building my foundation

Before getting into my experiences at Benton & Bowles, I need to share three important events that occurred around the start of my career.

> **1. My family grew.** Six months into the job at B&B, my wife Vicki and I were delighted to find out that we were expecting our first child. Our son Brian was born in April 1966. In December 1967, his brother Gregg joined the family. We were blessed. It also meant we would need extra income to replace Vicki's salary.

2. I joined a band. A friend of mine played in a local band, The Rogues, and they were looking for a bass guitar player. I had some rudimentary guitar skills and a mediocre singing voice but somehow I managed to land the job. I became a Rogue.[1] On weekends, we played the local clubs in Brooklyn and Staten Island for twenty-five dollars each per gig. I had fun, met interesting people, encountered some unusual situations (that's another book), and did not get a lot of sleep. Rolling into B&B on Monday mornings was a very big challenge. That lasted about two years.

3. I earned my MBA and began teaching. Early on in my advertising career, I knew that I wanted to teach college as my sideline. To have a shot at that I needed a master's degree. My impatience kicked in again and in September 1965, I enrolled at New York City College's Baruch School of Business. I attended evening classes for two-and-a-half years, earning my MBA in Marketing Management in February 1968. Six months later, I was teaching night school business classes at the New York City Community College in Brooklyn. The decision to earn my MBA enabled the second career as a college professor that has meant so much to me over the years. The opportunity to bring my business experience to the classroom and contribute to a student's education has been worth every dollar and hour spent on earning my MBA. Now I tell my students: Always be on the lookout for ways you can expand your repertoire, give back, *and* pay it forward. For me, teaching has been the gift that keeps on giving back.

Looking back, I realize that balancing all of these aspects of my life—work, school, band, and young children—was a bit ambitious and a big ask of my family. Today it's called managed multitasking. Back then it was called "doing what you gotta do to get shit done." Luckily, the best time to take on too much and have lots of balls in the air is early in your career. That's when you have the energy and drive to put your heart and soul into making it all work. More importantly, you develop a conviction and commitment mindset that strengthens your tenacity muscles. Both will serve you well throughout your career. They sure did for me.

---

1. Here's The Rogues' publicity photo. I was heavier then. https://bit.ly/roguesBklyn

Decision affirmed

My five years at Benton & Bowles were invaluable and set the stage for my entire career. When I checked the advertising major box at Pace and took the job at B&B, I had no idea if I would actually like it. After a few months, I realized the advertising business was for me. I was nurtured by some of the best Mad Men in the business. I was learning constantly, meeting great people, and I really enjoyed the work (and the play). I was confident that I made the right career decision.

Fortunately for me, my decision was affirmed. That doesn't always happen in life. For some people that first year or two in a new career can go in another direction. I urge young people in those early years to listen to your soul, your heart, *and* your head. Be honest with yourself. If your initial choice doesn't feel right, face it. Count your blessings that you've rescued your future. Whatever you learned will be an asset to you regardless. When you pursue progress, not perfection, you build more personal assets faster. Take your experiences with you and apply them to finding *your* place, rather than the *perfect* place. Everything is a stepping stone to something else. Don't settle. You will get there.

Wonderment and firsts

The B&B office was located at 666 Fifth Avenue, home of the famous Top of The Sixes Restaurant. I would get on the subway in Brooklyn, get off an hour later at the Fifth Avenue station, and step out into what felt like a fairy tale for me. Just steps away were The Museum of Modern Art, Rockefeller Center, St. Patrick's Cathedral, The Plaza, Central Park, The 21 Club, and Madison Avenue. I was right in the middle of the heartbeat of Manhattan and the advertising business. This was my new neighborhood. The energy and excitement were contagious and I loved it.

Working with people from different backgrounds, countries, and cultures was new and exciting to me. Every day brought fresh experiences and connections. I never knew whose office I would be in next. One meeting was particularly memorable. Part of my job was coordinating commercial talent payments and contracts with our TV and radio department. I was called into a meeting with the department vice president, Mr. Bartholomew. To my surprise, Mr. B turned out to be Freddie Bartholomew, the legendary child superstar from my favorite classic films: *David Copperfield, Captains Courageous, Swiss Family Robinson*, and many others. Man, was I impressed. Freddie grew up to be a very nice adult and a pleasure to work with. He was a star at B&B.

B&B was the catalyst for so many firsts for me. First flight, first business trip, first travel outside New York to cities like Cincinnati and Los Angeles, first commercial shoot, and so many others. Today, these firsts don't seem all that eventful but for this Brooklyn boy they were amazing opportunities and adventures.

But the "first" that made the biggest and most lasting impression on me? After six months I was given my first-ever job performance review (a good grade!) and received my first pay raise of ten percent. Ten dollars more per week! I really liked how that felt and was determined to make that raise the first of many.

Putting my hand up

I liked the fast-paced environment of the media department, but after six months I knew I wanted to get into account management. The account teams were the hub of the agency. The "account man" directed and managed the agency's work flow and output across all departments, was responsible for client relations, and, essentially, was the lynch-pin on an account.[2] What drew me to the role was how the account executives (AEs) regularly interacted and collaborated with the creative teams. The account execs developed creative briefs with the creative teams and provided the information needed to inform and inspire creative development. The most effective and valued account execs kept the administrative BS to a minimum and found constructive ways to be invited into the creative process. You had to earn it. I set my sights on being the AE that was invited in.

But at B&B it was almost impossible to make the move from media to account management. Rarely did they let a media guy go up to the account floor. Nevertheless, I was determined to leverage my media job to get where I wanted to go.

I needed to make my own breaks, so I volunteered with a few account supervisors to help with special projects and show them what I could do. I kept putting my hand up and asking, "How can I help?" and it worked. About nine months later, one of the top account people, Tom Griffin (who later founded his own agency, Griffin & Bacal) requested me for the assistant account executive position on two General Foods test products: Orange Plus (which failed) and Cool Whip (a great success!). With Tom's support, I made that coveted move from media to the account group and I knew right away that this was for me. Another decision affirmed.

In addition to all the analytics, administrative tasks, and strategic work required to run an account, I liked that it was much more people focused. If you couldn't get along with and motivate people you would fail as an AE. Fortunately, getting along with people came naturally to me so I felt comfortable with the relationship aspect of the position. I had found my niche. Then another of my mentors, Roy Bostock (who went on to be president of B&B and chairman of Yahoo!) promoted me to be a full account executive on the agency's flagship business: P&G. I was assigned to Zest soap and Charmin toilet tissue.

---

2. In the '60s, they were all "account men." Female account executives were a rarity.

Learning the fundamentals

Having made it to the account group, I decided to really dig in, be a sponge, and soak up as much as I could from as many people as possible. Starting in media had given me a leg up. I already had a good relationship with my media colleagues and was well-versed in media basics. Bringing those assets with me to my AE position meant I could focus my time on developing new skills in budgeting, market analysis, production and creative development. (See? Everything's a stepping stone).

I was fortunate to be assigned to powerhouse consumer goods companies like P&G and General Foods but, boy, were they demanding clients. P&G in particular required buttoned-up account managers on their business who were essentially shadow brand managers. Working with P&G provided a best practices grounding in the fundamentals of successful marketing communications management.

A key learning for me was the critical role of a formal written brand positioning statement. Positioning defines the brand's reason for being for consumers. Brand equity is built by living up to and into that positioning every day. It's the platform upon which all brand behavior and communications are built. The creative brief and creative development cannot proceed without a brand positioning statement—no exceptions. This marketing rule is just as important today.[3] I also learned that a key responsibility of the brand manager and agency account person is to ensure the following:

- Rock-solid brand positioning informed and refined by consumer insights
- Full embrace and cultural infusion of the positioning within the brand/agency teams
- Marketing communications that consistently and responsibly bring the positioning to life

This and other best practices I acquired back then have empowered me throughout my career and are even more relevant today (more on that at the end of the chapter).

Communicating with confidence

I worked with P&G brand managers every day on marketing planning, competitive analyses,

---

3. Today's marketers often dismiss the importance of positioning statements in order to satisfy the 24/7, real-time content demands of digital media. This results in fragmented messaging and a diffused brand. A strong brand positioning statement is more valuable and important than ever. In my USC class, I devote two lectures to the discipline and art of positioning statements.

and agency recommendations—lots of them. Every agency recommendation and point-of-view had to be in writing, clear and succinct. I still remember being constantly reminded by my supervisors that P&G did not tolerate "page-two" thinkers. You had to convincingly make the case on the first page of any recommendation; everything else that followed was support. That's a good practice for any type of communication, especially in today's short attention-span environment.

There was one rather daunting requirement of the job that could literally make or break your career at the agency: P&G's annual marketing plan budget presentation. It struck fear and trepidation into every account man. I worked closely with the brand managers to create the annual marketing plans for Charmin and Zest and wrote a significant number of sections. That was demanding enough, but the AE also had to present the plans to P&G's top management.

Just imagine what it was like at age twenty-five to be center stage with all those heavyweights scrutinizing my performance. It demanded weeks of stressful, nerve-racking preparation—and it was worth it. I learned the importance of preparation, cooperation, and collaboration. I learned not to be intimidated by big important meetings and presentations. After my first trial by fire I began seeking them out. Never pass on an opportunity to stand up and stand out. Prepare, work your ass off, be confident, take center stage, and go for it.

I learned that success in marketing requires:

- Self confidence
- The ability to develop and craft convincing written recommendations
- The presentation skills to sell them up the chain of command

These three skills are a winning trifecta; do everything you can early in your career to master them. In Asset-Based Thinking terms it's called developing your Signature Presence: the way your unique combination of passions, capabilities, qualities, values, and beliefs show up when you are at your best. Let *you* shine through and weave your Signature Presence into everything you write, say, and do. Then watch what happens.

My creative awakening

I was lucky to be in on the early development of one of the most successful advertising campaigns of all time: the Mr. Whipple campaign for P&G's Charmin toilet tissue.

"Please don't squeeze the Charmin!"[4]

The campaign debuted in late 1964 and was based on the premise that Charmin toilet paper was so irresistibly soft that people just couldn't resist squeezing it, especially in supermarkets.

---

4. Whipple campaign history http://bit.ly/2PhUpEX

Mr. George Whipple, portrayed by actor Dick Wilson, was the store manager obsessed with keeping his customers from squeezing the Charmin.[5] Not an easy task. And, of course, he couldn't resist it either and was often caught sneaking a squeeze himself.

Sounds silly? Sure. But it worked. It worked because the campaign focused on an entertaining, fresh, and simple way to express and demonstrate the primary consumer benefit: softness. The campaign lightheartedly asked people not to squeeze the Charmin so, of course, they couldn't resist. Reverse psychology works!

Most importantly, the campaign had what we called Whipple magic. Mr. Whipple captured people's hearts and earned their loyalty. The campaign ran for twenty years with over 500 commercials chronicling Mr. Whipple's trials and tribulations as the guardian of Charmin's softness.[6] The advertising delighted consumers, generated mega sales, and built a powerful brand. In 1978, Mr. Whipple was the third most-known person in America–behind President Nixon and Billy Graham–and "Please don't squeeze the Charmin!" was named the most recognized advertising slogan.[7] It was a huge success by every measure and a once-in-a-lifetime experience for me.

The creative director on the account was Sid Lerner, a very nice, talented guy who taught me a lot. Remember him for later. Working with Sid on Charmin opened my eyes to the power of consumer-benefit-focused creativity and how the brilliant execution of a campaign can be the key differentiator in building a successful brand.

The B&B creative philosophy at that time was, "One strong, simple selling idea dramatically presented." The Charmin campaign was a powerful example of that philosophy in action. Over the years Sid's wisdom and that B&B philosophy has stuck with me and I believe is even more relevant today.

From Sid, I learned the importance of nurturing and protecting the integrity of a campaign idea as well as how to grow its popularity and effectiveness over time. He also schooled me in the art of managing character-based campaigns. For example, we were always on guard for what was affectionately called "Whipple wear-out" with consumers. Exploring ways to keep the campaign fresh, relevant, and unexpected without pushing it too far was on ongoing process. Also, as was policy for P&G, we worked diligently on alternate campaigns so there would always be a back-up waiting if Mr. Whipple began to fizzle. Fortunately, he didn't. We developed six alternate campaigns—none of them came close to Mr. Whipple.[8]

My once-in-a-lifetime Charmin experience built my conviction in the power of an idea and

---

5. The inspiration for Whipple's name came from B&B's PR director-George Whipple. P&G paid him one dollar for his name and the rest is history. A steal.

6. Original Whipple commercial and pool-outs. https://bit.ly/WhippleCampaign

7. Charmin history: http://bit.ly/CharminHistory

8. Alternate Whipple campaign exploratory. Have fun. https://bit.ly/charmin-alternate

my commitment to being a champion of creative work. I have brought that mindset to every position I've had throughout my career since and it has served me very well. Be a champion of big ideas and become a creative evangelist as soon as you can—whether you're on the creative side or not. You will love the feeling and the creativity is contagious.

One more hand up

My final "putting my hand up" act at B&B involved new business, the lifeblood of an ad agency. There's a saying about agency-client relationships that has a ring of truth: You begin to lose a client the day after you get it.

Agencies grow with new clients or fizzle out. Standing still is not an option. New business wins also build morale and industry reputation. I knew that being part of a new business team would be a great experience, credential, and asset.

In June 1969, B&B was one of a few agencies pitching the Avis Rent-A-Car account. Avis' "We Try Harder" campaign created by Doyle Dane & Bernbach (DDB) was legendary and the firing of DDB was big news.[9] I joined a great management duo headed by B&B Chairman, Ted Steele, and Dave Kreinik. They quickly put together a pitch team and the agency was ready and eager for the competition.

Ron Wulkan, Avis' Vice President of US Advertising, spearheaded the agency search for Avis. Ron was a colorful, outspoken guy with an interesting background that included agency experience. All the agencies were summoned to a group briefing at Avis headquarters in Garden City, Long Island. It was a surreal event. The top management of Avis corporate and representatives of their local retail locations were assembled in a large conference room. The pitch teams from seven A-list agencies were ushered in—an impressive well-tailored cast of Mad Men. Most of the agency people knew each other so the atmosphere was friendly. But each agency was sizing up the competition and getting ready for a winner take-all competition.

Ron led the briefing and emphasized that Avis wasn't looking for an idea to replace "We Try Harder." They wanted recommendations on how to augment and extend the campaign line commitment. He provided each agency with briefing documents and outlined Avis' business objectives and expectations for agency staffing, services, and resources. A Q&A session followed with each agency trying to upstage the other with smarter questions. Watching a room full of Mad Men jockeying for top position was interesting. We received our marching orders and were given five weeks to come back with recommendations.

B&B's new business machine kicked in and all departments worked feverishly on what we called the "dog and pony show." We poured through the Avis documents, conducted field visits, interviewed Avis employees, shopped the competition, worked behind Avis counters, held

---

9. Article announcing the firing of DDB from Avis https://bit.ly/HertzversuAvis

consumer focus groups, tested creative ideas, and prepared our pitch. It's important to note that there were no digital tools available at that time. Everything had to be hand done and put on Kodak slides. Preparation lead times were much longer condensing timetables even more. There could be no last-minute slide changes. We knew that each agency was putting in the same kind of effort and were prepared for a very tough competition. The agency presentations were scheduled over a one-week period after which Avis would choose a winner.

Half a century later, the details of our recommendations are a bit hazy, but I recall that we presented alternative lines and few interesting ways to build out "We Try Harder." We also proposed a unique staffing structure that included field account people. All of this seemed to be well-received so we were optimistic.

Then something unexpected happened. On Tuesday, June 24, Ron Wulkan called Ted Steele to congratulate B&B on being selected as one of three finalists along with Gilbert Advertising and Marschalk. *What?* Three finalists! We were not anticipating a second round. Then he told us that each agency had forty-eight hours to review their original recommendations and come back to Avis headquarters on Friday, June 27, with revisions, additions, and new ideas.

Wow. We had to gear up again, reassemble teams, re-energize, and top the work we had already done. And so we did. B&B's new recommendations were built around a modified tag line: "If you think Avis tries harder, you ain't seen nothing yet." Andy Granatelli, the world-famous auto racing expert and founder of STP motor products was proposed as the Avis spokesperson. The campaign touted the fact that Andy rewrote the Avis maintenance manuals so customers could always be assured of perfectly running and well-serviced vehicles. Three days later on Monday, June 30, it was announced in *The New York Times* that B&B had won the business.

As per our suggestion there would be one account executive who would work with headquarters and one external account executive working in the field. I was assigned to be the headquarters account executive. What a thrill. Ironically, soon after winning the account, I left B&B to join DDB, Avis' former agency. More on that in the next chapter.

Looking back on that campaign now, it feels uninspired, clumsily executed, and not a big idea. But hey, it won the business and ran for a short time. Over the ensuing years Avis would go through a number of agency changes and campaigns. Ron Wulkan went on to be the Marketing Director of Rolls Royce and Avis resurfaced in my business life fifteen years later.

Being part of any new business solicitation is an amazing experience. It helps build a healthy competitive spirit, instills a "give it your all" work ethic, and fosters an appreciation for being a team player in pressure-packed environments—all assets that will serve you well in marketing. Personally, I loved it all and seeing the agency's disciplines and departments converge (twice) to bring our winning presentations to life was inspiring. It whet my appetite for more.

Over the course of my career I've experienced both the thrill of victory and the agony of defeat across a broad range of new business pitches. I was fortunate to land bigtime clients like Boeing, Nestlé, Quaker, The City of Beverly Hills, and Nintendo. There's nothing like getting the call to let you know you've won the business. *What a feeling.* The reality, however, is that the average industry success ratio is about fifteen percent. Dealing with painful defeat is inevitable. Whenever I didn't win an account, I made it a point to find out why and extract the lessons for next time. Then, I'd put it in the rear-view mirror and move on. You have to be realistic and resilient. There is always a next time.

Imitating shamelessly and often

Perhaps even more important than the credentials and experience I gained was my exposure to great mentors at B&B. I had the opportunity to learn from some of the best Mad Men of that time.[10] More than anything else, I credit my mentors with the success I've had in my career. In addition to those I previously mentioned, there was Bern Kanner, Dick Gershon, and Merrill Grant in media, and Joe Bacal, Dick Anderson, and Les Stark in creative. My top management mentors were Ted Steele, Vic Bloede, and Jack Bowen. I am grateful to all of them for their wisdom and friendship. What's more, I made other great connections at B&B that would pop up throughout my career like Eric von der Lieth, Dan Adams, Bruce Nevins, Charlie Decker, and Alan Pando. More on them later. These early connections were the first of many business relationships that would help form the connective tissue of my career.

Asset-Based Thinking taught me that whatever talents and skills you admire in someone, you already have within yourself. When you embrace this truth, you are ready and able to incorporate those admirable qualities into your repertoire of personal assets.

At first, you may only see a glimmer of those qualities you admire, but they are in you—*and* you want more of them. Well, the fastest way to learn anything is to imitate a role model, their values, beliefs, approaches, and behaviors. Then, ask questions and seek feedback about how you can improve. One of the most effective questions you can ask someone you admire is, "Wow, how did you do that?" They will immediately open up to you.

Make mentors matter—whatever stage you are in your career. Raise your hand, be a grateful student, and imitate.[11]

The end of a decade

I am very fortunate to have begun my career in the '60s. It was a special time, one in which a

---

10. To learn more about B&B, take a look at this book by Gordon Webber chronicling B&B's first 50 years: *Our Kind of People*

11. This includes reverse mentoring! Later in my career, I discovered the joy of learning from younger digital communications leaders. A real gift. More on that later.

generation rebelled and lost its innocence. The Vietnam War and the unrest that surrounded it was part of our daily lives. Fortunately, I was not called up in the draft and I count my blessings for that. The '60s was a decade of change, experimentation, and hope. The Age of Aquarius. Everyone was ready for the dawn of something new. All of this spilled over into the business world and made it a transformational time in the advertising industry. The creative revolution had begun and a new breed of ad agencies and ad people was emerging on the scene. It was a watershed moment and my timing could not have been better. Fast-forward forty-two years to 2007 and imagine my delight when AMC's *Mad Men* series premiered and became a hit. I had no idea then that I would be a Mad Man now. Stay tuned for more about *Mad Men*.

At the end of the decade, I was twenty-six and we were a family of four. I had five years of major league agency experience under my belt. I had learned marketing communications fundamentals from the best ad men in the business. An MBA and business school teaching experience had been added to my resumé. My knowledge, credentials, and confidence were set. I was ready to move onward and upward and to take on a bigger role in advertising's creative rejuvenation.

Mad Man Wisdom

- Your first job is but the first of many stepping stones. Don't sweat about it too much.
- Reaffirm (or de-confirm) your career choices regularly.
- Learn to juggle. Keeping a few balls in the air keeps you on your toes—especially early in your career. Have a sideline. Make time for a personal pursuit that fuels and fills your spirit.
- Find confidence and self-esteem-building pillars. Etch them in your psyche. (My first was the P&G budget meeting process.)
- Be a page-one thinker. Assume that no one's going to read your page two.
- Leverage your Signature Presence to be a persuasive, prolific communications ninja.
- Put your hand up. An inquisitive open mind gets you places.
- Latch on to creative people. Hone your creative judgment. Champion big ideas.
- Make mentors matter. Find yours and be one. Ask. Imitate. Imagine.

Marketing Truisms & Tips

Building Your Marketing Core

Spend most of your early career time developing the essential knowledge and skills that build your marketing core. Strengthen it throughout your career. Here are my suggestions for adapting five time-tested best practices from back then to build your marketing core now.[12]

MARKETING COMMUNICATIONS BEST PRACTICES	
THEN	**NOW**
Positioning = what the brand stands for in the mind of the consumer	Positioning = what the brand stands for in mind, heart, and soul of the consumer
Have deep product and service performance knowledge	Wrap all that knowledge in brand purpose and values
Be consumer-benefit focused	Be consumer-benefit and service-obsessed 24/7
Employ consumer segmentation modeling for targeting	Develop consumer persona maps for personalization–creating "segments of one"
Be data knowledgeable: analyze, measure, and monitor performance periodically, adapt as necessary	Be data-driven: listen, measure, and monitor performance constantly, iterate daily, innovate often. But also, avoid being data dependent. CAUTION: Build relationships by balancing privacy concerns with *serve-to-sell* targeting while looking for ways to establish better consumer relationships.

---

12. In my USC/Marshall Executive MBA digital marketing course program I did not use a text book. Instead I assigned two excellent books that you will find helpful:
Jim Stengel: Grow: *How Ideals Power Growth and Profit at the World's Greatest Companies*
Brian Solis: *X: The Experience When Business Meets Design*

Chapter 2 Footnotes

Scan QR codes for direct links to footnote content.

2.1 Rogues

2.6 Original Whipple Commercial

2.8 Alternate Whipple Commercial

2.9 Hertz vs. Avis Article

2.4 Whipple History

Chapter 3:

Magnify What's Best, Focus On What's Next

Five years into my career I was feeling pretty good about where I stood and ready for the next thing. I wanted to find my way into a leading-edge creative agency but was feeling a bit stuck. I was in my comfort zone at B&B and complacency was tempering my restlessness.

As it often happened in my career, the impetus for my next step came from outside, not within. Unexpectedly presented with the opportunity to join the best creative agency on the planet, I was forced to put myself and my situation under the microscope. When I did, a renewed appreciation of the professional assets I'd accumulated over the past five years came into sharper view—along with the conviction that it was time to cultivate some new assets. That magnification of the positive and forward-leaning focus ensured that when I made the move to Doyle Dane Bernbach (DDB), I felt not only uplifted and optimistic, but also strengthened by the positive things I would carry with me from B&B: great credentials, fond memories, good will, and wonderful, lasting relationships.

My time at DDB was action-packed and intense from day one. None of it intimidated me; I loved the excitement and the opportunity to put my experience to work in a new environment. It was all good. Then, one year in, a series of unexpected events occurred that disrupted my original expectations. Objectively, none of them were terrible but suddenly, it felt like I was starting all over again.

A bit flustered, I needed to steady myself and so I pushed aside the negativity and disappointment in order to concentrate on the potential upsides of my new circumstances. I began to view my situation as a new beginning. So my "checked all the boxes" new job turned out not to be what I expected. Instead, it had morphed into much more and I had the good fortune of going—and growing—along with it.

It just goes to show…when you magnify what's best and focus on what's next, you learn how to make the most of opportunities and rise to the challenges of the unexpected. A two for one!

The time and place

As my career moved into the 1970s two wonderful life events occurred:

> **1. I became a father for the third time.** Our son Jason was born in October 1972. Our family was complete—just like the popular TV

show of that era, *My Three Sons*. Our boys have always been a source of joy, pride, and strength to Vicki and me. They are wonderful, outstanding young men.

2. I was hired as Assistant Professor of Marketing at my alma mater, Pace University. This appointment launched my teaching career in earnest and it was thanks to two of my former professors and mentors: Dr. Stanley Mullin and Dr. Frank Fallon. They had invited me to speak at an alumni event at the university, which then led to a discussion about my joining the Pace faculty. In 1970, I was named an Assistant Professor of Marketing. It was such an honor. Getting to give back to the place where my professional journey began was a dream come true for me. I continued teaching at Pace for almost twenty years, which opened the door to subsequent teaching appointments. I've been lucky and privileged to be in the classroom with next-generation marketers for almost fifty years. It's been exciting and fulfilling, and my students have helped keep me on my toes and current. I learned early on that you can't fake it—in the classroom or the boardroom.

The '70s

In some ways the '70s were a spillover from the '60s with continued divisiveness about the Vietnam War and political unrest. The Watergate scandal and subsequent resignation of President Nixon had a major impact. Individualism became more important as people grew dissatisfied with wars and politics. Rules were broken and expressing oneself became the mantra. This was the decade that brought us streaking, pet rocks, and wildly colorful clothing.

The 1970s began with a minor recession and slow growth in marketing spending. In 1973, severe gas shortages hit the economy hard. That put pressure on ad agencies to manage costs more tightly, the consequences of which I experienced. But by 1979, ad expenditures had increased dramatically and total U.S. agency billings had tripled, reaching $28 billion (in 2019 total US expenditures were $244 billion). TV viewing had emerged as a centerpiece of American culture and it became the preferred advertising medium.

By the end of the '70s, the ad industry had embraced the use of computers in a big way, changing how agencies ran their everyday operations: billings, reporting, and more importantly, consumer research. The slide rules, calculators, and rooms full of reference books I used at B&B were replaced by machines and screens. Technology helped agencies gather and analyze valuable information, such as demographics, psychographics, and consumer preferences. I welcomed this shift to more discipline and accountability because it enabled a deeper understanding of the consumer, better strategic thinking, and finer-tuned communications plans. By today's standards of real-time precision data gathering, our methods back then seem rudimentary, but at the time, it was a game changer.

Regulations and government scrutiny also hit the marketing communications business. The biggest was the Public Health Cigarette Smoking Act, which required package warning labels and banned cigarette advertising on television and radio. Industry code review boards and agencies began to monitor advertising and often banned unclear, exaggerated, or untrue claims. The US Federal Trade Commission (FTC) initiated the practice of corrective advertising and public concern over the marketing of products to children on television led to the formation of Peggy Charren's non-profit group Action for Children's Television (ACT), which kicked opened the door to much needed scrutiny and regulations that continue today.[1]

But perhaps the most impactful and lasting developments involved the economics and business models of agency-client relationships. There was an accelerated pace of account shifts as clients demanded more accountability from agencies regarding their profitability and staffing effectiveness. This brought about a series of acquisitions with large agencies acquiring smaller creative shops. A number of large agencies also went public as the landscape shifted. Some agencies even diversified into auxiliary businesses to generate increased profits. DDB purchased a sailboat company—an acquisition that would directly affect me as you'll soon find out.

A step up to stand out

There I was, fresh off an amazing team experience winning the Avis account for B&B. I had hit my stride at the agency and was proud to have made a mark. I was in my comfort zone and assured that a move up to account supervisor would happen soon. Then, a head hunter contacted me about an opportunity at DDB for an account supervisor position. I met with DDB's HR person, Charlie Buck, at the famous Algonquin Hotel across the street from the DDB offices. Charlie's enthusiasm for DDB was infectious and the position he described was almost too good to be true: vice president and account supervisor on the Gillette account reporting to Derrick O'Dea, a well-respected, high-profile agency executive.

The new job checked all my boxes:

> best-in-class creative agency
> promotion
> more responsibility

---

increased salary

A VP title

DDB was a public company, which made the VP title even more attractive. Plus, DDB was unique. These were the pioneering Mad Men responsible for building the agency that literally changed advertising. DDB was leading the creative revolution with some of the most celebrated advertising of that time.

Unlike other large agencies, at DDB there was no doubt that creative was king; it drove both the operations and psyche of the agency. Everything and everyone was viewed as being in service to the development of great creative work—especially account teams. I felt this could be a big opportunity and my impatience and restlessness drew me to it instantly. I had two great meetings with Derrick and his boss, Ed McNeilly. I met Charlie again at the Algonquin and he offered me the job. I accepted on the spot. Charlie and I became friends and would meet often at the Algonquin. Charlie subsequently joined the management consulting firm, Canter, Achenbaum & Heekin. Jim Heekin, Sr. was a Mad Man era legend I admired so Charlie connected us. Stay tuned for how another Heekin would influence my career. Charlie remained a valued source of advice and connections over the years.

My decision-making process went like this: Yes, I had a great career ahead of me at B&B where the account person was king, but I realized that for every one of me there were three more who were just as good. I was merely one of a cadre of very well-trained packed goods account guys. Also creatively driven agencies like DDB were hot, and I knew they would dramatically impact the ad business. I decided that I could make a greater mark, grow faster, and go further at an agency where creativity dominated. DDB and Gillette provided an opportune doorway into that world.

I decided to move away from my B&B comfort zone and join DDB, but it was harder than I thought it would be to cut the cord. I felt an allegiance to B&B and knew I would miss the friendships I had developed. That weighed heavily on me. In Asset-Based Thinking terms, I got past that by magnifying what's best and focusing on what's next. Here's how that worked for me. I shut down the "what if" distractions…If I stay will a better position become available? What if I don't fit in at DDB or the pressure is too much? Then I sharpened my view of what I wanted next and why. I really wanted to move up to a supervisory position at a creative powerhouse agency and build my management skills. DDB offered that and more. So I kept my sights focused on the upside and eliminated peripheral doubts. I used that clarity to move past my anxiety, confident that I could leverage and adapt my experience and knowledge to make it work. I trusted my gut, gave myself a kick in the butt, and let go. Magnifying the best and focusing on what's next is a powerful mindset to help guide career decisions. Use it to shake off complacency, dispel doubt, and pursue progress. It has served me well.

Unexpectedly intense

I started at DDB in January 1970 and exited two years later—a shorter run than anticipated but definitely not short on learning, new experiences, and mentors. A hell of a lot happened in twenty-four months. It was not the experience I thought it would be—in a good way.

The DDB offices were housed in an older building on 42nd street between 5th and 6th Avenues. The no-frills offices were dated, spread across a few floors, and described by DDBers as "plain pipe rack," a big difference from the modern B&B digs at 666 5th Avenue. I suppose the proximity to Times Square, the NYC Public Library, Grand Central Station, the Algonquin Hotel, and other NYC attractions helped compensate for the décor's shortcomings.

In March, the DDB board of directors officially confirmed my appointment as a vice president of the agency. At twenty-six years old, I was told that I was the youngest VP in the agency's history (who knows, I still might have that distinction!).[2] It was a great moment of pride for me. Then, to my surprise, I was informed that as a new VP I would be given an office improvement allowance of $5,000 to decorate my office. My jaw dropped. That was four times the annual rent for our apartment. It was a big deal. I decided to think differently and go minimalist. I installed an industrial rubber black tile floor, traded a desk for a built-in corner work counter, and added a round glass conference table with modern chairs and a couch. I didn't like sitting behind a big desk and holding court. I preferred a more open casual environment, a preference that stayed with me throughout my career.

DDB's Gillette assignment included razors and toiletries and I was assigned the latter. At the time, the double-edged stainless-steel razor blade was state of the art technology. DDB had created a very successful award-winning campaign for the blades called, "The Spoiler."[3] It was classic, simple, powerful advertising created by two Mad Men legends: Dave Reider, copywriter, and Bill Taubin, art director. They also were the creative team I worked with on the toiletries account. Dave and Bill were elder statesmen at DDB with campaign credentials a mile long. At first it was a bit intimidating. Dave was serious and pensive. Bill was outgoing and open. It was all business and I respected the fact that my job was to provide them with everything they needed to develop great creative work and then present and sell their work to the client.

The Gillette toiletries brands I managed included shave creams, balms, and after shave lotions. There was nothing very unique about them so they were supported with smaller budgets. But there were two special brands that received substantial support:

> **The Hot One:** A self-heating shave cream that delivered soothing hot
> lather right out of the can. DDB created great advertising built around

---

2. Hank's DDB VP Press https://bit.ly/HanksDDBVPPress

3. Gillette Spoiler commercials https://bit.ly/GilletteSpoiler

the concept of "shaving too close for comfort."

Nine Flags: A unique specialty line of men's colognes and body creams. The cologne was packaged in small, ball-shaped bottles with long necks and brushed aluminum caps and sold individually in Styrofoam containers or as a full collection in a plastic case. Each scent was named after a different country, giving the cologne an international flag flair. The line was designed by world-famous designer, Massimo Vignelli.[4]

Just as I was settling into the Gillette account, the sky started falling at DDB...kind of. In December 1970, DDB President Joe Daly informed us that the agency would be resigning the Gillette account. *Boom!* In that instant I thought I was out of a job. Then Joe dropped the other shoe. Simultaneous with the resignation, the Warner Lambert company was awarding the Schick Safety razor business to DDB and I would be assigned as account supervisor, still reporting to Derrick O'Dea. *Bang!* Suddenly, it looked like I had an even better and bigger position. *Whew!* The official reason for the Gillette resignation was account unprofitability but I'm sure other factors figured into the decision. Here's an excerpt from *The New York Times* article covering the Gillette resignation:

"In making the announcement, Joseph R. Daly, D.D.B. president, having noted his sadness in parting and, the good relations with his departing client, added, 'But in the end we had to face the fact that it was impossible to provide the necessary service and still maintain profitability on the account.'"

Right then and there I learned a valuable lesson. Always be concerned with and, when possible, dig into the financials of any business or brand you work with. As you grow into management positions this is an essential job responsibility. Early in your career this information may not be readily available to you and not one of your responsibilities. The DDB resignation decision, for example, was made way above my level. But so what? Ask your superiors about financials in a respectful, constructive manner and it's very likely they will think more of you for doing so.

Next: more ironic twists.

In February 1971, Gillette appointed a new agency to replace DDB. Guess which one: Benton & Bowles. First Avis, now Gillette. And just as I left DDB in 1972, Avis pulled its business from B&B and returned to DDB. Three account shifts in two years! Welcome to the ad biz. Over the course of my career there would be more of these switch-ups that added spice and interest to my journey. My advice is to recognize and appreciate ironies in your life and

---

4. DDB created advertising as brilliantly designed as the product. "We wanted to import the world's one most exciting men's shaving cologne. We failed." Today, Nine Flags bottles are sought after collector items on eBay...I still have mine. https://bit.ly/nineflags

career. There's usually a lesson in there somewhere and at the very least it makes you smile and accept that sometimes shit just happens. Roll with it and lighten up.[5]

In November 1970, a month before the Gillette/Schick trade, DDB announced the purchase of the Snark sailboat company as part of the agency's diversification plans.[6] Yes, sailboats. Snarks were lightweight, affordable sailboats starting at $119 designed to have mass-market appeal. It was a pet project of DDB President, Joe Daly. One of the first things he did was assign an agency account team to the Snark house account. To my surprise, Joe selected me to head that team. In effect, I became the liaison between DDB and Snark management. I'd never even been near a sailboat and now I would be helping develop Snark's marketing programs. Anchors away!

In just a two-month window, the consequences of two industry trends—financial accountability (Gillette resignation) and revenue diversification (Snark acquisition)—landed squarely in my lap. Instead of being flustered by these sudden, unexpected events, I embraced the changes and decided to learn all I could from both of them. I magnified what's best, focused on what's next, and welcomed 1971 with Schick as my new client and Snark as an entirely new type of responsibility.

The Schick account

Gillette drove most of the product innovation in the razor category and Schick was the number two brand. Schick's competitive strengths were its ability to quickly follow Gillette with product tweaks and advancements, smarter pricing, and more agile marketing. We already had a wealth of shaving category knowledge and experience so we hit the ground running.

The priority brand assignment was the Schick Super Chromium blade, positioned directly against Gillette's Super Stainless Blades, the very brand that DDB's Dave Reider and Bill Taubin made a category leader with their award-winning campaign, "The Spoiler." Dave and Bill made it clear that they did not want to work on Schick since they had so much emotional capital invested in their Gillette work. Understandable. So the first priority was assigning a new creative team and building fresh relationships with them.

Creative director Bob Levenson assigned Roy Grace and Evan Stark to Schick. I hadn't yet worked them but I was thrilled that they would be the creative team. Evan and Roy were next-generation DDB creative stars who had already produced three Hall of Fame commercials[7]:

---

5. Forty-seven years later I would again resign Gillette. This time I made it personal. Stay tuned for that story.

6. DDB's Snark acquisition https://bit.ly/SnarkDDB.

7. Roy & Evan's commercials https://bit.ly/Roy-EvanCommercials

- Alka Seltzer, *Spicy Meatballs*
- Volkswagen, *Funeral*
- American Tourister, *Gorilla*

I knew this would be a different working relationship. Roy was a morning person; Evan was not. There were only a few hours in the day to get them together for meetings and there was never a dull moment. They expected a lot of their account people, asked challenging questions, and were always putting ideas on the table. Things could get intense, but they also had a great sense of humor that helped make meetings relaxed and productive. Roy and Evan knew that I had category knowledge and had worked well with Dave and Bill, so I was welcomed into the creative process.

At one point, we considered a competitive positioning for Schick centered on a closeness benefit. We ruled that out because Gillette owned that territory and the Federal Trade Commission's scrutinizing of competitive claims made it difficult to execute. Instead, we leveraged the fact that, generally, men do not enjoy shaving. Men like the results but dreaded the time and effort they had to put into it. We called it "divine discontent" and used that discontent as the emotional trigger for the campaign. The advertising focused on another very important benefit to shavers: comfort.

Comfort, however, was not easily demonstrated. Roy and Evan overcame that by creating a great campaign around the idea that a Schick comfort shave was the way to escape the annoyance and discomfort of their morning ritual. The premise was simple: A Schick shave was "so comfortable you'll actually look forward to your next shave."[8] The commercials utilized humorous situations showing men eager to shave. It was very DDB: a focused message with an entertaining twist, brilliantly produced. The commercials were well received by the client and performed well in the marketplace. Schick was a short but sweet experience made even more rewarding (and comfortable) by Roy and Evan. More on Evan later.

The Snark experience

Snark's management team, Jim McMullen and Alex Roth, were entrepreneurs more than twice my age. They ran the operation from manufacturing to distribution, to sales and marketing. I built a good relationship with both of them and spent most of my time helping develop promotion plans, trade advertising, and justifying marketing budgets with DDB management.

In that first year we didn't do much consumer advertising, but I remember one trade ad that received some notoriety. It featured a simple picture of a Snark against a plain background with the headline, "The Volkswagen of Sailboats." That ad pretty much summed up our marketing

---

8. Schick Commercials: https://bit.ly/ShickCommercials

platform for Snark: reliable, sensible, affordable, and fun. We also implemented a unique self-liquidator promotion with Kool cigarettes.[9] Consumers could purchase a Snark complete with a Kool logo sail for only $88 and a Kool carton proof of purchase. It was one of Kool's highest scoring ads and generated over 18,000 orders. This brief encounter was the only time I came near a cigarette account.

What I liked most about this assignment was working closely with successful entrepreneurs. Alex's and Jim's dedication to making a great product, cost controls, smart accountable marketing spending, and profitability made a big impression. They also involved me in sales calls with major retailers, a new experience for me. The importance of trade marketing to help build retail distribution and promotional support hit home, and I learned to value its key role in the marketing mix. Trade campaigns deserved the same creative rigor and attention as flashy consumer campaigns. Our "Volkswagen of Sailboats" trade ad opened a lot of retailer doors for Snark and changed the way I saw trade advertising.

That famous quote, "Nothing happens in business until you sell something," was on the wall at Snark. As far as Alex and Jim were concerned, every marketing communication had to contribute to a sale. Simple return on investment (ROI) advice that's still relevant in today's complex digital measurement landscape of likes, engagements, influencers, and attribution.

My Snark experience also gave me a glimpse into what it was like to be a client, albeit on a smaller scale. I realized there actually were a lot more things on my client's mind than advertising. I learned to respect and show an interest in the scope of my clients' responsibilities and always made it a point to ask if I could help. When you look for opportunities to contribute, you learn and earn respect.

My creative enlightenment

One aspect of working at DDB that impressed me greatly was being surrounded every day by legends in the business. I had the opportunity to meet many of them and work directly with some of the best. In addition to those I mentioned there were other great mentor moments. Because of my teaching experience, I was on a team that worked directly with renowned agency founder Bill Bernbach, creative director Bob Levenson, and DDB's head of HR on new employee orientation and training sessions. Being assigned to the Snark Sailboat acquisition, meant I worked directly with DDB President Joe Daly. I also worked with another great writer, Irwin Warren, on special projects. Remember his name for later.

I think I learned more about the development and integrity of creative work at DDB than at any other place I worked. Bill Bernbach felt that creatives should spend their time creating and not managing client relationships; that was the account person's job. He also believed

9. Snark/Kool ad. https://bit.ly/Snark-Kool

that the agency should recommend only its very best work, not its second or third best, so presenting multiple creative options was frowned upon. As the agency business became more and more competitive DDB fell into line with the rest of the agencies in presenting multiple campaign options. In retrospect, however, "only the agency's best" still seems like a good creative philosophy.

At B&B and most other agencies campaign options were the norm and the creative and account teams jointly presented the agency's creative recommendations to clients. But that was not the case at DDB. The creative teams expected me to present and sell their one best idea to the client…without them. Simply being the "delivery boy" for the creative work was not an option. I had to be fully versed in all aspects of the creative executions and totally committed to selling it. Period.

My boss, Derrick O'Dea, was particularly good at presenting creative work and helped me get over my initial self-doubts and trepidations about solo performances. He pushed me to get immersed in the details and nuances of creative work. I watched Derrick as he spent time with creative teams understanding their rationale and learning why they felt so strongly about their work. I imitated him shamelessly and often. I made sure I was fully convinced that what I was presenting was the one best idea for the brand. Then I rehearsed my presentation until I felt totally confident and comfortable with it. I learned to know it, own it, and make it personal. This is an empowering strategy for anyone involved in getting buy-in for a creative project.

It's rare that a client approves creative work as is. When that happens, the creative teams love you. Total rejection is also unusual. The reality is that most of the time creative approval is a give-and-take process of refinement and improvement. And that is why being a great listener is a key to success in marketing. When you're the agency person presenting the work, you must be a good listener so you can provide accurate and constructive client feedback that will help creative teams address issues and make improvements. It's a skill that doesn't come naturally and isn't taught in business schools. You have to work at it. Asset-Based Thinking teaches you how to "listen softer" by opening the lens of your attention and listening with your ears, eyes, and heart. The result is that the distance between you and the speaker fades and you get clearer more genuine feedback and direction. Practice listening softer to hear better, learn more, and engage smarter.

Going smaller to grow bigger

I'd been through some rapid-fire disruption and unexpected changes at DDB but I was generally happy and settling in. I was not looking to leave DDB when an opportunity appeared in front of me that was too good to ignore. In December 1971, I was contacted by Judy Wald, a search consultant who specialized in placing creative talent; she also helped a few smaller creative agencies find account people. Judy contacted me about a position at DKG: vice president, management supervisor on their largest account, Corning, and directing new business development. DKG was a much smaller agency than DDB but the step up to management supervisor would be huge for me.

DKG was founded by celebrated art director Shep Kurnit as Delehanty, Kurnit & Geller. Later, the creative team of Neil Calet and Peter Hirsch along with finance man Larry Spector became principals of the agency. In 1969, the name was changed to DKG. It was a respected medium-sized creative agency with a solid base of clients, including Corning, Sperry Remington, Getty Oil Company, and Westinghouse Broadcasting. DKG was winning creative awards, was well-known and well-positioned for growth. It was an invitation I couldn't refuse.

In exploring the new position, I met with the four agency principals and director of client services, Jack Foley. I liked what they had to say about their plans for the agency and the potential for equity down the road. I felt comfortable with them, especially Shep and Neil. Experienced, well-respected creative talent comprised the majority ownership of the agency, insuring that the priority was creative, something I had come to value at DDB. Likewise, my DDB experience contributed to DKG's interest in me. The signals and circumstances were positive but when I was offered the position, I didn't accept it on the spot.

There was considerably more risk in making this move than when I left B&B for DDB. A more senior position meant that more would be expected of me within a short window of time. It would be a prove yourself fast or exit fast test. With a growing family the stakes were high. But even back then I knew that the road to success was not paved with guarantees and at some point I'd have to take a risk. I was seven years into my career and decided that this was the right time. I minimized the financial risk as much as possible by negotiating a six-month termination clause. I encourage everyone to reduce personal financial risk when making job changes at any career stage. Understand termination clauses and terms and don't be shy about pushing for the best you can get. You will be respected for it.

Focus on my what's best attitude to help magnify what's next and put everything in perspective. It enabled me to get more comfortable with the risks and take that leap of faith. I joined DKG in 1972.[10]

Beating ageism

As I started this next phase of my career, ageism became a reality and I learned some lasting lessons. I know many future leaders will have similar experiences and here a few tips to help navigate them.

---

10. That same year Evan and Roy left DDB to become partners in Gilbert Grace and Stark, and Derrick O'Dea joined McCann, heading their Tokyo office.

With growing responsibilities and supervisory roles, I found myself managing and motivating colleagues and clients older than me. I often was the youngest person in the room leading meetings and making recommendations to people more experienced than me.[11] It was intimidating at first and here's how I learned to push through that anxiety and make my age an asset:

> 1. **Respectful recognition, not intimidation.** I always showed respect for and appreciated those with age and wisdom beyond mine.

> 2. **Confident humility, not "know-it-all" posturing.** I had worked hard to earn my place in the room and was proud of it. But I also acknowledged that I didn't know everything and wasn't afraid to admit it. I made up for what I didn't know with hard work and preparation.

> 3. **Persuasion, not preachiness.** I had confidence in the value of my contributions before communicating them.

> 4. **Genuine appreciation, not pandering.** I always thanked the people for their attention. I recognized when they said something that opened my mind.

Those four steps make up a powerful Asset-Based Thinking confidence-building process. It can help you bypass anxiety and build energy by recognizing who you are and how you add value. You are magnifying what's best, turning your assets into your adrenaline, and leading with confidence and enthusiasm, no matter your age.

As I headed to DKG one of Bill Bernbach's famous quotes echoed in my mind: "An idea can turn to dust or magic depending upon the talent that rubs against it."[12]

I was determined to be a magician.

Mad Man Wisdom

- Avoid the complacency trap. First-job comfort zones can cloud your vision and temper ambition. Be focused, confident, committed, and always a little restless.
- Prepare yourself to leave your first job. Have a goal, criteria, timetable, and be ready to step out and up.

---

11. Later on in life I found myself going through similar experiences, but in reverse. More on that later.

12. *Bill Bernbach Said* book of quotes. https://amzn.to/2XGJ8kk.

- Embrace risk on your terms. Taking risks builds character and confidence. Find your level of risk tolerance, mitigate as much as possible, and go for it.
- Expect the unexpected. Don't worry about what you can't control or see coming. S**t always happens and sometimes it's good s**t.
- Own your age at any age. The number is irrelevant. Leverage your assets, abilities, diligence, and confidence to make your mark.
- Master the art of listening softer. Make "eye to I" contact so people open up and reveal what they really think and feel.
- Always be searching for creative opportunities, especially in unexpected places. Building and honing your creative judgment is a never-ending journey.
- Put your emotional skin in the game. Get personally invested in your projects, especially creative recommendations.
- Remember what Bill said. Hang out with magicians and be one.

Marketing Truisms & Tips

Never Underestimate the Power of an Idea

Throughout my career I've been constantly reminded that ideas and creativity are the single, most important differentiator in the marketing mix. Trust me. They are and always will be.

Regrettably, in today's data-centric, analytics-first environment I've seen a tendency to let that devotion to creating magical ideas slip down the list of priorities. Don't fall into that trap.

One of the best testimonies to the power of creativity is a digital era success, Dollar Shave Club (DSC). Founder Michael Dubin set out to be a disruptor in an established, traditional distribution category, men's shaving, by employing a proven subscription-based internet business model.[13] He was not the first. Harry's and a few others were already there, but Michael unlocked the magic that made Dollar Shave Club a phenomenal success. I was a speaker at the 2012 Pivot Conference hosted by my friend Brian Solis and I conducted a filmed on-stage interview with Michael Dubin.[14] Here are some great insights and lessons learned from my interview.

First, Michael got the basics right:

- Solid business model embraced by a small cadre of committed people
- Abundant, readily available product supply

---

13. Michael preferred to call it a membership model because it implied personal connections.

14. My interview with Michael Dubin https://bit.ly/Hank-DubinInterview.

- Clear and efficient web and e-commerce customer experience
- Simple and relevant proposition: blades as good as the market leader at a lower price and conveniently delivered

Second, he concentrated his resources and optimized messaging for digital and organic social media delivery.

Michael made a risky marketing communication move by hitting Gillette head on and irreverently telling it like it is. Then he became a magician. He wrote and starred in DSC's brand video and produced it for only $5,000. It was direct, simple, sincere, personal, and very entertaining. It made a human connection and tapped into emotional truths. Michael transcended the message and became one with his target market; he became their champion. The video was a viral phenomenon and DSC's target audience became Michael's media. Momentum and good management took over and the rest is history. In 2016, DSC was purchased by Unilever for one billion dollars.[15] Even Michael acknowledged that none of that would have happened without his risky and magical $5,000 video.

---

15. DSC Unilever purchase http://bit.ly/DSCUnilever

Chapter 3 Footnotes

Scan QR codes for direct links to footnote content.

3.2 Hank's DDB VP Press

3.3 Gillette Spoiler Commercial

3.6 DDB Snark Acquisition

3.7 Grace/Stark Commercials

3.8 Schick Commercials

3.9 Snark/Kool Promotion Ad

3.14 Dubin DSC/Wasiak Interview

Chapter 4:

Widen Your Lens to Sharper Your View

In 1972, my resume was strong with top-tier large agency experience working on A-list packaged goods clients. The traditional next step would have been a move up to management supervisor on another big packaged goods account. My untraditional move to DKG required me to widen my lens and be open to different challenges that would broaden my horizons.

I ventured out of my public corporation comfort zone into to a new world of boutique agencies; from structure and silos to open, cross-discipline teams; from familiar, formulaic packaged goods discipline to less structured general consumer goods marketing. Plus, the new role would put my nascent new business development skills to the test. Pretty much everything was changing—and it was just the adrenaline jolt I needed.

At DKG I gained experience in product categories that targeted a wider range of consumers, required involvement in multi-level distribution, trade marketing, retail promotion, and heavy use of print media. I learned new skills from experienced clients with expertise in sales and product development. These bigger picture experiences also helped me realize that my packaged goods knowledge and skills transferred well to different businesses. I became even more confident that my marketing core was a solid, strong asset I could take anywhere.

Moving into a management position in a smaller, partner owned and managed agency was an eye-opener. At Benton & Bowles and DDB, layers of management insulated me from the realities of what it took to operate an ad agency. Previously, pretty much all my time was focused on managing my accounts and teams. At DKG, I saw how each account was linked and critical to the overall health of the agency. Financial stability and cash flow was a 24/7 priority that put stress and strain on relationships. No job was above anyone's level—we did whatever it took to get things done. When a new business lead came in everyone got excited and involved. I came to really appreciate that sense of purpose. DKG prepared me well for my next move up and for another investment I would make twenty-five years later.

It just goes to show…when you widen your lens you're never sure exactly what you will see. But you can be sure that the more you see, the better able you are to develop new skills and insights about yourself that push you forward.

Under new management

DKG's office was in the Time Life Building, directly across from Radio City Music Hall.

Surrounded by Rockefeller Center, the agency occupied the entire 38th floor. Each of the four partners—Shep Kurnit, Neil Calet, Peter Hirsch, and Larry Spector—had a corner office and the views were amazing. Our lux digs put my mind at ease about the agency's financial health.

I was also relieved that joining as vice president and management supervisor on DKG's largest account, Corning, my primary account was in good financial shape. In addition to my employment agreement's six-month severance clause, I received my first big perk: a company car and parking. I leased a Lincoln Continental!

I liked the energy on that 38th floor.

DKG came of age during the creative revolution with its award-winning Talon zipper campaign: "Your fly is open." Founder Shep Kurnit was a great judge of talent and surrounded himself with up-and-coming creatives. The legendary Jerry Della Femina, who spent a few years at DKG as a creative supervisor before he started his own successful agency, called us the agency "built on a zipper." Shep loved telling Jerry stories.

The environment at DKG was very different from B&B and DDB. Those were larger, more structured, "corporate" organizations while DKG was more like a family business. Everyone knew each other and our lives and responsibilities were intertwined. We worked hard to eliminate silos so there were rarely battles over turf. We interacted as people not job titles and I thrived in that atmosphere.

DKG was closely managed by the four partners. They generally got along well, but like any family, there were spats, blow-ups, and tensions among the "elders." Usually it was Shep (Chairman) and Neil (EVP creative director) on one side and Larry (President) and Peter (EVP creative director) on the other. Larry and Peter went to the same shrink every week. That seemed a bit odd to me. Shep often said he felt their therapist was a fifth silent partner.

I bonded closely with Shep and Neil. From the outset both were welcoming, warm, helpful, and valued the positive contributions that strong account managers could make to creative development. Shep was like a loving uncle and Neil like a big brother. They were amazing mentors and what's more, they felt like family. I am forever grateful for how much I learned from them. I got along well with Larry and we had productive working relationship, but Peter and I had a more tense and strained relationship.

I respected Peter as a great creative director and didn't have any issues with him. But, for whatever reasons, Peter did not connect well with me and he chose to work at arm's length. That was unfortunate and I always felt that I missed out on valuable learnings from him. It was the first and probably the only time that I experienced that kind of negative personal and professional tension.

Always remember that it is the people behind the business that create its success. That is why the relationships you develop will be some of your most valuable assets. That said, personality and personal conflicts are bound to happen in everyone's career. You just need to understand the underlying reasons, self-correct, and accommodate appropriately. And if these strained relationships are happening regularly, you need to be strong enough to face the fact that you may have some serious relationship issues that need correction. If not, you are guaranteed to miss out on opportunities and have a less fulfilling career.

While honest introspection is healthy, sometimes you also have to accept the fact that you just might not be someone else's cup of tea. Then you simply accept that you don't have to be bosom buddies with colleagues to get things done…it just takes more work. You have to accept that your interactions will be all business. Be fully prepared, be a great listener, and don't linger longer than you have to. That's how it was with Peter and me.

One thing led to another

Soon after I joined, the partners mutually agreed to part company with my immediate boss, Jack Foley. They felt he didn't have the marketing skills and presence required to manage the types of clients the agency was pursuing. Opportunity knocked and I was promoted to fill Jack's spot as senior vice president and director of client services. This was a big deal for me: a step up in responsibilities, title, salary, and a much bigger expense account. My sphere of influence and direct reports expanded dramatically and I was now managing all the account teams. This was the move up I had hoped for and I was ready to raise my game and take charge. I widened my lens again and identified what I needed to do to sharpen my management skills.

In my new role, one of my key responsibilities was keeping a close eye on the health and stability of our client relationships. For the older legacy accounts my involvement was internally directed, supporting the account teams as needed. On new business wins, my involvement had to be deeper. My new, more senior role was to assure clients that agency management cared about their business and to support the account and creative teams.

I held bi-monthly meetings with the account teams and made sure I participated in important client meetings whenever possible. I had to work hard at resisting the urge to do what I had been used to doing: taking charge of accounts and running meetings. One of the toughest things to do in moving up to a new job is to stop doing your old job. So, to avoid that trap, I met with the account teams before meetings to discuss if and how they wanted me to pitch in. Learning how to temper and adapt your management style as your responsibilities grow is a skill that is often overlooked by hard-charging young executives. Never forget that as a manager, it's not about you. You are in service to the teams you manage. Be sensitive to that need and responsibility. It will serve you well.

Eleanor Holtzman, director of research;, Marty Lipsitt, creative director; Stan Gerber, director of media; and Lester Goldstein, director of production; were high-powered, well-regarded leaders in their areas of expertise at DKG. We collaborated closely on client management and new business and I was very fortunate to have worked with them. In 1975, Shep gave each of us five percent equity in the agency and we became members of a newly created executive committee. Shep was a proponent of rewarding key players with equity opportunities as a way of providing skin in the game and keeping talent. *Wow!* Partnership. What a feeling.

Then came the icing on the cake. *Ad Age* named DKG Agency of the Year for 1976.[1] This was a huge industry accolade that put DKG on the map as a creative agency force. Prior winners included heavyweights like Cunningham & Walsh, Scali McCabe & Sloves, and Leo Burnet. I am very proud and fortunate to have been part of the DKG management team that earned that Agency of the Year honor. Little did I know that I would enjoy a similar, even better feeling of pride forty years later.

Cooking with Corning and flying with Alitalia

In my seven years at DKG, I worked with a variety of clients across many categories, ranging from packaged goods, travel, housewares, small appliances, beauty, automotive, alcoholic beverages. Each was different and I amassed a broad base of knowledge and experience. Corning and AliItalia are two of the more memorable ones.

Corning was primarily an industrial company that developed versatile, innovative, glass products, many of which played a big role in the space shuttle program. They were adept at converting these technologies into high-benefit, value-added consumer products like Pyrex, pyro Ceram (later Corning Ware), and various other kitchen and appliance products. DKG was the agency for Corning's major appliance, ophthalmic, and consumer products divisions.

Corning was very different from the package goods clients I'd worked with. Since their products were distributed through mass merchandisers and department stores, Corning's marketing communications programs were both trade and consumer-focused. That meant I had to learn another business model and manage a workload that encompassed both.

The first week on the job, I took a Mohawk airlines flight upstate to Elmira, New York, with my boss Jack Foley and Shep Kurnit, made the half-hour drive to Corning, and met with my new client. I would make that trip almost 100 times while at DKG. Unfortunately, that was before frequent flyer miles.

On that first trip I met division president Conrad Stemski and chief marketing officer Frank Fenno. Both were older than me and seasoned Corning executives. Conrad had risen through manufacturing and Frank through sales. I came to respect and admire both of them greatly. Being fellow Poles, Conrad and I had an instant connection. Frank was welcoming and we hit it off right out of the box and developed a great working relationship and friendship. I stayed on for a couple of days and also met the brand managers and marketing staff who welcomed

---

1. *Ad Age* announcement https://bit.ly/DKGAgency-of-Year

me and showed me the ropes.

I hit the ground running and got to work. And there was a lot of work. At any given time we were managing communications programs across ten different Corning brands. Corning was constantly monitoring consumer trends for unmet needs and ways to improve their products and every year they would introduce new shapes and sizes, updated decorative patterns, and specialty products to keep their brands fresh and growing.[2] All new product introductions came through DKG—no competitive pitches or other agencies were involved. The relationship was deep and the workload intense.

Trade marketing was an important priority. Prior to scheduling "pull" consumer marketing communications to drive retail traffic, DKG developed trade "push" programs like special display concepts and trade ads to build distribution and retailer co-op promotions. These efforts were concentrated around bi-annual housewares shows and Corning sales meetings.[3] The DKG team was embedded with the brand teams as an integral part of these events. I learned that if programs were not properly sold-in to the trade and aggressively promoted at point-of-sale the effectiveness of any consumer marketing was greatly diminished. This realignment and balancing of priorities was an important lesson for me.

Perhaps the biggest impact Corning had on me was its people and culture. Corning was based in Corning, New York. It was a small company town and most of the Corning employees were colleagues, good friends, and neighbors who valued their time together in and out of the office. It was an interesting dynamic and we made sure to respect and celebrate those connections in our relationships. For example, Corning CMO Frank Fenno and most of his team loved fishing. So did Shep Kurnit. Every summer Shep would organize a Corning fishing weekend that everyone looked forward to. It became a business and friendship ritual. In the summer of 1972, Corning suffered a massive flood that wreaked havoc on the community and severely damaged the world-famous Corning museum of glass. I flew up a few days later and it was inspiring to see how the company rallied its employees to help the town. They created a $400,000 fund to employ the town's youth to help residents clean up their properties. It was a side of a business and community relationships I'd not seen before and it impressed me greatly.[4]

Most of the brand managers were longtime Corning employees who had come up through manufacturing, product development, or sales. There was a fair amount of rotation between sales and marketing personnel resulting in turnover in the brand groups so we were constantly beginning new relationships. With Frank's blessing, I made it a point to have all new brand

---

2. Corning relied on focus group expert, Shoi Dickenson, to uncover insights and opportunities. I enjoyed watching Shoi work her magic with consumers.

3. The International Home + Housewares Show was the largest trade show of its kind and took place at Chicago's McCormick place each January and July. I attended fourteen of them. http://bit.ly/HousewaresShow

4. Short flood documentary. http://bit.ly/CorningFlood

managers spend a few days visiting the agency for a brand orientation. It helped establish DKG as a knowledgeable partner plus it created that personal connection from the start. And of course, they welcomed the opportunity to escape upstate New York for a few days enjoying fine dining, theater, and hitting NYC hot spots. A good time was had by all. Yes, it's okay to mix business meetings with pleasure…just make sure it's in the right proportions.

A few thoughts about meetings: Yes, there are too many meetings that are meaningless. I love this quote attributed to Star Trek's Capt. James T. Kirk:

"A meeting is an event where minutes are taken and hours wasted."

Approached smartly, however, meetings can be very meaningful relationship builders.

Throughout your career you will lead all kinds of meetings: informational status reports, innovation sessions, and so on. All too often these meetings are viewed as soapboxes to brag about accomplishments, overwhelm with facts and data, and advance personal agendas. In actuality, it should be just the opposite. Make meetings dialogues, venues for sharing stories, and opportunities for personal connections and rapport. In our brand orientation sessions for clients we made sure the meetings provided a platform for the new managers to tell their personal stories and layout their views on the business and agency expectations.

Four words that I use to help me plan my meetings are: Strategic. Social. Stories. Succinct.

The Corning assignment at DKG was a great example of an enduring client/agency relationship based on mutual professional respect and personal relationships. I was fortunate to be part of it. Unfortunately, these relationships are rare today. Corning stayed with DKG four years after I left. In 1983, Frank Fenno moved the account to…guess who? Benton & Bowles. Frank called and asked if I thought B&B would be a good choice. I gave him the thumbs up.[5]

• • •

DKG was responsible for all marketing communications for Alitalia Airline's largest and most competitive market, North America. We had limited budgets with media concentrated in newspapers, outdoor, and radio. Alitalia was government-owned and, unfortunately, that meant frequent strikes and service disruptions, which played havoc with our marketing and media plans. Chris Ebner, my account supervisor, did a masterful job managing the constant changes.

Neil Calet and creative director Joe Tantillo conjured up a hard-working campaign that branded Italy as Alitalia's Italy: authentic, in the know, and a step above the normal experience. The tag line was, "Alitalia's Italy. All you ever dreamed of. And more." So yes, there were no

---

5. Corning B&B announcement https://bit.ly/BBCorning

great creative breakthroughs—just a constant flow of solid hard-working messaging.

The more interesting and rewarding aspects of Alitalia were working with an international client, learning the airline business, and my relationship with Ricardo Machiavelli, head of marketing for the US market.[6] And oh yeah…the delights of first-class international travel and amazing family travel experiences in Italy were wonderful fringe benefits.

There was often tension between the Alitalia home office and US management about budgets and promotional tactics. This occasionally required trips with Ricardo to Alitalia's home office in Rome to secure buy-in to our plans. Observing Ricardo navigate resolutions to issues was a masterclass in maneuvering and negotiation. It was in his DNA.

Here's one example:

Alitalia traditionally promoted well-known gateway destinations like Rome, Milan, and Florence. Unfortunately, these were also the most competitive gateways and Alitalia was often at a disadvantage in terms of flights and rates. One of Ricardo's promotion ideas featured Sicily as a first stop gateway and feeder for Alitalia flights to other Italian cities. Since none of the competition adequately serviced Sicily, Alitalia would be the default choice. A brave idea. A tough sell since Alitalia's executives essentially viewed Sicily as an inferior destination. As we prepared for the formal meeting Ricardo gave me insight into Alitalia's culture. The real decision making happened in one-on-one sessions before or after the meeting. He called them the "real meetings."

I watched Ricardo deftly line up individual support in private meetings. He persuaded his colleagues to agree to his plan with the condition Sicily's travel bureau contribute substantial funding for the promotion. What he didn't tell them was that he had already obtained the Sicilian tourism board's agreement to do just that. At the formal meeting when we laid out the program, Ricardo announced the deal with Sicily. Alitalia management felt like they had won and the program was approved. It was a success.

Getting consensus and agreement to out-of-the-box thinking can be challenging. Often it requires being skilled in the art of persuasion and knowing how to work the room—or in Alitalia's case, work the system. Since then I've always looked for opportunities to have those "real meetings" in constructive and positive ways. Every business and company has their own way of doing "real meetings." Judiciously seek them out. Manage them wisely.

In addition to my business dealings with Ricardo, Vicki and I became good friends with he and his wife Fiorella. They personified the *La Dolce Vita* lifestyle of sophisticated, jet-setting Italians and we thoroughly enjoyed their company in NYC and Italy. Those were special times and we stayed in touch well after my exit from DKG.

---

6. And yes, Ricardo was a direct descendant of the infamous Niccolò Machiavelli.

New business: win some, learn always

We were always pitching new accounts. Each prospect represented a new challenge, and an opportunity to learn a new category and to meet smart successful people. Here's how we worked. After the lead came in, I would manage the agency team and one of the creative partners, Neil or Peter, would take the creative lead. Then we brought in research and media directors Eleanor and Stan and the full agency team got to work. It was an intense pressure-packed process. I loved the adrenaline rush.

I particularly enjoyed our winning the Arm & Hammer account. It was an opportunity to leverage my packaged goods experience. Arm & Hammer baking soda was already an iconic kitchen staple; now they were seeking an agency to launch Arm & Hammer laundry brands. CEO Bob Davies and CMO Burt Staniar were leading the search. Both were top-notch successful executives and I was eager to work with them.

The Arm & Hammer brand was loved by consumers. It stood for purity and simplicity and the laundry detergents were formulated accordingly. The pitch did not entail developing spec creative work. Rather, agencies were asked to provide credentials and strategic thoughts on how best to position Arm & Hammer brands in the category. Neil Calet took the creative lead and presented our point of view about leveraging brand heritage and values when appealing to women, using DKG's work on Corning as examples. The DKG team bested a field of tough competitors to win the business.

In developing the creative briefs, we worked closely with Arm & Hammer CMO Burt Staniar. He was Colgate-trained, smart as a whip, had a great sense of humor, and we developed a nice friendship. Two things that really impressed me about Burt were his understanding and respect for brand values and his involvement in the creative process.[7]

Burt made sure our briefs reflected brand values, had simple yet powerful brand voice guidance, and left room for creative leeway and invention. It was a good checklist that I still use today. He was firm but not heavy-handed and took the time to personally get these views across to Neil and his creative teams. He was very effective.

Working with Burt reinforced my belief in the importance of living up to and into brand values. It reaffirmed the fundamental critical role of the creative brief and, as importantly, the effectiveness of bringing it to life for creative teams through one-on-one dialogue and conviction. Delivering and communicating briefs in a personal and heartfelt manner always motivates creative people to step up higher.[8]

In today's marketing world, much is made of the importance of purpose-driven marketing—and that's a good thing. Brand purpose is powerful. But it's essential to recognize that brand

---

7. Burt would go on to be CEO of Westinghouse Broadcasting Company and Knoll.

8. Importance of the Brief video that I use in my USC class. http://bit.ly/TheBriefImportance

purpose must be built on the foundation of brand values and in marketing communications, it must link back to the product or service benefits.

First delight

The two other new business experiences permanently etched in my memory both involved alcoholic beverage companies: Brown-Forman Distillers and Ernest & Julio Gallo. One was a delight and one was a disaster. Here's the story of the former.

DKG was invited to pitch for Brown-Forman's Old Forester bourbon, one of the leading premium brands in the category. McCann Erickson was already the agency for their Canadian whisky brand, Canadian Mist, and it was decided that Old Forester needed its own agency.

Brown-Forman had recently moved to a brand management system and Dan Schusterman, newly appointed VP managing Old Forester, spearheaded the agency search. Dan was one of Brown-Forman's star sales executives and not a classically trained marketer. He wanted a full-service agency to manage the brand's marketing communications. The request for proposal (RFP) required recommendations on marketing strategy, promotions, creative, and media. Peter Hirsch was the creative partner assigned to the pitch. This was my first big test with Peter, and I was eager to do well. The pressure of a new business pitch can bring out the best or worst in people. In this instance it brought out the best in Peter (and me) and we worked cooperatively to put together a winning effort.

Like many of the agency team, I had never tasted bourbon so I had a lot of market learning to do. Fast. We were invited to Louisville, Kentucky, for a brand orientation that included a distillery tour. The distillery tour was invaluable and we were impressed with the expertise, dedication and craftsmanship behind the brand. Old Forester was a superior premium bourbon.

It had a loyal following in the Bourbon Belt but it was not a well-known brand outside its core markets. The key communications objectives were to build awareness and "wake-up" the brand.

The Bureau of Alcohol Tobacco and Firearms (BATF) regulated the advertising of alcohol brands and the only media allowed at that time were print, outdoor, and point of sale. Peter created a hard-hitting campaign that passed BATF scrutiny, tested well, and won the business. The campaign was a Peter Hirsch gem. DKG became a Brown-Forman agency alongside McCann.

Peter's idea was to position Old Forester as more than a premium tasting brand. Rather, it was an experience—something you do. He made the brand a verb with a great call-to-action tag line: "Go Forestering."[9] Then he took on other whisky and bourbon brands with a competitive feistiness that was embraced by consumers and loved by the sales force (and cleared

---

9. "Go Forestering" ads https://bit.ly/GoForestering

by the BATF).

We created a library of ads each of which featured a powerful close-up of a man's hand holding a bottle of Old Forester, topped by a clever headline and paid off by the brand's tag line "Go Forestering." Here are some of my favorites:

> When You Prefer Your Wild Turkey With Cranberry Sauce
> When You're Russian Away From Vodka
> When Your Old Grand Dad Is Ready For Retirement
> When You Have No Initial Reaction To V.O.
> When You Stop Taking A Shine To Smirnoff Silver
> When Crown Royal Isn't Your Bag?

Go Forestering

The campaign translated beautifully to outdoor and was a great attention grabber at retail point-of-sale. The Go Forestering campaign ran for almost four years and did its job. In 1977 it was replaced with a "reason-why" based campaign inspired by our distillery visits. The new tag line was "The great whisky made like great wine" and the Old Forester bottle was always shown lying down like a wine bottle.[10]

After winning the account, my first order of business was to hire an account supervisor with alcoholic beverage experience. Tony Codella came on board, made great contributions to the business, and helped educate me on the intricacies and nuances of managing a whisky account. But it was my client, Dan Schusterman, who took me under his wing and really taught me the alcoholic beverage business and connected me with industry leaders.

Marketing communications were just one factor in a complex alcoholic beverage business that was highly regulated and distribution driven. In addition to federal taxation and regulation of alcoholic beverages, each state had its own set of taxes, rules, and laws. Brown-Forman brands were sold into retail channels by a network of local and state distributors who managed a large portfolio of brands. Constant monitoring and interaction to keep them briefed on marketing plans was critical. Big retail chains and large on-premise accounts also received enhanced promotions that required sell-in.

Tony and I went to all the Brown-Forman annual budget meetings with the sales managers, made distributor presentations and retail calls. Dan made sure we got to know Marvin Shanken, owner of Impact, the industry's leading research and information resource. Dan opened the door to all those invaluable assets and resources and had a profound and lasting

---

10. Old Forester. Like Wine Campaign: https://bit.ly/ForesterLikeWine

impact on my career.

On a personal level, Dan made me feel like part of the Brown-Forman family and introduced me to key executives like Lee and Owsley Brown, Roger Coleman, Bill Street, and Bill Carroll. Dan and I became long-time personal friends and I owe a lot to him. Dan made it possible for me to make the transition from agency to client and that changed the trajectory of my career. More on that later.

Make appreciation matter in your career. In Asset-Based Thinking it's called raising your AQ, appreciation quotient. I'm not sure Dan realized the extent of his impact on my career and I wish I had let him know the depth of my gratitude more often. We all get caught up in the pace of life and work. Step back sometimes and express gratitude in the moment. You and the recipient will love the feeling.

Now disaster

Next is the story of one of the strangest business experiences I've ever had.

Shep received a call from Wally Bregman, VP of advertising and marketing at Ernest & Julio Gallo Wineries. Shep knew Wally when he was president of the Norman Craig & Kummel agency. Actually, Shep knew everybody. He was that kind of guy. Many of the agency's new business leads started with a call to Shep.

Gallo already had an agency of record, Y&R, but they decided to solicit ideas from a couple of agencies for a new mid-priced wine brand. Gallo was and still is a powerhouse alcoholic beverage company but they were notorious in ad circles for being one of the worst clients on the planet. They rode agencies very hard with unreasonable demands and were often abusive and condescending to agency personnel. So, why would we even consider working with them? Well, Wally presented an interesting proposition.

Gallo would pay the agency a one-time fee (as I recall it was around $65,000) to develop a brand concept and rough creative. If it was accepted, they would negotiate a further buy-out fee for use and production of the concepts. No longer-term agency relationship was involved.

This was a first and we found it interesting. It was an opportunity to draw upon our alcoholic beverage experience, perhaps create some great advertising, and earn additional income beyond the fee without enduring the agony of ongoing Gallo "punishment." Plus, Wally Bregman was a business heavyweight with whom we wanted to build a deeper relationship. It was a go. The first thing I did was clear it with Brown-Forman to make sure they didn't view it as a competitive conflict. They gave their OK and we got to work.

Given Peter's involvement with Brown-Forman it was decided that Neil would be the lead creative. The parameters of the assignment were pretty simple. Three weeks to develop and present a campaign. No agency credentials or dog and pony show. No more than two agency representatives to present the ideas to the Gallo executive committee in a one-hour meeting. So far so good.

The creative teams developed an interesting concept that put a premium twist on the term house wine. We positioned it as the "home wine" of the Gallo family, the wine they enjoyed every day as part of their family get-togethers and meals. Neil and I were the presenting team and off we went to Gallo headquarters in Modesto, California. We opted for a mid-afternoon meeting so we could take the early bird flight out of New York to San Francisco, drive to Modesto, and still have time to make final preparations for the meeting.

Wally and his team sat on one side of the conference room table and Neil and I were on the opposite side. Then Ernest Gallo and his son Joey entered and took the seats at the head of the table. When Wally introduced us we noticed something different about Joey Gallo. He was packing. In the inside pocket of his suit was a holstered gun. Definitely a first for me.

I began our presentation with the usual consumer review, strategic discussion, positioning statement, and creative brief. Per Wally's direction, I kept it short, sweet, and to the point so Neil could get to the creative quickly. Neil was a captivating presenter and had a wonderful easygoing way of bringing creative concepts and storyboards to life. Just as he was getting rolling, however, it became apparent that he was losing Ernest Gallo's attention. Then, the unthinkable happened.

Suddenly, Ernest was in full sleep mode. Not the occasional nodding off but full-on sleep punctuated with grunts and snores. We gestured to Wally asking what to do; Wally looked at Joey and they said carry on. And so we did. No one dared disturb Ernest.

As Neil was wrapping up, Ernest Gallo abruptly woke up, looked around the room and declared that he didn't like any of the work (that he slept through). He and Joey got up and left the meeting. *Holy shit.* Neil and I were dumbfounded but everyone else seemed to take it in stride. Wally asked Neil to finish and we wrapped up the presentation. Later, we met Wally in his office. He apologized and handed us a check for the agreed-upon fee.

We headed back to the sanity of New York a bit bewildered and amused. That's the last we heard from Gallo. Later on, Shep showed us an article about the idiosyncrasies of Gallo, which mentioned Ernest's penchant to fall asleep in afternoon meetings. He joked that Neil and I shouldn't take it personally. But who knows? If we had opted for a morning meeting maybe Ernest would have loved our idea. But then, I wouldn't have this wonderful story to share.

Lesson learned: Expect the unexpected and make the most of it. Every so often you may be lucky enough to experience a bizarre disaster that will add spice to your life story.

All in on NYC

In 1973, my wife Vicki and I purchased our first house in Greenbrook, New Jersey. It was a nice place to live, but it meant a ninety-minute commute to work—on a good day. As my DKG responsibilities grew this commute became too wearing so we moved to Manhattan.

New York City was struggling financially, neighborhoods had deteriorated, and real estate values were depressed. Most of our friends and family cautioned us against the move. They said it wouldn't be a positive environment to raise our three sons. They told us we'd lose our shirt on the purchase of a co-op apartment. But Vicki was certain it was the right time for a change and we followed her instincts. We agreed on the upper West Side since it was more casual and diverse than the East Side and there were reasonably priced, large apartments available in classic landmark buildings.

In 1977, we purchased a nine-room co-op at the Beresford on 81st and Central Park West. We had a great view of Central Park and were right across the street from the Museum of Natural History and the Hayden Planetarium (perfect for the boys). The Beresford was a New York City landmark, home to the likes of Beverly Sills, Isaac Stern, Peter Jennings, Rock Hudson, Tony Randall—and now, the Wasiaks.[11] A bit mind-boggling and almost too good to be true. I never knew who I would share a cab with in the morning. Also, three great marketing and media executives were neighbors and friends. Bob Forbes of the *Forbes* magazine family lived next door, Sy Lieberman the research guru was right above us, and corporate branding expert Alan Siegel of Siegel & Gale just a few floors up. Occasionally we'd have some fun talking shop. We lived there for fifteen years and it turned out to be a wonderful, opportunity-filled experience and the best lifestyle and real-estate investment we ever made. It was a magical time in New York. We made the most of it and our entire family thrived in the city.

Along with my increased responsibilities came the fun and enjoyment of client entertainment. Lots of it. It was an important part of the agency business in those days and New York was electric. Caught up in the excitement, I succumbed to the urgings of two friends from Brooklyn, Billy and Joey, who were opening up a bar on First Avenue between 56th and 57th streets. They told me it would be a perfect gathering place for ad agency people. A can't miss opportunity. They convinced me to invest with them and I became a ten percent owner for $5,000. The name of the bar was (wait for it) *Trumps*. No kidding. No comment.

We had some fun and initial success but, as happens with these ventures, it quickly fell on hard times. Later, it became painfully apparent that Billy and Joey were dispensing substances other than alcohol from behind the bar. I should have seen that one coming. Relationships became strained and about eight months after we opened Billy called to inform me that Trumps had a fire and we would be forced to close. *Whew!* Fortunately, no permanent harm was done and I was relieved to walk away with only a $5,000 loss.

I had made a textbook stupid mistake. I got caught up in my own ego, forgot lessons learned from youthful missteps, and turned off my inner compass. I knew that Billy was a

---

11. Beresford History http://bit.ly/TheBeresfordCPW

shady character, but put that aside for the bragging rights of owning a bar on Manhattan's east side. A recipe ripe for failure. You can take the boy out of Brooklyn, but you can't always take Brooklyn out of the boy. Lesson learned again: Friends with "can't miss" opportunities usually miss…big time. Sideline, hobby investments driven by vanity are always a bad idea. Keep your inner compass turned on and tuned in to avoid a stupid mistake like mine.

After that dumb diversion, I limited my client entertainment to more established, exciting NYC venues. Vicki and I frequently entertained clients and their spouses at the theater and dinner. I think we saw *A Chorus Line* and *Annie* about five times each and got to know Sardi's famous restaurant quite well. I also made sure that I had memberships to the hottest clubs like Studio 54, Xenon, and Regine's. I still have my membership cards. Studio 54, in particular, was the scene of many memorable nights.[12] Clients enjoyed going there and Vicki and I loved it. In the early days, at least, my membership card helped ease the way past the crowds. Admittedly, I sometimes partied a bit too hard in the name of client entertainment, but, hey, it was a sign of the times.

The reality is that hard work, long hours, and sacrifices are the building blocks of success. If you are working your butt off, it's okay to take advantage of sensible opportunities to combine hard work with pleasure. Just do it a little more wisely and restrained than I did.[13]

Looking to the future

At the beginning of 1979, I looked out at the horizon with the lyrical wisdom of Kenny Rogers playing in my head:

> *You've got to know when to hold 'em, know when to fold 'em,*
> *know when to walk away, and know when to run.*

With almost seven years in at DKG, I felt it was time for me to step back, widen my lens again, and sharpen my view of the future. I was growing less certain about what I saw on the horizon at DKG. We had accomplished a lot. Business was growing and we had earned Agency of the Year honors. I was working with great people some of whom would intertwine and re-connect with me throughout my career. All good there. But other factors were creating doubts about my future growth path.

The harsh realities of being a minority partner came into focus. The executive committee meetings were becoming contentious. The occasional dissension among the senior partners forced the minority partners to take sides making it uncomfortable for me. Most of the time I

---

12. Studio 54 http://bit.ly/Studio54Celebrity

13. My disco & Trumps memorabilia https://bit.ly/HankNYCMemorabilia

was on Shep's and Neil's side of the table. It also became apparent that big decisions regarding financials, investment for growth, and profit sharing happened outside the executive committee (you know, those unofficial "real meetings"). More importantly, there was no clear pathway for growth in responsibilities or additional equity. My five percent equity was nice but the big payoff would only materialize if the agency was sold and that was not in the cards at that time. When I left DKG my equity was purchased by the agency for a modest amount based on book value of the company per my employment agreement. No issues.[14]

I was approaching thirty-six years old and restless, but also complacent. I wasn't in a hurry to make a move. Then, you guessed it. Fate intervened with another phone call. This time it was Bill Genge, the CEO of KM&G International, a large, successful well-established communications agency based in Pittsburgh. They heard about me from B&B's Vic Bloede and Bill wanted to get acquainted. I didn't know Bill, but his reputation was stellar. We set a date and the events that followed completely changed the trajectory of my career and our family's life.

Always leave a connecting bridge behind you

You've heard the expression don't burn bridges behind you. That's sound advice but it belies a deficit-based mindset. Instead try Asset-Based Thinking to take it a step further. Whenever you exit and move on to another position, always leave a strong, connecting bridge back to the past. One that both you and others can cross with confidence and positivity. All of those bridges will lead to one lifelong journey of experiences that power your learning, success and fulfillment.

You've probably also heard the expression, "It's a small world." In marketing, it really is. I'm not talking about those superficial "What I can do for you?" connections that pop up. Rather, I'm referencing the people with whom you find genuine mutual respect and rapport. The connections that bring knowledge, joy, and real value to your life. I'm talking about the people who bring smiles to your face whenever you meet them, even after many years have passed. You can't manufacture those types of connections. They happen organically in your career and have uncanny ways of reappearing at different stages of your life when you least expect them and often, just when you need them. The joy of serendipity.

You really never know when they are going to happen, they just do—and if you've been building connecting bridges your entire career, you will be open to receiving their unexpected gifts. With the benefit of hindsight I realize how blessed I have been by my connections and I'm eagerly awaiting more to come my way.

---

14. Long after I left, DKG changed its name to Calet Hirsch Kurnit Spector and was sold to Ross Roy in 1986.

Mad Man Wisdom

- Some business relationships take extra work to be successful. Accept, introspect, correct, and redirect.
- Never underestimate the power and value of your experience. It is more transferrable than you think.
- Resist the urge to continue doing your old job. Move on and grow into your new responsibilities.
- Learn how to work the room and work the system. Figure out when and where the "real meetings" are taking place.
- Change the way you see meetings. Use them to build relationships and respect. Keep them strategic, social, succinct, and tell stories.
- Don't be thrown when the unthinkable happens. Once-in-a-lifetime experiences, good or bad, are great character builders.
- Collect and treasure personal connections. Make them part of the fabric of your life.
- Build bridges behind and ahead of you. The past is more than prologue; it can be fuel for your progress.
- Raising your AQ (Appreciation Quotient) is a never-ending journey. Share and declare your appreciation of others in the moment. Be grateful for the assets they add to your life.
- Surrender to serendipity.

Marketing Truisms & Tips

Values and Ideals: The Roots of Powerful Brands

In my University of Southern California (USC) classes we spend a substantial amount of time discussing purpose-driven marketing as a way for a business or brand to bond with consumers based on shared needs and interests. But before diving into purpose, I make sure students have a strong grounding in foundational brand values and ideals. They are linked but different. Purpose-driven marketing is a strategic element of a communications platform. Brand values are the organic roots from which purpose-driven marketing grows.

Consumers have always adopted brands based on their value (i.e., price/benefit ratios) and values (i.e., shared emotional connections). But today that linkage is essential to success. Studies show that the majority of consumers prefer brands that sincerely embrace a greater good ethos as part of their DNA. Brand values must flow seamlessly from brand benefits. If not, they become gratuitous appendages.

I use an excellent book by Jim Stengel, former CMO of Proctor & Gamble called *Grow, How Ideals Power Growth and Profit at the World's Greatest Companies* as the basis for brand values discussions.[15] The book offers compelling factual evidence that values and ideals-driven brands outperform competitors across all business categories.

In the book, Jim differentiates between values and organizational mission statements. He defines mission statements as "widely held set of beliefs and expectations about what you deliver and how you deliver it validated by customers' experiences." Mission statements are important, but unfortunately, all too often they are non-differentiating lists of clichés and platitudes. To avoid those pitfalls, Jim provides a clear and crisp description of brand values and ideals.

"The ideal is the business/brand's inspirational reason for being. It explains why the brand exists and the impact it seeks to make on its consumers and the world."

Brand value statements are short, powerful, easily understood, and emotional. You read it, you get it, you feel it. Here are just three examples cited in the book:

P&G's Pampers are a lot more than convenient diapers to keep your kids dry and clean. Pampers exists to help parents *care for their babies' & toddlers' healthy, happy development.*

Red Bull is more than a satisfying pick-me-up of caffeine. Red Bull exists to *energize the world!*

IBM is more than hardware, software, and consulting services. IBM exists to *help build a smarter planet.*

Living up to and into brand values differentiates great brands from good brands. Inwardly, brand values create your culture. Outwardly they define your brand. Hence the importance of living it on the inside before taking it outside. It is critical that the path to purpose-driven marketing follow this linear path:

Meaningful Organizational Mission Statement —> Brand Value Proposition —> Brand Values Articulation —> Purpose-Driven Content Platform

Unfortunately, many marketers make the critical mistake of reversing the order. They start by developing brand purpose content based on what is currently in vogue and capturing attention and buzz. Then they retrofit to find what could possibly relate back to brand values. That's a sure recipe for failure. More to come on that later with my take on Gillette's 2019 "The best a man can be"campaign.

---

15. *Grow* by Jim Stengel https://amzn.to/2M9jeDd

Chapter 4 Footnotes

Scan QR codes for direct links to footnote content.

4.1 DKG Agency of the Year

4.5 B&B Wins Corning

4.9 Go Forestering Campaign

4.10 Old Forester: Made Like Wine Ads

4.13 Hank's NYC Memorabilia

Chapter 5:

Elevate Anticipation and Desire Above Anxiety and Doubt

The '80s are called the Me Decade, the Yuppie Decade, and the Decade of Greed. Remember Gordon Gekko's infamous "Greed is good" declaration in the movie *Wall Street*? It was certainly a unique time to be alive and in the business world. In those ten years, I experienced a mix of triumph, turbulence, and transition. It ended up being my Transformation Decade.

It all started with my casual meeting with KM&G International (aka Ketchum) CEO Bill Genge in early 1979, which led to my appointment as President of Ketchum New York—what a milestone! KM&G International was a solid agency managed by good people with top-notch clients and ample resources to be successful. My anxiety was at a minimum, my anticipation levels were high, and I had no doubt that I would smoothly settle into my position. But just as I was hitting my stride at Ketchum, the unexpected happened again in a really big way. I was offered a C-suite marketing position at a client company I admired and had loved working with: Brown-Forman.

Sometimes you have to make watershed decisions that impact your career and family simultaneously. This was mine. The new opportunity felt like a dream come true for me but it came with a big "but." It meant we would have to leave the life we loved in New York and move to Louisville, Kentucky. This decision affected five lives, especially those of our boys who grew up as NYC kids. Anxieties and doubts immediately popped up and we weighed them against the magnitude of the opportunity.

In making the decision, my wife Vicki and I tried to focus on future career and lifestyle benefits instead of fixating on what we would lose in the move and what would happen if it didn't work out. This enabled us to better weigh pros and cons and examine acceptable scenarios that mitigated some of the anxiety and risk. Then, with eyes wide open we chose to move to Louisville and to make it work for us. Later on, when a convergence of opportunity and necessity pulled us back to New York, we were also able to adjust and keep moving forward. It turned out to be a fast and fateful roundtrip.

It just goes to show…when you elevate positive anticipation and fulfilling desires above anxiety and doubt, handling big changes becomes less daunting. You're able to spend more time advancing and less time worrying.

Ahhh the '80s

The '80s began with heightened tensions between the East and West, the Iran hostage crisis, gas shortages, and a severe economic downturn. Fortunately, the economy quickly rebounded and we entered into a sustained period of economic growth.

"Bigger is better" became the mantra and huge corporate mergers abounded. Of the 100 largest advertisers in 1980, only a third were still independent by 1990.[1] To keep up with their clients, agencies needed to increase size and scale so they also grew through the most dramatic set of acquisitions in the industry's history. *Ad Age* called it the "Decade of the Deal" and the "British Invasion" with UK companies gobbling many top US agencies. I, too, would be swept up in these mergers as the decade evolved.

Technology had a dramatic impact on marketing communications. Cable reshaped the TV industry and networks saw their share of audiences slip to under sixty percent. MTV became the new music culture while the VCR enabled viewers for the first time to record their programs for later viewing and, most impactfully for the industry, bypass commercials. Direct-response home shopping services like the Home Shopping Network and QVC emerged and infomercials popped up everywhere. To maximize ad efficiencies, agencies shifted from 30-second to 15-second commercials making twice as many commercial slots available and adding clutter to the airways.

Coke's "Mean Joe Green," Pepsi's "Taste of A New Generation," and Wendy's "Where's The Beef?" were among the noteworthy campaigns of the decade.[2] Political advertising also entered a new era with President Reagan's 1984 re-election campaign: "It's morning again in America."[3] The Reagan re-election team, led by Mike Deaver, wanted to appoint an ad hoc all-star team of ad land's best talent instead of a traditional agency. Deaver enlisted ad man Jim Travis to build what was called the Tuesday Team and they created that historic campaign. Two prominent members of that team, Jim Travis and Hal Riney, would end up playing a role in my career.[4] But perhaps the most dramatic marketing strategy and commercial was the Orwellian Apple Macintosh "1984" commercial created by Chiat Day.[5] It premiered during the 1984 Super Bowl and launched the Macintosh revolution.

---

1. In 1980, the only top 10 US agency owned by a holding company was Interpublic's McCann-Erickson. By 1990, only two of the top 10 agencies remained independent: Young & Rubicam and Grey.

2. Classic '80s commercials https://bit.ly/80sCommercials

3. Reagan campaign https://bit.ly/ReaganCampaign

4. Article about the Tuesday Team https://bit.ly/TuesdayTeam

5. *1984* commercial https://bit.ly/Apple1984Commercial

Earning the top spot

KM&G International, better known as Ketchum, was the 23rd largest agency in the United States. It was headquartered in Pittsburgh with offices in New York and San Francisco, each with a President and CEO. KM&G's CEO Bill Genge was interested in me for the position of President and CEO of Ketchum New York and member of KM&G International's board of directors. I met Bill and other Ketchum executives over six weeks and I liked them all.

In March 1979, Bill offered me the Ketchum NY position. I accepted and started in April 1979.[6] When my wife Vicki told our six-year-old son Jason I had a new job as president he asked, "of the United States?" Not quite, Jason, but it was definitely a big leap in my career. It took almost fourteen years and three jobs before, at age thirty-six, I earned the President and CEO title I'd been striving for. Now, the buck would stop with me and my leadership and decision-making skills would be put to the test. Sure, I had a little anxiety, but I knew that I had a solid and diverse base of experience and had learned from the best in the business. I traded anxiety for positive anticipation and confidently stepped into the role I'd been preparing myself for. It felt great!

I liked everything about this position: a CEO title, A-list clients, a top creative director, an open, ethical corporate culture, and a great boss, Bill Genge. The exit from DKG went smoothly. My bridge to the past was clear and I felt confident my colleague and client friendships would endure. I do remember, however, that DKG partner Larry Spector made it a point to remind me of the one year non-compete clause prohibiting my solicitation of DKG clients and hiring DKG personnel. I respected and honored that commitment through all the changes that would follow. In the course of a career, you will be called upon to make commitments to employers, colleagues, clients. Some will be contractual, but most will be verbal or handshakes. Commitments mean something and living up to them builds trust, self-respect and personal power.

Ketchum New York had well-appointed offices on Park Avenue South and 36th Street—a bit more south and a longer cab ride than I'd grown accustomed to. I'd found myself back at a larger more traditional agency with a much different vibe than the free-wheeling DKG and DDB. I embraced the change and eased myself into this lower key, more structured environment.

Ketchum New York was in reasonably good shape and operating at a profit. My creative partner was celebrated art director Walter Kaprielian who helped get me up to speed and introduced me to clients. We were a great team and developed a lasting friendship. In fact, a short ten years later, Walter would come back into my life in a new role. KM&G CEO Bill Genge was a classy, low-key executive. He became a mentor and showed me a refreshing "not

---

6. Bill told me twenty-two candidates had been personally interviewed before they offered me the job.

New York" sensitivity, wisdom and style. Plus, he liked that I was teaching at Pace University and encouraged me to keep that going. His remit to me: Breathe energy into the agency, set and achieve more aggressive growth and profit goals, energize the new business effort, and fine tune staffing as needed. A hefty list of opportunities (note that I didn't call them "challenges").

Taking care of business: old and new

The cornerstone accounts of the agency were Johnson & Johnson baby products division, Japan Airlines, Air Jamaica, General Foods, Schering Plough and…ready for it? Avis' commercial division. I just couldn't get away from Avis. I had experience in all of these categories so my learning curve was short and my credentials were respected by Ketchum's clients.

Given my Alitalia experience I focused first on our two airline accounts: Japan Airlines (JAL) and Air Jamaica. They could not have been more different. As with Alitalia, both were their country's flag carrier and run by the government. The JAL client was conservative and methodical. Communications plans were coordinated closely with management in Japan and in synch with JAL's global footprint. Air Jamaica was a delightfully different story.

Air Jamaica's culture was more open-ended, less predictable, and operations were sometimes affected by periods of political unrest in Kingston. Its management was headed by a mercurial, larger-than-life Jamaican, "Biggie" Machado. Ketchum's mandate was to make sure that all marketing communications reflected the fun-loving, welcoming, and celebratory culture of the island and its people. Thinking out-of-the box was encouraged. Our tagline for Air Jamaica was, "We make you feel good all over," and that attitude was reflected and delivered in all communications and in-flight experiences.

Air Jamaica passengers experienced Jamaica the moment they set foot on the plane. Jamaican music, headphones, colorful cabins, free local welcome drinks, authentic Jamaican food, and friendly outgoing cabin personnel. It was topped off with a fashion show featuring Jamaican designers proudly staged by the flight attendants with the aisles as their runways. One of the first things I did was take a weekend trip to Jamaica to get a feel for the experience and yes, I felt good all over. The airline was ahead of its time in bringing brand culture to life and unabashedly having it enwrap the customer experience. And this was before the days of the internet, mobile devices, and Instagrammable moments. I can only imagine the user-generated content that would have been shared. At USC one of my classes is entitled *Culture is Marketing Currency in The Digital Era* and I use Air Jamaica as a precursor example from the analog days.

Working with Johnson & Johnson's baby products division was a very different yet equally gratifying experience. I'd long admired J&J for their integrity and consumer commitment and used their marketing programs as best practice examples in my Pace classes. J&J's powerful "patients above profits" values and credo permeated their marketing:

We believe our first responsibility is to the doctors, nurses, and patients, to mothers and fathers and all others who use our products and services, In meeting their needs everything we do must be of high quality. We must constantly strive to reduce our costs in order to maintain reasonable prices, Customers' orders must be serviced promptly and accurately. Our suppliers and distributors must have an opportunity to make a fair profit.[7]

In 1982, J&J lived up this credo when they recalled thirty-one-million packages of Tylenol because of product tampering deaths. Before that no one recalled anything. They raised the bar on corporate responsibility and consumer safety.[8]

Jim Scowcroft, the J&J management supervisor, effectively ran the day-to-day account operations. I focused my attention on building a relationship with the division head Pat Lonergan. Pat was a long-time, well-regarded executive who lived and breathed J&J's credo. I admired how Pat put that credo into practice by making sure his brand teams and agencies were well-versed and committed to reflecting J&J values in marketing communications. It was another great learning experience that further reinforced my belief in the power of living up to and into brand values.

My approach to ramping up new business activities was measured. For the first few months I worked with the business development group in Pittsburgh to ensure we had the right supplemental research and media resources in place. Then, my creative partner Walter and I revved up the Ketchum new business machine and got to work. In the next twelve months we landed new assignments from General Foods and J&J, followed by successful pitches for Hanes Hosiery, ACCO Industries, and British West Indies Airlines (BWIA). Now we had three airline accounts! In addition to new revenue these wins were confidence builders.

Feeling good about what we could deliver, and being past my twelve month non-compete restriction, it was time to reach out to a few of my prior clients to see if there could be a role for Ketchum New York. My first call was to Dan Schusterman at Brown-Forman Distillers to set up a familiarization visit. As a courtesy, I called Larry Spector at DKG to let him know what I was doing. He appreciated the heads-up and jokingly wished me well in taking away one of McCann's assigned brands. I got the message...don't mess with DKG's brand assignments.

An offer I couldn't refuse…maybe?

Dan was receptive to my call for a meeting and said that he would like to include Bill Carroll, Chairman of Brown-Forman's import division, the Jos. Garneau Company. I knew Bill and

---

7. J&J Credo http://bit.ly/JJCredo

8. J&J Tylenol recall https://bit.ly/JJTylenolRecall

welcomed that opportunity. Dan requested that we keep it low key, so I came solo and we had the meeting at Bill Carroll's home. I put together a credentials presentation deck that we could review across a table and off I went.

I arrived at Bill's and over lunch we had a great time catching up. When I suggested that I take them through my presentation they looked at me and said, "Don't bother." Then they lowered the boom. Bill told me they brought me to Louisville under false pretenses. He wanted to hire me not the agency. My jaw dropped.

Since Brown-Forman's management was already well-acquainted with me Bill had received clearance to float the offer of Executive Vice President, director of marketing and brand management of the Jos. Garneau Company based in Louisville, Kentucky. I was absolutely floored. Once I regained my composure, I told Bill I was flattered and definitely interested. I was offered a doorway into the client C-suite working with people I knew and respected. *How could I not be interested?* With a wink, Dan excused himself and Bill and I continued our discussion. Bill explained that I would report directly to him and that the current president of Garneau, Mason Tush, would remain in place. Mason was a long-time Brown-Forman executive with a sales background and close to retirement age. No promises were made but I could see the handwriting on the wall.

When I returned to New York and told Vicki she was equally shocked and happy for me. But this would be a monumental move for our family and there were some big hurdles we would have to get over before it could become a reality.

Here's the short version of what unfolded over the next month:

Bill and I worked out the details of my package and I had reassuring conversations with Brown-Forman executives and brothers Lee and Owsley Brown. Their great-grandfather founded the company back in 1870. The more they talked about my role and responsibilities, the tradition, values, and culture of the company the more excited and enthused I became. Vicki and I flew to Louisville to get a feel for the place. We also dealt with heavy doses of anxiety, doubt, and uncertainty. We loved our New York life and were closely attached to our co-op apartment at the Beresford. The boys loved the city and we worried about uprooting them from their friends and schools. I was also sad about leaving my professorship at Pace behind. What if after we packed up our entire lives things didn't work out at Brown-Forman? What if we just didn't like the Louisville life? What would we do then?

We managed to put the "what-ifs" aside, let anticipation and desire drive our thinking, and laid out a plan that could hopefully get us over these hurdles and mitigate our risk. We petitioned the Beresford's co-op board for permission to sublease our apartment. These were rarely allowed, but after a few discussions they granted a sublease of up to three years as long as the tenant was approved by the board. Our friend and real estate broker Phyllis Koch took over and a few weeks later we had a great tenant lined up and approved: a top-level German diplomat posted to the United Nations and his family of five. The sublet amount was $4,000 per month, just what the we needed to cover our carrying costs and expenses for the apartment. What a relief—we had our escape valve back to New York in place.

I was totally transparent with Brown-Forman about the terms of our sublet arrangements and that was acceptable to them. I accepted the offer and soon we were off to bluegrass country!

The hard part

Fourteen years after being shut out of my client-side dream job right after college, I had landed an EVP marketing position at a premier alcoholic beverage company. My prior track record with Brown-Forman and respect for their management bolstered my confidence that this was the right move. Nevertheless, resigning from Ketchum was difficult. I was happy in my position and had an upward trajectory to increased responsibilities. Perhaps more significantly, CEO Bill Genge and I had developed a close personal relationship. I knew this would be a blow to him and I felt like I was letting him down.

When I called Bill to tell him I was accepting the position at Brown-Forman he asked that I not close the Ketchum door completely until he and I could meet personally. We met at Ketchum New York a few days later. I felt it was important to tell him the unusual circumstances surrounding my being offered the job so he knew I hadn't been actively looking to exit Ketchum. Bill appreciated that and asked if there was anything they could do financially or organizationally to get me to stay. I expressed my appreciation and stressed that I was not running away from Ketchum but being pulled toward a position and career move I'd always wanted.

That evening Bill took my wife Vicki and me to dinner to gauge her comfort level in making the lifestyle move to Louisville. Bill was genuinely concerned for our well-being and I greatly appreciated the way he handled us personally. We told Bill we understood the risks and explained our arrangements. He thanked me for my contributions and we agreed on a one-month exit schedule.

My time at Ketchum came to a short, bittersweet end but there were no hard feelings. Bill and I stayed in contact and enjoyed some great conversations in the years that followed. He was one of the classiest, nicest people I had the privilege of working with and I let him know that whenever the opportunity arose. I sometimes share this experience with my students and others as a teaching moment about moving on in your career. My golden rule: Never use the leverage of a new job offer to extract additional salary or responsibilities from your current employer. It's unfair to both companies and rarely results in long-term job satisfaction.

Essentially, there are three major reasons to leave a job:

1. Irreconcilable differences or dissatisfaction (e.g., environment, salary,

responsibilities, or future advancement.) that push you to make a change

2. External out-of-your control situations that require you to change (e.g., family illness)

3. New more exciting, better fit opportunities that you find or that find you (e.g., that dream job you've always wanted or a relocation to the city of your dreams)

Whatever the reason, once you've decided to exit be true to yourself and stick to it. If your current employer asks if there's anything they can do to get you to stay listen appreciatively and exit gracefully. Remember to always leave those connecting bridges.

In business there is truth in the notion that no one is indispensable. As I moved into top management I, too, dealt with instances of valued employees moving on to new positions. Those resignations created short-term difficulties but we always found a way to compensate and move ahead. I rarely, if ever, asked what I could do to make them stay. Instead, I asked what we could have done differently to keep them in the company. I learned from their responses and made changes as appropriate.

My new ole Kentucky home

We purchased a home in the suburbs of Louisville and lined up schools for the boys.[9] The moving vans pulled up outside the Beresford on July 2, 1980, and dropped off our belongings in Kentucky three days later on July 5. We moved in, celebrated my thirty-seventh birthday and off I went to work.

Working at Brown-Forman was a game-changer. Moving from the agency side to the client side was not common and could be a difficult adjustment. My transition was easier since I was comfortable with Brown-Forman management, already knew many of my direct reports, and had a good understanding of the alcoholic beverage business.

Brown-Forman headquarters were housed in a traditional colonial style building. The Garneau office was directly across the street in a totally different environment. It was an amazing space located in a hundred-year-old landmark building previously used to store barrels of aging bourbon. They had converted it into a wonderful, modern, open, light-filled office building while keeping its landmark status. The mix of history with the present brought a great energy

---

9. We selected St. Xavier as Brian and Gregg's high school - run by the very same order of Xaverian brothers that taught me. They liked that.

to the offices and I loved it.[10]

The Garneau company was a very profitable $250 million import division of Brown-Forman with an A-list portfolio of brands, including Martell Cognac, Veuve Clicquot Champagne, Old Bushmills Irish Whisky, Noilly Prat Vermouths, Ambassador Scotch, Pepe Lopez Tequila, Bolla and Cella Italian wines, and Anheuser German wines. It was an interesting mix of premium priced and luxury brands with global footprints. Some were centuries old and still owned and managed by descendants of the founders. Working with some of the world's oldest and most respected companies and families was special and very different from my more mainstream consumer packaged goods experiences.

My initial responsibilities as EVP marketing at the Garneau company included managing substantial consumer-focused marketing budgets, partner agency management, and coordinating with brand owners and suppliers in Europe. My agency experience prepared me well, and I easily adjusted to the client-side mindset and workflow. Then in mid-December my boss Bill Carrol had another very pleasant surprise for me. He informed me that Mason Tush, the current division president, was retiring and that I would be named Garneau President immediately. What a Christmas present![11] [12]

Again, I was thrust into a dramatically expanded sphere of responsibilities sooner than I anticipated. I now had full profit and loss (P&L) and operational responsibility for a $250 million-dollar division. In addition to directing marketing, I would be managing a sales force, distributor performance, finance, government compliance, and supplier relations. Everything I had hoped for. Sure, I was anxious and nervous, but I relied on my prior experience in similar situations to elevate my positive anticipation and confident desires. I pushed aside anxiety and self-doubt and jumped in.

Bill let me know he had complete confidence in my ability to do the job and assured me I would get all the support I needed. And he delivered. I was fortunate to have great colleagues who went all-out to show me the ropes. The brand teams were already doing a great job managing marketing, so I immediately stopped doing my old job. I put all of my initial energy into learning financial operations, working with the sales force, and interacting with suppliers and brand owners. I also had to fill three top positions quickly. I recruited Ray Dryden, former brand director at Abbott Labs, as SVP and director of brand management. I hired Brown-Forman's first female brand manager Mimi Zinniel.[13] And I promoted a strong

---

10. Garneau building information: https://bit.ly/GarneauBldg

11. Mason's retirement was sooner than he wanted.

12. My friend and colleague, Dan Schusterman, was simultaneously promoted to President of Brown-Forman's whisky division. We joked about being friendly rivals. Garneau Promotion: https://bit.ly/WasiakGarneauPresident

13. The alcoholic beverage business was dominated by male executives. Bringing in Mimi was well-received. I felt good about that.

sales manager, Joe Herpin, to SVP and director of sales. Joe, too, would circle back into my life after my Brown-Forman days came to a close.

I looked, listened, asked tons of questions, and was overwhelmed with the support and encouragement I received. I got myself up to speed quickly thanks to the support of others. But adopting this "help me" mindset was a bit difficult at first. I had to get beyond old notions that asking for help would undermine my leadership. I admitted to myself that I couldn't do this alone and realized that it was actually my responsibility to ask for help. I saw it as a sign of strength and adopted a posture of sincere, confident humility. The response was amazing. No matter what stage you are in your career realize that you can't do it alone. Turn necessity and humility into your strength.

Nothing happens until someone sells something

I've often said that Brown-Forman was where I grew up and really learned what it takes to run a business. Now rather than generating revenue from client fees and billings, I was responsible for generating sales of tangible goods: bottles and cases of alcoholic beverages. It required big thinking, hands-on work, and attention to detail.

The planning and budgeting process was rigorous. Sales goals and budgets were developed from the ground up in an intense two weeks of meetings with sales managers. Substantial expense and operating budgets were tightly managed and monitored. Bi-monthly sales and budget meetings were essential. Financial reporting was complex. Grueling travel schedules visiting markets and overseas suppliers were an essential part of my job. Personnel management was structured and had to be coordinated with corporate HR policies and procedures. I learned the value of formal employee evaluations and talent development. Yes, my client-side job was definitely different, more challenging, and tougher than anything I'd done on the agency side. But I was finally "walking in the client's shoes" and loving every step.

As you step into management positions two opposing voices will whisper loudly in your ear:

- Focus on the big picture
- The devil is in the details

My time at Brown-Forman taught me that it's not an either/or choice. It's about balance. I had to adjust my thinking, recognize when and how to rely on trusted colleagues for information and advice, and better manage my time to strike the balance that was right for me. It was not easy but it was essential. It required discipline, flexibility, and trust. And as I became more disciplined in my approach to balance, my confidence grew by leaps and bounds.

Motivating the salesforce to make quotas and stretch goals was an important part of the job. Beyond bonuses, we incentivized the sales force by rewarding top performers and their significant others with trips to our suppliers in Europe. These were first-class adventures and Vicki and I had the pleasure of hosting two of them. One year we visited Italy and Ireland and the other was a whirlwind trip to France to visit Martell and Veuve Clicquot. In addition to being great morale builders, these trips were inspiring reminders of the heritage, care, and craftsmanship behind the brands we marketed.

We were given private tours of the centuries-old cellars of Cliquot. We walked the Bolla family's vineyards. We stayed at Chanteloup, the elegant Martell estate, where since 1715 they've crafted their cognac. We watched the craftsmen at the oldest distillery in the world, Old Bushmills, established in 1608. Awe inspiring. I've mentioned the importance and power of brand values a few times. When values are wrapped in the gravitas of heritage and tradition their impact is magnified even further. I was fortunate to be associated with brands that had that special aura. Hopefully, you will be lucky in that regard as well. If not, identify heritage brands you admire, and study them for lessons and inspiration.

Absorbing the culture

The working environment at Brown-Forman was very different from what I was accustomed to. I had seen glimpses of it while working on Old Forester at DKG but living it every day took some adjustment. There were a lot more meetings and structure and the atmosphere was always polite and congenial. The day started very early, wound down around 5:30 p.m., and late nights were rare. Just the opposite of the typical workday at an agency.

A typical day in the office included pre-lunch drinks in the executive lounge, followed by an elegantly served lunch in the executive dining room (no wine), with end-of-day get-togethers in my conference room. These were firsts for me. The collegial environment was great for getting to know each other and casual business conversation. But it also required me to take a deep look inwardly and modify my behaviors.

I felt sluggish and less sharp in the afternoon after our elaborate lunches. I also realized that hosting end-of-day cocktails sent my staff home in their cars buzzed or worse.[14] I followed the lead of CEO Lee Brown, who did not drink in the office and cut back on the after-work conference room activity. Alcohol was obviously an inherent part of the job and Brown-Forman supported moderation in its employees and marketing messages. For the most part, common sense and good judgment prevailed.

---

14. This was before MADD and the crackdown on drunk driving. For last call, bars in Louisville even offered "travelers" for their departing patrons.

The company town—Southern style

Brown-Forman was deeply embedded in the Louisville community and I benefited from those connections right away. I was introduced to the dean of the business school at the University of Louisville and was hired to teach undergraduate marketing classes. Yes! It was a nice change to be teaching on a "real campus" versus a city building and in a classroom with a non-New York mix of students. I enjoyed that for three semesters.

A substantial part of social life also involved Brown-Forman colleagues and business-related activities. When Garneau distributors or suppliers came to town they were hosted and feted in grand Louisville style. There were weekend get-togethers in colleague's homes, company events, and parties at Louisville's finest private clubs. And of course, there was Louisville's signature event, the Kentucky Derby, held the first week in May.

Derby Week was an all-out cultural happening and Brown-Forman was a big participant. Each year Garneau would invite one or two of our suppliers and we rolled out the red carpet. Vicki and I had the pleasure of hosting the Bolla family, Jacques and Dominique Martell, and Jack McGowan and Jonathan McSweeney from Irish Distillers. We experienced the Derby in its full glory and splendor. Those memories are still with us.

Garneau also sponsored another Louisville horse race, the Bolla Hardscuffle Steeplechase. Held three weeks after the Derby it was a select and classy event. Everyone in Garneau was encouraged to attend and it was a great morale building perk.[15] Yours truly had the honor of presenting the winning $25,000 check and trophy each year. I joked with my sons about how new this horseracing stuff was to me. The closest I'd been to a racetrack was driving by Aqueduct raceway on the Long Island Expressway or going to the off-track betting parlor (OTB) with my dad. But as they say, "When in Rome, do as the Romans do." And so we did and we had a ball.

The gift of volunteering

Everyone in management positions at Brown-Forman was encouraged to get involved and volunteer in the community. Alice Cary, wife of Brown-Forman CEO Lee Brown, was involved with the Louisville ballet. When she found out that Vicki and I were season ticket holders to the American Ballet Theater in New York I was recruited to join the Louisville Ballet's board.[16] The Louisville ballet was in the process of developing a long-range strategic plan, an effort that was being led by another volunteer, Mike Miles, the CEO of Kentucky Fried Chicken. Mike

---

15. Bolla Hardscuffle article https://bit.ly/BollaHardscuffle

16. This Brooklyn boy fell in love with the ballet at Lincoln Center. I did not give up our subscription when we moved to Louisville.

was a highly skilled, seasoned executive and a prominent member of the community. I was thrilled when he enlisted me to work with him on the strategic plan. Working with Mike was another special opportunity to learn from the best. Remember Mike; he and I would work together again in a much different situation.

The Louisville Ballet gave me my first taste of volunteering and it whet my appetite for more. Since then, volunteering has had a deep, lasting, and profoundly positive effect on my life. Being a volunteer has helped me appreciate how good life has been to me and instilled a sense of fulfillment and desire to give back. Volunteering has made me better at everything I do. Everything. In business it has taught me the importance and true meaning of "mission" and how making it the driver of all behavior and action is critical to success. In my USC classes and whenever I interact with career starters I emphasize the importance of volunteering. I push people hard to be active and involved volunteers at organizations with which they have an affinity. Volunteer early and often in your life, and you will thank yourself for the rest of your life. I promise. My only regret is that I didn't volunteer earlier on in my career and with more consistency.

Two years in and things could not have been going better for me at Brown-Forman. I loved the company and working with an eclectic mix of amazing people. I was learning and growing as a businessman. My family was soaking up the best of what Louisville had to offer and we made the most of those amazing trips to Europe. Vicki did her best to adjust to the role of corporate wife but I saw that it sometimes could be wearing. I was travelling more than I was home so I didn't miss New York too much. My family, however, was a bit more homesick. We occasionally said "y'all" but our New York accents were still intact. It was a good thing, too. Stay tuned for why.

Mad Man Wisdom

- Trust is your most potent asset. Make keeping commitments one of your strongest character traits.
- Exit positions with integrity and class. Holding an employer hostage never works.
- Contingency plans help clarify and focus career decisions. Use them to overcome fear and doubt.
- Look for your "grow-up" career moments and step up to seize them.
- Discover and leverage the brand values in whatever business you're associated with.
- Seek help with confident humility. No one can do it all alone. Make others your assets.

- Master the art of balancing macro and micro thinking. Delving deeper often makes the big picture brighter.
- Connections are the gifts that keep on giving. Prepare yourself for colleagues resurfacing and impacting your life at every career stage.
- Volunteer. Volunteer. Volunteer. Help others while you discover more about yourself.

Marketing Truisms & Tips

Culture Is Priceless Marketing Currency

Companies now live in glass houses. There are no secrets. Digital, mobile, and social media changed all that. Whatever is going on, positive or negative, will ooze out. And that's why great companies put their cultural DNA on display for all to see.

One of the most powerful and prevalent factors influencing C-Suite thinking and marketing strategies is a renewed energy and emphasis on the importance of culture. It is increasingly tied to marketplace success. The hard assets that make companies competitive are important but they are merely the costs of entry. You can't show up without them. Enlightened leaders recognize that human soft assets are the differentiators that separate the great from the good.

Company culture must be defined and led from the top and then liberated to permeate every nook and cranny of the company. It should embody how a company operates, why people want to work there, the reasons partners and suppliers enjoy doing business with them, and why customers trust and purchase from them.

One of the exemplary companies I admire and reference often is Zappos, the online shoe and clothing retailer.[17] My friend Erica O'Grady introduced me to Zappos CEO Tony Hsieh and he and I were on the same digital conference program in 2010.[18] Tony gave a great presentation on company culture and success at this conference and here were my key takeaways:

1. Make sure all the customer satisfaction "cost-of-entry" basics are in place.

2. Be able to articulate your committable core values. Some of Zappos' include: create fun and a little weirdness; to be adventurous, creative and open minded; and to be humble.

3. Define your purpose and ethos simply. Zappos is to "Deliver

---

17. Zappos was purchased by Amazon in 2009 for one billion dollars.

18. Erica is wonderful serendipitous connection you will hear more about later.

happiness through WOW service."[19]

4. The three pillars of Zappos' business success are: Culture. Customer Service. Clothing. Those first two should apply to all businesses.

5. Everyone should contribute to articulating and living the company culture. In fact, Zappos employees wrote the company's first Culture Book in 2009 and publish an updated version every year.[20] Zappos employees are also encouraged to blog about their work experiences and be active on social media.

6. Hire with a *Culture First* mindset. After Zappos new hires finish an intensive orientation and training program they are de-briefed and then offered $2000 to leave the company. If someone accepts it is viewed as a well-spent two grand as it means the culture is not something they feel passionate enough about to stay.

7. Culture is your brand. Be real and there's nothing to fear.

In the Q&A that followed, skeptical "suits" in the audience commented that all the fun, personalized happiness stuff was great for Zappos but not for serious companies like theirs. Tony's response was simple.

"Yes, it's right for Zappos and probably not right for yours. It doesn't matter what your culture is. Just have one you deeply believe in, then live up to it and into it every day."[21]

Tony closed his presentation by referencing the secret to success given by rapper Puff Daddy to Biggie Smalls, aka Notorious B.I.G.: "Chase the dream, not the paper."

Culture is the company dream lived every day.

---

19. Tony Hsieh's book on Zappos *Delivering Happiness*. http://bit.ly/DeliveriHappiness

20. Link to 2018 Culture Book http://bit.ly/ZapposCultureBook

21. Tony loved our book, *Change the Way You See Everything*. I sent him copies for the Zappos employee library. Book: http://bit.ly/HankABTBook

Chapter 5 Footnotes
Scan QR codes for direct links to footnote content.

5.2 1980's Classic Commercials

5.3 Morning in America Commercial

5.4 The Tuesday Team Article

5.5 Apple 1984 Commercial

5.8 J&J Tylenol Article

5.12 Wasiak/Schusterman Promotion

5.15 Bolla Hardscuffle Article

Chapter 6:

Priorities Provide Perspective to Power Your Decisions

My time at Brown-Forman Distillers was going as planned, and I was getting some great confidence-building experience and expertise. Then, circumstances out of my control arose that changed the game for me and my family. My triumphs were overshadowed by turbulence.

When the safety-valve sublet of our apartment at the Beresford hit a snag I was forced to make another big career and life decision. I had to find the right balance of personal and professional priorities for this new set of circumstances. Professional ambition had been the impetus for my decision to join Brown-Forman and move our family of five from New York City to Louisville, Kentucky. Now, I had to reexamine my priorities from a different perspective. While I was content with work and life in Louisville, it was not the longer-term lifestyle of choice for my family. Family was the driver behind my next move and so back to New York City we went. Our "Ole Kentucky Home" became our old Kentucky home and we found ourselves back at the Beresford on Central Park West.

Initially, I didn't have a clear direction or plan on how I would find a new job in NYC. Then an unexpected opportunity found me at precisely the right time. A stroke of good luck led me to a different corporate life just when I needed it, and I was appointed chief operating officer (COO) of one of Norton Simon's subsidiary companies, Somerset Importers, based in Manhattan.

But it wasn't smooth sailing from there. Uncontrollable circumstances came into play again in a very different way. I found myself dealing with a round of bad luck and corporate politics that put me in unfamiliar—and unwanted—territory. Leaving Somerset required me to evaluate my priorities once again, but now from a perspective of vulnerability. I didn't like where I was and I had to figure out where I wanted to go from there.

There are no guarantees in life. But what my experience goes to show is that getting your priorities nailed down first will help you make better decisions for the future. Nothing ever goes as anticipated, but when you let your priorities provide perspective, you can get yourself unstuck and keep moving in the right direction.

Two great campaigns

As president of the Jos. Garneau Company, I was in charge of $250 million in sales, five brand teams, a sales force, promotion department, and substantial marketing budgets. Luckily,

Garneau's marketing communications were in relatively good shape when I arrived and there were no major issues that required immediate attention. Our agency, Richard K. Manoff, had recently been purchased by British agency Geers Gross and relationships with the brand teams were satisfactory.[1] Manoff created solid advertising for all of our brands including very successful television campaigns for Bolla and Cella, Garneau's biggest brands.[2] The agency's creative director was a colleague from my DDB days, Irwin Warren.

Ciao Bolla!

Bolla was introduced to the US market as a well-priced mainstream brand. It totally changed the way imported wines were marketed by de-mystifying the category for consumers. Most imported wine brands had an array of different types, varieties, vintage years, and pricing in their portfolios. This was an insular strategy that added mystique to a brand, but it confused and complicated consumer purchase decisions. Bolla eliminated confusion by offering three varieties each priced the same: one white (Soave) and two red (Valpolicella and Bardolino). It was a brilliant and effective marketing strategy. Bill Juckett, the Bolla brand director, was smart, really understood the business and did an excellent job.

As Bolla grew and the import category became more competitive, we decided to focus advertising on reinforcing Bolla's Italian origins, family heritage, and quality. Manoff created a campaign with a unique twist. Franco Bolla, the well-respected head winemaker became the brand spokesperson. Franco was handsome and charismatic but his English was poor. Irwin's solution was to have Franco tell the Bolla story in Italian with English subtitles and a narrator's voice seamlessly interacting with Franco's mellifluous delivery. Commercials were shot at the elegant Bolla estate in Verona, Italy, and Franco's performance was brilliant.[3] We arranged publicity tours for Franco, he gained some celebrity creds in the United States and the campaign sold a hell of a lot of wine.[4]

A character that built a brand

Cella was a mass market, casual, Lambrusco-style sparkling wine that competed with Riunite, the category leader. Despite being significantly outspent by Riunite, Cella enjoyed higher consumer awareness. The reason was a very successful campaign developed by Irwin Warren.

---

1. This was the first acquisition of a US agency by a UK company and the start of the '80s British Ad Invasion.

2. Brown-Forman shared 50% ownership of Bolla with the Bolla family and owned 100% of the Cella brand.

3. Franco Bolla commercials. *Ciao*! https://bit.ly/FrancoBolla

4. Every woman on those sales force incentive trips at the Bolla estate couldn't wait to meet Franco. My wife Vicki was first in line!

The centerpiece of the campaign was Cella's version of Franco Bolla: Aldo Cella.

But Aldo was the polar opposite of Franco. He was the larger-than-life, bon vivant, black sheep of the fictional Cella wine family who effusively spread the word about Cella…especially to beautiful women. Aldo was a perfectly crafted comedic stereotype of the short, stout, bubbly Italian, always wearing a white suit, hat, and a smile. The campaign hit a sweet spot and magic happened.

"This is Aldo Cella. He is not tall. He is not pretty. He is not powerful. But he knows what women like. Cella Lambrusco."

Aldo and his signature line, "Chill A Cella" became a phenomenon.[5] We quickly recognized that Aldo was a huge brand asset that could live well beyond thirty-second commercials. Leveraging Aldo's popularity, Ron Tamassini, Cella's brand director, managed one of the most effective, well-coordinated public relations and promotion campaigns ever in the alcoholic beverage business. It was a multi-pronged effort that touched Garneau employees, distributors, retailers and, of course, consumers. We created a twelve-month calendar of Aldo appearances choreographed to consumer and trade promotional periods and showcase events. And wherever Aldo went, he made a grand entrance, received standing ovations, and collected new fans. The media couldn't get enough of him, especially the morning shows.[6]

We were fortunate to have a great actor, Jimmy Manis, in the role of Aldo Cella.[7] Jimmy loved Aldo and made the character his own. His appearances were rarely, if ever, scripted and we trusted Jimmy to live up to Aldo's character with playful discretion. I can't recall any incident where we had to do Aldo damage control. Whenever Jimmy appeared as Aldo Cella he stayed in character the whole time. And whenever Jimmy as "Jimmy" was asked about Aldo he deflected the questions saying he didn't know the man. Nobody else could have been Aldo.

Working with the Garneau team on Cella was a masterclass in how to successfully build a sustainable, character-driven brand marketing program. I'd seen glimpses of the power of character spokespersons with Charmin's Mr. Whipple but Aldo took it to another level. Aldo became the fun-loving personification of Cella, part of the brand equity, and, in today's parlance, an influencer.[8]

Aldo (and Irwin Warren) taught me some simple and very valuable lessons about leveraging the power of character-driven branding. First, don't equate it with celebrity spokespersons. Celebrity spokespersons are essentially borrowed interest and live outside the brand.[9] Second, for effective

---

5. Aldo commercials. Smile. https://bit.ly/AldoCella

6. Aldo *Good Morning America*. Priceless. https://bit.ly/AldoCellaonGMA

7. Jimmy Manis remembrance website http://bit.ly/30trh1L

8. In today's climate, Aldo might be considered sexist, but I'm convinced with skillfully crafted adjustments Aldo would be a success today, especially on social media.

9. One of my favorite B&B creative directors, Dick Anderson, said that creative teams resort to using celebrities when they don't have a big idea.

character-driven marketing the character *is* the big idea and lives inside the brand. So he, she, or it must have a deep, textured persona that is relevant, convincing, and entertaining. There must be respect and belief in the character, without it the brand character can easily turn into a brand caricature. Finally, everything depends on the casting of the character. The talent has to be a perfect fit and committed to making it personal. Casting is the make-or-break decision. Don't compromise. I hope you're lucky enough to have the opportunity to be involved with creating future Aldos or Mr. Whipples. They will be your friends forever.[10]

Firing my future and hiring my past

Unfortunately, the management situation and quality of service at Geers Gross deteriorated rapidly. There was turnover in the account teams, top management was distracted pursuing additional acquisitions, and balls were dropped. We expressed our concerns but the agency made little progress addressing them. The situation came to a head after Geers Gross merged another previously purchased agency, Martin Landey Arlow, with Manoff. The merged agency had other spirits brands that spawned conflicts of interest. In addition, the acquisition brought another creative director to Geers Gross causing Irwin Warren to leave the agency.

With relationships deteriorating and the trusted creative person responsible for the Bolla and Cella campaigns gone, I had a big decision to make: Fire Geers Gross and risk losing creative momentum on our brands or keep them hoping they could get their act together. I placed the priority on having a strong, dependable agency partner for the longer term over the short-term risks of disruption and we replaced Geers Gross as Garneau's agency of record on all of our brands. Bob Gross, chairman of the agency, was very unhappy and let me know it…more than once.[11]

Leading my first and only agency search was a great experience. I'd always been on the pitching side and now here I was on the receiving end. Believe me, being pitched felt a lot better than pitching. First, Dan Schusterman, president of Brown-Forman's whisky division, and I agreed that Garneau needed its own agency; we would not consider any of the whisky division's agencies. Then, I worked closely with the brand teams to set the parameters. We felt it was important to work with larger agencies with deeper media capabilities and decided to split the account between two agencies: one for Bolla wines and Martell cognac, and one for Cella wines and Old Bushmills Irish whisky. Separating the wine brands was the top priority and Bushmills and Martell were added accordingly to even out the workload. There was enough revenue to support both and, more importantly, we would have two resources providing input

---

10. Irwin created another successful character driven campaign for Breakstone dairy products with Sam Breakstone. Sam and Irwin came roaring back into my life a few years later.

11. This was my first but not last encounter with Bob Gross. Our paths crossed again in an ironic and fateful turn of events.

and points of view about the wine category.

I was adamant on two other points:

> 1. We would work on a fee basis rather than commission. The commission system, in place since the mad men days, compensated agencies by receiving a percentage (usually 15%) of the brand's media budget. This left agency income and service levels subject to the ups and downs of budgets and most clients were moving away from that system. The fee system compensates agencies based on a mutually agreed to scope of work and deliverables. The fee covers the costs of staffing and overhead plus a profit. It also includes potential for additional compensation for exceptional performance. This was relatively new at that time and has since become the standard method of agency compensation.

> 2. No spec creative. We already had campaigns that were working and there was no need nor desire to change. It would be a useless exercise and I was not a believer in the value of spec pitches anyway.[12] Instead, we asked the agencies to present their credentials on building premium image brands, and provide thoughts on strategies for success in the wine category, future research recommendations, and specific staffing plans.

The full Garneau management team attended each agency presentation and three agencies made the final cut: Benton & Bowles, Ogilvy, and Ted Bates. I asked to have one-on-one meetings with the agency CEOs, Jack Bowen, Ken Roman, and Bob Jacoby, respectively. I wanted to get to know them better, discuss their personal views about their agencies, how they saw our business fitting in, and their expectations of us as a client. I already knew Jack well from my days at B&B so I spent more time with Ken and Bob.[13] These were great discussions with true Mad Men that left a lasting impression. The process took five weeks and we decided on Benton & Bowles and Ted Bates. I was comfortable with both agencies and left the brand assignment decisions to the brand directors, Ron Tomassini and Bill Juckett. They selected Benton & Bowles for Cella and Bushmills and Ted Bates for Bolla and Martell. It was gratifying to hire the first agency I worked for, Benton & Bowles—a sort of a homecoming for me.

I took away a great lesson from this agency hunt experience: There really is no such thing

---

12. Agencies are one of the few businesses that compete by giving away their ideas as a condition of being hired. Ridiculous. Here's a video illustrating the absurdity. https://bit.ly/NoToSpec

13. In 1984, Bob Jacoby engineered the sale of Bates to Saatchi and pocketed $100 million dollars and was ousted as chairman two years later. https://bit.ly/JacobyOuster

as an agency-client relationship. Companies, and particularly creative service companies, don't have relationships; people do. Companies have policies, procedures, contracts, and offices, but it is the people who provide the spirit, energy, and drive, that spawn great ideas and form trusted, enduring personal and professional connections. Great creative work alone is not enough. If trust and confidence are lost, the relationship will deteriorate. In today's data, algorithm, and AI-influenced business culture there is a worrying tendency to "institutional-ize" versus "personalize" relationships. That's a recipe for failure. If you believe as I do that a company's culture is priceless currency, then you need to champion a company ethos of people over process and procedure. Keep that in mind when considering working, hiring, or doing business with any company.

A big decision I did not want to make

All was good at Garneau. We had made our numbers two years running, staffing was expanded and enhanced, our agency roster was strong, and performance evaluations were on the mark. My industry reputation was growing. A prominent communications trade media publica-tion, *Marketing and Media Decisions*, published a guest editorial cover story about me and the Garneau Company.[14] I coordinated with Brown-Forman's public relations team and key Garneau executives and made it a team effort. The magazine editorial folks visited our offices and interviewed the Garneau team. We crafted the article as a platform to articulate Garneau's philosophy, expertise, and leadership in building premium brands. I was also asked to provide my personal principles for brand building. Looking back on them today, most are still relevant and followed by successful brands.

Then Marvin Shanken, the beverage industry guru and owner of Impact Communications' *Market Watch* invited me to be a guest speaker at his company's premier wine seminar event, Premium Wine Marketing in the '80s. It was held in San Francisco and featured an impressive line-up of speakers. I was honored to be invited.[15] I delivered a well-received presentation and was pleasantly surprised that my friend and colleague from Benton & Bowles, Bruce Nevins, was in the audience with his business partner, Jim Stevens. They were starting a wine import company and asked if they could call on me for advice. I said, "Of course!" That chance meet-ing would soon turn into another career-shaping event in my future.

My future outlook was bright. Then, major storm clouds gathered over Central Park West in New York City. Our sublease tenant was called back to Germany and vacated our apartment earlier than expected. The Beresford immediately notified us that we would not be allowed an extended period for another sublet. We were left with three options:

---

14. The picture of me on the cover is in front of my office bar. https://bit.ly/HankMediaDecisions

15. Marvin was a friend I respected for his expertise and success as an entrepreneur. https://bit.ly/Shanken

1. Sell the apartment.

2. Leave the apartment vacant and absorb the expenses.

3. Exit Brown-Forman and return to New York jobless.

None of these were attractive options. It took a very short conversation with my wife Vicki to realize that the first one—selling the apartment—was off the table. This was a no-go for her. Not going to happen. Option two, carrying two residences was not a sustainable option without major adjustments in lifestyle and living arrangements. Option three meant finding new employment in New York, which wouldn't be easy and would take time.

As part of my discussions with Brown-Forman I floated the idea of splitting my time between headquarters in Louisville and Garneau's New York sales office. We could move the family back to New York, and I would keep an apartment in Louisville and get to NYC as often as possible. This was a no sale with Brown-Forman *and* my family.

We could carry the two residences for about six months, so I used that time to figure out a solution. I brought my boss Bill Carroll into the loop. He was upset, but said he understood the circumstances when he hired me and reinforced their desire to have me stay. But this time around, it was clear that family priorities outweighed business considerations and financial factors. Privately, I accepted that one way or another my time at Brown-Forman would sadly be coming to an end, how and when remained to be seen, however.

A not so divine intervention

Suddenly, out of the blue, the storm clouds started to disappear. The skies brightened with a call from Wally Cook, senior vice president at Norton Simon Inc. (NSI). I hadn't yet put out any feelers for NYC jobs so I was surprised to get the call. Wally said my name had come up in conversations with beverage industry leaders as someone NSI should get to know. Wally asked if I would be interested in discussing a position as Chief Operating Officer (COO) of one of their subsidiary companies, Somerset Importers, based in New York City. *Wow!* Talk about a well-timed call.

Somerset was a prestige alcoholic beverage company that imported Johnny Walker Scotch, Tanqueray Gin, Pimms, and other brands. It also owned Old Fitzgerald bourbon and the San Martin California winery. An impressive roster. When I mentioned the Somerset possibility to Vicki, without hesitation she said go for it.

Norton Simon was a high flying conglomerate whose roster of companies included Hunt Wesson Foods, Max Factor beauty products, Halston Fashion Enterprises, Glass Containers

Inc, the United Can Company and…wait for it, Avis. Yes, Avis again.[16] NSI's CEO David Mahoney, was a highly regarded, charismatic, larger than life executive. David was a "rock star" in big business. When I met with Wally Cook in New York he told me he was leading the search under David Mahoney's direction. David was an ex ad guy so my agency background and mix of packaged goods and alcoholic beverage experience appealed to him.

The COO position was a new one that Norton Simon's management felt was needed… more on why later. The responsibilities were essentially the same as at Garneau but with a broader product portfolio and larger sales revenue. Wally discussed the special circumstances surrounding the search. While I would be reporting to Somerset CEO John Heilman, David Mahoney wanted to personally identify the best candidate for the job. He felt that Somerset needed a top manager with an experience base beyond alcoholic beverages. He also made it clear that success in the COO position would lead to the CEO position in a very reasonable time frame and that future possibilities at NSI were plentiful. I'll tell you what that meant for the current CEO John Heilman in a bit.

I met with David Mahoney twice while Wally and I worked out the major components of my employment agreement. Then I met with John Heilman to get his endorsement and button up some details. Priorities and perspective converged with possibilities and potential at just the right time and the deal was done. Option three came to fruition without the anxiety and hassle of a job search. Our family was relieved and excited. I have to admit that I felt pretty good about myself, too. Being hand-picked by David Mahoney to run one of his companies was an ego booster.

My resignation and exit from Brown-Forman was smooth and problem-free though we did have to leave some good friends and relationships behind. I had regrets and speculated about the future I might have had with Brown-Forman. That's to be expected when you leave a company you respect and admire. We said our goodbyes without any big fanfare and I did all I could to keep my Louisville bridge open and clear.

Back in the Big Apple in a big way

The move back to Central Park West went well and it almost felt like we had never left. New York City was booming, the Beresford was better than ever, and we were welcomed back home.[17] The boys got settled in their respective West Side schools: McBurney for Brian and Gregg and Columbia Grammar and Prep for Jason. I let Dr. Frank Fallon at Pace University know that I would be returning to New York and was eager to pick up where I left off as a professor. Frank liked that I had kept up teaching at the University of Louisville and I was

---

16. NSI profile https://bit.ly/NSIProfile

17. We had a new neighbor: John McEnroe now occupied the tower penthouse in our elevator line!

welcomed back to the Pace faculty. I began teaching classes that fall. It felt good to be back in familiar territory.

I knew that getting myself established at Somerset would be a delicate balancing act between reporting to CEO John Heilman and my interactions with the larger NSI organization. I soon found out why David Mahoney felt the need to create the COO position. NSI recognized that the alcoholic beverage industry was changing and brands were increasingly employing packaged goods marketing strategies as regulations started to ease. Marketing plans required innovation, constant monitoring, and iteration. Distributors were consolidating and handling more and more brands making the need for regular, consistent interaction with distributor top management a high priority. I'm sure that was the role that David wanted me to fill.

John Heilman was more of a big-picture guy—pretty hands-off and somewhat aloof. He preferred center stage in industry circles but didn't get his hands too dirty back-stage. Our relationship was respectful, cordial, and all business. Basically, he tolerated having me in the company because he knew David wanted me there. It was a bit awkward but expected. He knew I was a threat.

I was fortunate to have a great support from Frank Cirona, Somerset's CFO. Frank was a long-time Somerset executive with an impressive knowledge of the business. He was well-respected and listened to at NSI. He knew the circumstances of my hiring and we worked together very well. Frank was a great asset for me to lean on and he really helped me get into the swing of things. Once again, I saw how seeking the help of others made me stronger. Whenever you face challenges and difficult situations be confident that there are allies available to help. When you open yourself up to the possibility of help, chances are they will find you.

Joining Somerset meant a return to office life in Manhattan. There was no executive lounge, dining room, or parking space, just a classic modern office on Park Avenue and cab rides to work. On the operational side, my transition to Somerset was relatively uneventful. Some areas of the brand teams needed upgrading and we accomplished that quickly. The bulk of our advertising was handled by Smith Greenland, a respected mid-sized agency. I had a casual acquaintance with Leo Greenland, owner of the company and we got along fine. The account teams knew the brands well and had strong working relationships with the brand teams. All was good there. I already knew most of our distributors through Brown-Forman so I acclimated to that part of the job quickly. The big need was for a new director of sales. We filled that position with an experienced sales executive from Seagram, Dick Mutter. Dick knew his stuff, had a great reputation in the industry, and hit the ground running. Dick and I worked very well together as a close-knit team. Remember Dick Mutter's name for later.

Another first-order priority was to visit with and get to know our owner/suppliers, especially the Distillers Corporation, headquartered in London. Their senior executive teams were seasoned global managers who were gracious and welcoming. I also visited the Johnnie Walker distilleries in Kilmarnock, Scotland, to get the feel for the craftsmanship behind those world -renowned Scotch whisky brands. Impressive. With that exposure under my belt I worked with the brand, sales, and financial teams to build the next fiscal year budget and marketing plans. We developed solid and aggressive plans that were approved by our suppliers and NSI.[18]

Being an executive at a Norton Simon company also meant being involved in charitable support activities. David Mahoney and his wife Hilie were a big part of the New York phil-anthropic social scene and Vicki and I found ourselves being invited to a stream of black tie charitable events. We enjoyed meeting other NSI executives and had great conversations with some high-powered people. It also reminded me of how much I enjoyed my volunteer work with the Louisville Ballet and lit a spark in me to do it again.

Above and beyond my control

The summer of 1983 turned out to be one I would want to forget. On June 7, David Mahoney called a meeting of the Norton Simon board of directors to propose that he and a group of NSI executives offer a leveraged buyout (LBO) to take the company private. Valued at $1.65 billion it would be the largest LBO in history.[19] If the buyout was successful David Mahoney's group of executives would remain in command and could get between one-third and one-half of the stock in the new private company for relatively small investments of their own money.

All of us at Somerset were stunned and knew that, if successful, it would be an exciting game-changing event. NSI would no longer be subject to the financial rigors of public com-pany quarterly earnings and Somerset, being a strong cash flow high return-on-asset division, would take on even more importance. I was rooting for David's success big time.

But my excitement didn't last too long. Three weeks later, a rival suitor, the Esmark Corpora-tion, bettered the Mahoney group's offer and walked away with the company. Disappointment. Then, even more disappointment. David Mahoney resigned immediately.

Win some, lose some was not the emotion I was feeling. My champion at NSI, David Mahoney, was gone and others I knew on his team would no longer be calling the shots. I realized my situation would be changing under new corporate ownership and so meeting Esmark chairman Don Kelly and his team was high on my agenda.

This time the sky did fall

Before the ink could dry on the Esmark/NSI deal John Heilman made his move. Without any notice, I was summoned into John's office with Greg Gleason, Somerset's attorney, also

---

18. Somerset's budgeting was similar to Brown-Forman's but with less rigor in the development of sales quotas.

19. *NYT* article https://bit.ly/NSILBOArticle

present. No hellos or small talk. John told me that I was being terminated immediately, and I should clear out my office. Sure, I had expected some change in my standing with John, but this knocked me for a loop. Greg said they would honor the termination clause in my contract and asked me to sign a document acknowledging the conversation.

Then my Brooklyn came out. I knew it was all over but I wasn't going to go down easily. I looked them both in the eye and told them that this was all bullshit. My employee evaluation was excellent and there had been no mention of performance issues. I had successfully completed our planning and budgeting process and had just received a raise. I demanded that they provide me with the cause for my dismissal. They couldn't.

I got up, told them what they could do with the document they wanted me to sign and that they would be hearing from my attorney about a wrongful termination suit. I cleaned out some of my files, was escorted out of the office, and never returned. Right after my termination, John called my SVP of sales Dick Mutter into his office and terminated him as well. Dick's only transgression was being aligned with me.

John Heilman had executed the perfectly timed coup. He eliminated me as a potential threat before new management could even get to meet me. Esmark's management had a lot more pressing and urgent matters on their plate than my termination so this was a done deal. In retrospect, I understand why John wanted me out of the way. I was next in line for his job. He had never wanted me there in the first place. What I could not condone, however, is the manner in which John acted. He was spiteful, nasty, and purposely wanted to humiliate me. There were other more professional, high-road dignified ways he could have handled me and my termination. John could have had a civil conversation explaining the facts of life. With new ownership there was only room for one leader in the company and as CEO that would be him. It was a new ballgame and my position was being eliminated. Tough luck. Now let's talk about the best way to make your exit quick and with minimal disruption to the company and you. That wouldn't have taken any more time or effort and it would have been the classy thing to do. Same results with a better lasting impression. But John chose the low road and I lost all respect for him because of that.[20]

Here's the short story of how it ended: I consulted an attorney and decided to exit gracefully making sure that at a minimum I received everything I was contractually entitled to. We contacted NSI legal and worked things out. First, the press release about my leaving would state the I resigned over differences in management philosophy.[21] Since there was no defensible cause for my termination NSI had no trouble getting John Heilman's agreement. My severance was enhanced slightly and I was provided office space in one of NSI's other locations, secretarial help, outplacement services, career counseling, and extended medical benefits.

---

20. Just one year later, Esmark sold Somerset to Distillers Corporation for $250 million. I never spoke to John Heilman again.

21. Somerset departure article https://bit.ly/SomersetExit

Reality bit hard

Truth be told, the damage from my untimely and unwarranted termination was more than a bruised ego and a dent in my finances. I was shattered. This was the first time I'd been fired from anything—not even my little league baseball team. All my previous career moves had been made on my terms and in my timeframe. I was always in control and looking forward to what would unfold next. Now I wasn't in control. I was entering turbulent, unchartered territory and had no idea what would happen next.

In order to set my priorities and make the big career path decisions necessary, I needed a clear head. I had to get my feet back on solid ground. Before I could do that, however, I had to get over two big hurdles: beating myself up for making the decision to join Somerset and being pissed off at John Heilman. It took some time, soul-searching, and introspection but I got over both.

The more I reflected on joining Somerset, the more I realized that I had actually made a great decision for that time and place in my life. Yes, it came crashing down, but that was through no fault of mine or the others I trusted in making my move. That's life. It was a unique opportunity to be in the NSI corporate environment and around a guy like David Mahoney. Short, sweet, and no regrets. In Asset-Based Thinking terms, I shifted from a beat-up to build-up mindset and worked hard to stay there.

Next, I got over my anger towards John Heilman by trading places with him in my mind. That helped me accept that John had the right to act in his own best interest, even though he did so in an unnecessarily negative and vindictive manner. Then I asked myself how I would have acted in a similar situation—definitely not the way he did. I put my anger aside by committing myself to never treating anyone that reported to me in that way or tolerating that type of behavior in any company that I managed. Experience, good or bad, is often the best teacher. If and when you experience setbacks, decisions not working out, or encounters with low-road managers these Asset-Based Thinking mindset shifts can help: Shift from *Beat Up* to *Build Up* and *Trade Places*.

With those two issues settled in my mind I was ready to do something I had not done in almost twenty years: look for a job.

Mad Man Wisdom

- Like it or not, the world around you evolves. Priorities change and so do you. Fully commit to your top priority and you will find a way. Be half-hearted and you will find excuses.
- When the chips are down and you have to choose between personal/

family priorities or professional priorities there's only one choice. You know what it is.

- Surprise, serendipity, and even setbacks make your journey interesting and worthwhile. Embrace them with an inquisitive open mind to find the assets in any situation.

- When dealing with people in difficult, confrontational situations, choose civility. The low road leads nowhere.

- Steady yourself to ready yourself for what's next. Career setbacks are hard to take but not the end of the world. You will survive and can thrive.

- Build Up is always a better approach than Beat Up, whether dealing with yourself or others.

- Prepare for discussions with people by trading places with them in your mind. It creates empathy that helps you to soften bad news or makes good news even better. A win either way.

- When reality bites resist the urge to immediately bite back. It never hurts as much the second day and restraint yields healthier results.

"There's nothing wrong with getting fired." –Ted Turner, founder of CNN and TBS.

Enough said!

Marketing Tips and Truisms

Cultivating Creative Service Resources

At some point in your business life, especially in marketing, you will work with or for a creative services organization. The digital transformation of business has greatly expanded the breadth, scope, and specializations of these companies to include everything from traditional agencies to mobile marketing specialists, social media content management, live-streaming services, and so on.

There are plenty of great choices and making the right choice at the right time requires a skillful evaluation of hard and soft assets. Organizations like the Association of National Advertisers (ANA) and the American Association of Advertising Agencies (AAAA) publish company information and management profiles as well as excellent, detailed best practices guidelines and support on how to engage, evaluate, and manage these resources.[22] Take advantage of them. These tools help navigate the foundational, rational, and professional benchmarks necessary

---

22. ANA/AAAA Guidelines https://bit.ly/ANAAgencySelectionGuide

to make decisions and selections—the cost-of-entry hard assets.

Sizing up soft assets requires a more personal, nuanced, gut-feel approach. There are no formulas or checklists to fill out—and that's a good thing. As part of your due diligence you will be given client references. Call all of them. Then step back to see the bigger picture and get a feel for the aura that surrounds the company. Here are my top three macro tips learned from working with, for, hiring, firing, and founding creative service companies:

1. Engage with companies that have a people-first mindset, one that values people over process, procedures, and their databases. That mindset can only flourish if it starts at the top. Spend time with top management, find out if they hire with a culture-first approach and how they do it. If you feel like you're getting company talking points rather than a conversation about the company's "why," you will have your answer.

2. Get a feel for the culture beyond the website and social media pages. Ask if you can walk around their office unescorted. Feel the vibe and talk to people. Drop in unexpectedly. See how they react. Find employees that have left. Talk to them. Culture isn't something a company does, it's who and why they are.

3. Partner with a service company that operates with an in-service client attitude with management that puts their emotional skin in the game. They recognize that their company exists to help make their clients' business lives better, more successful, and more productive. In-service companies instill an "above and beyond the brief" work ethic. Look for that in case history presentations and how success stories are told. That sense of pride will transcend the numbers.

There's a great Mad Men era quote from ad legend Fairfax Cone, founder of Foote Cone & Belding (FCB), that captures the essence of what powers and drives a creative services company. "Our inventory goes down the elevator every night."

In the best creative service companies, when the "inventory" gets in the elevator the next morning, it's usually a bit early and they're feeling even better about the ride up than the day before. Stand by the elevator and catch that morning vibe. Going up?

Chapter 6 Footnotes
Scan QR codes for direct links to footnote content.

6.3 Franco Bolla Commercials

6.5 Aldo Cella Commercials

6.6 Aldo Cella GMA Appearance

6.12 No Spec Pitch Video

6.13 Bob Jacoby Article

6.14 Hank's Media Decisions Article

6.16 NSI Profile

6.19 NSI LBO Article

6.21 Somerset Exit Article

6.22 ANA Agency Selection Guidelines

Chapter 7:

Lose Control, Gain Traction, Move Forward

The good news was that we were back in New York City and settled into our home at the Beresford. The boys were doing well in their new schools and Vicki was back working at her friend's salon on Columbus Avenue. I was teaching again at Pace and reconnecting with colleagues. The bad news was I had been unceremoniously terminated from my job and unemployment hung like a dark cloud over everything else.

It took a little time to distance myself from that cloud before going all-in on finding the next big step in my career. I knew that whatever that step was, it didn't have to be perfect, but it had to be progress—a promising opportunity right for me and my family. I availed myself of all the resources provided in my severance package from Somerset and started my search.

I set my priorities on finding a client-side job and soon took an entrepreneurial leap of faith in the wine business with a former friend and colleague whom I admired and respected. Through no fault of mine or my friend it turned out to be a short leap. Circumstances changed and I decided to move on. I looked at it as a minor speed bump and got back on the job search road.

Sooner than I expected, a terrific opportunity crossed my path and I jumped at it. I landed a top executive position in a first-class company in the beauty and fashion businesses. New industries, new learnings, new opportunity, and new payroll checks. *Whew!* Then a meeting with a former agency CEO turned into an almost surreal job offer that pushed me to rethink everything and return to the agency business.

All of these moves were triggered by being fired, losing control, and hitting the lowest point in my career. Regaining control and traction required a couple of attitude and self-confidence reboots. I did that through a healthy mix of discipline, self-tough love, and the help of others. It all turned out to be just what I needed to get me moving forward again. It just goes to show…losing control over one aspect of your life doesn't have to overwhelm your entire spirit.

What now?

I prepared to navigate a never-before travelled road: unemployment and looking for a job. My first step in gaining some traction was realizing that I was the only one in control of my attitude. I had to get past that dirty word, "unemployed."

I had been working since I was fourteen years old. I was raised to think of unemployment as a stigma: your fault and your obligation to get reemployed as fast as you can. Even though I was forty years old, I was uneasy about telling my parents—not because they would be disappointed in me, but because it would worry them. I explained that our family had a financial cushion and there was time to find my next opportunity. My reassurances helped, but mom and dad worried anyway…that's just the way they were.

Truth be told, I was worried too. I'd lost control of my career path and was looking for a job in a sluggish but improving economy. To move past this setback I knew I had to keep trusting and believing in myself. I did a couple of things that helped me keep calm and focused.

First, I took time to do something very unfamiliar for me: nothing. We had rented a house at Breezy Point in Queens that summer and I decided to spend my first unemployed month at the beach without feeling too guilty about it. Sea air, time with my family, and beer helped a lot.

Next, we decided that my next position would have to be in the New York metro area. We weren't going anywhere until the boys were ready to go off to college. Period. That ruled out going back over the Brown-Forman bridge.

The other big decision I had to make was whether to look for a client or agency gig. I needed to pick a direction. That decision, however, required a lot more thought and would have to wait. I had to temper my impatience.

By mid-September I was settled in the office space provided by Norton Simon Inc. (NSI) as part of my severance package. Located on Park Avenue in the heart of mid-town, my office mates were a few other displaced NSI executives. We had all the administrative services we needed and a great coffee machine.

Being in this type of office environment was a first for me. My office mates were fine but the atmosphere lacked the energy and people interaction I was accustomed to. It was like being in a sad waiting room all day, every day. Nevertheless, I was grateful to have the resources available to help me do all the stuff I needed to do to find a job: update my resumé, line up references, contact head-hunters, network, etcetera. Necessary but not enjoyable.

I also used the career counseling services provided in my severance package, another first for me–a career shrink. It involved two days of psychological testing, skills tests, questionnaires, and personal interviews, which was actually enjoyable. Introspection and absorbing other's opinions and advice was helpful and refreshing. The bottom-line assessment by the counseling team was that I was well-suited for both agency and client companies but I would be happier and enjoy more success and fulfillment at an agency. They recommended I focus on agency opportunities first. Of course, I ignored that advice and decided to concentrate on client-side positions—even though there were fewer of those available and landing the right one would likely take longer. My brain was telling me that I'd worked too hard making the transition to the client side. Having more of that exposure would broaden my skill set, deepen my expertise, and be a leverageable asset wherever my career took me. I wasn't ready to give up on it yet.

I put aside my trepidations, focused my attention on finding the right client job, and dove in. One of the search consultants I contacted was Sid Stryker. He and I had been in touch over the years so Sid was familiar with my background and experience, and I trusted him. He specialized in high-level executive placements in fashion, beauty, and alcoholic beverage companies. Sid was very helpful and encouraging and we began exploring interesting options in alcoholic beverages, beauty, and cosmetics. Finally, I was gaining traction and moving forward. Then along came another one of those pleasant surprises.

Getting my feet on the ground

Remember my friend from my B&B days, Bruce Nevins? I had reconnected with him at the Impact Wine Seminar two years prior. Well, he called me with an interesting proposition.

Bruce and his partner Jim Stevens had launched their new companies, Premium Products Sales Company (PPSC) and Premium Wine Imports-Chevalier (PWIC), and had ambitious development plans. PWIC, the wine company, was a joint venture with Nicolas, a successful wine and spirits producer and retailer in France.[1]

PWIC also had the importing rights to two Neil Empson Italian wine brands, Bollini and Gabbiano.[2]

Bruce felt that I would be a great addition to their partnership and we began our discussions.

I was a great admirer of Bruce and what he'd accomplished. Bruce was an account executive at B&B who left to join Levi's and built a great track record as a key member of their marketing team. Later he gained fame and accolades as the genius behind the launch and success of Perrier in the United States. Bruce gained notoriety for both his marketing acumen and being one of the most eligible bachelors on the NYC and Los Angeles social scenes. He had a celebrated relationship Margaret Trudeau and was dating Shelly Hack of Charlie's Angels fame when we reconnected. Bruce was an interesting guy to be around.[3]

We started serious discussions in November of 1983 and by December had worked out the structure of a partnership deal. I would be president of PWIC and vice president of PPSC with shares in each. I was offered a reasonable salary, a discretionary expense account, and a car. The income was sufficient to cover my expenses and the big opportunity was in building the business for future sale to Nicolas, our joint venture partner. I would be placing my bet on that scenario. (Maybe it would be the next Perrier?) I had been bitten by the entrepreneur

1. About Nicolas http://bit.ly/304MiDd

2. Bollini was a chardonnay positioned against California brands as "The Chardonnay For Every Day." Partner Picture https://bit.ly/PWICPublicityPhoto

3. Bruce's ventures and adventures. https://bit.ly/BruceNevinsArticles

bug and Bruce, Jim, and I signed a letter of understanding in mid-December.

As you progress in your career you undoubtedly will have the opportunity to forgo current compensation for some form of equity, especially in today's digital start-up culture. My advice is to take advantage of those opportunities whenever possible. You have to strike the right balance for your individual circumstances and recognize that there are no guarantees of future returns. Nevertheless, here's why you should take the leap. Equity forces you to put your skin in the game and become invested financially and emotionally in the success of the company. You feel that your job matters so you work harder, smarter and look beyond your area of responsibility. You eagerly put ideas in the "suggestion box" for management. In the next stages of my career, I had mixed results following this philosophy, but never regretted my decisions. Rolling the dice adds excitement to your life. Stay tuned for more about that.

I started working at PWIC offices in Greenwich, Connecticut, in January, while they put together the formal contract. The reverse commute from NYC to Greenwich was bearable and I began to get a feel for working with Bruce and Jim. They made a smart, savvy creative thinking team and our chemistry was great. Vicki and I also enjoyed some nice social time with Bruce and the glamorous Shelly Hack.[4] I told you he was an interesting guy to be around.

Not long after, our joint venture partner, Nicolas, started having financial difficulties and rumors of a possible sale to Remy Martin surfaced. It set off big alarm bells for me. Now I knew the reason why it took three months to get my contract written.

Looking twice before I leaped

Remy Martin already had a US importer and their ownership of Nicolas would make PWIC redundant. It would seriously jeopardize the company's financial stability. I was losing confidence in the deal and after a lot of soul-searching I concluded that it was too big a risk to take.

I told Bruce and Jim that I would not execute the contract. I explained that I couldn't dedicate myself fully to a company in which I had lost confidence and felt this was the best course of action for all concerned. They understood, appreciated my candor, and asked if I could suggest anyone to replace me. In fact, I did.

My senior vice president of sales at Garneau, Joe Herpin, had left the company and his strong sales and distribution expertise would be a great asset to Bruce and Jim. I felt very confident in recommending Joe and made the introductions. Luckily, it was a good match and Bruce offered Joe essentially the same package as mine. Joe viewed the position through a different lens. He saw this as an opportunity to increase his salary, get that important title of President, and a potentially lucrative equity position in the company. It was a different risk/

---

4. When Bruce and Shelly visited our Beresford apartment our boys were over the moon! What teenage boys wouldn't be?

reward relationship for Joe and he joined the company.[5] I felt good about how it all worked out and that we parted on excellent terms.

Here are a few things I learned from this experience that can be helpful as you contemplate career moves. I discovered that somewhere in me was an entrepreneur waiting for the right time and opportunity to come along. I also realized that the risk/reward relationship was a critical decision-making component, not to be taken lightly when making that entrepreneurial leap. I tucked that away for future reference. Listen for those inner voices whispering to you from time to time—they might be right.

I also recognized that my gut-feel decisions sometimes don't pan out the way I thought they would. I took time to objectively take stock of what happened: Was my judgment flawed from the beginning? Was my due diligence shoddy or did changed circumstances alter the path I had envisioned? Introspection teaches valuable lessons that help you grow wiser.

In the end, I concluded I was comfortable with my gut-feel decision, my due diligence was good (primarily, at least), but changed circumstances beyond my control altered the game for me.

I realized that no matter how good things looked initially, when I "lost that lovin' feeling," I had to walk away. I had to work up a lot of resolve to back out of our agreement at the eleventh hour. It was tough, especially since Bruce and I were friends. But as we say in Brooklyn, "You gotta do what you gotta do."

I also discovered that there is great wisdom in the adage, "It's never a done deal until it's a done deal." And often that's a very good thing.[6]

Moving on to mood enhancement

When my PWIC entrepreneurial leap didn't go as planned I started questioning myself again. While the three months with PWIC wasn't a disaster, it was a setback in terms of time and confidence. I put it behind me by recognizing that this setback was an opportunity to recalibrate, get back on track, and recommit myself to landing a client-side position. Fortunately, during that time, Sid Stryker had kept exploring options for me. *Maybe he knew something I didn't?*

About a week after exiting PWIC, Sid presented what he felt was a great opportunity with Charles of the Ritz (COR). COR was a $550-million-dollar fragrance and cosmetic company owned by the pharmaceutical giant Squibb. COR marketed a range of prestige and mass brands such as Yves Saint Laurent (YSL), Jean Nate, Bain de Soleil, Enjoli, and Forever Crystal. The CEO of Charles of the Ritz, Bob Miller was establishing a new division, Environmental Fragrance Technologies (EFT), and Sid connected me with Bob.

---

5. Joe wrote a book about his exploits, *BOOZE BIZ Confidential*, that includes his time at Premier. https://amzn.to/30aOwAU

6. Remy Martin subsequently purchased Nicolas, eliminating future buyout windfalls for the partners. Happy I bowed out of this one.

I met with Bob and he laid out the EFT story and his vision for its future. COR had recently purchased an innovative, patented fragrance dispensing technology from inventor and entrepreneur, Don Spector.[7] Don and the COR team developed a unique product presentation, the Aroma Disc System, which had been introduced a few months earlier for the 1983 holiday season. It included an electronic diffuser that looked like a small CD player and a range of high-tech fragrance discs packaged like mini CDs. The player heated the disc, causing the scent to emerge from the player, and a fan gently pushed the scent into the room. The fragrances were playfully titled with experiential names such as Fireplace, Seduction, Mountain Top, A Dozen Roses, After Dinner Mints, Ocean Breeze, Passion, and Movie Time. The initial marketing program promoted those music and mood associations, and created substantial awareness and buzz.[8]

Bob was committed to building EFT into a substantial $100-million division in three years. His objectives:

> 1. Double sales of the Aroma Disc and related products in two years

> 2. Leverage COR's fragrance technology and expertise to create new household and beauty products and applications through expanded channels of distribution

> 3. Tap into Squibb's pharmaceutical research to create innovative health and well-being applications that opened up new distribution channels

It's important to note that electronic fragrance products like Glade Plug-Ins and similar devices weren't mass marketed until 1999. There was no aromatherapy category of any consequence—that wouldn't go mainstream until many years later. EFT was on the leading edge of these categories and well ahead of its time. That appealed to me: innovation and opportunity mixed with uncertainty.[9]

I liked Bob's vision for the division and he made me a sweet-smelling offer I couldn't resist: President of EFT and EVP of Charles of the Ritz. The opportunity to apply my experience and expertise to new categories of business and work in a prestige beauty company was exciting. I was back and pumped up. I couldn't wait.[10]

---

7. Don is a brilliant, larger-than-life innovator dubbed "the most prolific living inventor you never heard of." Working with Don was an adventure. http://bit.ly/DonSpector

8. Aroma Disc: Article https://bit.ly/AromaDiscArticle Commercials https://bit.ly/AromaDiscCommercials

9. The Aroma Disc is now classified as "Retro-Tech" along with film cameras and Game Boys. Who knew?

10. My wife Vicki was looking forward to a constant flow of perfume. YSL's Opium was tops on her list.

On April 4, 1984, I showed up at the COR offices at 54 West 57th Street and got to work. I loved the commute, just three short stops on the F train, and the neighborhood. Central Park was a short walk, the Russian Tea Room was just steps away, Carnegie Hall was around the corner, and the New York Athletic Club (NYAC) just a few blocks West. (I couldn't wait to use my membership more!) I looked forward to working in new categories of business and stepping into a different company environment.

The COR offices were pretty standard, well-appointed, and much like I was accustomed to. The vibe and culture, however, were much different than Somerset and Brown-Forman. The COR culture reflected the softer aesthetic of its brands and the people marketing them. It was a more female-influenced work environment and culture. "Guy talk" was much more tempered. It was a welcome change of pace for me.

The fashion and beauty industry is well-known for its abundance of awards shows honoring industry leaders and designers and charitable galas. I found myself putting on a tuxedo a lot more than I ever had.[11] At one of those events I met Ralph Darian, executive director of the Greater New York Council of Boy Scouts of America and had a great chat about the organization.[12] One thing led to another and I was invited to join their board of directors.

I was eager to do volunteer work again and jumped at the chance to join a high-powered group of NYC leaders in politics, business, media, and philanthropy. It was an honor and privilege and I remained on their board for six years. A very special and rewarding experience. Serving on the board of directors of any non-profit is an honor and gratifying. It doesn't have to be a large, well-known organization. If their mission lines up with your passions and interests, go for it. Contributing your time and expertise to help deliver their mission to market is powerful and provides the opportunity to interact with leaders from different walks of life and professions. You learn from them and they learn from you. Reciprocity at its best. That's the way it was for me with BSA and it would be taken to an even higher level years later when I joined the board of the American Heart Association. More on that later.

The members of the EFT team were experienced and talented COR executives from sales, marketing, finance and production. They welcomed me to the team and were a pleasure to work with. Don, the inventor, would also pop in from time to time to provide advice and add some spice to the mix. Marketing budgets funded some advertising, but the majority of dollars were allocated to retail trade promotion, in-store displays, and public relations. EFT brands were distributed in mass merchandisers, department stores, and chain drug stores.

I spent most of my time making retail calls, attending trade shows, doing public relations interviews, and working on new product and business applications. I also had to finalize

---

11. Image was everything. Female executives were provided a wardrobe allowance to keep them garbed in the latest COR designers' fashions. Male executives were left to fend for themselves.

12. I was never a Boy Scout but our boys were Cub Scouts.

production contract details with our Aroma Disc production partner, Remington. I had negotiated service contract agreements on both the agency and client sides but this was my first time negotiating a production contract. It involved nailing down everything from product specs, production quantities, and delivery timetables, to warranty details and pricing.

Remington's flamboyant CEO, Victor Kiam, was leading those discussions and I met with him at his home.[13] His choice. Being on Victor's literal home turf meant he could be firm yet keep the discussions friendly and "homey." The casual environment helped us to iron out details without much difficulty. Victor and I also enjoyed talking about my Remington experience at DKG prior to his purchase of the company. We spent as much time chatting about that as the contract. He was famous for his commercials announcing that he liked the Remington electric razor so much he bought the company.[14] Here's what I took away from my first production contract negotiation experience:

> **1. The best contract negotiations are those in which there aren't winners and losers.** A deal won on the basis of screwing the other party almost always results in a strained relationship and the other party doing the bare minimum to fulfill obligations. The winner should be the outcome that results in mutual satisfaction. Sure, be tough and firm but eliminate the need to win and do a victory dance.

> **2. Venues matter.** Discussions and negotiations don't always have to be in an office around a conference table. Select place and time wisely and make it work for you. And whenever possible make it face to face. In today's Skype and Zoom world it's easy to opt for convenience and expediency. But even with those remote tools, selecting the setting in which you place yourself says something about you.

Working with the marketing team on the Aroma Disc was enjoyable and fun. Phil Crosland was the marketing director. A talented, great guy with an excellent marketing background and a wonderful sense of humor, Phil was a big asset. The Aroma Disc had a light-hearted, smile factor that attracted media attention and was a nice change from alcoholic beverages. An important part of the media strategy included live product placements on select TV and radio shows to generate buzz and additional PR. We had a live placement on the Johnny Carson Show with Johnny and Ed McMahon demonstrating the product during an entertaining

---

13. Victor was also owner of the New England Patriots NFL team from 1988 to 1991. https://nyti.ms/308iaa8

14. Victor Kiam Remington commercial https://bit.ly/KIamRemingtonSpots

two-minute segment.[15] We used live announcer commercials on music and talk radio stations including the Howard Stern and Don Imus programs. I met with both hosts at their offices to explain and demo the product so they could improvise live commercials. Don and Howard really got into the whimsical nature of the product, which made it one of my most enjoyable media meetings. They particularly liked talking about the Seduction and Passion discs—you can imagine how that went. Don and Howard were even better on air and our sixty seconds of purchased media time often turned into entertaining, unpredictable, and occasionally "bleeped" two minutes or more.

In addition to the Aroma Disc, EFT also marketed a high-end line of fragrance-diffusing devices designed by the legendary fashion designer Giorgio Sant'Angelo.[16] They were functional pieces of his art that dispensed his signature fragrances. Giorgio was always creating, designing, and sketching ideas. It was a special experience visiting with him in his studio for meetings and getting a peek into the fashion world. He was inspiring to be around. Vicki and I enjoyed the pleasure of Giorgio's company often over the years and kept in touch until his passing in 1989.

EFT's work on new technology applications also led to new and unexpected areas of product development. We explored distribution channels and applications in which olfactory stimulation could provide benefits. Some of these were:

- Schools – helping with student attention and participation
- Retail stores – drawing in customers and amplifying in-store experiences
- Real estate sales – enhancing sales appeal
- Nursing homes – calming and relaxing residents

Our parent company, Squibb, was also researching olfactory stimulation in healthcare involving cognitive function in patients with Alzheimer's, dementia, and autism. The results were very encouraging, but obviously a long way from being viable products.

I had a busy first year and then it was time to meet with my boss Bob Miller for my annual review. He rated my performance as outstanding and gave me very nice salary increase. The only area Bob identified for improvement was reacting more quickly to negative financial results. I agreed with him. It was not my strong suit. As is customary in these reviews Bob also asked for my views on the EFT business and my goals at COR. I was direct and to the point.

First, I let Bob know that I thoroughly enjoyed working for him and respected his leadership. Next, I told him that my assessment of EFT as a longer-term viable business was not bullish. Consumer demand for the Aroma Disc was waning and future division growth required substantial R&D investment to develop new applications backed by significant marketing

15. Johnny Carson segment clip https://bit.ly/JohnnyCarsonAromaDisc

16. About Giorgio Sant'Angelo http://bit.ly/31oag9T

support. Without it, growth potential was limited. Bob appreciated my candor and I got the feeling he agreed with me. Finally, I told him that I viewed my future at COR positively and wanted to be considered for a leadership role in another division or corporate management. Bob reaffirmed his confidence in me and agreed we should revisit everything in ninety days.

We continued pushing ahead for the next few months but Bob and I had not yet had our follow-up chat. Then I got a sense of why. Speculative news reports started circulating about Squibb revamping its corporate portfolio to focus exclusively on healthcare. If true, that would definitely trigger a sale of COR. Understandably, Bob had a lot more to think about than me. Where there's smoke there's usually fire. I'd been down this road before so I kept my antenna up for developments.

My believe-it-or-not moment

While I was smelling the roses, ocean breezes, and other wonderful aromas at COR I received another one of those fateful calls. To paraphrase Winston Churchill, it would turn out to be "an irony wrapped in an enigma inside an oddity."

Bob Gross, Chairman of Geers Gross (the agency I fired while at Brown-Forman) called and invited me for a drink at the Plaza Hotel. I had no idea what to expect. I speculated that he was either going to give me a long-awaited punch in the nose for firing him or pitch me for the EFT business. Punch or pitch—that was all I could come up with.

I arrived early and watched Bob as he walked in using a cane. He was much frailer than I remembered. We sat down, ordered a drink, had about two minutes of pleasantries, and then Bob got right to the point in his characteristically blunt manner. Bob said he wanted to hire me as President and CEO of Geers Gross NY. He told me to leave all the "client bullshit" behind (his words) and get back into the agency business with him. *Wow!*

Visions of my meeting with Brown-Forman's Bill Carrol popped into head. I remembered that I went into my meeting with Bill having certain expectations that unexpectedly turned into the CEO position at Garneau. Suddenly, the advice I received two years ago from that career counselor flooded my mind…"I would be happier and enjoy more success and fulfillment at an agency." I was speechless for a minute. Then I asked Bob why now and why me? Here's what he said.

Why now? Geers Gross had purchased another agency, Kurtz & Tarlow, bringing substantial billing to the agency but also management unrest and uncertainty. Bob wanted a new, strong CEO to step in, bring stability to the agency, and mold it into a solid cohesive unit.

Why me? Bob didn't like being fired by me but admitted I treated the agency fairly under the circumstances. He felt my experience on both the agency and client sides was big asset and that I would join the "new" Geers Gross without any baggage. Plus, it was unexpected and would get attention in the trade press. Bob always liked getting attention.

Bob's offer certainly got my attention and we spent the next two weeks hammering out a potential deal. I would be President of Geers Gross NY (then about $150 million in billings) with full operating control and hold a seat on the publicly listed company's board of directors in London. I would receive a great salary, stock options, a car, and a country club member-ship.[17] Now I had a very important choice to make: stay put and ride out the uncertainties surrounding COR or make a big move back to the agency world.

My wife Vicki, though equally flabbergasted with the offer, advised me to "go with your gut." It wasn't lost on me, however, that in a period of six years I had had four different positions and neither my psyche nor my career resumé could weather another short-term job. I needed stability and traction in my life. My thought process went like this:

My client-side experience had been amazing and I'd gained invaluable skills, experience, and connections that I could take with me wherever I went—these were especially valuable assets in an agency management position. I'd been on the other side of the fence and liked it, but in the end, deep down in my heart I wanted to return to where my passion and roots were: the agency business. I missed the people, the creative insanity, the diversity of businesses, and the unpredictability. I realized that it's never too late to follow past good advice.

And so, Madison Avenue, there I went…again.

Next came my resignation from COR. By now, after six resignations one would think it would be a piece of cake. Well, it wasn't. I'd never left my previous positions unhappy or under negative circumstances (except for Somerset) and it's not easy to part company with people you admire and enjoy working with. But, ultimately, you have to do what's best for you. I met with Bob Miller and explained the circumstances that led to the Geers Gross job offer. He, too, appreciated the irony. Bob graciously accepted my resignation and I agreed to stay on the job for a month. I moved on with my bridge open and grateful for the learning and guidance I received from Bob.

As it turned out, my trepidation about Squibb's divestiture of COR was justified. A year later Bob Miller unsuccessfully tried to lead a leveraged buyout of COR and Squibb sold the company to Yves Saint Laurent (YSL) for $630 million. Bob was replaced as CEO. I felt badly for Bob, but grateful I didn't go through that buyout agony again. In the sage words of Yogi Berra, it would have been "*déja vu* all over again."[18]

Even today I look back and scratch my bald head in wonder about the crazy twists of fate that unfolded in those eventful six years. I visited Brown-Forman to pitch their business for Ketchum and instead they hired me. Then I fired our agency, Geers Gross. A few years later at COR I met with Bob Gross of Geers Gross thinking he was pitching me. Instead, he hired

17. I joined North Hills Country Club. My handicap was 16.

18. COR Sale to YSL https://bit.ly/CORSaleToYSL

me as CEO of the agency that I had previously fired. The media had a ball covering my return with headlines like "Geers Gross Appoints An Old Nemesis" in *The New York Times* and "Fired to Hired: Wasiak in at Geers Gross" in *Ad Age*.[19] Sometimes reality is stranger than fiction.

Walking my feet to 42nd Street

The Geers Gross offices were in the Daily News Building at 227 East 42nd Street, a historic, thirty-seven-story Art Deco tower and home to one of the greatest lobbies in New York City. Right in the middle of the lobby is an illuminated twelve-foot globe that revolves beneath a black glass dome. Movie fans may recognize the building as the offices of the fictional newspaper *The Daily Planet* in the original Superman movie.

The building was a bustling media hub and a top NYC tourist attraction. Showing up to work was a never-a-dull-moment experience.[20] The Geers Gross offices were on the top two floors and we had a private elevator at our disposal. Bob spared no expense in renovating the space with lots of marble and a spectacular spiral staircase connecting the two floors. The executive floor was very well-appointed and Bob's office had its own bathroom and shower—off limits to all but Bob. Impressive and expensive. Too expensive as I would come realize later.

Initially, the management situation was chaotic. The principals of the most recent agency acquisition, Don Kurtz and Dick Tarlow, were working out their exit arrangements, which complicated my entrance. Neither one of them had any interest in helping me get acclimated or introducing me to clients. I chose not to engage in their drama. I ignored the negative energy and left sorting that mess out to Bob Gross. He did, but at a hefty cost to the agency.

I focused on getting myself established at the agency and with clients and assessing staffing needs. The good news was that there were great people who were very helpful and supportive heading most departments: Russ Gilsdorf (media), Nancy Jo Kimmerle (research), Terry Galvin (production), and John Koutsantanou (finance and operations). The account teams were in good shape with a very solid group management supervisor, Dennis Fogarty. I identified the immediate need for another group management supervisor to work alongside Dennis and filled that position with Chris Ebner whom I'd worked with previously at DKG.

A dream that almost came true

About a month after I arrived, Neil Calet, my friend and DKG partner invited me to lunch. Shep Kurnit had left the agency so it was now called Calet, Hirsch, Spector (CHS). Neil told me that the partners were considering selling the agency and had started buyout discussions

---

19. Wasiak Geers Gross Press https://bit.ly/HankGGPress

20. Daily News Building http://bit.ly/30bxrqJ

with the Ross Roy agency. One thing led to another and I suggested that perhaps Geers Gross could be a better acquisition partner. Neil loved the idea and cleared it with his partners Larry and Peter. Bob Gross agreed and CHS sent us their most recent financials. John Koutsantanou, our CFO, and I quickly met with the Geers Gross financial teams in London to crunch the numbers.

We let CHS know that we were prepared to offer $5 million paid over three years with CHS being absorbed into Geers Gross. There were no client conflicts and the numbers worked very well since we could eliminate duplicate positions and excess overhead. One of the key stipulations was that Neil would agree to stay on at Geers Gross as the agency's creative director. Larry and Peter would phase out of the agency on a timetable of their choosing. Working with Neil again was a dream scenario for me and both he and I were eager to make the deal. Sadly, the dream did not come true. Ross Roy put a better offer on the table and acquired CHS in January 1986. *C'est la vie!*

Getting down to business

Once the dust finally settled with Kurtz and Tarlow, it became apparent that the agency was in need of new creative leadership. I needed a creative partner I could count on and work with to build the agency. Bob Gross agreed and we discussed potential candidates. This is when things got even more interestingly ironic. We came up with a great tailor-made solution and decided to recruit my friend Irwin Warren. (You might recall that Irwin had left Geers Gross while I was at Garneau.) At the time, Irwin was a creative director at BBDO. Irwin and I met and he loved the idea, the irony, and the opportunity. We worked out his package and he rejoined the agency in March 1986.

I was hired by the agency I fired. Then I hired the creative director who had "fired" Geers Gross. The circle of irony was complete. If circumstances hand you an unexpected, unorthodox opportunity to make a bold move, take it. Decisions based on fate, karma, or whatever you choose to call it are often less rational and more risky. But when it works you can't beat the feeling. Twists of fate and circumstance certainly made my life more interesting and career more fulfilling. We had a powerful management team in place and another story for the press.

One of the highlights of agency life for me has always been the people connections—the inventory that goes down in the elevator every night. Geers Gross certainly had its share of talented and dedicated people with whom I would stay connected over the years. I was pleasantly surprised to find three former DKG colleagues in the creative department: Ron Becker, Tom Wai-Shek, and Joe Tantillo. It was especially nice to be working with Joe Tantillo again. Joe was a great creative director, we enjoyed our time together at DKG, and he was always available if I needed a fill-in for my Pace classes.[21]

A new, fateful connection was Griffin Stenger. Griffin was a young aspiring art director in the print production group eager to make a move to the creative department. I had a sign in my office that read, "If you have an idea I want to hear it." Griffin had ideas...lots of them.

One day, he popped in with an idea for our Rhone Poulenc client. They manufactured ceiling caulk, not exactly the most exciting subject matter for an ad. But Griffin took it on and created a print ad concept that everyone liked and that led to a junior art director position in the creative department. I was happy for him. Stay tuned for the chain of life-changing events that would emanate from Griffin's promotion at Geers Gross.

There is a great lesson in Griffin's persistence and belief in himself. Don't be shy about sharing your ideas within and outside your areas of responsibility. Bring only your best and be enthusiastic and humble. Reach as high as you can on the influence ladder while always respecting the chain of command. You will get noticed, receive great feedback, and maybe even get the recognition and promotion you deserve. Done this way, there is no downside. Be an idea ninja.

The melding of three acquisitions left Geers Gross with a solid list of clients including Kraft Foods, Fuji Film, L'Oréal, Lea & Perrins, United Biscuit, Bass, and a few smaller accounts. It was a solid base from which to grow. My first priority, of course, was meeting clients and I focused on the larger clients first.

The Kraft Dairy group was headquartered in Philadelphia and led by a great CEO Tom Herskovitz. Fuji USA was managed by experienced photographic industry executives, Bernie Yasanaga, CEO, Carl Chapman CMO, and advertising manager, Tom Charbonneau. All good there. L'Oréal was a bit more complicated since these were businesses in which exiting partner Dick Tarlow was involved and he did very little to help. Geers Gross assignments included great fragrance brands like Chaps, Polo, Vanderbilt, Paloma Picasso, and the Biotherm skincare line. It took a bit more time and with the help of our great account teams lead by Robin Fry and Phyllis Califano, both Irwin and I built the relationships we needed. The bridges I had built helped too. My experience at COR was a good credential and a few COR colleagues made calls on my behalf to people they knew at L'Oréal.

Now with the all the past management issues settled at Geers Gross, I felt in control and confident that we had a great team in place to move forward. Bob and I agreed that we would not pursue any new agency acquisitions and we set simple but ambitious growth goals: solidify and add new assignments from existing clients and bring in substantial new business. And we did, big time. I was back where I belonged.

---

21. Geers Gross LinkedIn alumni group http://bit.ly/30Br0Jx

Mad Man Wisdom

- Sometimes losing control is just what's needed to get you back on track. Always being in control is not realistic and over-rated.
- You alone control your attitude. When unexpected events knock you off your feet, take time to clear your head before you get up. If you don't, chances are you will fall again.
- Setbacks suck but they are temporary. Think of them as set-ups for your come back and the road ahead becomes smoother.
- Don't get sucked into other people's negativity. You win by walking away from their toxicity and finding your own better way to get things done.
- Be an Idea Ninja at every stage of your career. Envision an "Ideas Welcome" sign on your supervisor's door. Knock only when you're ready. Enter boldly and humbly.
- Conversely, be an Idea Magnet. As you progress in your career hang that "Ideas Welcome" sign over your door. Recognize, respect, and reward those who come across the threshold. Hey, you never know.
- Lose the winner-takes-all mindset. When you are working out agreements, contracts, or whatever, make a mutually beneficial outcome your goal. It will lead to less stress, more confidence and better results.
- Never ignore a gut feeling, but never believe it's enough. Surround that feeling with challenging thoughts and diligent evaluation. Then, re-check your gut. If it's positive, go for it.
- Don't finalize any moves or commitments until you are one hundred percent confident. It's never too late or bad business to walk away when doubt overwhelms your decision. In the end, it's better for everyone involved.
- If you're lucky enough to encounter an "irony wrapped in an enigma inside an oddity," run towards it and go where it takes you. It's almost certain to make your life more interesting and memorable.

Marketing Truisms and Tips

Principles For Brand Builders

In the prior chapter I referenced a feature story written about my role at the Garneau company that included a section entitled "Wasiak's 15 principles for brand builders." I chose the term "brand builders" rather than "building brands" to emphasize that brands don't build themselves.

They are carefully planned and constructed over time by marketers who make it personal.

At Geers Gross I incorporated those principles into a 10-point branding check list for our clients. Here's that check list tailored to reflect today's consumer and marketplace dynamics.

1. Confirmation of want, receptivity, and viability: Be convinced there is a positive and receptive environment, sufficient consumer desire, demand potential, and margins to fund adequate marketing spending. All four are essential.

2. Make it better than it has to be: Commit to the highest product and service quality possible. This is the cost of entry and essential to optimizing the price/value relationship and delivering sufficient margins to ensure sustainability.

3. Market with a "segment of one" mindset: Identify precise, receptive *persona* clusters. The responsible use of rich data and AI make hyper personalized connections and experiences possible.

4. Articulate a clear brand frame of reference and point of difference: The trade must know exactly where to place the brand "on the shelf" and the consumer must know where it stands versus competitive options. Answer this question for the consumer: Why is this brand right for me?

5. Wear a transcendent brand halo: Identify and articulate organic, sincere brand values and be committed to them as guideposts for directing brand purpose. Always live up to and into them.

6. Create and proliferate a powerful brand positioning: Define what the brand stands for (and delivers) in the mind, heart, and soul of its consumer. Its functional and emotional reason for being must be brought to life at every consumer touchpoint. Tell the brand story 24/7.

7. Be real and sincere or fail: You can't fake or manufacture authenticity.

8. Make long-term brand commitments: Brand positioning is built to last and withstand short-term marketplace fluctuations. It's the DNA of a brand. Have a game plan to keep it fresh and relevant that includes product or service enhancement and extensions.

9. Vigilance + Defense = Brand Protection: Branding longevity requires constant monitoring across all aspects of the marketing mix. Vigorously defend the brand positioning from encroachment by competitors.

10. Recognize and respect that people build brands: Cultivate a brand builder mindset in every person that touches your brand—inside and outside. Celebrate and reward their commitment.

Ultimately, the power and effectiveness of branding comes down to execution. That's where the creative magic happens and it determines whether brands rise from good to great or fall from good to ordinary. Execution requires discipline, judgement, and asking the right questions. Here's how a great creative director I admire summed up his agency's approach.

"The first and most important question we ask ourselves about
any content we create is always, 'Is it right for the consumer?' If the
answer is no, it's off the table, regardless of how much we love it.
If it's yes, we confidently craft it to perfectly fit the brand."
—Gregg Wasiak, Concept Farm

Chapter 7 Footnotes

Scan QR codes for direct links to footnote content.

7.2 PWIC Publicity Photo

7.3 Bruce Nevins Articles

7.8 Aroma Disc Article

7.8 Aroma Disc Commercial

7.14 Victor Kiam Commercial

7.15 Aroma Disc Johnny Carson

7.19 Geers Gross Wasiak Articles

Chapter 8:

Trade Enraged For Engaged

My move to Geers Gross set in motion a series events I never could have anticipated. The period from 1985 to 1990 was a personal and professional roller coaster. My situational swings went from excited and exhilarated, to disillusioned and defiant, to calm and collected. It was an eventful, colorful, and sometimes stressful ride that I'm grateful for having taken.

The first twenty-six months at Geers Gross NY were action packed and exhilarating. We built a strong team, a blue-chip client list and new business momentum. I even got recruited for a side hustle: board member of R&J Emmet, producer of Irish Cream liqueurs, to assist them in going public.

Then the rug got pulled out from under us. Chairman Bob Gross suddenly decided to sell Geers Gross NY to Interpublic (IPG). We were blindsided, shocked, and exasperated. Rather than being masters of our own destiny we would be absorbed into IPG's flagship agency, McCann Erickson. I was angry, disillusioned, and initially defiant. It was a done deal so I had no choice but to calm down, collect myself, and face reality, so I could make the most of this next (albeit unwanted) move.

The terms of sale required me to make a two-year contractual commitment to Interpublic and McCann. That meant dedicating the next two years of my life to a position that was being forced on me. I had to choose between being a pissed off obstructionist or a compliant contributor to the acquisition's success. After the initial shock, I chose the latter. I let go of my anger and decided to do my best to make the transition as smooth as possible for our staff, clients, and for myself. I made a personal commitment to be an engaged and valuable member of McCann's management team and make the most of the upside rather than lament the downside. I'd be co-managing a major iconic agency with much larger staff, deep resources and a very blue-chip client list. It was a huge opportunity to up my game.

It just goes to show…being engaged will always get you farther than being enraged. When your world turns upside down the best way to get back on top is to take a breath, recalibrate, and move forward. Enraged closes doors. Engaged opens them up.

An unexpected extracurricular opportunity

I was nine months into the job and I was pleasantly surprised at how comfortably I slid back into the agency side of the business. It was invigorating to be back in a less structured, less systems-driven business. I didn't realize how much I missed the creative energy and fluid, unpredictable nature of a people-driven agency environment. I had to readjust from selling "stuff on a shelf" from a company back to selling ideas from people.

Now, having walked a mile in my clients' shoes I had street cred with both my clients and Geers Gross colleagues. I knew firsthand the importance of adding value and seamlessly integrating the agency into the flow of a client's other responsibilities, of knowing when to stay out of their way, not create unnecessary issues, and of being a confidant if needed. That empathy made a huge difference for me and I constantly tried to instill that in the Geers Gross management teams.

"How can we be viewed as more than just the agency and be valued as 'just the right agency' for our clients?"

That "being in service" mindset I spoke about earlier took on even greater meaning. It felt good to be back where I belonged. Fortunately, there were no major client issues, staffing was set, and we were in high gear with our new business machine. I was hitting my stride, comfortable in a productive positive rhythm, and I had an open runway ahead of me. Then, another Brown-Forman connection came back into my life that would disrupt my rhythm and lead to wonderful life experiences and new career expertise.

Jonathan McSweeney, whom I had hosted for Derby Week during my time at Brown-Forman in Louisville, had left Irish Distillers and was now a regional manager at R&J Emmet, producer of Irish Cream liqueurs. Emmet's was a moderately priced alternative to Bailey's and the US was its largest market with annual sales of 193,000 cases. Emmet's principal shareholder was financial heavyweight and dealmaker Dermot Desmond. Management was taking the company public and felt a non-executive director with US alcoholic beverage experience would be an asset. Jonathan recommended me!

I met with Joe Lynch, Emmet's managing director at the Helmsley hotel in New York. We hit it off right away. Joe laid out the company's plans and explained that my participation would entail attending a few board meetings a year in Ireland and helping liaise with Emmet's US importer 21 Brands, a subsidiary of the McKesson Corporation. In addition to Dermot and Joe, there were three other respected board members.[1]

I was flattered and very interested but anxiety crept in. I was concerned that I might be taking on too much since I already had three responsibilities on my plate: Geers Gross CEO, teaching at Pace, and serving as a Boy Scouts of America board member. Then I elevated anticipation and desire above anxiety and doubt. I switched from feeling restrained to a "discover my capacity" outlook.

Being associated with this heavyweight group of Irish businessmen, putting my alcoholic

---

1. Board members included chairman, John Lynch, CEO of the Irish Productivity Center; David Fassbender, managing director of Industrial Credit Corporation; and Fred Spengeman, director of finance at R&J Emmet.

beverage experience to work from a brand owner perspective, and visiting Ireland made the opportunity too hard to resist, and I liked Joe Lynch a lot. I decided to stretch myself a bit more, cleared it with the Geers Gross board, signed up for the Aer Lingus frequent flyer program, and jumped in.

The public offering went smoothly and, initially, our board activity was pretty routine. But things heated up when McKesson decided to divest itself of 21 Brands. There was a change of ownership provision in our contract and we wanted to be prepared with alternatives if the new owners had conflicts or other issues. Joe and I took two important steps. First, we hired the law firm of Baer Marks & Upham to represent us in the event of any litigation. Next, we spent a few months meeting with importers and eventually decided that Age International would be a good partner if we made a change. Age International, headquartered in Frankfort, Kentucky, was owned by industry vets Bob Baranaskas and Ferdie Falk, the first guys to create a single-barrel bourbon: Blantons.

When it was announced that Remy Martin would acquire 21 Brands, we pulled the brand. We felt Emmet's would get lost in Remy's premium brand portfolio and went full steam ahead with Age International. Rather than a traditional importer/supplier relationship we agreed to set up a joint venture marketing company with a staff of four. The joint venture retained all of the importation margin, paid Age a handling fee of $5 per case with the remainder allocated to staffing and marketing support. The arrangement was unique and it required a collaborative management approach with the owners of Age. My patience was tested often and my diplomacy skills worked overtime. It required me to stretch myself even more, but it was a successful and educational experience.

Then the legal battles began.

McKesson and Remy filed for an injunction blocking our termination action, but it failed in court. Next they filed suit for breach of contract seeking millions in damages. We wanted to avoid lengthy, costly, court proceedings and decided to offer a structured settlement of one million dollars. Joe, myself, and our attorney, Andy Crisses, visited the McKesson offices to present our offer. The three of us walked into the conference room and were greeted by a team of twelve (!) lawyers on their side of the table. That bizarre scene is still vivid in my mind.

It was a short meeting. They rejected the offer, subsequently filed suit, and the case rumbled through the courts for three years. In the meantime, our joint venture became operational and successfully increased Emmet's sales to 301,000 cases by 1991. That success enabled Dermot Desmond to engineer the sale of R&J Emmet to Diageo, owner of Bailey's Irish cream.

The sale ended my board participation and began Dermot Desmond's meteoric rise to fortune and fame. Today, Dermot is the fifth richest man in Ireland with a net worth of two billion[2] euros.

---

2. Dermot's life and exploits, *The Kaiser* https://amzn.to/2kZhf9r

It was nice to witness the birth of a billionaire! Fortunately, the sale of Emmet's didn't end my relationship with Joe Lynch. In 1994, Joe started another Irish Cream company, First Ireland Spirits, and he invited me to serve on the board. I worked with Joe and his team on the launch of two successful Irish cream brands, Feeney's and O'Mara's. Joe and I remain great friends today.

The joy of open bridges to the past is that you never know when one of your connections will cross over and bring possibilities you never would have pursued on your own. My connection with Jonathan McSweeney led to my joining a dynamic team of Irish businessmen at R&J Emmet and experiencing taking a company public. I was fortunate to be able to balance all of that with my day job at Geers Gross.

This experience also helped develop my aversion to lawsuits. After the sale, Diageo and Remy settled the 21 Brands lawsuit out of court after spending almost $800K on legal fees. My takeaway? A realistic compromise is always smarter than an unrealistic fat lawsuit.

Unfortunately, lawsuits are an inevitable part of business life. Some are truly unavoidable but most are colossal wastes of time, money, and human capital. This quote from Songwriters' Hall of Fame member David Porter says it all.

"Litigation is the basic legal right which guarantees every corporation its decade in court."

My Irish adventure was exciting, educational and rewarding. Looking back on it today, what I value most is not the experience or how it boosted my credentials, it is my special thirty-five-year friendship with Joe Lynch.

And now, back to my day job

I was fortunate to step into Geers Gross at a time when client relationships were relatively stable so I was able to concentrate on our large clients and new business. Each client had its unique story, but Fuji and Kraft were especially memorable.

Fuji

For those of you reading this who were born in the digital age, Fuji was the first Japanese producer of photographic film—you know, those film canisters you put in old-timey cameras that you have to develop in a dark room?

Fujifilm management included CEO Bernie Yasanaga, ad manager Tom Charbonneau, and CMO Carl Chapman. Geers Gross' top creative team, Joe Tantillo and Tom Wai-shek, worked on the business with a strong account team headed by Chris Ebner and Mike McCartan. The relationship was solid. The agency developed a successful award-winning campaign, "Breakthrough," featuring dramatic visuals created with Fuji film that challenged the viewer to determine if it was real or Fuji.[3]

Joe and Tom also developed a contingency back-up campaign that labeled the leading film brand as yesterday's technology. It featured older users (i.e., grandmothers and grandfathers) showing poorer quality pictures taken with "the leading brand" vs. the same photo taken with Fuji film. It was a light-hearted, fun competitive comparison. The copy went something like this.

"Don't use the same film your grandmother did. Step into today with Fuji advanced color film."

Fuji CMO Carl was an experienced photographic industry veteran and was very supportive of Geers Gross. Nevertheless, after listening to our presentation, he took a minute, looked Joe in the eye and growled, "My wife is a grandmother!" He was a man of few words and we knew the campaign was dead. Carl's simple pointed comment reminded me of the famous quote from ad legend David Ogilvy: "The customer is not a moron. She's your wife." Respect.

A Fuji experience that had a special personal impact was spending time with my childhood idol, New York Yankee great Mickey Mantle (#7).[4] We hired Mickey as a Fuji spokesperson for a trade-oriented campaign. Mickey would appear at the Fuji booth at the annual industry trade show, attend the Fuji sales meeting, visit a few key retailers and record two radio commercials. Mickey's fee was $75K. A bargain![5]

Tom Charbonneau, Chris Ebner, Mike McCartan, and I once enjoyed a private dinner with Mickey. Imagine how I felt spending an entire evening laughing it up with THE Mickey Mantle. He had a well-deserved reputation for his drinking prowess so it was a long, enjoyable evening.

At the dinner, I ordered the Italian wine brands that I previously imported, Bolla and Bollini. Mickey wanted to learn more about Italian wines so there I was educating Mickey Mantle. Go figure. The next week, I shipped him a case each of those wines. Mickey sent a very nice thank you note: "Salute." Unforgettable.

Mostly we talked baseball. What stood out most was Mickey's displeasure at the comparisons between himself and Yankee slugger Reggie Jackson, also known as "Mr. October." Mickey complained that baseball pundits loved to point out that he struck out a lot, but rarely mentioned that Reggie held (and still does) the record for most career strike outs of any major

---

3. Fuji advertising https://bit.ly/FijiAdvertising

4. About Mickey Mantle http://bit.ly/2pJ2zgn

5. When Mickey appeared at the Fuji trade show booth the lines for a photo op (with Fuji film, of course) were out the door all day long.

leaguer.[6] Mickey wasn't angry or jealous; he just lamented that the full story was rarely told. After all that Mickey had accomplished, I was struck by the fact that this gnawed at him. Hey, nobody's perfect…even number 7.

Kraft

Geers Gross enjoyed a long, positive relationship with the Kraft Dairy Group based in Philadelphia. The key brand assignments were Breakstone, Light n' Lively Yogurt, Sealtest, Breyers, and Frusen Glädjé ice creams. Dennis Fogarty, the agency's management supervisor, was doing a fantastic job running the business and had established a great rapport with Tom Herskovitz, the division's CEO. At about the time I arrived at Geers Gross, Mike Miles was named CEO of Kraft and all the company's divisions reported to him. Yep, the same Mike Miles I knew from my time at Brown-Forman and the Louisville Ballet board. Again, a past positive connection working its way back into my life.

I knew Mike well so I could easily connect with him if there were opportunities or issues to discuss. I also knew that Mike got to the office very early, about 6 a.m. Chicago time, which meant 7 a.m. NY time. When I wanted to connect with him I arrived at Geers Gross at 7 a.m. and called his direct line. He usually answered. If it went to voice mail I left my direct number. When Mike called back, I was at my desk to answer the call. This was before cell phones so there was no faking it. I learned that sometimes small things like a shared work ethic make a big difference when working with clients. It's a good practice to know and respect their contact and engagement preferences. Being in the right place at the right time always helps make conversations better.

Our showcase Kraft dairy brand was Breakstone, founded in 1882 by the Breakstone brothers in a storefront on Manhattan's lower east side. Earlier while at Manoff, creative director Irwin Warren created a campaign for the brand that built on that heritage. TV advertising featured the demanding, cantankerous store owner, Sam Breakstone, obsessed with making the very best cottage cheese and sour cream. Nothing was ever good enough for Sam. He wouldn't settle for anything less than the best and always got his way. But Sam would also get his comeuppance at the end of each commercial when an angry dog would growl and pull at his pant leg.[7]

The campaign had been running successfully for ten years.

Kraft CEO Mike Miles visited Geers Gross for a business review meeting. We didn't envision any major issues and were looking forward to engaging with Mike. All was going well and we saved our best brand review for last: Breakstone. We took Mike through a business review

---

6. Career strikeouts/rank: Jackson 2597/1, Mantle 1710/36

7. Breakstone commercials with dog. https://bit.ly/BreakstoneDog

then proudly showed the Sam Breakstone commercials. Mike was silent for what seemed like an eternity and then said, "I really don't like those commercials."

We were stunned. Mike said that a Kraft brand should not have a spokesperson who is so mean that even dogs hate him. We thought he was kidding, but Mike was dead serious. He did not approve of Sam being attacked by an angry dog. You can imagine everyone's incredulous reaction. Irwin was apoplectic. In ten years there had not been any negative reactions to the dog. Heck, we all loved the dog! Nevertheless, the brand teams diplomatically agreed to take Mike's comments into consideration for future commercials.

Guess what happened? We dumped the dog.

Our next pool of commercials followed the same format but featured different "dog-less" fun ways for Sam to get his comeuppance.[8] The campaign continued its successful run even though the brand team received a few letters inquiring about the missing dog. More importantly, Mike Miles was pleased that we listened. I was reminded of two useful lessons. First, when developing and evaluating creative options there is more than one way to skin a cat—or dump a dog as it were—and still keep the integrity and effectiveness of a campaign. In the ad business necessity is often the mother of invention. Second, it's always good to make the CEO happy.

Kraft purchased the Lender's bagel company in 1986. Lender's was a family-owned business known for great-tasting frozen bagels with a strong franchise in Northeast markets. Based on our positive track record with the Kraft dairy group, Geers Gross was assigned the business without a pitch. Lender's was based in Greenwich, Connecticut, which required three-hour drives for client meetings. None of us looked forward to those. Lender's did not have an agency and instead worked with a creative consultant. Guess who? My colleague from DDB, Evan Stark.

Both Irwin and I knew Evan and respected him. Evan had created a campaign that featured animated characters of the company's owners, Murray, Sam, and Marvin Lender.[9] They were charming commercials that Dennis and I thought worked very well, but Irwin did not share our viewpoint. Nevertheless, we worked with Evan and continued the campaign.

Kraft had inserted their own management team at Lender's and developed aggressive market expansion plans that required a rethink of the creative approach. We were asked to develop a campaign with stronger appetite appeal while keeping the authenticity and heritage of the Lender family. Evan was not happy but Irwin jumped at the chance to put his mark on the creative. We had met with the real-life Murray Lender a few times and Irwin felt he would be a convincing brand spokesperson. Murray was great on camera, came across as likeable, believable, and boy could he sell the great taste of Lender's bagels. Murray was a success.[10]

---

8. Breakstone commercials. No dog. https://bit.ly/BreakstoneNoDog

9. Lender's animated commercials https://bit.ly/LendersAnimation

10. Murray Lender commercials https://bit.ly/MurrayLender

Here's an interesting postscript: At times Irwin could be a bit demanding but we accepted that as part of his creative persona. After his Murray Lender success Irwin asked to be rewarded with special travel arrangements for meetings at Lender's headquarters. So, instead of driving three hours we took a few helicopter rides to Greenwich at the agency's expense. We called it Irwin Air. A bit extravagant, but it definitely added excitement to our day. Remember this: Always do your best to keep your creative director motivated.

Our new business hit parade

With great staffing, client success stories, and a strong creative reel we generated an enviable growth record at Geers Gross. In just two years, we added additional assignments from Kraft (Sealtest, Polar Bars, Lender's Bagels), L'Oréal (Ralph Lauren fragrances) and Lea & Perrins. We topped that off with seven significant new business wins: Nintendo, Quaker, Curtice-Burns Foods, Manufacturers Hanover Bank, Wamsutta Home Furnishings, Diana Ross Enterprises, and Schmidt's Beer. The first and last two had a special impact on me.

Nintendo: the resurrection of video games

Winning Nintendo gave me the opportunity to be part of a team that rescued a decimated video game category. First, some context. In the early '80s the Atari 2600 gaming console enjoyed great success. Then came the infamous video games crash of 1983 brought on by the recession and waning consumer interest. Atari eventually went bankrupt and the category was on life support.[11]

When we landed Nintendo in 1986 there was still a negative stigma attached to video games. Prevailing wisdom was that the lack of trade and consumer interest in a new gaming system would make it dead on arrival. Skeptics were everywhere. In fact, some agencies elected not to even pitch the account.

The Nintendo Entertainment System (NES) was a compact 8bit console that came with peripherals that helped set it apart from past video game systems: Light guns for shooting games and R.O.B., a robotic operating buddy.[12]

The Nintendo team in Redmond, Washington, included Ron Judy, Gail Tilden, Peter Main, and CEO Minoru Arakawa, whom we called Mr. A. Dennis Fogarty and I headed up the agency team. We were a tight knit core group of NES evangelists ready to defy the odds.

The Nintendo team in Redmond made two brilliant strategic moves. First, Nintendo

---

11. Atari: The video games crash http://bit.ly/33KxXKb

12. NES product details https://bit.ly/NESProductDetails

eliminated retailer resistance and risk by agreeing to buy back unsold consoles.[13] Next they introduced a now-standard practice of licensing third-party developers to produce and distribute games for Nintendo's platform insuring a steady flow of new games. Mr. A pushed this hard. He had great instincts about marketing games and knew the key to success would be a catalog of quality games. Hardware was just the enabler.

Initially, we targeted young gamers and parents with a family fun and excitement positioning to convince consumers NES was worth the $90 to $100 price tag. Parents had to be reassured that the NES wouldn't wind it up in the closet next to Atari collecting dust. Introductory commercials were essentially very well-done product demos featuring the accessories and game play.[14] They connected and NES was an instant success.

Then, with the introduction of powerful games like Super Mario Brothers and Legend of Zelda, advertising focused on game play excitement with the tag line, "Now You're Playing With Power."[15] The category exploded with a new generation of gamers and the rest is history.[16] It's not an exaggeration to say that without the successful of launch of the Nintendo Entertainment System, video gaming as we know it today would not be around. In 2019, the video game industry generated a record global revenue of $152 billion with $37 billion in the US. Nintendo continues to be ranked as one of the top four video game companies. Text a big H&K and GRATZ to Nintendo the next time you play Pokemon, Grand Theft Auto, Call of Duty, or Madden NFL 20 on your Nintendo Switch, Xbox, Play Station, iPhone, or Samsung Galaxy.

Nintendo innovated again in 1989 with the smash hit introduction of Game Boy, a handheld portable video game console that took gaming out of the home. We created fast-paced commercials featuring untethered gamers enjoying Game Boy excitement and competition.[17] Game Boy sold a whopping one million units in just three weeks.

Nintendo was a busy, non-stop action account that everyone loved working on. For me, it was a once-in-a-lifetime opportunity to be part of an amazing team that defied the odds and made history. I learned a lot about the video game business, managing trade resistance, the importance of customer experience over systems, and much more. Perhaps the two most important lessons were these:

1. History doesn't have to repeat itself. If you build a better mousetrap

---

13. Nintendo executives convinced the largest toy retailer, Toys R Us, to support NES opening the door to broader distribution.

14. NES introductory commercials https://bit.ly/NESIntroCommercials

15. NES game play commercials https://bit.ly/NESGamePlayCommercials

16. Podcast: Nintendo; Saving an Industry http://bit.ly/NintendoSavingAnIndustry

17. Game Boy commercials https://bit.ly/GameBoyCommercials

(or gaming system, for that matter) the world will beat a path to your door.

2. To paraphrase Margaret Mead, "Never doubt that a small group of thoughtful, committed people can change an industry; indeed, it's often the only thing that ever does." Years later Nintendo would come back into my life in a surprising and purposeful way. Stay tuned for that story.

Quaker: Sticking it to the big guys

The big ad agency mergers of the '80s often created conflicts requiring clients to reassign brands to new agencies. This created ill will on the client side, and it was a hot topic in the trade press. Due to a merger the Quaker Oats Company was forced to find new agencies for a number of its brands. The Quaker CMO leading the search was another Benton & Bowles colleague, Charlie Decker. Connections! They screened eight non-merger agencies and Geers Gross and Chiat Day came out on top. We were in good company. Geers Gross was assigned the Quaker Puffed Rice and Puffed Wheat brands and the development of a new cereal brand. When our win was announced in the trade press I made the most of the merger dissatisfaction with a banner headline declaring, "We are the happy beneficiaries of mega-merger fallout." It felt great to say that. I was also looking forward to working with Charlie again. He was a sharp marketing pro who understood the value of brand equity.

Developing concepts for a new Quaker cereal required a deep dive into the dynamics and value of the Quaker brand equity since it was both a product line and corporate brand. We were struck by consumers' exceptionally high expectations of healthy, quality products surrounding the Quaker name and the depth of brand trust. In developing new cereal product concepts, a key litmus test was to ensure that the new brand would fulfill those expectations. It had to deliver what we called "Quaker Goodness" for the product line brand *and* add value to the corporate brand equity (more on that later). Our creative exploratory was comprehensive and included a wide range of concepts to measure variables including taste descriptions, the Quaker name's linkage to oatmeal, heritage, product names without Quaker, and so on. Each concept was evaluated for both its efficacy as a new stand-alone product and value-add potential for the corporate brand. It was a complex set of permutations that gave birth to Quaker Oatmeal Crunch. I used this as a new product development best practice example in my Pace classes. Here's a link to a video of the concepts.[18]

---

18. Quaker concept videos https://bit.ly/2Bl2XHO

Schmidt's Beer: Bad taste backlash

Jos. Schmidt was a hundred-year old brewery in Philadelphia. Schmidt's was a Northeast regional beer brand with a 97% stereotypical, macho, heavy beer drinking customer profile. At the time, Budweiser was aggressively marketing to this target with its own style of macho advertising. Schmidt's CMO, John Paul Jones (yep, that was his name) wanted to mount an aggressive campaign to build its market share with this target group. The brand did not have the massive marketing budgets of competitors so we concentrated support in New York and Philadelphia metro markets with an aggressive radio campaign. The brief: Create awareness and use tongue-in-cheek humor to generate buzz with our macho beer drinking target. And, oh boy, did we!

Commercials featured copy extolling Schmidt's full-bodied beer taste with an unexpected twist. Rather than discuss who should drink Schmidt's, the commercials described customers who shouldn't drink the brand. Remember, this was the mid-'80s when social norms were just starting to come out of the dark ages and commercial standards parameters were quite different. Regardless, we pushed the envelope way too far. With those caveats, here's sample copy from one of the radio commercials:

> *It's not for guys who like to crochet or dust. It's not for guys who like to drink with their pinkies extended. It's not for prissy women. It's not for interior designers. It's not for men who want to be prissy women. Schmidt's: A beer you'd be proud to serve your friends, unless they're ballet dancers.*

The commercials generated controversy even before they aired. One of the actors we brought into the agency to read for the voiceover, David Groh, read the copy, took great exception to it, then went right downstairs to the *Daily News* offices to show the scripts to reporter Anne Adams. A few days later, just as the commercials started to run, an article appeared in the *New York Daily News* with the headline, "A Beer With A Sneer."[19] We were taken to task and skewered for being insensitive, anti-gay idiots.

Some stations pulled the commercials. The National Gay and Lesbian Task Force picketed outside our building for two days. I received lots of hate mail and other assorted items from people expressing their dissatisfaction. Account supervisor Chris Ebner received a gift-wrapped package of human excrement. That got our attention.

We admitted we screwed up, pulled the commercials, and started airing new spots. These new commercials embraced the same creative macho beer drinker strategy but identified a different group who should not drink Schmidt's beer: yuppies. Yuppie was a slang term for

---

19. Schmidts Beer Articles https://bit.ly/ScdmidtsBeerArticles

young, preppy, college-educated, urban professionals in well-paying jobs living in big cities—the '80s version of today's hipsters. Poking light-hearted fun at yuppies was fair game back then.

Here's sample copy from one of those commercials:

> *It's not for guys who take a bath with a rubber duckie. It's not for guys who understand Shakespeare. It's not for guys named Biff who name their daughter Muffy. Schmidt's. A beer you'd be proud to serve your friends, provided they don't belong to a birdwatching society.*

Yes, the commercials were toned down and more "acceptable" but they still had a disrespectful, snarky tone that rubbed some people the wrong way. The campaign ran its course without major controversy but not before earning a spot on *New York Magazine*'s annual round-up of top ten NYC *Winners & Sinners*.[20] You know which list we were on. Four years later the campaign was parodied in a *Saturday Night Live* skit called *Schmitt's Gay Beer*.[21] Times had changed. They were not picketed.

The lessons we learned from Schmidt's are powerful. Yes, back in the '80s, times were different—but that doesn't justify our initial effort for the brand. It was dumb, offensive, hurtful, and looking back I should not have allowed those commercials to run. They should not have even made it to the idea stage, no less to aired commercials. Bad taste is bad taste in any decade. Also, it again drove home the point that there is always another way to execute a creative brief—ways that can very often be better than that first seemingly perfect idea. I would have to remind myself about this almost twenty years later as a happy farmer.

Last, making fun of or putting down people that don't use your brand is more often than not, a bad idea. Remember the "my wife is grandmother" comment from Fuji's Carl Chapman? Offending people doesn't work in any decade. As an Asset-Based Thinker I realize that it's better to recognize the positive characteristics and qualities of people who use or should use your brand. Telling a competitive brand user that she or he is clueless or a behind-the-times luddite for using that "other" brand may get awareness but it doesn't create an inviting positive impression.

When weighing your options in the creative process, choose to celebrate rather than denigrate.

Diana Ross Enterprises: A superstar's missed opportunity

My most unique client relationship was with Diana Ross Enterprises. Yep, that Diana Ross. In mid-1987 Tom Bowles, a financial consultant working with Ms. Ross, hired us to develop

---

20. Schmidts NY Magazine https://bit.ly/SchmidtsNYMag

21. *SNL* Gay Beer Skit http://bit.ly/SNLScmidtsGayBeer

recommendations for building the Diana Ross brand beyond music and entertainment.

Tom and I worked out a fee arrangement to conduct consumer research on Ms. Ross' appeal to female consumer segments and categories and sketch out possible brand positionings. Our research director Nancy Jo Kimmerle did a great job fielding comprehensive attitude and awareness research and identifying potential category fits.

Consumer awareness and attitudes about Diana Ross were high and overwhelmingly positive in every regard and across all demographic groups—there were no issues with crossover among ethnicities. Neither Nancy Jo nor I had ever seen celebrity perception numbers that high. The Diana Ross brand was viewed as the epitome of elegance. It was daringly sexy, of the highest quality and style, and glamorously aspirational. The three categories identified for development were fragrance, eye and lip make-up, and luxury apparel. The Diana Ross brand was a potential powerhouse in these categories. We were eager to give her the great news and scheduled a meeting at the agency.

Diana arrived with her security person and drew a crowd. I met them in the lobby and we took the private elevator to our offices. I gave her a brief tour of the agency and Diana could not have been more polite and cordial with everyone she met. We met in our smaller, cozy conference room and presented the research. Diana asked great questions. I remember being struck by how surprised and giddy with excitement she was with the overwhelmingly positive results. After the meeting we walked down 42nd street to have lunch at the Helmsley hotel. That two-block walk was quite an experience. By the time we got to the hotel we had picked up a small crowd of adoring fans. Diana was magnetic and gracious as she charmed her admirers.

We were given the go-ahead to develop concepts and worked with Tom on compelling pitch proposals for fragrance and apparel companies. We agreed our relationship with L'Oréal/Cosmair would be a good place to initiate discussions. We met with Diana one more time, reviewed proposals, and started planning meeting strategies and timetables. Then circumstances changed within Diana Ross Enterprises. Diana became pregnant with her third child and wanted to direct her efforts elsewhere; meanwhile, Tom Bowles decided to move on.

There was no question in my mind that a Diana Ross fragrance would be a huge success. We communicated for a couple of years while I was at McCann and I continued urging Diana to launch her personal fragrance brand. But it never happened and life moved on. Thirty years later in 2017, I was delighted to see that Diana finally introduced her fragrance brand, *Diamond Diana*. Kudos to Diana and her team. The name is perfect, the packaging dramatic and elegant and the fragrance profile "designed for those who enjoy being in the spotlight," is right on the money.[22] Better late than never!

---

22. Diamond Diana HSN introduction http://bit.ly/2AO41k8

A bombshell and betrayal

In September 1987, just after my two-year anniversary at the agency, Chairman Bob Gross called me into his office for a chat. Things were going well and I was expecting to have one of our usual update meetings. Bob looked uneasy and got right to the point. He said, "I know you're not going to like this, but hear me out. Geers Gross Ltd. is selling the New York agency to the Interpublic Group (IPG) and Geers Gross New York will be absorbed into McCann Erickson New York. Oh, but don't worry Hank, you will be just fine. IPG will assume your contract." *BOOM!*

What? Don't worry? How the hell did this happen? I had no idea Bob had been shopping the agency.

I stood up and vented. As a board member I should have been involved in these discussions. I demanded an explanation. Bob told me that the agency was carrying too much debt (over $5 million dollars) and the UK financial institutions were threatening to call in their loans. Selling the New York asset was the best way to get the company's finances straight. Bob's exorbitant spending on the New York office renovations, the spiral staircase, the private elevator, and payouts to prior agency acquisition principals had finally taken their toll. In retrospect, I realize that I should have pushed to be more involved in the corporate financials. My mistake.

I told Bob I was not on board with the sale and needed time to get my head around it. We had killed ourselves for two years getting New York humming and were poised for more growth. I was not ready to hand the agency over to IPG. This made Bob angry and anxious since he knew that if I didn't cooperate, it could seriously jeopardize the deal. Bob was absentee management in New York; it was me, Irwin, and the management team who held the client relationships.

I brought Irwin into the loop and he shared my point of view: no sale, no thank you. I spent the next few weeks digging into the details of the acquisition and building a safety net clause into my Geers Gross termination agreement. If I was not employed at McCann at the end of my two-year contract, regardless of the reason, Geers Gross would pay me severance compensation. During our discussions Bob constantly reminded me of my fiduciary obligations as a board member and the potential legal ramifications of jeopardizing the sale. Despite his warnings, Irwin and I frantically tried to find financial partners to back a leveraged buyout (LBO) of the agency but there just wasn't enough time. I had to accept the reality of the sale. I felt betrayed. Bob had not been honest and transparent with me. Was this Bob's payback for having fired him so many years ago when I was at Brown-Forman? I was enraged.

Trading enraged for engaged

I had to recalibrate, work myself into a positive mindset, and make the most of a situation not of my choosing. I started thinking about the new people I'd meet, working with new big-name clients, the additional media and research resources at my disposal, and having a quicker subway ride. Who knows what else I'd discover?

My first priority was to clarify and firm up my employment contract with IPG. Phil Geyer, IPG's CEO, invited me to his office to meet with him and my future boss, John Dooner, head of McCann New York. It was my first time meeting both of them and I didn't know what to expect. Phil and John were cordial and respectful of my feelings. They listened to my misgivings and we had a good discussion. Both seemed pleased that I would be joining the McCann management team. We agreed that my title would be EVP deputy general manager of McCann New York reporting to John.

The terms of sale required me to make a two-year commitment to IPG and McCann, and they were willing to explore ways to enhance the compensation and benefits aspects of my contract.

We were now on the same page! Phil escorted me down the hall to meet IPG's head of human resources with whom I would iron out contract details. Guess who? Kent Kroeber, the HR person that hired me for my first job at B&B in 1965. Go figure.

Kent is a great guy, a straight shooter, and I was comfortable working with him. He made letting go of my rage easier. I decided to dedicate myself to making the transition as smooth as possible for our staff, clients, and for myself. I made a commitment to become a valuable member of McCann's management team and see where that would lead over the two years of my contract. I traded enraged for engaged and prepared myself to walk through a new door to McCann. But before I could step over the McCann threshold there was work to be done.

Announcement anxiety

My next challenge was managing the transition with Geers Gross clients and staff. Bob was adamant that we not give our clients any heads-up and keep the pending sale a closely held secret. He was nervous about sparking client objections before the deal was announced. I understood his concerns but strongly objected to that approach. We owed our clients the respect and courtesy of a private conversation a day or two before the announcement to explain the deal and assuage any concerns. And, selfishly, I would be the one taking the heat and managing any fallout as Bob exited back to London. Giving the client forewarning would definitely make my job easier. But Bob prevailed and the acquisition was announced

November 3, 1987.[23]

In the days following the press announcement, I spent my time reassuring clients that the key people servicing their business would be moving to McCann and we wouldn't lose a step. I also pointed out that being part of IPG would open up a broader array of resources and talent—something I was personally looking forward to exploring. Some clients were annoyed about not receiving advanced notice and a few groaned about potential disruption, but overall our clients took a healthy wait-and-see posture.

The internal announcement was made by Bob Gross and me a day before the public release. It was not a joyful day. People were upset and disappointed that they suddenly had to rethink their futures. Many had previously worked at larger agencies and joined Geers Gross to escape big agency bureaucracy. Now they were being thrust back into that environment, not knowing what to expect. At the beginning of January 1988, we would leave the Daily News building and move to McCann New York. We had eight weeks to reflect, commiserate, and prepare. I was determined to do my best to make it a Happy New Year.

Mad Man Wisdom

- Discover your capacity. Don't feel constrained by your current workload and responsibilities.
- When opportunity knocks loudly and you're not sure you can handle it, say yes anyway. You can figure out the "how" tomorrow.
- Make your own history. Be on the lookout for your opportunity to join a small group of thoughtful, committed people that can change things.
- In creative execution there's a fine but clear line between edgy and offensive. That line will turn red when you reach it. Don't be color blind.
- There is no "only one way to do it" limitation in content development. Therein lies the magic of creativity.
- In marketing communications it's okay to laugh at yourself. It's bad manners (and bad business) to laugh at your competitors—or their users.
- If your trust is betrayed, being enraged is understandable…but regroup and reengage quickly. Being enraged closes doors. Getting engaged opens them.

---

23. IPG Geers Gross Purchase https://bit.ly/IPGBuysGersGross

Marketing Truisms and Tips

Feed The Brand Equity Piggy Bank

Brand equity is a company's single-most valuable asset. At the same time, it can be a fragile asset—especially in today's consumer-driven digital marketplace where amplification happens instantly.

I devote two of my USC class lectures to demonstrating how brand equity is a powerful marketplace "influence" driven by consumers. We discuss how brand equity assets are built over time and in today's digital business environment that timeframe can be relatively short. For example, Gillette, the shaving product behemoth owned by Procter and Gamble, took decades to build its brand equity. Meanwhile, Dollar Shave Club (DSC), the shaving product subscription company that took the industry by storm in 2011, built its brand equity asset in just five years. P&G's competitor, Unilever, jumped the waiting line and purchased DSC in 2016 for one billion dollars.

But creating brand equity assets is only half the job; maintaining and continuing to build on those assets is the other half. I use the old-fashioned piggy bank metaphor to reinforce the importance of this critical concept.

The core principles of this strategy are:

1. No net withdrawals. Ever!

2. Make deposits constantly. Any amount.

Here are my five key tips to successfully implement this strategy:

1. There are no little things. Think through all brand activity to avoid making stupid mistakes. Unfortunately, stupid happens and comes in all sizes…big and little. They all matter and add up.

2. Employ value-based pricing strategies that increase the brand's overall consumer value as well as the bottom line. Brand equity should never be used as a motivation to simply charge more.

3. A product or service line extension must first stand on its own consumer benefits. Brand equity should be icing on the cake that heightens consumer appeal thereby lifting overall brand value. Brand equity should not be the foundation of line extension success.

4. Every brand action should give back more than it borrows from brand equity. At a minimum, the action should have a neutral effect on equity assets. Neutral effects should follow a 5:1 rule. Positive equity contributions should outnumber neutral actions five to one.

5. Regularly measure brand equity activity and results just like other important business metrics. Build the results into performance evaluations—that will get people's attention.

Finally, consider this. There are only two ways to get money out of an old-fashioned piggy bank: turn it upside down, shake it like crazy, and hope something will fall through the slot, or take a hammer and smash it. In marketing, neither of those alternatives is acceptable.

Chapter 8 Footnotes
Scan QR codes for direct links to footnote content.

8.3 Fuji Commercials

8.7 Breakstone (dog) Commercial

8.8 Breakstone (no dog) Commercial

8.9 Lenders Animation Commercial

8.10 Murrey Lender Commercial

8.12 Nintendo Product Details

8.14 Nintendo Introductory Commercials

8.15 Nintendo Game Commercials

8.17 Nintendo "Game Boy" Commercials

8.18 Quaker Creative Exploratory

8.19 Schmidt's Beer Articles

8.20 Schmidt's NY Magazine Article

8.23 GG IPG Sale Articles

Chapter 9:

Stay Calm, Carry On, or Move On

Once the initial shock of the acquisition passed, all of us at Geers Gross got into our "dealing with reality" mindset and carried on with our jobs. That didn't mean the next few months weren't challenging personally and professionally. We had to continue servicing our clients making sure no balls were dropped. Meanwhile, everyone (including me) was apprehensive about the transition to McCann. As the CEO, keeping myself and everyone else calm was my top priority.

We closed out 1987 packing up our office belongings and misgivings and started 1988 unpacking and dealing with our misgivings. Navigating McCann's sprawling office space, dealing with the agency's own brand of bureaucracy, and acclimating to its boys' club in-your-face culture was difficult. There were definitely hiccups along the way but, overall, I was proud of how well everyone rose to the occasion. Unfortunately, we did suffer one major account defection as a consequence of the acquisition: Fuji. That loss hit hard.

My new job as co-deputy general manager took some getting used to, but I had a good partner in Gene O'Sullivan. And with the CEO pressures and the responsibility of running an agency off my shoulders, I actually got to relax a bit, make some time for extracurricular activities, and get to know myself better. Then, out of the blue, I was promoted to a bigger job overseeing McCann's aligned creative agency partners.

Rather than viewing the new gig as unexpected, additional stress, I saw it as an opportunity to widen my lens, learn more about other marketing disciplines, and connect with a different cadre of creative talent. All in all my "stay calm and carry on" mindset served me well and I was enjoying my time at McCann, but as my two-year anniversary approached I came to that inevitable fork in the road: One arrow was marked "stay on" the other "move on." I had to make my biggest career decision yet.

I chose to leave McCann with the confidence and conviction that moving on and taking the road less travelled was what I needed to do. It just goes to show…regardless of the stress, uncertainties, and misgivings that come your way, staying calm and carrying on will lead to the right path for you.

Closing the door on Geers Gross

When the time came to vacate Geers Gross, packing up the agency was relatively easy. The only "inventory" we had to move were people and files. The agency employed 125 people and 105 would be transferring to McCann. A few decided to leave and there were some redundancies in back office services. All of the people made redundant were treated well. My biggest disappointment was that John Koutsantanou, our CFO, would not be joining us at McCann. We had a great relationship and I would miss his advice and counsel (more on John to come later). There was no big farewell party, but I did host a lunch for our management team and gave each person a Tiffany watch as a memento. No tears, just some nice reminiscing and stories. There was artwork on the walls and some of the pieces were given to the staff as keepsakes. I have three pieces in our home; a daily reminder of what once was.

To ease staff anxiety, I suggested that someone from McCann management visit Geers Gross before the move to deliver a "welcome to McCann" pep talk. Disappointingly, that didn't happen. However, John Dooner, GM of McCann New York did one smart thing that helped mitigate some of the unease. John convened a dinner with key Geers Gross management to get better acquainted and presented them with shares of IPG stock. It was a small amount but that didn't matter. It sent a well-received welcome to the family message.

Absorbing all of us into McCann's office space was a challenge and not everyone was happy with their new digs. There was no giant globe in the lobby…I missed that. There were some bruised egos and, unfortunately, a few of my colleagues felt like second-class citizens in their new departments. Geers Gross EVP creative director Irwin Warren and I did our best to mitigate those feelings, making the rounds those first few weeks to check in with everyone. We settled into our departments and responsibilities and got down to work.

Same clients, new agency, different culture

Getting acclimated to life at McCann proved to be onerous in a few areas: the physical space, hierarchal structure, procedures, and McCann's culture in general. McCann New York employed over a thousand people spread over multiple floors. At Geers Gross interactions and meetings happened with a quick walk down the stairs or the hall. At McCann it meant elevator rides, lobby door keys, and appointments. Geers Gross operated as a cohesive unit; we were a tight-knit group. At McCann there were fiefdoms and people fiercely defended their turf. Respecting the chain of command was demanded. We all had to adjust and carry on, like it or not. Getting used to the personality vibe of McCann was the biggest and most interesting challenge.

When acquisitions or mergers happen the culture of the acquirer takes hold quickly and the acquired agency's culture evaporates just as rapidly. The door to the past closes and a new one opens. That's just the way it is. Systems integration is relatively easy. People and cultural integration takes a lot more work and personal attention from both sides. I experienced that as the "acquirer" at Geers Gross and now I'd be facing it as the "acquiree" at McCann. Same process, different realities.

Back then, the agency business was known for its male-dominated culture, and McCann was notorious for its over-the-top maleness. John Dooner instilled a "we will not be denied" and "do whatever it takes" attitude when it came to our clients' businesses. Not that that was a bad philosophy; actually, it was one I also embraced. But like most management mantras, its effectiveness depended on how it was interpreted and executed. At McCann, it meant being a rough, tough competitive boys' club where colleagues would "stab you in the front."

Needless to say, day-to-day business could get a bit intense. When there were disagreements or turf battles, civility went out the window. The "f**k you," "a**holes," and "SOBs'" flowed freely. Thick skins were definitely an asset. I had experience with that rough rhetoric from my Brooklyn days so I could stay calm and let it roll off my back but many of my Geers Gross colleagues didn't like it at all.

The *Mad Men* TV series featured an unflattering view of McCann management in one of its episodes calling them "a bunch of black Irish thugs." In reality, though, my new colleagues were, for the most part, hard-charging guys who were good at their jobs. Yes, there were a few crude, abusive jerks, but they eventually got stabbed—some in the front, some in the back. There were also very talented and equally strong women at McCann at that time including one of my heroes Nina DiSesa, creative director. Nina is one of the most talented and effective creative people I know. I learned a lot watching her nurture creative talent, interact with McCann's management, and work with clients. She believed in her people and their creative work, took the time to know her audience, and knew how to read the room. One of the best in the business!

First things first: clients

I was looking forward to working with a management team of heavy hitters: Bob James Chairman/CEO McCann Worldwide; Jay McNamara, President McCann Worldwide; John Dooner, McCann NY CEO; and my co-deputy GM, Gene O'Sullivan. Irwin jokingly called us the four Irish horsemen...and Hank.

My initial priority was getting Geers Gross clients settled at McCann. Once that was done I gradually added oversight responsibilities on other accounts. I did my best to bring the "four Irish horsemen" up to speed on Geers Gross (now McCann) clients so we could schedule introductory meetings. Overall, our meetings went well and during my tenure at McCann there weren't any significant issues or major client defections, except for one, Fuji.

Fuji operated in the competitive photo film category dominated by Kodak. They were always fighting to get trade support, attention, and shelf space. Being a large and significant client to their agency was important to Fuji and they expected a deep commitment to their business. Creative capabilities, personal attention, and trust were what they were looking for in an agency partner and indeed what they received from Geers Gross. Fuji's president, Bernie Yasanaga, trusted us enough to send his daughter to work and train at Geers Gross.

After the acquisition, Fuji management was very concerned about being a much smaller fish in the big McCann pond. I reassured them that we had the full support of McCann management and arranged an introductory meeting with Bob James, McCann Worldwide CEO. Bob was a strong leader and driving force behind McCann's rise to global dominance.[1]

I hadn't spent much time with Bob, but I knew he was not a touchy-feely guy. I briefed him on Fuji management's concerns and expectations and set up the meeting. Unfortunately, Bob was not at his best in that meeting. It started out as a dialogue, but then Bob began extolling the success of McCann, its global strength, organizational resources, and, worst, talked to the Fuji management team about how fortunate *they* were to be part of the McCann system. He hardly spent any time talking about their business, service expectations, and the subjects most important to them: personal commitment and creativity. Instead, Bob discussed the uphill battle the company would face in fighting the success of mighty Kodak. I could see the walls going up.

There was a definite culture disconnect and I believe the fate of the Fuji account at McCann was sealed at that meeting. Not surprisingly, Fuji put their business into review two months later. It was a hotly pursued account in which McCann participated, but I knew it was a lost cause. Hal Riney New York emerged as the winner. Like Geers Gross, Riney was a smaller, independent creative agency and Fuji would be the New York office's largest account. The biggest fish in a smaller pond! Personal attention and creativity. (More about Riney later.)

For McCann, the account loss was not financially significant, but it was a very big blow for all of us on the Fuji team. We lost a valued and cherished business partner. Soon after Fuji's exit, Chris Ebner, management supervisor on Fuji and Manufacturers Hanover, left the agency. Chris and I had been through a lot together at DKG and Geers Gross and I was very sad to see him go.

The other client introduction meetings with McCann management went well and the account teams did a great job integrating our clients into the McCann system. For me, the Fuji experience reinforced some simple, yet important guideposts for getting off on the right foot with clients or business partners:

> 1. Be well-prepared to talk about *their* business. Make it more about *them*, not you.

---

1. By 1993, the McCann network had expanded to ninety-nine countries. It was the number one agency in sixteen countries.

2. Follow the two-to-one rule: Listen twice as much as you talk.

3. Tell the client how important they are and then tell them again.

4. Confident humility works all the time.

5. First impressions are often lasting impressions. Sometimes you only get one chance.

Over the years, whether on the client or agency side, I constantly reminded myself that creative service companies can't exist without their clients. All the resources and capabilities that make an agency successful are only as good as the people that use them and the results produced for their clients.

Dual (Not dueling) deputy general managers

In my first year at McCann NY, Gene O'Sullivan and I shared the deputy GM role. Gene was an experienced, well-respected ad guy and we got along well. From the outset we agreed to work together and complement rather than compete with each other. Both of us lived up to that commitment. We also served on the McCann NY executive management committee.

McCann was the largest agency and revenue contributor in the Interpublic Group (IPG). Financial performance and making the numbers were Gene's and my top priorities. We focused on client relationships, account management personnel, revenue, and profitability. I concentrated on Geers Gross clients plus Sony electronics, Mennen, Nabisco, and new business. Gene took charge of Coke, AT&T, other major accounts, and new business.

Integrating myself into existing McCann accounts required a big mindset shift. I'd spent the past few years eliminating excess layers of management. Now, I was the excess layer of management. I accepted that it wasn't necessary to be involved in everything. I did my best to tread lightly, not disrupt already well-run accounts, and concentrated on how I could add value. My McCann colleagues appreciated that. Taking a step back had the added benefit of reducing my stress level. "Relax Hank, you don't have to do it all" was my new mantra. Here's a snapshot of a few interesting lessons I learned on my new accounts.

Mennen

Mennen was a successful men's toiletries company and McCann handled their Speed Stick deodorant and Afta after shave lotion brands. Mennen's CEO, Hal Dannenberg, was a smart, well-respected executive who liked to be involved in the creative process. Gunnar Wilmot was the management supervisor and a rising star at McCann. He had an excellent relationship with Hal and was great at involving me in creative work sessions and client meetings when he felt it was appropriate. We had good chemistry, mutual respect, and were an effective team.

McCann's creative work for Mennen was basic, hard-working packaged goods advertising—nothing dramatic or award winning, but very effective. There was one aspect of Mennen's branding that really intrigued me: their tag line/jingle. Every commercial ended with a simple "Byyyy Mennen" three note jingle and on-screen copy. If you're of a certain age you probably heard it in your head as you read the words. It was one of those sign-off signatures that became embedded in your mind .

"By Mennen" was one of the top ten most recognized brand slogans or signatures in the '80s and '90s. It was famously uttered by George Costanza in a 1993 Seinfeld episode (now a meme!).[2] Hal Dannenberg liked to remind us that this device was a critical, essential element of Mennen's brand equity, almost like a seal of approval. How it flowed in at the end of each thirty-second commercial was just as important as the twenty-six seconds that preceded it. This simple pneumonic was both a brand identifier (By Mennen) and a call to action (Buy Mennen).[3]

Brilliant. Here's what stuck with me: There are no little things when it comes to building brand equity. Attention to executional details matters and everything is interconnected.

From then on, whenever I looked at brand plans and creative ideas I asked myself, "Where are those three little notes?" They were hard to find.

Sony

Sony electronics was an account that always had drama attached to it. The director of advertising Jeff Brooks was a tough client who required a lot of attention. There were regular crises and urgent meetings that wore down the account teams. If nothing else, my presence relieved some of the pressure by simply giving Jeff another person to call, commiserate with, and occasionally yell at.

The saving grace of the account for me was that underneath all that tumult, Jeff was a smart guy who really knew the electronics business. He shared his insights with me and I appreciated that. Jeff was also very interested in the video game business and eager to hear about my Nintendo experience. I realized that sometimes just "being there" is enough to make a difference in a business relationship. As Woody Allen said, "Eighty percent of success is showing up." On

---

2. Mennen commercials and George meme https://bit.ly/ByMennenVideos

3. Brand signatures became a lost art but finding favor again. It's now called Sonic Branding. Using the power of sound and music to transcend language and culture as a brand identity equity. Best exemplified by Avon https://bit.ly/AvonSonicBranding.

Sony, I showed up, listened, shared, and learned.

Nabisco

McCann's Nabisco assignments included the Ritz cracker brand. I enjoyed working on Nabisco for two reasons. First, I was and still am a Ritz lover. I ate Ritz every day as kid. Second, Nina DiSesa had taken over as creative director on the account and I was eager to work with her. It would be my first time working with a female creative director in my twenty-three years in the industry. A sad commentary.

The current brand campaign for Ritz featured happy families enjoying Ritz with different toppings and the tag line, "Everything tastes better on a Ritz," followed by the Nabisco three-note corporate logo (Nabisco's corporate brand pneumonic was good but it didn't make the same connection as "By Mennen"). The agency was asked to explore new creative options and Nina convinced the client to make it more of a brand positioning exploratory.

Ritz was a strong, stand-alone brand so broadening and deepening its appeal would feed the Nabisco brand equity piggybank. Nina's direction was to focus more on Ritz's inherent taste and deliciousness, not its use as a carrier for toppings. It was a smart strategic call that led to an interesting range of ideas and executions—everything from "tastes so good it should be called a cookie;" to "all I want is Ritz," which built on a "growing up with Ritz" theme (I think my story inspired that idea); a fun "Why question perfection?" analysis of Ritz; and "When you want a cracker, you want Ritz," brought to life in a range of executions. The "When you want a cracker, you want Ritz" concept depicting family sharing moments was the winner. Here they are in a video case history.[4]

There were two important things I took away from this experience:

> 1. Challenging the status quo energizes creative teams and often brings unexpected positive results. Nina pushed the creative teams to think out of the Ritz box (sorry, couldn't resist that) and we were able to see how far we could push the brand promise.

> 2. Working with a female creative director didn't make any difference (talent is genderless) but working with Nina DiSesa specifically was a very special experience. Her seduction and manipulation (S&M) approach worked like a charm.[5]

---

4. Video with all the tested Ritz commercials. Good behind the scenes learning https://bit.ly/RitzCreativeExploratory

5. In her bestselling book, *Seducing the Boys Club*, Nina recounts her experiences breaking through the testosterone at McCann. She shared her secret to winning over (and surpassing) the big guys, what she calls S&M: Seduction and Manipulation. http://bit.ly/SeducingTheBoysClub

More fine people

In addition to the people with whom I directly worked I was fortunate to connect with three McCann colleagues who would have a positive impact on my future: Gene Kummel, Marcio Moreira, and Bruce Nelson.

Gene Kummel, McCann Chairman Emeritus, had traveled the world building McCann into a global powerhouse and in 1988, he was inducted into the American Advertising Federation Hall of Fame[6]. Gene was actually a mentor to one of my mentors at DDB, Derrick O'Dea. When I joined McCann, Derrick called Gene and asked him to look in on me. He loved that I was teaching at Pace and we made an instant connection. Gene was also into giving back to the next generation; he was chairman of the Advertising Educational Foundation, which focused on learning programs and mentorships. Gene had great stories to tell and was very generous with his time and advice. I made it a point to drop in on him whenever I could.

Marcio Moreira was a larger than life gregarious ad man and a highly respected international creative director at McCann. When I arrived he was already a twenty-year McCann veteran responsible for overseeing all of the agency's global creative work. Marcio was gracious and welcoming and helped me navigate the ins and outs of McCann's global network. Our friendship would blossom and play an important role a few years later.

Bruce is a rare breed of ad guy that has that magic mix of creative brilliance and big strategic thinking. In fact, at McCann he held key positions as creative director as well as strategy director. Bruce had extensive experience across a broad array of categories including financial services. I was looking forward to working with him. My wish was fulfilled when McCann was asked to pitch a for a special assignment from Fidelity Investments.

At that time Peter Lynch was running Fidelity's very successful Magellan Fund. One of his practices for identifying company's in which to invest was actually visiting the company and "looking around." Bruce used the simply profound intent of that principle to develop a powerful campaign idea: Common Sense. Uncommon Results. A perfectly "human" articulation of Fidelity's philosophy. The client loved the idea and we were awarded the project. Bruce and Irwin created a series of commercials that brought the idea to life for the everyday investor and the campaign ran for a few years. I took away an interesting lesson working with Bruce. Even in complex, high stakes categories such as finance and investments simplifying and humanizing brand characteristics and benefits is possible and powerful. Simplify. Humanize. Works in any decade. Bruce and I would reconnect again and we still enjoy a great friendship today.

---

6. Advertising Hall of Fame: Gene Kummel http://bit.ly/KummelAdHallofFame

Less pressure, more "me" time

Sharing deputy general manager responsibilities at McCann had one great benefit: It took the pressure and demands of being CEO off my shoulders. Sure, I had important responsibilities but the buck no longer stopped with me. That made a difference. I became more relaxed as I gradually realized I could step back and smell the roses on occasion.

I was always being invited to media parties and galas and as a BSA board member had an open invitation to the Boy Scouts' luncheon events. At Geers Gross I had convinced myself that I didn't have time and passed them up. Now at McCann, I made the time—three events had a profound impact on me, albeit for very different reasons.

1. Opulent diversion

Kathy Keeton, wife of *Penthouse* founder Bob Guccione, was a smart savvy magazine executive whom I knew and respected. She launched a science magazine *Omni* and I was a big supporter of the publication with my clients.[7] Kathy sent a congratulatory note when I joined McCann inviting my wife Vicki and me to dinner. I was surprised to find out that the invitation was for a small dinner party at their spectacular 20,000 square foot East 67th Street mansion. It was the largest single residence in Manhattan with dual spiral marble staircase, priceless art, and sculpture everywhere and a lavish indoor pool on the lower level. Stepping into this amazing place was an unforgettable experience.[8]

There were ten of us at the dinner and Bob's younger sister Geri Winston was among the guests. The food was wonderful, the conversation stimulating, and Bob and Kathy were gracious hosts. What I remember most, however, were drinks after dinner in the upstairs lounge. The centerpiece of that room was Judy Garland's gleaming white and gilt piano. Imagine the people that sang songs around that piano. I actually was allowed to sit at that piano and pecked out the only song I knew: "Twinkle Twinkle Little Star." A big thrill but no applause.

Vicki and I struck up a friendship with Bob's sister Geri and we were invited to the spectacular fiftieth birthday party Bob hosted for Geri and her twin sister at the mansion. It was an elegant affair spread across two floors with a string quartet playing around the indoor pool. This was not your everyday family birthday party. We had a ball. What I originally thought would be a nice dinner with a publisher turned out to be a once-in-a lifetime experience leading to new friendships and an opportunity to channel my inner Judy Garland. You never know.

7. Kathy Keeton: The forgotten female genius at *Penthouse* http://bit.ly/KathyKeeton

8. Guccione mansion http://bit.ly/GuccioneNYMansion

2. Poignant admiration

We attended *People* magazine's celebration gala honoring individuals featured on their 1987 magazine covers. You can imagine the celebs and VIPs at the event. There was a formal ceremony followed by dinner with the honorees seated among the guests at tables of ten. Vicki and I were blessed to be at the table with the most inspiring, heroic cover person there: Ryan White.[9]

Sixteen-year-old Ryan was on the cover because of the discrimination he suffered while suffering from AIDS. A hemophiliac, he contracted the disease at age twelve through blood transfusions. Ryan desperately wanted to go to school but was denied access by the school board because of his illness. He and his mom fought the system and won, and Ryan became a spokesperson and champion in the AIDS crisis battle.[10] He looked very grown up in his tuxedo—he radiated maturity, humility, and a quiet strength—but really, he was just a young kid wanting to enjoy what was left of his life. We had a wonderful conversation about a lot of stuff–not AIDS. I couldn't help but think about our boys and how devastating it must have been for Ryan and his mom. Sadly, about three years later Ryan was featured on another *People* magazine cover chronicling his passing, one month before his high school graduation.[11] I'll never forget that evening. It left a lasting impression and serves as constant reminder to appreciate my blessings.

3. Powerful inspiration

The Greater New York Council of Boy Scouts held afternoon fund raising events called Lunch-O-Rees. Businesses sponsored tables and scout troops attended. The program included the usual hotel fare, a short film, event chair comments, and the introduction of "guest of honor" scouts by a board member. The scouts' speeches were amazing and there wasn't a dry eye in the house after they finished. At one Lunch-O-Ree I was the board member who introduced a very special group of scouts: members of our Scouting for the handicapped program. They spoke to the audience about how the program changed their lives and proudly displayed their merit badges. The energy, enthusiasm, courage, and skills demonstrated by these scouts were awesome. The emotion in the room was palpable and everyone was humbled in their presence. The tears flowed, the applause was deafening, and the checkbooks opened wide. As I took it all in, I realized that none of it would have been possible if it wasn't for the passion and persistence of my fellow board member, Vivian Harris.

Vivian was a prominent philanthropist, community leader, and a powerful advocate for

---

9. *People* magazine cover story http://bit.ly/PeopleRyanWhite

10. HRSA profile: http://bit.ly/HRSARyanWhiteProfile

11. *People* magazine story http://bit.ly/RyanWhitePassing

ill and disabled children. Her mission was to make scouting accessible to handicapped boys; there was definitely a demand but no program existed to administer it. Vivian was relentless in overcoming the NYC public school bureaucracy to get clearance, recruiting, and training special scout leaders and lining up funding. Vivian got the program up and running with about 2,000 Scouts. At the time of the Lunch-O-Ree that number had grown to over 20,000.[12] I saw firsthand how the "power of one" focused on a bold vision can move mountains (and even the NYC Board of Education!). To top it all off, Vivian was also a founder and president of Ronald McDonald House New York.

In Asset-Based Thinking terms I put Vivian on my Mount Rushmore of people I look up to. When we place people there it means that the qualities we admire in them are the qualities we have in ourselves waiting to bubble up and put into practice in our own lives. I drew on Vivian's inspiration years later when I became an American Heart Association volunteer (more about that later).

If IPG had not acquired Geers Gross I most likely would have missed out on these amazing experiences and my life would be less full. It made me realize that my initial bitching and moaning about being acquired served no purpose. Fortunately, I was able to see the silver lining soon enough to have and cherish those experiences with Kathy, Ryan, and Vivian. About fifteen years later, I would remember this lesson when I once again had to find the silver lining in another dark McCann-related cloud.

More meetings, less me time

In late 1988, NY CEO John Dooner added the title of CEO of McCann North America to his responsibilities. John was a very proactive manager and quickly implemented major changes that positively impacted me. I was named EVP, Allied Communications and new business development for McCann North America and a member of a newly formed North America executive committee responsible for the overall profitability and professional quality of McCann's network and new business. The committee included John Dooner, EVP Craig Middleton, CFO Bob Cabezas, and myself.[13]

I was now responsible for overseeing McCann's direct marketing, sales promotion, public relations, and healthcare communications agencies as well as chairing the corporate new business group. Oh yeah, and I also remained on the New York executive committee and continued overseeing Sony, Nintendo, Manufacturers Hanover, and other accounts.[14] *Phew!* I went to a ton of meetings and travelled extensively, dramatically curtailing my me time. I was stretched thin.

---

12. The Scouts memorialized Vivian's work with the Vivian Harris Award. https://bit.ly/VivianHarrisAward

13. Gunnar Wilmot replaced me as EVP deputy general manager of McCann NY. A well-deserved promotion.

14. Internal announcement memo. https://bit.ly/McCannPromotion

My Allied Communications oversight role was essentially checking on financial performance and advising on the operations of McCann's aligned creative agencies. I had no real decision-making power or operating responsibilities. It was frustrating just being involved around the edges of these companies. I preferred the responsibility and challenge of running businesses and being at the center of the action. Meetings, meetings, and more meetings were just not my style. To energize myself, I adopted a ready-to-make-a-contribution attitude. Sure, we looked at the numbers but here's how I added more purpose and productivity to our meetings.

1. Starting meetings with a creative show-and-tell so pride in their work set the tone. Recognition and praise go a long way.

2. Brainstorming ways to increase their revenue by bringing in non-advertising assignments from McCann's clients, essentially making revenue exchange a two-way street. We added direct marketing projects from Nintendo and sales promotion assignments from Manufacturers Hanover Bank.

3. Being each agency's advocate with the McCann North America executive committee to ease or eliminate pain-points and operational barriers. Helping get bureaucracy out of their way went a long way.

I also used these meetings as learning experiences that would add to my expertise and give me a better understanding of the total marketing communications landscape. I especially enjoyed spending time with the creative directors of our allied agencies. They were just as passionate and enthusiastic about their direct mail piece, display promotion, or latest PR coup as the ad agency teams were about their print ad spectaculars, TV spots, and Super Bowl commercials. Again, it reinforced my belief that ideas and people are the drivers of marketing success.

The last day before the rest of my life

By October 1989, I had to start facing my future. My two-year contractual obligation to IPG would be fulfilled at the end of the year and I had to decide whether or not to stay at McCann. I was torn. While I hadn't yet found my niche there, I enjoyed being part of the organization and was working with talented people. Plus, John Dooner was a good boss and doing his best to find the right fit for me.

On the other hand, having gone through my share of mergers and buyouts, I felt a bit burnt out and fed up with corporate life. My wife Vicki and I were thinking about a change of pace and seriously considering leaving Manhattan. Our three sons were either in college or recently graduated and self-sufficient. And if I left McCann, termination compensation triggers would activate and provide me with a nice financial cushion.

I reconnected with my Somerset colleague Sales SVP Dick Mutter, who was also at a crossroads in his career and we talked about our mutual desires to be more in control of our destiny. Creating a business together was an intriguing possibility. All of this was swirling around in my head. I had to stay calm, focus, weigh my options, and make yet another career decision. Stay at McCann or move on. And move on to what?

First, after much soul-searching, I made the decision to leave McCann. I involved my friend and creative partner Irwin in my decision making process since he knew me well. I trusted his judgment and, also, I didn't want him to be surprised. I owed him that. Irwin supported my decision and told me that he was going to stay at McCann. It was the right decision for him. Irwin went on to have a stellar career at McCann until his voluntary retirement in 2007.

I had lived up to all of my obligations and then some and knew I could leave with my head held high. That was important to me. The "what next?" part of my decision was more complicated and I put that aside until after my McCann swansong was behind me. I announced my resignation to John Dooner on December 1, explaining that I was not leaving due to discontent or for another agency opportunity. I wasn't sure what I would do next but I needed to step back, wipe the slate clean, and start fresh. John was a little surprised, but I think he was probably expecting it eventually. He could not have been more understanding and gracious. John was genuinely sorry that McCann couldn't find the right fit for me and he valued my contributions and friendship. The feeling was mutual. We both agreed that this didn't necessarily have to be the end of our story—and happily it wasn't (stay tuned for that).

John agreed that I could let my Geers Gross clients know about my leaving before the public announcement. I told John that our biggest potential client issue was Nintendo since Dennis Fogarty, the Nintendo management supervisor, had left McCann a few months earlier. Dennis was with me on Nintendo from the very start and was highly valued by the client. My leaving would exacerbate the situation, as was duly noted by John (Postscript coming next chapter).

My next step was to properly execute my termination contractual requirements. I delivered a formal notification of my resignation to Geers Gross to activate the termination compensation clause. I received a notice of acceptance from Geers Gross attorneys. I didn't hear back from Bob Gross for a couple of weeks. He wished me well.

Next was another visit to my old friend Kent Kroeber, head of HR at IPG to work out my exit details. My meeting with Kent was bittersweet. Two years earlier we had reconnected to create my McCann entry plan agreement and now were meeting to expedite my exit. Fortunately, my employment contract was clear and specific and IPG agreed to deliver on everything in the agreement. There were no issues. I had Kent Kroeber to thank for that. We also agreed to keep in touch.

I made my calls to our clients and was very touched and humbled by their understanding and genuine well wishes for my future. That made moving on a little easier for me. On December 7, John Dooner sent out a nice complimentary staff memo and the announcement appeared in *The New York Times* and trade press the next day.[15] I really appreciated how graciously John handled my leaving McCann. Talk about leaving a connecting bridge behind you. It's a good feeling when you're treated well upon joining a company, but it's an even better feeling when you are treated just as well on your exit.

The next week was very emotional for me. My Geers Gross buddies hosted a wonderful good-bye lunch, created a farewell video, and I shed some tears. I received a number of "wishing you well" notes from clients, colleagues, and industry friends. I was pleasantly surprised to get a nice note from my old Norton Simon boss David Mahoney. It's times like these when you really appreciate and treasure the personal connections that make up the fabric of your career. I saved a few of those notes, including one from Jim Smith, EVP and creative director at McCann's direct marketing agency. I'd only worked with Jim for about a year in my role as director of allied communications but his words hit home.

Here's an excerpt:

> "In the five years I've been here, you are one of the very, very few
> McCann executives who showed any interest at all—except in our
> profit picture. We appreciate the work you got for us with your clients.
> And the respect you showed us as advertising professionals…all the
> creative folks here wish you well."

Jim's thoughtful note validated how I approached my job as "overseer" of McCann's allied communications companies and reinforced my core beliefs about managing and working with creative service partners:

> People are the most valuable "inventory."
> Creativity is the prime asset.
> Appreciation is a valued form of compensation.

---

15. McCann exit article & announcement https://bit.ly/MCCannExitAnnouncement

A poignant personal retrospective

Joining Geers Gross in 1985 was a very good and fateful decision. The ensuing five years were action-packed with ups and downs that challenged me to mature and grow as a businessman. I worked with amazing colleagues, a diverse mix of clients, and amassed more valuable experience than I ever imagined. It eventually came to a graceful and positive exit from McCann that would have future benefits. But there is one other serendipitous, fateful consequence of my Geers Gross tenure that is impossible to value. In fact, I'm sure this story would not have been written had it not occurred.

In 1988, my son Gregg was in his junior year at Syracuse University's Newhouse school of communications and totally committed to being an advertising copywriter (more about Gregg's career later). He discussed doing a study abroad semester at Syracuse London in the fall. We created a better option: instead, Gregg scheduled a summer study course at Syracuse London and combined it with a creative internship at Geers Gross. Two for one: credits and experience.

That summer, Gregg attended classes at Syracuse London's Faraday House two mornings a week, and interned at the Geers Gross office on St. Marten's Lane the other week days. He was back in New York for the fall semester. Meanwhile, thirty-five of his Syracuse classmates enjoyed their fall study abroad semester in London and on December 21, 1988, left to return home on Pan Am flight 103. That flight was taken down over Lockerbie, Scotland, by a terrorist bomb. There were no survivors. All 259 passengers perished along with eleven people on the ground. The shock, sorrow, and outrage was felt around the world and hit especially hard in Syracuse.[16]

Gregg's graduation ceremony in 1989 paid tribute to those thirty-five students at a very moving and emotional ceremony in which a Lockerbie town official addressed the class. Our family was spared the agony of a lost child and our good fortune will never be forgotten. If I hadn't worked at Geers Gross and been able to get Gregg a summer internship at the London office our son would most likely have done the fall semester abroad and been on that flight with his thirty-five now deceased classmates. We were blessed by timing and circumstance.

Upon graduation, Gregg landed a copywriter trainee position at a blue chip agency, Lintas. He did it all on his own. I didn't know anyone at the agency. So, here was one of my sons entering the Mad Men business twenty-five years after my debut. It was proudful, delightful, and fateful. More on Gregg's career and me later.

I left McCann just before Christmas ready to celebrate the holidays with my family. My wife Vicki's birthday is on Christmas day, making it an especially important time of year for us. Our Christmas in New York was particularly magical that year. January 1 ushered in a

---

16. Lockerbie remembrance http://bit.ly/LockerbieRemembrance

new decade and I was looking at a wide open road ahead of me. I was forty-six, heading into the '90s without a job (this time by choice) and with the flexibility and freedom to move my career in any direction I chose.

I was ready to start the first day of the rest of my life.

Mad Man Wisdom

- Turn complain into calm and carry on. When the rug gets pulled out from under you, bitch and moan fast then get over it.
- Company culture is a fact of life in business. It doesn't change to suit you. Adapt, leave, or be miserable. Your choice.
- When meeting new people, listen twice as much as you talk. It will speak volumes about you.
- When working with or sharing responsibilities with colleagues have a complement rather than compete attitude. 1+1 = 3.
- Adopt an "add value" mindset whenever you're asked to pitch-in or called-in to meetings. Make your words and actions count.
- Talent knows no gender. Jettison your stereotypical expectations and encourage others to do the same.
- Show up with your Signature Presence. You can make a difference and be a positive catalyst.
- Carve out your personal Mount Rushmore. The people you put on it will bring out the best in you. Guaranteed.
- Count your blessings, big and small. They add up to a more appreciated life.
- As Yogi Berra once famously said, "When you come to a fork in the road, take it!" You know what I mean.

Marketing Truisms and Tips

Question: What's More Important: Strategy or Execution?
Answer: That's the wrong question.

The facile answer is, of course, "both." To be successful in marketing you must have both. Strategy and execution have a symbiotic relationship; it's not an either/or choice. This quote from renowned Taiwanese entrepreneur Morris Chang nails it.

"Without strategy, execution is aimless. Without execution,
strategy is useless."

In the context of both being important, perhaps a better question is, "Which has the greatest potential to be a differentiator and accelerator?" I come down on the side of execution and espouse management guru Peter Drucker's simple point of view:

"Strategy is a commodity; execution is an art."

My strategist colleagues should not be upset by Mr. Drucker's quote. Identifying strategy as a commodity by no means diminishes its importance and value. Here's a simple analogy. Gold, platinum, and silver are all very valuable commodities. Mining them takes great skill and resources. Their ultimate consumer value is realized when craftsmen refine them for functional uses or artists mold and shape them into items people want and treasure. Mining is strategy; molding and crafting is art. The good news is that in today's digital world, the power of both strategy and art have greatly increased. On the strategic side, data-driven marketing tools and processes enable even more incisive and powerful strategic thinking. For artists, digital tools have exploded a new range of creative possibilities. And with split-second deployment and real-time feedback, personalized creative executions at scale are now possible.

In a prior chapter, I discussed how Michael Dubin, founder of Dollar Shave Club, was both strategist and artist. The strategist in him created a sound, nimble subscription-based business model for his internet company. The artist in him viewed the value proposition as joining a more personal, membership-based tribe and created and brilliantly executed a $5,000 commercial that was the differentiator and accelerator.

Everyone is different. I enjoy hanging out with strategists and artists, but I choose to spend more time cultivating the artists. Discover what works best for you.

Chapter 9 Footnotes

Scan QR codes for direct links to footnote content.

9.2 Mennen Ads & George Meme

9.3 Avon Sonic Branding Video

9.4 Ritz Creative Exploratory

9.12 Vivian Harris Award

9.14 McCann Promotion Press

9.15 McCann Exit Press

Chapter 10:

Take the Detour. Arrive at a Better Destination.

After leaving McCann, the road to the rest of my life was paved with connections, unexpected opportunities, and introspection. It was a new decade and I was ready for a major change in direction. It took some soul searching to decide what that direction was, however, and then time preparing the road to get there. Along the way I made wonderful new connections with advertising superstars I admired and reconnected with valued friends and colleagues. And when it came time to choose, I decided on a detour I'd been wanting to explore for some time.

I followed my entrepreneurial urge and started an alcoholic beverage company, Capstone International, with my colleague from Somerset Importers, Dick Mutter. I left the hectic pace of the New York advertising business behind and moved to St. Petersburg, Florida. I was forty-eight years old and ready to enjoy the leisurely semi-retired lifestyle I'd often dreamed about.

My detour lasted an enjoyable and fulfilling four years and then it came to an unanticipated but necessary end. It enabled me to reassess my priorities and dreams so when serendipity opened up a new road, I could look at it with a fresh perspective. At age fifty-two, I took a new old road, one that led to Los Angeles and my McCann encore.

It just goes to show…a detour at the right time can lead you to a much better place.

The '90s

My exit from McCann and detour away from the agency business happened as the marketing world entered the '90s, a decade of rapid change and expansion. In 1995, those changes exploded, ushering in the digital era. Almost every aspect of the industry was altered: media, messaging, agency structure, and consumer dynamics. The internet had been around since the 1980s but it didn't start evolving into a marketing force until 1994. Netscape's internet browser took it mainstream and search tools like Infoseek and AltaVista enabled users to easily browse millions of websites.

Internet advertising really heated up with the launch of *Hotwired*, the first online magazine that really took off.[1] It was also the beginning of online shopping and everyone in marketing rushed to alter their business models in order to harness this amazing resource. The great promise of "e-tailing" fueled the rapid growth of countless dot-com companies including eBay

---

1. In 1996, the Internet Advertising Bureau (IAB) pegged internet advertising spending a scant $157 million. In 2019 that number was $124 billion!

and Amazon. People hardly took note when Google came on the scene in 1998, but when it went public in 2004, everyone noticed!

The rise of the digital age meant that consumers had more choices, more control, and greater ability to interact with information and media. As a result, mass media offerings became more sophisticated and expensive. Agencies reacted by developing integrated marketing capabilities through expanded allied communications services and building out technology resources and expertise. The most significant change occurred when big agencies began to spin off their media departments to provide full media services enabling them to work with clients outside the parent agencies. For example, McCann established Universal McCann as their unbundled media agency.

The number of websites grew exponentially and by the end of the decade pundits were predicting the imminent demise of traditional media. Less than a year later, the dot-com bubble burst; only the strong survived as the industry corrected itself.

It's fair to say that the 1990s laid the foundation for marketing communications as we know it today. The digital era was upon us. By the mid-'90s these changes had reawakened my passion for marketing and put me on a path to a new and better destination. I was reenergized and ready to be part of helping shape its future. But first, let's go back to 1990 and my post-McCann detour.

I moved on

My last day at McCann was just before the Christmas holidays of 1989. Figuring out my next move involved a trifecta of factors:

> Career: Yet another corporate or agency move to clutter up my resumé?
> Family: Kids have all left the nest. Time for a relocation and new lifestyle?
> Personal: Don't BS myself. What did I really want?

It took more work and preparation to come to a decision than originally thought. In the meantime, I had the opportunity to celebrate my successes with some awesome client colleagues.

In February 1990, I was invited to lunch by my Nintendo friends for a formal farewell get-together. It turned out to be one of the most heartwarming days of my career. They presented me the Super Mario Award of Excellence.[2]

It read:

---

2. Super Mario award https://bit.ly/MarioAward

Presented to Hank Wasiak in recognition of his outstanding contribution to the success of the Nintendo Entertainment System.

Minoru Arakawa, President

Mr. A said it was their way of expressing Nintendo's thanks and memorializing my contributions. *Wow!* I didn't expect anything like that and was deeply touched and honored. Much more than a plaque, it was a beautiful expression of gratitude that I will always treasure. This award gave me instant gamer creds with my sons, Pace students, and later, my grandson Lucas. Nintendo and this award would come back into my life years later. Stay tuned for that.

Side note: In June 1990, just four months after that lunch, Nintendo moved their account from McCann to Foote, Cone & Belding (FCB). I saw that one coming.

And now back to my life ruminations…

My first decision was to put career resumé clutter concerns aside. Another full-time big agency or client job was simply not a priority. Luckily, my hard work over the past three decades had earned me the privilege of being able to make a decision driven by lifestyle factors and following my gut.

Taking control of my destiny kept on rising to the top of my priorities. The entrepreneurial bug was starting to bite again, but this time it was different. In my first venture with Bruce Nevins at PWIC, I joined as the third partner in an existing wine company and was buying into someone else's vision and business plans. This time Dick and I would be launching a company from scratch and shaping it to our shared vision and business objectives.

So Dick Mutter and I began serious discussions about starting an alcoholic beverage company.

But setting up an alcoholic beverage company was not as simple as hanging out a shingle. It required sorting through regulatory red tape while we worked on business plans, identifying potential suppliers, lining up distributors, and other miscellaneous operational details. Most importantly, we had to apply for and obtain the required federal, state, and local permits and licenses, all of which required extensive background checks. Any glitches with those government approvals and it was game over. In addition, the process would take six to nine months before Dick and I could make a go or no-go decision. As this due diligence was proceeding, I hedged my bets by keeping active in New York advertising circles. It didn't take long for opportunity to knock.

Temptation, opportunity, and income

Right after the holidays, I received two calls that got my attention. A mutual friend connected me with Tom McElligot. Tom was a creative star in the ad business and in 1981 cofounded the very successful Minneapolis agency, Fallon, McElligot, Rice, now known as Fallon.[3] Tom had recently left the agency and, like me, was contemplating his next moves. I was an admirer of Tom's work and jumped at the opportunity to chat with him. We spoke a few times, got along well, and discussed the possibility of an agency partnership; account guy and copywriter was a good yin-yang relationship. But Tom was committed to staying in Minneapolis and while I was open to leaving NYC, Minneapolis was not for me (brrrr). We agreed that the moon and the stars did not align on this one. *C'est la vie*, but I was still very fortunate to have met Tom.

I've always made it a point to "take calls" from people whether I knew them well or not. You never know what interesting opportunity or challenge could be on the other end of the phone. Sometimes these calls opened the door to things that benefited me directly and other times to ways that I could be helpful to others. Either way I got something out of the engagement.

Admittedly, my default position of always hitting the "yes" button sometimes led to distraction overload, loss of focus, and a too long to-do list. In today's 24/7 digital world, keeping up with connections on social media and LinkedIn can be overwhelming. My advice is to adopt a sensible "take calls" mindset that includes being skilled in knowing when and how to say no. It isn't easy. Now when I receive calls, I do few things to manage my "yesses." If I know the person or they say someone I know referred them to me, I always take the call. That's simply respect for the relationship. If I don't know the person, right after saying hello I politely ask why they're calling me and how they got my name. After that, it's pretty easy to sniff out whether it is a sales call you don't want or a connection worth lingering longer for.

When people ask if they can pick my brain I'm flattered and always reciprocate by picking theirs. I look for ways to make every call have value, even some of those sales calls. After I say I'm not interested I ask a quick question that interests me, like:

> How's the mortgage business this week?
> What percentage of your calls lead to an action?
> Are men more likely than women to give to your charity?

I'm always surprised at the things I learn in that extra minute. Whoever you connect with, make that connection work for you *and* for them. Time well spent.

Next I received a call from Jim Travis, CEO of the Hal Riney agency. Jim and Hal were founders of the *Tuesday Team* that created Ronald Reagan's groundbreaking "Morning In America" campaign discussed in chapter five. Hal Riney was One of the hottest agencies around and had taken the Fuji account away from McCann two years before. I absolutely wanted to hear what Jim had to say. We met for lunch and Jim cut right to the chase. Hal Riney New York was growing and Jim was looking for a president to run the agency. He

---

3. McElligot article http://bit.ly/McElligotArticle

thought I was the right guy for the job.

Jim was good friends with my partner, friend, and surrogate uncle at DKG, Shep Kurnit, so I assumed Shep was the genesis of Jim's call. But the real catalyst was a pleasant surprise. Carl Chapman, the CMO of Fuji, had sung my praises to Jim and Hal and suggested they meet with me. It was a wonderful feeling to know that a client thought that much of me. Another example of how positive bridges from the past opened up new opportunities for me.

I was flattered and told Jim that under different circumstances I would jump at the opportunity to work with them. I was open about my plans to start an alcoholic beverage company and explained that there were hurdles yet to cross before I could bring that to fruition. Jim understood, asked me to keep an open mind, and set up a meeting with Hal Riney in New York. I was looking forward to meeting with one of my creative heroes.[4]

Hal and I met for dinner and spent the evening getting to know each other. It went very well. Throughout dinner I was mesmerized by Hal's smooth, familiar voice. He had narrated some of the agency's iconic commercials including those for Perrier. His grandfatherly voice was part of the television landscape and images of those Perrier commercials kept popping into my head. Jim and Hal made an interesting proposal that I accepted. I joined Riney for a four-to-six month consulting role, essentially functioning as interim president focusing on new business.

The role was perfect for me. I would have an office at the agency, be paid a nice consulting fee, and work with people I admired. Then an article appeared in the trade press erroneously stating that I had joined Riney NY as president.

"Hal Riney & Partners has ended a two year search for a general manager of its NY office and tapped former McCann Erickson executive Hank Wasiak as the new president of Riney New York."

Yikes! I immediately heard from the folks at McCann since I had told them and everyone else I would not be taking a full-time management role in another agency. My exit agreement did not prohibit me from doing that, but nevertheless it was important for me to set the record straight. Fortunately, Riney issued a release clarifying that I was merely hired as a consultant, things calmed down, and I got to work.

Right away I found myself leading a new business pitch for the Carvel ice cream account. I loved that assignment. I had grown up eating Carvel soft serve ice cream. We started work on the pitch and I had the great fortune to work with legendary creative director, Helayne Spivak.[5] She was like the Jewish version of Nina DiSesa.

Helayne grew up in the business during the '70s. She had a wonderful sense of humor, a sharp wit, and was a creative dynamo. Helayne and her team developed a great campaign

---

4. Hal Riney Legacy: http://bit.ly/Rineylife

5. Helayne is now executive director of the VCU Brand Center. http://bit.ly/AdLegendHelayneSpivack

around the concept of "Carvel - it's everybody's soft spot," featuring entertaining snippets of classic Americana life moments. We won the business and the campaign began airing in May (and no, Hal Riney did not do the voiceover narration).

Toward the end of my engagement with Riney NY, Dick's and my vision for our alcoholic beverage venture was getting closer to being a reality so I decided not to extend my consulting role. Jim understood, we parted on great terms and kept in touch over the years. This short unplanned stop on my journey—my detour from my detour if you will—left me richer and wiser with valued new connections.

Sometimes people are faced with the choice of looking for a "real job" or accepting consulting assignments. I advise people to look at that choice through a different lens. "Real" is in the eye of the beholder and consulting relationships provide opportunities to make meaningful contributions and positive impact. They build expertise, strengthen a resumé, create new relationships, and often lead to full-time employment opportunities. The digital age has opened up a plethora of new opportunities, especially for the digitally savvy. In 2020 digital parlance it's called the "side hustle" and there even are resources and online communities dedicated to "side hustle success." (Really. Google "side hustle" and see what comes up). Whatever you call it, make sure your antenna is up so you can heed Bill Bernbach's advice to rub against the very best, the magicians—even if it's only for a short time like I did.

While we were putting the pieces of our entrepreneurial puzzle together, yet another short-stop consulting opportunity came along. This time two past bridges to colleagues and friends converged into one. Walter Kaprielian, my creative partner at Ketchum had left the agency and was now a principal in his own agency Kaprielian O'Leary (K&O). Meanwhile, John Koutsantanou, the CFO of Geers Gross New York, had left after the sale and joined the Gegenheimer Group, a company that invested in communications agencies. They had just acquired K&O and John offered me a consulting gig as adviser to his company and K&O. It was a perfectly timed opportunity to work with two close friends in a mutually beneficial relationship: I could help John and Walter better position their company for growth and they could provide my fledgling company office space and creative and production resources for our launch promotional materials.

Sadly, while we were working together, John and I received the bad news that Bob Gross had passed away. Irwin, friend and former Geers Gross creative director, and the two of us got together to reflect and share some memories. Sure, Bob had his faults but he was also a visionary whose agency acquisitions launched the British invasion of the US advertising world. Bob and Geers Gross played a pivotal and positive role in enabling the three of us to be where we were at that time. We relived some poignant moments and mourned his passing.

Crossing the Rubicon to semi-retirement

At the end of July, Dick and I completed our due diligence and made the "go" decision to launch our alcoholic beverage company. One of the reasons we were both so gung-ho about it was the important commonalities between Dick and me.

We were the same age—I mean exactly the same age. Both born on July 5, 1943 in NYC.

We were married with three children of about the same age and out of the nest.

We had alcoholic beverage industry experience and complementary skills.

We were colleagues at Somerset so we already knew how to work together.

We both desired to relocate to the west coast of Florida.

We were also aligned on company vision and lifestyle expectations. We wanted to build a small, niche company that would generate sufficient revenue to support our current lifestyles. The cost of living in Florida was substantially less than New York making that an attainable goal. Becoming the next Garneau or Somerset alcohol beverage behemoth was not our objective. Been there. Done that. We wanted to be semi-retired with the ability to balance work and play. We recognized that building an alcoholic beverage company from scratch required hard work and perseverance; at the same time, we agreed the business should not overwhelm us. It doesn't get any more compatible than that! I had no qualms about launching a business with Dick. I put the marketing and advertising business in the rearview mirror and went full speed ahead on the road to entrepreneurship.

Building a new life in Florida

We chose Capstone International as our company name; it signified that our new venture was our crowning achievement, the culmination or finishing touch on our long, successful careers. We settled on St. Petersburg, Florida, as home base and registered our company on August 20, 1990. For the next ten months we operated out of New York until we were ready to relocate to Florida in July 1991.

The time was right for a move to Florida. Our oldest son Brian had just relocated to Los Angeles to pursue a film career. Gregg was in his second year as a copywriter at Lintas with an apartment on Manhattan's upper west side, and our youngest son Jason was attending the Ringling School of Art in nearby Sarasota, Florida. Also, our co-op at the Beresford had greatly appreciated in value and we were ready to cash in. Our real estate broker, Phyllis Koch, put the apartment on the market in March and it sold almost immediately. Our move out date was July 1.

The moving vans pulled up to the Beresford for the fourth and last time that day. In the interim, we rented a Manhattan apartment in a Rutherford Place landmark building on 2nd

Avenue between 17th and 18th Streets. Originally opened in 1902 as the Lying-In Hospital, it had been converted to unique residential apartments in the 1980s.[6]

Filled with history, it turned out that the building had a very special significance for me. When I told my eighty-year-old mother where we rented the apartment, she very nonchalantly said, "Oh, that's where I was born."

So there we were, eighty years later, living where literally everything started for me. My epicenter. You can't make this stuff up—fate, karma, coincidence, divine intervention, whatever. Whenever I walked into the lobby of that building I thought of Josephina Candida Sierra circa 1910. Special coincidences like this make life interesting and more profound.

Another special coincidence occurred at that time. My son Gregg was hired by James Patterson, creative director at J. Walter Thompson (JWT) as a copywriter. Patterson would soon leave the ad business to become one of the best-selling authors in the world.[7] At JWT Gregg met Jim Heekin, JWT's president, and worked with two art directors: Ray Mendez and Griffin Stenger. You may recall that Griffin was that young kid knocking at my Geers Gross door with all those ideas. Little did I know then that Griffin's promotion to art director would lead to his being teamed up with Gregg a few years later. Stay tuned for how all of these connections intertwine and converge even further.

Leaving New York was bittersweet. Vicki and I were excited about starting a new life but our family grew up on Central Park West and we would miss the comfort of our home. Moving also meant that I was closing out my twenty-year career as assistant professor at my alma mater, Pace University. The seeds for both my business and teaching careers were planted at Pace and I remain eternally grateful for the opportunities, experiences, and friendships that blossomed there.

I had a wonderful farewell lunch with my Pace mentors; they encouraged me to continue teaching and offered to write recommendation letters. I didn't waste any time taking them up on their offer. With their help I quickly landed teaching assignments at the University of South Florida and Eckerd college. I taught classes at both institutions during my time in Florida. Looking back I find it interesting that even in my semi-retired mode I had to have multiple items on my plate. I liked being busy with what I liked to do. Still do. It was a precursor of things to come.

We purchased a condo in a nice St. Pete Beach waterfront golf community, Isla del Sol. The Mutters purchased a condo in the same community and Dick and I found affordable office space a mile from our homes. Loved the commute! I purchased a 1963 Ford Fairlane convertible making my top-down ride to the office even more enjoyable. With everything in place, Dick and I got to work building our company.

---

6. At one time 60% of all births in Manhattan occurred at Lying-In Hospital http://bit.ly/LyingInHospital

7. Jim's website http://bit.ly/PattersonWebsite

Building Capstone from the ground up

Building our company involved a mix of confidence and concern. The confidence came from being well-versed in the alcoholic beverage industry and having the skills and experience to manage an import company. The concern emanated from the realization that the breadth and depth of operational details were daunting. I'd always been a hands-on manager but this new venture would require digging in up to my shoulders, especially at the beginning. I turned those feelings into a healthy tension that kept me on my toes. Here's how we did it.

First, we locked in on our vision and business development strategy:

> **Vision:** Become a leading niche brand company marketing a select portfolio of brands across the spirits and wine sectors of the alcoholic beverage industry.
>
> **Strategy:** Focus on four areas of business development in this order:
>
> 1. Importation and US agency contracts for premium/mid-priced brands
>
> 2. Development and marketing of Capstone owned brands.
>
> 3. Marketing agency for smaller "orphan brands" in large conglomerates
>
> 4. Acquisition of brands and trademarks

With that settled we enlisted K&O's help in creating our company logo, letterhead, and brochures. They designed a classy modular brochure that we mailed to overseas brand owners, wholesalers, trade publications and other key industry executives announcing the launch of our company.[8] This was before classy websites and digital marketing tools so we did it the old-fashioned way with printed promotional materials, direct mail, and phone calls. It felt great to drop those brochures in the mail.

Next we established banking relationships to secure the lines of credit necessary to finance the purchase of inventory and carrying of wholesaler receivables. We presented our business plan to Barnett Bank and they came on board as our banking partner in January 1991. Dick and I used our personal assets as collateral until the company began generating revenue. We really did put our skin in the game.

In previous management positions, I focused on revenue and profit. Cash flow was managed

---

8. Capstone Brochure https://bit.ly/CapstonePromoBrochure

for me. As entrepreneurs we had to flip that equation and follow the sage advice of management guru Peter Drucker.

> *"Entrepreneurs believe that profit is what matters most in a new enterprise. But profit is secondary. Cash flow matters most."*[9]

Each start-up business has its unique cash flow needs and pressure points. Our critical first step in managing cash flow was to layout the runway of cash required to operate the business for nine months assuming no revenue. Our biggest pressure points were large purchases of inventory from foreign suppliers and excise tax payments. That required meticulous sales forecasting to inform the detailed inventory purchase schedules we used as the basis for operating plans. We also became very skilled at cajoling and charming suppliers for the most favorable payment terms. Importantly, we involved our financing partner, Barnett Bank, in our planning so they were invested with us in the event of any issues. Then we checked reality versus plan every week.

There were only a few instances where we pushed our lines of credit to the maximum and faced a cash flow issue. Fortunately, Dick and I were able to manage them by providing short-term capital infusions. Put all of these on your cash flow checklist: Runway. Pressure points. Sales/inventory forecasting. Financing partner involvement. Monitoring.

Whenever I'm asked for advice about entrepreneurship, partnership, or starting a company I tell people that the founders should have two words tattooed on their foreheads: *Cash Flow*. So, every morning when they look in the mirror it's the first thing they see, pay attention to, and manage. Eight years later I would call on those cash flow lessons in the launch of another entrepreneurial venture.

Now, who does what?

Our to-do list was long so we decided to divide and conquer. Things we had to learn ranged from setting up international shipping and securing bonded warehouse facilities to navigating government bureaucracies and understanding foreign currency exchanges and hedges. In our prior corporate positions, support for most of those tasks was on our internal speed dial. Now, it was just the two of us and we were the answer at the other end of the phone. We were familiar with most of it at a high level but now we had to get into the weeds and learn by doing. We were fortunate to have colleagues from Somerset and Brown-Forman whom we could call on for advice and to help us when we were stuck. Dick and I learned an important lesson quickly: Suck it up and ask for help often. We did and were never disappointed.

---

9. Drucker Article http://bit.ly/DruckerArticle

Our four big buckets of responsibilities were:

- Generating sales by securing import rights to existing brands and creating Capstone proprietary products
- Hiring and working with distributors and sales representatives
- Financial and cash flow management
- Operations and logistics

We shared responsibilities for securing new brands, financial management, and operations. Dick took the lead on sales/distributor relationships and I took the lead on new product development. We trusted each other to pull our weight and we did. I cannot emphasize enough the importance of compartmentalizing workload responsibilities, setting expectations, and having each other's back. Not doing those things opens the door to chaos.

Building brands and revenue

In a relatively short period of time we secured distribution rights to Macorix Dominican rum, Chabanneau cognacs, Chatelle brandy, and Nice French liqueur. Next we were appointed by an Australian company, International Wines & Spirits, as importer for their brands: Bushman's Australian vodka, Sambuca di Parma and Apollo ouzo. Bushman's was the first and only vodka from Australia with a unique package and cute mini koala bears as promotional items. Then we pulled in John Barr scotch whiskey from Whyte & Mackay. John Barr was a quality affordably priced scotch packaged in a square bottle and positioned against Johnnie Walker. Both Dick and I enjoyed that irony that we would be directly competing with Johnnie Walker, one of the brands we helped build while at Somerset. We were now representing and marketing brands from five different countries.[10]

Securing these distribution contracts was exciting and gratifying, but creating and developing new products was where I drew most of my satisfaction. I had worked on conceptualizing and marketing new products, but this was different. We had to take a product from idea to prototype to production to distribution to consumer sales. I'd not done that before. It was challenging and invigorating. Dick and I brought two distilled spirits products to market in a complex and challenging environment in which government was heavily involved in all four, now five, Ps of the marketing mix.

Product – All product formulations and packaging required federal approval.

---

10. Capstone brand pictures https://bit.ly/CapstoneBrandPhotos

Price – Federal, state, and local taxes were levied on products significantly increasing prices to consumers.

Place – We had to adhere to a wholesaler-based distribution system and controlled retail availability.

Promotion – Some marketing channels, like broadcast, were totally off-limits and there were significant restrictions on trade and consumer promotions.

People – Our products were for adult consumption only.

Some of the restrictions are less stringent today but alcoholic beverages remain a tightly regulated product category. Nevertheless, we fulfilled that component of our growth strategy and successfully introduced two Capstone owned brands: Barkeeper's Call and Carezza.

Barkeeper's Call

Barkeeper's Call was a line of premixed alcohol ingredients for popular complex cocktails. It had a simple value proposition for on-premise bars and restaurants owners: boost bartender productivity and increase profitability by reducing liquor overpouring.

The first product in the line was Long Island Iced Tea, a very popular drink at that time that contained rum, gin, vodka, tequila, and triple sec topped off with sour mix and a splash of cola. Potent and profitable. With Barkeeper's Call the bartender only had to make one alcohol pour then add the sour mix and cola. We spent six tedious months developing the formula, lining up a production and bottling resource, developing labels, and securing Bureau of Alcohol Tobacco & Firearms (BATF) approval. Working our way through the BATF bureaucracy took a little longer since this was a first-of-its-kind product. We filed for a trademark in November 1990 and it came through in September 1991.

Barkeeper's Call was well-received by distributors since it provided a new product story for existing accounts and did not compete with other brands in their portfolios. For Capstone it was an entrée brand into wholesalers that didn't require significant marketing expenditures other than trade pricing incentives. Our first product delivered steady sales at a nice margin and helped get our company off the launching pad.

Carezza Cappuccino Cream Liqueur

In 1992, coffee shops were booming. Starbucks had just gone public and the cream liqueur trend was also growing. There were coffee liqueurs available like *Kahlua* and *Tia Maria* but no cream-based coffee brands were yet on the market. We saw this convergence as an opportunity to create a first ever cappuccino cream liqueur. We originally approached Starbucks to license their brand name but they were adamantly against any alcoholic beverage association. So we created our own proprietary brand of authentic imported Italian cappuccino cream liqueur.

We received some good advice from my friend Joe Lynch, former colleague and CEO of R&J Emmet, who told us to focus on delivering the very best combination of taste, texture, and mouth feel. Each was important and had to be in sync. We worked on product development with a top-notch family-owned distillery, Fratelli Francoli in Ghemme, Italy, and they produced an absolutely great-tasting product. Next, we selected a unique bottle shape, named it Carezza ("caress" in Italian) and worked with K&O to design a festive label featuring an outdoor trattoria scene.[11]

Everything came together nicely. We secured the necessary BATF approvals, registered the trademark, produced promotional materials, and began selling Carezza to wholesalers in the first quarter of 1993. We knew building a consumer franchise in a competitive category without major marketing budgets would take time, however, so we concentrated our efforts in control states where we could quickly get retail exposure in high cream liqueur development markets.[12]

In just two years we brought two innovative niche brands to market. It was a very gratifying experience for Dick and me. We joked that it probably would have taken twice as long at Brown-Forman or Somerset. Being a small, nimble company we didn't have to deal with internal bureaucracy, red tape, and approvals.

My mid-decade introspection

Dick and I had spent the past four years building our company with relatively little friction. Things were moving along as planned but as we entered our fifth year the partnership began to fray around the edges through no fault of either one of us. A convergence of four factors hitting at the same time made me edgy and restless:

> **Entrepreneurial ennui:** Most of our time was now spent on sales, distribution, and administrative details. Dick was much better at sales than I and he enjoyed it. I found it tedious and wearing. Dick and I spent a lot of time together working in close quarters and sometimes our patience with each other would wear thin. There weren't any huge issues, just a bit too much constant contact and claustrophobic rote.

---

11. Carezza package photos https://bit.ly/CarezzaBottlePhoto

12. Seventeen US states entirely control the wholesaling or retailing of alcoholic beverages within their borders. Known as alcoholic beverage control (ABC) states.

Early retirement rethink: I semi-retired at forty-eight years old and four years later at fifty-two the lyrics of that classic Peggy Lee song started playing in my head, "Is that all there is?" I wasn't unhappy at Capstone but I was questioning the whole package that I had created for myself. Small business entrepreneur, play/work equilibrium, laid-back leisurely lifestyle, Florida vibe. The allure and vibrancy of that vision at age forty-eight had faded into complacency and lethargy at age fifty-two. I felt that there was a lot more left for me to do.

Marketing FOMO: For the first few years in Florida, I separated myself from the advertising business and NYC. But watching the digital era unfold in the mid-'90s drew me back into that orbit and I started absorbing as much as I could. I saw the writing on the wall for marketing's digital rebirth and my fear of missing out started creeping in.

Florida fatigue: One of the reasons we selected southwest Florida was its retirement-friendly lifestyle. Initially, it was a welcome change and ambiance but it progressively became boring and monochromatic for me. Vicki grew to dislike it intensely.

That was my prevailing state of mind and I was struggling coming to grips with it.

A (phone) call to action

In April 1995, with this uncertainty and restlessness swirling in my head, I received an unexpected but welcomed call from my old friend Kent Kroeber, head of HR at IPG, the holding company that owns McCann. Kent owned a vacation home in Naples, Florida, and suggested we meet to catch up. I looked forward to spending time with a valued friend and we met for lunch at the Tampa airport. Never in my wildest dreams did I expect what Kent put on the table. He asked if I was ready to come back to the agency business and re-join McCann. Seriously!

I was blown away. He couldn't have known my current state of mind, but he sure hit me with the right question at the right time. I ordered a double martini. Here's the scenario Kent laid out: John Dooner, my former boss, was now head of McCann Worldwide and Jim Heekin (former president of JWT who joined McCann in 1992) was in charge of a significantly expanded North American network. Meanwhile, McCann Los Angeles was in need of a new general manager.

John Dooner saw this an opportunity to create a new position: EVP manager of McCann West/general manager, McCann LA. The role would encompass McCann's offices in LA, San Diego, San Francisco, Seattle, and later offices in Texas and he felt it would be a perfect fit for me. Man, did that get my attention.

I told Kent I was definitely interested but needed time to sort things out with my wife and make a big decision about Capstone. Kent understood and said that in the meantime he would prepare an employment package for me to consider. Since John had already blessed this I knew that things would move fast and there was a lot to think about—quickly.

Once again my wife Vicki and I were faced with a career move involving a major relocation—this time all the way across the country. Luckily, I had no trouble selling a move west to Vicki. She really wanted to get out of Florida and knew that I was languishing. Vick loved the idea of relocating to Los Angeles since our oldest son Brian, now married, was living there. I was also intrigued by LA and stepping back into the advertising business was a very enticing opportunity. Next, I had to convince myself to walk away from the business Dick and I created and coach myself on how best to handle that.

Walking away

Dick and I had a lot of blood, sweat, tears, and some cash invested in Capstone. The business successfully fulfilled our original goals and we were proud of what we had accomplished. I knew I'd be leaving a lot on the table by walking away from the business I helped build. Nothing had changed with the business, however I had changed. I had given it my best shot but as I looked at the horizon, I just couldn't see myself doing this long term.

My initial meeting with Dick didn't take too long. We knew each other well enough to get right to the point. It was a bit tense at first but we talked it out and agreed to make it an amicable and orderly exit. I would wrap up any issues that required my attention, we would notify suppliers and business partners, and start the process of amending registrations, permits, and licenses. Our attorneys drew up the partnership dissolution papers, Dick and I agreed upon a fair stock buy-back purchase price. I took my last Ford Fairlane ride to Capstone's office on June 23, 1995.

Dick would be the sole beneficiary of the company we created and we both knew he would have no difficulty managing Capstone on his own. Plus, he would have more income enabling him to hire help if needed. Soon after my departure, Dick hired his daughter, Ann, a very bright and eager recent Miami University graduate, to work with him. Dick taught her the business and they made a great team. Ann stayed on with Dick at Capstone and over the years they built a great family business. I was delighted by their continued success.

I learned again that it's okay to walk away from a business venture when it's done the right way and for the right reasons. I also reaffirmed something about myself. Even in a semi-retired mode that included running a small business and teaching, I couldn't sit still. I needed to do more.

Like any relationship, a business partnership can have great plans and promise, but even under the best of circumstances it might not work out. No matter how trying or gut wrenching the decision, it's possible to walk away and keep open positive bridges to the past. Be brutally honest with yourself about why and totally open and specific about your reasons and feelings with the other parties. Honesty and time are great assuagers. And don't beat yourself up about it. It's better to walk away and move ahead than to force-fit something that's not working for you.

Westward ho!

Things moved quickly with McCann. Kent and I met again and finalized my employment agreement. John Dooner gave me a congratulatory call and invited me to New York to meet with Jim Heekin (my new boss) and Phil Geier, IPG's chairman. I knew Phil well and was looking forward to getting his "welcome-back" pat on the head. My son Gregg knew Jim from JWT and held him in high regard, but I was a bit apprehensive about meeting Jim for the first time since John Dooner had already hired me. (Visions of my David Mahoney arranged meeting with Somerset's John Heilman popped into my head.) Gladly, my initial meeting with Jim went great and it marked the beginning of a wonderful business relationship and friendship that I still cherish today. Jim is one of the very best in the business. We settled on a mid-July start date for me, although Vicki stayed behind for a few weeks to manage our departure from St. Pete.

My detour was over. I was back on the main road to an exciting West Coast destination eager to make my McCann life even better the second time around.

Mad Man Wisdom

- Cultivate opportunities to celebrate successes. Both the celebrated and celebrators benefit.
- Adopt a manageable "take calls" mindset. Listen for opportunities to be helped and to be of help. Don't text or type. Talk. Make it personal.
- Create opportunities to connect with the stars of your chosen industry, the magicians. Even short encounters can leave an indelible impression.
- Every career path is marked with detours and side roads. Notice them and take the detour when the time feels right. But always remember the way back to the main road—just in case you need it.

- Sometimes winding down is the best way to get yourself back up and back on track. It's okay to make a career rest stop.
- When the entrepreneur bug bites don't swat it away. Let in linger. Look it in the eye and see the what it's envisioning for you. Then decide your next action.
- Sometimes even your surest instincts can morph into uncertainty. Don't fight it. Use those reflective moments to transform and adapt your plans.
- Breaking up is hard to do in business, but staying longer than you should is even harder on everyone involved.

Marketing Truisms & Tips

The Soft Side of Entrepreneurship

The urge to be your own boss crosses many peoples' minds during the course of a career. For some it's a burning desire and they push to find those opportunities. Others are destined to just dream about it. I fell somewhere in between. For me it was more like a recurring, curious impulse and itch. I briefly tested the waters with Bruce and Jim then waited until the right time and circumstance came along to dive in head-first with Dick. In both cases, it was with partners whom I knew well, respected, and liked. Even so, neither venture went according to plan. I don't view them as failures, however. They fulfilled my at-the-time needs and I learned and grew from both experiences.

There's a plethora of excellent "how to" books for aspiring entrepreneurs that provide solid operating and structural blueprints for success.[13] By all means use them. My advice and lessons learned are on the personal, soft-asset side of the equation. There are no formulas and templates for those—just a lot of honest self-evaluation, gut feelings, and common sense.

Here's what Dick and I did right that made our partnership work:

- Envisioned the life we wanted for ourselves and molded our start-up and partnership to fit that vision, not the other way around
- Checked all the right personal compatibility boxes
- Operated in a business sector we knew well and in which we could use our complementary skills
- Stayed in synch on vision and business plan
- Clearly delineated our operational responsibilities and workload

---

13. Two that I like are *The Art of the Start* by Guy Kawasaki https://amzn.to/2LqicBk and *The Lean Start Up* by Eric Ries https://amzn.to/2rht6m3

- Got comfortable and confident being the person on the other end of the phone
- Asked for advice and help often from a trusted circle of colleagues and friends
- Got over ourselves and self-promoted
- Handled difficult situations by staying focused on the rewards

Our business was working well; it just stopped working for me. What I could have done better was self-assess sooner, face my changing priorities earlier, and better plan my exit. I should have discussed my waning interest in the business and Florida with Dick earlier. It wouldn't have changed my decision, but we would have more time to smooth out operational and contract separation details. Fortunately it worked out okay and I was lucky that my next opportunity found me at just the right time.

Oh, one more thing. Don't forget to get that *Cash Flow* tattoo!

Chapter 10 Footnotes
Scan QR codes for direct links to footnote content.

10.2 Super Mario Award

10.8 Capstone Brochure

10.10 Capstone Brand Pictures

10.11 Carezza Package

Chapter 11:

Pefect Time For a Second Time Around

I was lucky to step back into marketing communications when the seeds of digital disruption were being planted. Positive bridges to the past transported me to the ground floor of an exciting new world of marketing communications. I am very grateful to John Dooner, Jim Heekin, and Kent Kroeber for giving me the opportunity to return to McCann.

My second time around at McCann brought about some of my most enjoyable and productive years in business. I was energized to be back. My mind was open to any and all possibilities and I embraced the challenges of new technology. It felt like 1965 all over again.

My McCann encore lasted eight years and unfolded in a three-act saga with surprising twists, turns, and stepping stones. It just goes to show…careers really can be better the second time around. It's up to you to take it as far as you can for as long as you want.

Before recounting a few informative stories from act one of my McCann encore, I'll share three significant events that impacted my career reboot. Each had a powerful and profound effect on my outlook on life and business.

Panic: HELP!

Vicki and I made our initial trip to Los Angeles in July 1995. We rented a temporary apartment in Westwood on Wilshire Boulevard, an easy ten-minute drive down Wilshire Boulevard to the McCann office. Vicki returned to Florida to arrange our move and I stayed in LA eager to restart my agency career.

It turned out to be an unexpectedly difficult transition. I was beginning to get myself acclimated when I noticed that I just didn't feel right. I had trouble focusing, couldn't sleep, and was overwhelmed by uncertainty, stress, and anxiety about the decision I made. I felt increasingly scattered and tense. At first, I wrote it off to new job jitters. I told myself that the new job had been my choice so it was up to me alone to handle it. Boy, was I wrong.

One weekend I completely lost it. I couldn't sleep because I was too busy obsessing about everything that could go wrong and lapsed into a full-blown panic attack. I'd never experienced anything like that. Losing control was not my style. I was stronger than that!

One Saturday morning, I wandered aimlessly along Wilshire Boulevard and stopped in to the Holiday Inn for breakfast. The waitress came with the check and asked if I was staying at the hotel. I said, "Yes," and gave her what I thought was my room number. She came back and told me I was not registered at the hotel. I had given her the number of my apartment. I had lost all sense of where I was.

Struggling to reorient myself, I finally made it back to the apartment. I called Vicki and told her I was in trouble. Thankfully my son Brian was living in LA. Vicki called Brian and he took me to the emergency room at UCLA medical center. My heart rate and blood pressure were through the roof. I was diagnosed with acute anxiety and panic attacks and given medication to calm down. They kept me under observation until I was stable enough to be discharged. I left the hospital with lingering anxiety, but at least I was functional.

I was referred to UCLA psychological services for an appointment right away. Fortunately, I was able to be out of the office a few days in order to get the help I urgently needed. It was more than run-of-the-mill anxiety that was plaguing me. I was diagnosed with depression and anxiety and prescribed a combination of medications to treat them. After about a month of medication and doctor visits I finally felt back in control. Counseling, medication, and family support kept me from going over the edge.

At the time, I didn't tell anyone at McCann about my troubles and until now, only my family, physicians, and a few close friends knew what had happened to me. Today, I feel compelled to tell this story to help others face their own mental issues. In the past, my "always be in control" mindset had helped me face difficult, stressful situations. You know, that Brooklyn machismo never-admit-a-weakness-or-need-for-help attitude. But when my life changed, I unexpectedly changed and it all caught up with me.

The good news is that after this SOS I made it through the storm, resumed my second-time around and went on to enjoy some of the most productive and fulfilling years of my life. Completely "losing it" compelled me to face the reality that I couldn't go back to "normal." I had to find a new and better path forward. I started paying much closer attention to my mental state of mind, periodically sought counseling when I needed it, and accepted that medication would be a continuing part of my mental health regimen. I learned how to purposely integrate "chill time" into my day by listening to and discovering new music. Over the years I integrated the therapeutic power of reiki, meditation, and yoga into my life. All of this and family support kept me on the path. I am blessed that I was able to find my way.

My plea to you is to be alert to the signs and symptoms signaling that you might need help coping. Shaping your life and building your career can be stressful and impacts different people in different ways. My initial signs of trouble were sudden anxiety, a constant flood of self-doubt, loss of control, and feeling overwhelmed. Be alert to any similar triggers and talk about your concerns with the people you love and trust. Don't try to do it alone. Hopefully, unlike me, you will be able to slide through the rough spots without professional help or medication. But if you can't, don't be ashamed. That's what they are there for—to help.

A few years later, when I went through another rough patch I was fortunate to meet Dr.

Kathy Cramer, an acclaimed psychologist and leadership coach. She introduced me to Asset-Based Thinking and helped positively propel me in a new direction. More about that later.

Help is a powerful word. Don't be afraid to use it.

Pure joy

Two months after my mental break we were given news that brought incredible joy and fulfillment into our lives. In October of 1995, our son Brian and his wife Lisa announced that they were expecting a child. We would be blessed with our first grandchild! Jubilation. Suddenly everything became brighter and positive anticipation took hold. Our grandson Lucas was born on May 25, 1996. If I needed validation that our move to LA was meant to be this was it. *Being there* was our special gift. We held Lucas the day he was born and he became an essential and wonderful part of our life from that day forward.

Lucas is simply the best grandson one could ever hope for. I could fill this entire book with Lucas stories and the joy that he has brought into our lives but I'll spare you the gushing grandparent speech. As any grandparent knows there is a special connection you have with your children's children that goes deep. Here's a quote from a celebrated ad exec whom I knew, Lois Wyse, that summed it up for me.

"Grandchildren are the dots that connect the lines from generation to generation."

Our future had arrived.

Purpose

About a year after my arrival at McCann Erickson Los Angeles (MELA) President Clinton announced his welfare-to-work legislation. The initiative transformed welfare from an entitlement program to one that incentivized and motivated recipients to begin working and exit the welfare rolls. The President's call for businesses to actively hire welfare recipients and support them on their road to self-sufficiency resonated with me. I saw it as a great opportunity to be part of the solution and an article in the *LA Times* moved me from agreement to action.

The article profiled three Angelenos who were actively working to find jobs, getting off the welfare rolls and becoming self-sufficient. Two of the three landed jobs; one did not. Carol Martinez was a divorced mom with three young kids committed to lifting herself up. Her story touched me and I decided to do something about it. I had our HR director get in touch with Carol and bring her in for an interview. I made it clear that unless there were extraordinary extenuating circumstances, we would hire Carol and do our best to help her succeed. Carol did well in her interview and she was hired for an office administration role at McCann LA.

Our HR director suggested that it would be a great confidence booster to provide Carol with a stipend to help her purchase some office clothes, so I chipped in some cash. On July 21, 1997, Carol began her career at McCann as a floater for the receptionist and definitely didn't need any extra help on her road to success. She was a self-starter with an endearing personality who quickly assumed more responsibilities. Carol was soon promoted to receptionist followed by a promotion to office operations coordinator. The McCann LA office went through a number of changes in the ensuing years and Carol was promoted to assistant office manager. Twenty years later in, July 2017, McCann dramatically downsized the LA office and Carol's entire department was laid off.

Carol's successful twenty-year career at McCann was filled with recognition, promotions, and friendships. This successful, dedicated working mom put her three kids through college. Each of them has started on their own career paths thanks to their mom. All Carol needed was a helping hand up. A job. Seeing Carol succeed and watching her children grow into wonderful adults has been a highlight of my life. I'm very proud of Carol and value her friendship. We all still keep in touch.

In your life and career, look for opportunities to make a positive impact on a person's life. That opportunity can pop up when you least expect it. When it does, reach out, grab it, and be the helping hand up. Believe me you will always get back more than you give. Without a doubt, Carol is the best hire I've made in my entire career.

"Unless someone like you cares a whole awful lot, nothing is
going to get better. It's not." —Dr. Seuss

Back in the ad biz

The next five years on the west coast was a wonderfully productive and successful period in my life. We purchased a 1930s home in Hancock Park and loved living there. It was only a seven minute drive to the office—no LA freeway nightmares! My job as EVP manager of McCann West and General Manager of McCann LA lived up to everything I'd hoped it would be and more. One of the reasons is that John Dooner, head of McCann Worldwide, shaped it to fit my strengths and combined two management functions important to me: direct P&L and operating responsibility for MELA and oversight assistance for other ME west coast agencies. It was a perfect mix for me. My time allocation was about 75% MELA, 25% McCann West.

During these five years McCann went through a series of top management changes that directly impacted me. Here's the timeline:

1. In January 1998, my boss Jim Heekin moved to London as regional director for McCann's European operations. It was clear that Jim was being groomed for the CEO position. My new boss, Don Dillon, was a twenty-year McCann veteran with a great track record.

2. In October 1999, John Dooner replaced Phil Geier as CEO of IPG, the public holding company that owns McCann and other communications agencies. John's promotion had a ripple effect that reached me. Jim Heekin replaced John as CEO of McCann Worldwide, Don Dillon took over Jim's spot as regional director for McCann Europe in London. Tony Miller, head of the MacLaren/McCann agency Toronto replaced Don Dillon as head of McCann North America as my new boss.

Did you follow all that? Three different bosses in five years. Fortunately, I respected and liked each of them and had no trouble adjusting to the changes. There was some noteworthy connective tissue between myself and Don Dillon. Don is the younger brother of a successful copywriter and creative director, Brian Dillon.[1] Brian was a good friend and colleague from DKG and we often chatted about his younger brother Don. Now he was my boss. Don and I made an instant connection and began a nice friendship. More on how these moves intertwined next chapter

The best way to share my experiences is by responsibility. Running McCann LA was fulfilling and rewarding. Overseeing McCann West was, for the most part, good but had some trying moments that challenged my positivity and patience.

The LA ad scene

The Los Angeles advertising landscape was very different from New York's. It was smaller in terms of billings and revenue and less geographically concentrated but more communal and tight-knit. People got to the office earlier and left earlier—not as much of a workaholic attitude. The lunch and restaurant scene was part of the business culture. My three favorites were Morton's, The Ivy, and Pane Vino. Most client meetings meant drives in your car rather than cab rides and you actually had to stop for pedestrians in crosswalks. My new company car was a turbo-charged hunter green Camaro convertible. Why not? It was LA.

I received many wonderful welcome wishes and helpful advice from my IPG colleagues, old friends, and new industry faces. Dennis Holt and Michael Kassan at IPG's Western

---

1. Brian and Don's father was legendary ad man Tom Dillon former CEO of BBD&O, member of the Advertising Hall of Fame. Great advertising pedigree.

International Media and Dailey's Cliff Einstein and Brian Morris welcomed me to the family.[2] Gerry Gibbons, head of the Western States branch of the American Association of Advertising Agencies (WSAAA) was especially helpful and I joined the WSAAA board soon after arriving.

I was pleasantly surprised to be contacted by Alan Pando, a former Benton & Bowles and DDB colleague. Alan was one of the senior account managers who took me under his wing. Twenty years later, he was running DDB West and again being helpful and supportive. He graciously offered to connect me with leaders in the LA ad community, people who were generous with their time and advice. It served as good reinforcement and a reminder to me of why I liked the ad business: the people. There was only one exception: Bob Kuperman.

Bob was a respected former DDB creative director, now head of Chiat Day in Los Angeles working with legendary ad man Lee Clow. I was looking forward to meeting him. I called Bob, told him about Alan Pando's referral and suggested that I take him to lunch. It was a short call. Bob essentially told me that he had no interest in meeting with me since he and I would inevitably be competing for business. *Really?* Nice chatting with you Bob.

I brushed it aside, appreciated my other positive connections, and chalked it up to a valuable lesson learned. Regardless of career stage or personal success we all need support and advice. I got a lot more help by asking than if I had allowed Bob's dismissal of me to scare me off. More importantly, it reminded me that one of the biggest responsibilities of leaders and managers is to openly give advice and support whenever asked. Get over yourself and don't worry about protecting your turf. Proudly share your accomplishments and expertise. How you respond will leave a lasting impression.

One of the perks of my new job was a country club membership. I set my sights on joining Wilshire Country Club since it was reasonably priced and located near our home in Hancock Park. Wilshire's membership process was lengthy and required referrals and sponsorship from club members. I didn't think I knew anyone at Wilshire so I looked over the membership roster. *Guess what?* My old friend and B&B colleague Eric von der Lieth (aka Duke) was a member and chairman of the membership committee. Eric and I reconnected and he paved the way for my application to be accepted.

Being a member at Wilshire was one of the highlights of our life in Los Angeles. It rekindled my friendship with Eric—which is still going strong twenty-five years later—and opened the door to wonderful new relationships and business connections. I was an engaged and involved member, succeeded Eric as membership chairman, and later served on Wilshire's board of directors. By the way, during that time Bob Kuperman applied for membership at Wilshire. His application was not accepted. (More about Wilshire later.)

---

2. Dennis Holt and I would connect again for interesting collaborations.

Talented people + great clients = satisfaction & success

McCann LA was an agency waiting to break out and live up to its potential. There were talented people in all departments and the client list was blue chip. All the agency needed was energetic leadership and I was in the right place at the right time with the right energy.

The account teams were strong: Peter Serchuk provided solid creative leadership, our CFO Jerry Duran was rock solid, and my assistant Kristin Anderson was a gem. I beefed up our resources with the addition of a great account planning director, Cathy Clift; moved one of McCann New York's best media directors George Hayes to be media director for MELA and ME West; and added creative director Kathy Kozai to the creative department.[3] We were a strong management team and each played an essential role in MELA's success.

MELA had a great line-up of clients across a number of categories, including Nestlé (packaged goods), Cathay Pacific (airlines), Sony Pictures (entertainment), and Northrup, Allied Signal (aerospace/industrial). Initially, I focused my attention on Nestlé, Sony, and new business. It paid off. The agency prospered, I learned and grew professionally, and formed lasting personal relationships with special people.

Successful businesses are guided by clearly articulated missions, goals, operating procedures, and so on, but the degree of success is dependent on people working together to bring them to life. Relationships are the foundation of business success and I constantly remind myself that people, not companies, build them. This is a really important mindset, especially as digital and data become more prevalent. Thankfully, there seems to be a revival in the importance of "being human" in business today. Attach yourself to the humanization of business mindset and you will grow faster and prosper.

Success starts at the top

Nestlé was an extremely important account for McCann. It was in the top three for global revenue and McCann LA's (MELA) largest account. MELA was the agency for a number of brands in the beverage, food, nutrition, and pet care divisions. In 1995, Nestlé USA's (NUSA) annual sales topped 50 billion dollars across a broad range of categories and brands. NUSA was consistently a top performer in Nestlé's global portfolio with great brands, strong management, and outstanding leadership.

Nestlé USA was a classically structured packaged goods company with separate divisions each run by a Senior Vice President and brand management teams supported by operations management and marketing services. Its Glendale headquarters were a short twenty-minute drive from the office and virtually all of our client meetings were at their offices. I was there

---

3. When George relocated back to the east coast he was succeed by Tom Schepansky.

at least once a week. In addition to the short drive there were two other benefits attached to Glendale meetings. The Nestlé company store was in the lobby where I could stock up on my favorite Nestlé brands. I rarely left without a bag full of candy and an ice-cream. Nestlé also had a full-service company cafeteria where everyone from the CEO to the secretary enjoyed their lunch. It was always busy and a perfect place to casually connect with Nestlé's management. And, of course, the food was excellent.

Making my mark and being successful with Nestlé was a cornerstone of my job. The company came to hold the same cherished place in my career as Nintendo. Like Nintendo, the Nestlé relationship was built on mutual respect, shared goals, open communications, and recognition and rewards for "jobs well done." It was the kind of relationship that makes you want to give them your very best—and we did. I could fill a few chapters with the experiences from my NUSA days but I'll devote the rest of this chapter to a few of that left the deepest impressions.

You've heard the axiom, "the route to success in businesses and companies starts at the top"? That truth was definitely a reality at Nestlé USA. The person at the top was Joe Weller.[4] Joe is a personable, caring person, sharp as a tack, and an honest, straight shooter while also being a disciplined and motivational task master. Joe is a man of integrity with a powerful moral compass that he brought to his job every day. He was respected and loved by his employees and MELA staff alike.

Joe held a prominent place on my Mount Rushmore of leaders I admired. I often looked to him as a role model as I faced challenges in my career. One small "lead by example" action that Joe took is still fresh in my mind today. He felt that NUSA had settled into a time-wasting "excessive meeting culture" that was getting in the way of an individual's time to think and create. He took that head-on by establishing Friday as a no-meetings day. Joe personally never took meetings on Friday and often made the rounds checking-in to show people how serious he was about it. I happened to be in one of those "unauthorized" Friday meetings discussing Carnation Infant Formula advertising. Joe popped his head in the door and said with a smile, "Hey folks, no Friday meetings," but the meeting kept going a bit longer. Joe popped in again, this time without a smile. He just looked at us and the meeting was over.

In the larger scheme of things, no Friday meetings was a small gesture, but it sent a big message about the value of individual thought and creativity and that Joe practiced what he preached. Ever since then I recall the look on Joe's face to remind me to avoid time-wasting meetings and call them out whenever I can.[5] I also had the opportunity to get to know Joe's family and began a relationship with his son Jeff, occasionally providing business and career advice. We still keep in touch. The apple didn't fall far from the tree. Joe would also be a much

---

4. Joe wrote a great management book, *Blueprint For Success*. https://amzn.to/2QzEQdo.

5. Fun short video about meetings. https://bit.ly/meetingsnomore

appreciated source of support a few years later.

Joe surrounded himself with top-flight managers who shared his vision. He set the positive collegial tone at the top and NUSA's management practiced it day-in day-out in their working relationships. Working with them was both a pleasure and an education. One of the people at the top of my list was Al Stefl, NUSA's Senior VP Director of communications. Prior to joining Nestlé, Al had a successful agency career and Joe valued his expertise and counsel.

In large companies with separate divisions and a brand management structure, there is often tension between corporate communications and division brand management with each "protecting their turf." That wasn't the case at NUSA. As an ex-Marine, Al brought a valuable discipline and sense of mission to marketing communications that was respected and valued at Nestlé. He assembled a great team and the division managers relied on Al's counsel and expertise. Observing this dynamic taught me a valuable lesson: The best way to break down organizational walls is to earn trust. You do so by adding value, being politely persistent, and consistently confident. You had to earn your way in to Al's trust, but once earned it you could always count on him for guidance, straight talk, and support.

A pleasant coincidence paved the way for me with Al. My friend and colleague from B&B days Eric von der Lieth (whom I had reconnected with at Wilshire Country Club) was a close friend of Al. They were "neighbors" in Malibu. This unexpected intersection at McCann LA enabled the rekindling of a special friendship with Eric and the beginning of wonderful new one with Al. Both are still part of my life today. When "six degrees of separation" moments appear in your life embrace them. They add a sense of discovery and often lead to wonderful, enduring experiences. You will find these "second time around" incidences increase as your career progresses, especially in today's hyper-connected social media environment. Jump on them (with a careful eye) when they pop up. More to come on this.

Food, felines, beverages, and babies

MELA's Nestlé relationship included assignments in the nutrition, beverage, food, and pet care divisions. While operating procedures and management structures were similar across divisions, Joe Weller encouraged each division manager to put their personal style and stamp on their divisions. And they did. Working with each of the division heads demonstrated the benefits and wisdom of Joe's not mandating a "one size fits all" management style. This mindset is especially important in managing and motivating today's millennial work force that values personal freedom and flexibility. However, there is a caution. To be effective, there first must be a structure, procedural ground rules, and performance expectations in place. Whether you're the "manager" or the "managed," insist on this before unleashing the "do your own thing" juggernaut.

Our food division assignments initially included the Carnation, Contadina, and Libby's brands.

Marketing spending was limited and MELA created targeted, seasonal print campaigns in women's service magazines. Then, opportunity knocked. At just the right time, Nestlé acquired the Ortega Mexican food brand. MELA was asked to pitch for the account against other NUSA agencies. It was an early test of our recently formed new business team. Everyone stepped up and we won the business. A nice win, confidence builder, and positive reinforcement for our MELA teams. It was the beginning of an impressive series a major new business wins for the agency.

Cats: the experience

I particularly enjoyed working with the pet care division under the leadership of John Harris and brand management director Tom Buday. MELA was assigned the cat food brands (Friskies and Fancy Feast) and our sister IPG agency Dailey worked on the dog food brands (Alpo and Mighty Dog).

Fancy Feast is a super-premium gourmet wet food brand. Friskies is mid-priced wet & dry food brand. Both were strong brands with very distinct consumer franchises and marketing plans. I found it ironic that I was marketing cat food brands since I had a severe allergy to cats. Initially I didn't tell the client about it but was soon "outed" on my first visit to Nestlé's pet food palatability test lab…yep, lots of cats tasting cat food. I scratched and sneezed my way through the visit. We had good laugh about it and the next time I brought plenty of Benadryl.

Working on Nestlé's pet food brands required an interesting shift of perspective and opened the door to valuable brand management best practices that I still use today and teach in my USC classes. Again, I was fortunate to have an outstanding agency management supervisor by my side, Bob Sutter, to help me learn the business. Here's a snapshot of a few lessons learned.

The ultimate "consumer" of pet food is, of course, the pet and if the cat didn't like a particular brand of food it was a no-go. Yes, cats really are finicky eaters. Since the pet caregiver/purchaser cannot share their cat's eating experience, making the precisely appropriate emotional brand connection is paramount. This required an understanding that the pet/pet-carer (not owner) relationship resembled the parent/child bond. Nestlé and MELA understood intimately the nature of this bond through the infant nutrition brands. John Harris instilled the importance and respect for that mindset into everyone associated with Nestlé's pet food brands. This helped direct the development of smart, sophisticated market segmentation models that informed and enabled *empathetic consumer profiles*, similar to the consumer personas we use today. These personas were the north stars that directed all brand behavior—from division brand portfolio management, to product development and marketing communications.

Each brand built a proprietary brand pyramid that started with a base of physical product attributes and rational benefits and laddered up to the pinnacle emotional brand benefit. It was the blueprint for the development of the brand marketing plan. More about this tool in the Marketing Tips section at the end of the chapter.

When it came to creative execution John insisted that all advertising respect and celebrate the inherent natural characteristics and behavior of cats that pet-carers enjoyed and cherished. This direction was baked into all creative briefs. Manipulating their behavior—singing cats, cats doing flips, dancing cats—was a no-no. Nestlé respected cats for being their wonderful, quirky, loveable selves, and John's direction insured those values were reflected in Friskies and Fancy Feast communications.

Again, I was reminded of the importance of specificity in creative briefs. Rather than limit creativity, John's parameters focused brand content on bringing the true pet-carer/pet bond to life and it worked. Fancy Feast was NUSA'S most profitable brand and Friskies was the leader in its market segment. This was an early lesson for me in what today is called brand authenticity. Messaging that is real, sincere, and rooted in organic brand benefits and behaviors always beats borrowed interest and trying too hard for attention. I give great thanks to John Harris and Benadryl for making these learnings and lessons possible.[6]

Beverages: Nesquik, Taster's Choice, and more

The beverage division marketed Nescafé, Taster's Choice, Nesquik, Coffee Mate, and Juicy Juice. When I arrived the coffee brands were headquartered in San Francisco and the division head was Ed Marra, former EVP of sales and marketing for Nestlé's Stouffers division. Ed was a brilliant marketer with personal flair, presence, and a competitive spirit. His management style was emotional and motivational. Ed's personal mantra was "passion to win." He closed all his correspondence with that message. He was always pushing the agency to think out of the "Nestlé box." I enjoyed working with Ed and we built a friendship that grew deeper over the years. In June 1997, Nestlé consolidated the beverage brands and relocated the division to its Glendale headquarters with Ed Marra still at the helm and Rob Case as brand director. Now all of NUSA brands were handled out of McCann LA, which made servicing the account easier and my life a little better—fewer trips to San Francisco and more frequent interaction with Ed.

Nesquik is a global beverage brand marketed as Nestlé's Quik in the US. NUSA was in the process of migrating the brand name to Nesquik and bringing communications in alignment with global guidelines. The brand icon was, and still is, a colorful, perky cartoon bunny featured prominently on packaging and marketing communications. The bunny, named "Quicky" outside the US, was synonymous with the brand. MELA worked with the marketing teams on the rebranding and creating communications plans to reach an emerging consumer segment: male teens and tweens. They had grown up with Quik and research showed that a smartly

---

6. My business relationship with John blossomed into a wonderful friendship. John joined me as a member of Wilshire Country Club. We had the same handicap: 17.

"cooled up" bunny and improved ready-to-drink packaging could connect with these young adults. The Quicky name didn't resonate with US consumers so we kept the Nequik Bunny moniker. The bunny's cool factor was amped up visually, presence in convenience stores where our target shopped was expanded, and sales increased.

Ed directed the agency to develop new outreach recommendations to expand the user base but none of them hit the mark. So Ed put his own out-of-the-Nestlé-box proposal on the table: a beverage division/Nesquik sponsorship of a NASCAR racecar and driver, Jeff Green. A big multi-year, multi-million dollar commitment. The team's reaction was lukewarm. It was no secret that Ed was an avid auto racing fan so many of us viewed this as Ed's fulfilling his racing fantasy. Ed kept his foot on the gas pedal, pushed passed the doubters, and did the sponsorship deal.[7]

Deal done, Ed's passion to win enthusiasm kicked in. He motivated everyone at NASCAR and Nestlé to go the extra mile to maximize the relationship. The oversized Nesquik bunny racing down the track on Jeff's car was dramatic and generated buzz and publicity. One of the team members jokingly suggested we name the bunny "150mph Quicky." The sponsorship turned out to be a success and continued for a number of NASCAR seasons.

An out-of-the-box idea is almost always met with a cloud of resistance and cynicism. It takes the confidence and persistence of the person behind the idea to clear away the clouds letting the potential shine through. But, that's only half the challenge. Next comes the even tougher job of motivating people to give it their all to turn the idea into action. That requires a deep belief in yourself and relentless personal commitment. I saw all of that manifested in Ed's "passion to win" mantra. It was a lot more than a sign-off on his memos. Ed believed it, lived it, and turned cynicism into collaboration and success. Next time you hit a wall of resistance to your ideas imagine 150mph Quicky racing down that NASCAR track.

Taster's Choice instant coffee was part of my Nestlé responsibility and creative was managed out of McCann New York. The Taster's Choice campaign was one of the most talked about and successful of that time and it was exciting to join the team that created a legendary campaign. It was even more special to me since my old friend Irwin Warren was the creative director genius behind it. Here's a snapshot.

The campaign originated in the UK where Taster's Choice was named Gold Blend. It featured a couple, Tony and Sharon, who lived in the same apartment building and met when she knocked on his door to borrow some coffee. Michael introduced her to Taster's Choice and the romance unfolded from there in a series of thirty-second commercials. The campaign was a huge success in the UK and we wanted to adapt it for the US market.[8] Irwin and his team delivered, big time.

---

7. Nesquik/Nascar announcement https://bit.ly/3b7k1NW

8. Taster's Choice articles https://bit.ly/tasterschoicepress

Irwin kept the essence of the character plot and the same UK actors using American accents, but he brilliantly adapted the story line to fit the US market. The 30-second cliff-hanger dramas had plots and staging as engaging as any hour-long soap opera and greater staying power than many. Launched in the US in 1990, the Taster's Choice saga was an explosive success in the US and McCann produced thirteen "episodes" that played out over seven years until July 1997.[9] Bringing the campaign to an end was a consequence of Nestlé's strategic decision to concentrate resources behind the Nescafé global brand and NUSA shifted its efforts towards the re-branding of Nescafé Taster's Choice. Fittingly, the end of the saga received even more hype and publicity than the campaign itself.[10]

Rubbing elbows with the Taster's Choice campaign was a thrill and reinforced a few of my marketing beliefs. First, big ideas travel very well, especially when they tap into an emotional truth. But even then, rarely can big ideas be cut and pasted from one market to another. The creative brilliance lies in massaging, nuancing, and shaping the content to make the precise emotional connection for each market and situation. That's where the magic happens. Reiterating my favorite Bill Bernbach quote is very relevant here. "Ideas can turn to dust or magic depending upon the talent that rubs against it." For Taster's Choice, that talent was Irwin Warren.

Next, storytelling is still one of marketing's most powerful communication and connection tools. I emphasize this in my USC classes and use Taster's Choice as a best practices model. On one hand, today's digital environment of short attention spans and channel/platform fragmentation present challenges. On the other hand, it has given rise to the even more powerful art of transmedia storytelling: The designing, sharing, and participating in a cohesive story experience across multiple traditional and digital delivery platforms. Digital has enhanced creative storytelling power by enabling consumers to insert themselves into the story arc. The possibilities are endless. I sometimes wonder how Irwin would have adapted his Taster's Choice campaign to transmedia storytelling. Brilliantly, I'm sure.

Happy, healthy, hungry babies

The Nutrition Division marketed infant and adult brands including Carnation Good Start Infant Formula and Sweet Success diet products. The SVP was Ernie Strapazon and Doreen Ida filled the brand director position. Ernie was a low-key manager with a wry sense of humor who brought a relaxed discipline to a complex business. Behind his casual management style was a well-grounded recognition of the important role of Nestlé's nutrition brands in family life. Ernie constantly reminded his teams that Nestlé was one of the few companies that could build a "cradle to grave" relationship with consumers. The gateway to this special relationship

---

9. Enjoy this Taster's Choice campaign compilation reel. https://bit.ly/tasterschoicecompilation

10. Taster's Choice finale article https://bit.ly/tasterschoicefinale

began with Nestlé's infant formula brands and Ernie made sure that we all understood its significance and importance. Nestlé accumulated a wealth of knowledge and product development expertise around infant nutrition, supported by powerful insight into the mother/child bond and family dynamic. While times may change in terms of social norms and parenting practices the underlying specialness of that bond is always there.[11]

I had marketed Johnson & Johnson infant care brands while at Ketchum but this experience was deeper and more profound. Now I was working on a brand that was literally present at the beginning of life and birth of a family. I had a lot to learn. The agency teams led by Diane Kuyoomjian and Linda Jackson ensured that essential consumer insights were embedded at the agency. Both were strong management supervisors with excellent client relationships and terrific at bringing me up to speed on the business.

Nestlé's "being in-service to moms" mindset was embedded in everyone involved with the division. They encouraged me to sit in on focus groups with first and second-time moms to get a better feel for the dynamics. While the underlying brand benefits were generally the same for all moms, the appeals to first-time moms, especially working women, were very different. Creating customer relationship management (CRM) platforms and communications for first-time moms required a sensible and sensitive blend of rational and emotional intelligence. For example, the issue of breast feeding versus formula was front and center for new moms and NUSA's guiding mission was to support moms with information to help them make the right personal decision. This was job one. Specific brand benefit communications occurred later in the CRM cycle as appropriate. Brand teams delivered "hi-touch" marketing communications in a still nascent internet environment without social media.

The "serve not sell" mindset is taking hold in marketing today and that's a good thing. Enabled by real-time, granular consumer behavior data, brands have an unprecedented opportunity to turn "hi-tech" into "hi-touch" at scale. Again, it's all about relationships and fostering an emotional connection. When I discuss this topic in my USC class, I often reference my emotional bond lessons learned from sitting in those mom focus groups. Empathetic connections fuel serve-not-sell marketing and can only happen when the emotional and rational quotients coexist. Always remember that on the other side of that *click, dm,* or *like* is a person first, a sale or transaction second.

That was the beginning of my west coast story. I pushed through some personal challenges, experienced the joy of our grandson Lucas and settled in to a new, breezy California lifestyle. I joined a great MELA family of colleagues and Nestlé became an important part of my business and personal life. The next part of my second-time around was an interesting mix of different client experiences, the thrill of victory, and management challenges capped off by a totally unexpected opportunity.

---

11. Similac commercial dramatizing the motherhood bond. https://bit.ly/similacmomsunite

Mad Man Wisdom

- Be alert to signs and signals that you're pushing too hard (e.g, lingering over-the-top anxiety or constantly feeling overwhelmed and hopeless). Listen to yourself. Know when to ease up and put your health and well-being first.
- Help is a powerful word. Reach out, let others in and lean on them for support. No one is invincible—even me, even you.
- Being a helping hand-up for others raises you up higher. Sharing your advice and counsel increases your value even further.
- Create your leadership Mount Rushmore. Observe, appreciate, and envision how you would look alongside them.
- There isn't one best or perfect leadership style template. Develop your signature leadership style and presence.
- Cultivate your "in-service" mindset. Master the art of hi-touch marketing. Each brand application is unique. There is no formula.
- Build storytelling capabilities into your communications skill set. Out-of-the-box big ideas are risky and always a hard sell. Winning people over is half the fun.

"A cautious creative is an oxymoron." —*George Lois*

Marketing Tips & Truisms

Build A Pyramid

The brand pyramid should be one of your go-to marketing communications power tools. It's the marketing blueprint that provides answers to fundamental strategic questions related to how the brand will exist and operate in the market. In addition to its functional benefits, I like the emotional imagery associated with pyramids.

- Pyramids take time to build and also endure over time.
- From a distance pyramids are an imposing monolith…up close you see they are built stone by stone.
- Their construction required planning, precision, and perseverance.
- They were built by people not machines.

There are plenty of pyramid templates available that can be adapted to fit the needs of a particular brand. I still find the one we used for Nestlé the best. Here's the template and an example of how it looks for a cat food brand. Also, in the footnote below there is a link to a brand pyramid built by my class for Tai Pei Frozen food and another developed at the Concept Farm for a Disney branded egg.[12]

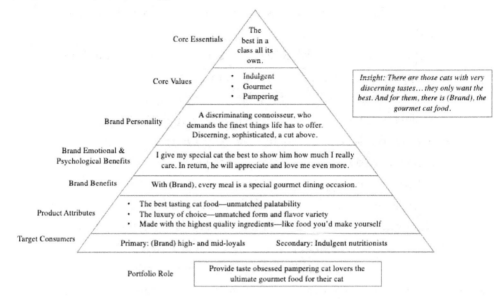

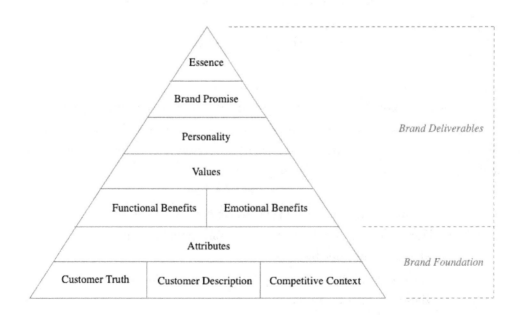

Chapter 11 Footnotes

Scan QR codes for direct links to footnote content.

11.5 Meetings

11.8 Taster's Choice Articles

11.9 Taster's Choice Compilation

11.10 Taster's Choice Finale

11.11 Similac

11.12 Brand Pyramid Examples

Chapter 12:

Turning Good Timing Into Opportunity

My first five years at McCann Erickson Los Angeles (MELA) were filled with more opportunities and challenges than I imagined. After my family and I weathered my personal storms, the business side of my life kicked into high gear. We had built a powerful team at MELA, our relationships were solid, our new business track record was spectacular. With each new client came new lasting connections and unexpected opportunities. I gained valuable experience in new categories of business from aerospace to entertainment, fast food, fitness, music, tourism, and more.

At the same time, the digital rumblings changing the practice of marketing communications were growing stronger and deeper. Much of that change was being driven by tech companies and agencies on the west coast. My fortunate timing enabled me to have a bird's eye view of it all.

Very often timing sets the stage for how you and your career will develop—sometimes it's with you, other times it's not. Either way, you can't let timing control you. In Asset-Based Thinking terms it's called "agreeing with your reality" and shaping it to your benefit. Timing was mostly with me during this period at MELA and I seized the day. It just goes to show that when hard work and good timing converge, opportunities multiply and your optimism amplifies.

Lights, camera, action

To be a player in the LA market, an agency needs a movie studio, or car client. McCann Detroit already worked with General Motors and MELA was fortunate to have one of the largest movie studios on its roster, Sony Studios. We managed all the media planning and buying for the studio and its burgeoning after-market video sales division. Remember video tapes, Blu-Rays, and DVDs distributed months after a film's release in Blockbuster Video stores? A vastly different landscape than today's almost simultaneous digital and streaming release dates.

A studio's CMO is responsible for marketing the release of each film and putting butts in theater seats on opening weekends—easily one of the most pressure filled CMO jobs in business and often a revolving door. That pressure and stress was reflected and magnified at the agency. Establishing a positive relationship with Sony's CMO was a top priority.

Here again, I was lucky to have an unexpected one degree of separation relationship that paved the way for me at Sony. This open bridge to the past was my dear friend and DKG partner Neil Calet. In the mid '70s when I would be in Neil's office at DKG he would occasionally be on the phone with his cousin Sid, a marketing executive with Gulf & Western's Paramount Pictures. Neil sometimes put us on the speaker phone for some three-way small talk. When Neil learned that I was heading to McCann LA he called and said, "Hey Hank, remember my cousin Sid? Well, he's now your client." *Wow!* Sid was Sid Ganis, the highly respected president of marketing at Sony.[1] Neil connected the dots for us and Sid and I were no longer just voices at the end of each other's speakerphones. Cousin Sid was now client Sid.

I remember the first time I walked into Sid's office. He greeted me with a big smile, a hug, and graciously welcomed me into the Sony family. Sid's kindness, support and advice was invaluable and he had a big impact on my success at MELA. About eighteen months later Sid left his position at Sony and set up his own successful production company, Out of the Blue Productions. He also went on to serve four years as president of the American Academy of Motion Picture Arts and Sciences. We kept in touch and both Sid and his wife Nancy would circle back into my life a few years later (another interesting story).

Sid was replaced by another talented and respected studio executive, Bob Levin. Prior to joining Sony, Bob had a stellar career at Disney. I picked up where I had left off with Sid and developed a great relationship with Bob. He taught me a lot. We connected again years later when Bob became a fellow adjunct faculty member at USC's School of Cinematic Arts. Fight on!

Opening weekend pressure

Sony Studios, located in Culver City, was a short ten-minute drive from McCann. I was there at least once a week for client meetings, some of which took place in Sony's executive dining room, usually including a celebrity sighting. I enjoyed walking around the studio lot, peeking into sets and watching the craftsmen at work. That was a special treat for me and helped ease the pressure. Memories of those moments help remind me that behind the glare of the job stress there were hidden moments of relief, joy, and reward. When times got tough I put on my Asset-Based Thinking sunglasses and found personal moments of distraction and satisfaction. Try it. You will like the way you look.

At that time the studio was introducing about ten theatrical release films per year. In essence, launching ten new products, each competing with films simultaneously being released by other studios. Each release required its own marketing brief, creative content, media plans and consumer awareness tracking protocols. The intensity and pressure to drive audiences to theaters on opening weekend—"putting asses in theater seats"—was enormous. Opening weekend performance was, and still is, the critical driver for the entire life of the movie. It

---

1. Sid Ganis IMDB Bio https://bit.ly/SidGanisBio

influences domestic box office as well as all downstream international and aftermarket revenue. There was a big conference room at Sony with a very large whiteboard graphically displaying the marketing and competitive activity leading up to opening weekend. It helped studio executives and the agency stay on top of constantly in-flux media and an incredibly competitive marketplace. Each film fielded critical in-market tracking of awareness, attitude, and opening weekend "purchase intent" against key demographic groups. Media buys and creative content were adjusted accordingly to shore up under performance or exploit opportunities.

The opening weekend experience for the release of *Jerry Maguire* is still fresh in my mind. Released in 1996, it starred Tom Cruise, Renee Zellweger, and Cuba Gooding Jr. The film was about the trials and tribulations of a sports agent and positioned as a romantic comedy/drama sports film. It straddled the line between being perceived as a chick flick and guy sports film.[2] Awareness and interest was constantly tracked with both male and female audiences and the marketing team used this data to meticulously choreograph media and creative content placement. The real-time in-market response was impressive, with the film grossing 274 million dollars and earning Cuba Gooding Jr. a best supporting actor Oscar. In my USC classes I use *Jerry Maguire* as an example of "real-time content marketing" long before availability of the sophisticated digital data and monitoring tools of today.

Managing people under pressure

McCann's Sony account teams were led by Cheryl Lodinger and Terry Powers. Cheryl had overall responsibility for the account and focused on broadcast media. Terry managed newspapers and outdoor. Both were strong, experienced, and respected at Sony. Their working dynamics were quite different, however. Terry was a team player, always looking for ways to be of help and take on additional responsibilities beyond Sony. Cheryl, on the other hand, was a challenge.

Cheryl was very protective of the Sony relationship and her role on the account. She operated as if the Sony account was "hers" and McCann resources and people, me included, were there to service her needs and demands. If there was client contact or agency action that Cheryl was not informed of beforehand, there was hell to pay. Cheryl was the gatekeeper and key master, period.

The best account people have deep commitments to their clients and take their relationships and responsibilities personally. Managed correctly, this sense of ownership helps instill an air of accountability and urgency at the agency. Both Terry and Cheryl had that level of commitment, but Cheryl's modus-operandi was a bit extreme. My relationship with Sid Ganis somewhat insulated me from the wrath of Cheryl, but her demeanor and attitude rubbed me the wrong

---

2. *Jerry Maguire*: http://bit.ly/MaguireScenes

way. At first I resented it. I soon realized, however, that given the intense pressure and per-sonality-driven relationships of studio accounts Cheryl's MO was exactly what was needed in her role. I put my ego aside, upped my daily patience quotient, and adjusted my in-charge mindset from "resent and react" to "respect and respond" in order to make our relationship work. And it did. The account ran smoothly, I was less stressed, and Cheryl and I got along just fine. Earned mutual respect goes a long way, a valuable lesson that has stuck with me.

Managing and motivating people is an especially critical skill in marketing communications. People are the assets who come to work every morning and their knowledge, expertise, and mindset are the "machines" that power successful relationships. Management and motivation challenges vary widely and it's difficult to follow a one-size-fits-all prescription. Terry and Cheryl were both excellent managers on the same account, but my managerial approach to each was quite different. There's a plethora of people management best practice guidelines and advice that you should make use of. Ultimately, however, you have to develop your personal style and adapt it as responsibilities increase.

These are the top three personal assets I cultivated as I climbed the ladder of success.

> **Consistent moral compass.** I adhered to my beliefs on the importance of respectful teamwork.
> **Sincere empathy.** I mentally "traded places" with Cheryl and appreci-ated the difficulty of her job.
> **Confident flexibility.** I was secure enough in my own skin to adapt my mindset to Cheryl's MO and not feel threatened.

Discover yours and stick with them.

I valued my time working with Sony. I gained high-level experience in a new, evolving cat-egory that helped me navigate marketing's transition to the digital era. I was fortunate to have worked with two of the very best studio executives in the business: Sid Ganis and Bob Levin. One quote from Bob Levin about the movie studio CMO's role stuck with me.

> "Understand one thing about your role as a person in marketing. If a movie is successful, it was a great movie. If a movie fails, you did a bad job marketing it. And I've never known that philosophy to ever change over my period of time doing it."

I think about Bob's wisdom when people question the relevance and role of marketing and I read about CMO job tenures continuing to decline. According to a recent Spencer Stuart study in 2019, the average tenure of CMOs was forty-three months, the shortest of any C-Suite resident. The pressure to perform is intense. Some things never change.

New business hit parade: *déja vu*

MELA built an enviable record of client retention, added new assignments from Sony and Nestlé and racked up impressive new business wins earning us the award for the best agency performance in McCann's North American network. New business wins were a result of an "all-hands-on-deck" attitude and extraordinary efforts by a terrific, talented team of people. They inspired me and together we built momentum and success. Guiding that talent and dedication was our five-point strategy:

1. "New business is everyone's business," was our mantra.

2. We leveraged our expertise, especially in dominant local industries like aerospace and entertainment.

3. We made an aggressive push for local clients with our offering of big agency resources and local, personal attention.

4. We cultivated relationships with consultants who assisted clients with agency talent searches, especially Strategic Resources Inc. (SRI) CEO Mike Agate was a former manager of McCann LA and fellow Wilshire CC member.

5. We raised our profile and involvement in the LA ad community. I joined the American Association of Advertising Agencies western region board.

The agency was focused and well-prepared to meet the demands of multiple, sometimes simultaneous new business pitches. In five years, we added ten new clients to our roster, an impressive, eclectic mix of global, national, and local accounts.

These wins generated significant new revenue, raised the agency's profile, bolstered morale and garnered substantial trade press. I particularly liked this *Adweek* headline:

"McCann Winning Streak…McCann's Los Angeles office wins fourth account this year!"[3]

It reminded me of the winning streak we enjoyed at Geers Gross a decade earlier. The competition was intense and winning was invigorating. I'll share a few of the wins that left lasting impressions.

---

3. MELA wins http://bit.ly/MELAWins

McDonnell Douglas and Boeing

Soon after my arrival we were invited to pitch the McDonnell Douglas account. McDonnell Douglas was a manufacturer of aircraft for commercial markets and the second largest supplier to the US military. This was an opportunity to leverage MELA's aerospace experience with clients like Allied Signal. Our management supervisor Dave McAuliffe was well-versed in the industry. Creative director Peter Serchuk also had a great feel for the category. They were the driving force guiding the agency's presentation.

The agency search was commissioned by McDonnell Douglas CEO Harry Stonecipher and managed by two savvy, experienced executives: ad manager Tom Young, a former fighter pilot, and his boss, SVP Fred Hill. They culled the final agency candidates to four: J. Walter Thompson (the incumbent), Ketchum Advertising (my prior employer), Keiler and Co., and MELA. Harry's mission was to change the image of the company among investors and customers, and build employee morale in their communities. He provided this simple challenge to the agencies: "When I watch one of our ads or when I see one of our ads in print, I want the hair to raise up on my arms."

We delivered on that emotional quotient big time and won the business in November 1995. Fred and Tom encouraged us to push the emotional envelope and together we developed breakthrough work. Rather than feature the technical capabilities and performance of the aircraft, our campaign focused on the pilots, families, communities, and passengers whose lives and well-being depended on them. Real-life situations were dramatized and paid-off by a unifying campaign idea and tagline: "McDonnell Douglas will."[4] It received rave reviews and won awards because it summed up everything McDonnel Douglas employees do and distilled it to an emotional human connection.

One commercial featured F/A-18 Hornet pilots landing on an aircraft carrier. The narrator, actress Jessica Walter, lists the loved ones awaiting the pilots' return and asks, "Who will bring them home?" The answer: "McDonnell Douglas will."[5]

Other commercials featured a young girl waiting for her grandmother to arrive aboard a jetliner, a group of school children (future pilots, engineers, and aircraft builders) waiting in the rain for their school bus, and disaster victims waiting for urgent relief supplies. Emotional voiceover copy poignantly asked who can be trusted with each of these responsibilities? "McDonnell Douglas will."

In today's marketing parlance, our campaign is an example of "humanizing brands," "authentic story-telling," and "emotional bonding." In today's marketing world, every product or service, from industrial brands to consumer services, can and must make these sincere

---

4. McD campaign article http://bit.ly/MCDWillArticle

5. McDonnel Douglas Commercials http://bit.ly/McDCommercials

connections to be successful. Marketing communications enabled by data discovery and digital personalization tools provide ample opportunities for brands to create their unique brand-centric emotional story. An essential first step is "listening softer" to consumer data and feedback to tease out the emotional essence that informs messaging. The Coca-Cola Company describes this as "data whispering."

As legendary radio personality Paul Harvey used to say, "Now, for the rest of the story." In December, just nine months after the "McDonnell Douglas will" campaign launched, Boeing announced it was acquiring McDonnell Douglas and it would be folded into Boeing. Suddenly, just like that, our corporate campaign became irrelevant and the scope of our assignment was in limbo. After the completion of the merger in August 1997, one of our champions, Fred Hill, exited the company, but we continued working with the military division on special projects.[6]

Eighteen months later, in May 1999, Boeing announced it would be consolidating all of its advertising with one agency and we were invited to pitch the corporate account. Here we go again…same song, second verse, different name.

This was a hotly contested high profile search led by Boeing's communications VP Judith Muhlberg. It was an intense four-month pitch period that came down to four big agency finalists: McCann, Bozell Worldwide, Publicis, and Young & Rubicam. Our team stepped up yet again and we won the business. An even bigger win the second time around. We "agreed" with both the good and bad timing of each situation and our persistence and patience paid off. Winning an account once is tough enough, winning it twice in three years is a special accomplishment.[7] That's the serendipity of the marketing communications business…you never know what's around the corner.

In-N-Out

In-N-Out is an iconic Southern California brand. Founded in 1945 by Esther and Harry Snyder, it is still family run and stores are still company owned. No franchises. There are 347 locations and they outperform all competitors in sales, profitability, and customer satisfaction, and for good reason…they have an almost fanatical dedication to quality, tradition, and service with a smile.[8]

Not much has changed since 1945. Everything is fresh. Everything. The stores are bright, clean, and cheerful. Employees are the highest paid in the fast-food industry and always greet customers with a big hello and a smile.

---

6. Fred joined JP Morgan Chase as EVP communications. We stayed in touch. In 2018, he published a great mystery novel, *Bank Notes* https://amzn.to/2K3bvra

7. Boeing Win http://bit.ly/BoeingArticle

8. In-N-Out History https://bit.ly/InNOutStory

In-N-Out's marketing budget of $5 million dollars was dwarfed by its competitors. The majority of spending was on outdoor, radio, and tactical promotional materials. Their slogan, "Quality You Can Taste," was sacrosanct. It was a relatively small account and wouldn't be a source of new showcase creative. Yet every agency in town hungered for the business. Being on the inside of the In-N-Out cult meant local bragging rights and the opportunity to contribute to an iconic brand's continued success. Over thirty agencies put themselves up for consideration.

The agency search was led by VP of operations Carl Van Fleet. Carl was a great brand evangelist and lived the brand from the inside out. After an extended nine-month review, five finalists made the cut: Dailey & Associates (another IPG agency), Cohen/Johnson, Odiorne Wilde Narraway Groome, incumbent Weller, O'Sullivan, Zuckerman & Lightcap, and McCann LA. Each agency presented recommendations on marketing communications strategy and client references. No spec work was required.

Carl and his team held a series of strategy recommendation and chemistry check meetings with the finalists. Myself, creative director Peter Serchuk, planning director Cathy Clift and media director George Hayes led the pitch. We meshed well with the In-N-Out team and came out on top but our appointment wouldn't be official until we received the blessing of the family's principle owner and CEO Guy Snyder, son of the founders. I was looking forward to meeting him but didn't know what to expect.

It was a low-key meeting. Guy asked about our backgrounds, In-N-Out experiences, and thoughts about the brand. Each of us expressed our personal pride in becoming part of the In-N-Out family and our responsibility to respect and live up to the brand's fifty-year heritage of commitment to quality and customer service. We meant it. Our sincerity resonated with Guy. The deal was sealed and In-N-Out was added to MELA's roster.[9] Our meeting with Guy reinforced important principles that I embraced. The best way to begin an agency-client relationship (or any business relationship) is to listen first and often, make the conversation about them, not you, and be sincere in what you say. Remember, you can't rehearse sincerity.

We were fortunate that another IPG company, Western International, was In-N-Out's media agency. They helped us get up to speed on the business and I could count on the support of their top executives, Dennis Holt and Michael Kassan. They were part of my welcoming committee when I first arrived in Los Angeles. MELA created brand advertising, a steady stream of tactical promotional materials, and communications that supported In-N-Out's philanthropic and community programs. Community involvement was an integral part of the brand's DNA and they often held charity fundraising events. We made sure the agency had a presence at many of them. I always came away impressed by the family feeling, depth of mutual respect, support and appreciation demonstrated at these events. At one event I was lucky to be the

---

9. In-N-Out Win http://bit.ly/InNOutWin

winning bid on a custom made In-N-Out jacket. I liked it so much I had a mini-version made for my three-year old grandson, Lucas. Take a look.[10]

Another learning I applied to In-N-Out was putting your skin in the game to build trust and add value. We agreed to a fee-based compensation system and I asked Carl if they were open to including some form of incentive compensation. Carl liked the concept. As the starting point we prepared our initial fee proposal based on a mutually agreed-to scope of work and estimated billable hours. That worked out to a $40K monthly fee.

I proposed that MELA cut that fee by 15% ($6K/month) in exchange for a mutually agreed to incentive compensation program. Carl agreed. So far, nothing unusual. Then Carl made a suggestion that I jumped on. He proposed that 80% of the incentive compensation be tied to the same bonus program as store managers and 20% be based on qualitative agency performance measures. Carl explained their bonus system measurements simply: burgers sold (revenue) and smiles (customer satisfaction). Given what we knew about In-N-Out's sales and customer satisfaction track record this seemed like a safe bet. And so we aligned our bonus with their management—if they did well so would we. It turned out to be the one of the best compensation deals I've ever made.

Every year we earned a minimum 50% bonus against our base fee (+$204K) bringing the agency's total annual compensation to $612K. That's an average $132K per year additional compensation versus the original $40K/per month. Both In-N-Out and McCann came away happy. My client side experience taught me that aligning your company's incentives and rewards with your client's is usually a safe bet. It's very rare that top management doesn't earn a bonus. More about In-N-Out at the end of the chapter.

The Beverly Hills Visitors Bureau

The Beverly Hills Visitors Bureau was another uniquely LA opportunity. The Bureau's annual marketing budget of $3M was funded by hotel taxes levied by the city. The agency search committee included hoteliers and city officials and was led by Peter O'Colmain, GM of the Regent Beverly Wilshire hotel. They reached out to thirteen agencies and narrowed the finalists to four: D'Arcy Masius Benton & Bowles (DMB&B), Evans Group, Pulsar, and MELA.

Each agency was asked for strategic recommendations and a creative campaign to build awareness of Beverly Hills as unique destination. Peter Serchuk, creative director; Cathy Clift, planning director; and I led the agency's pitch and hit the sweet spot that landed the account. Our, "Some Things Can Only Happen Here," campaign captured the specialness of Beverly Hills and commercials and print ads leveraged its celebrity aura.

Research revealed that people believed Beverly Hills had fantastic shopping, dining, and

---

10. My Jackets http://bit.ly/In-N-OutGear

hotels but felt they were only available to insider movers and shakers. Our campaign positioned Beverly Hills as a one-of-a-kind destination within a destination (Los Angeles) and rolled out the red carpet for savvy travelers. The campaign visualized how visitors could enjoy the same amenities and delights as the celebrities who live and work there.

Wolfgang Puck starred in one of the commercials shot at his world famous restaurant Spago. Legendary actor Charlton Heston agreed to do the voice over.[11] His signature delivery of the campaign theme line, "Beverly Hills. Somethings can only happen here," was the perfect punctuation.[12] I got to meet with Charlton Heston at his Beverly Hills home to review the campaign and work out production details. Sitting in his living room surrounded by his memorabilia was like being in a Hollywood time capsule. Right then and there our tag line became a reality for me. Yes, some things could only happen in Beverly Hills!

The assignment opened up valuable relationships with hotel management and unexpected business opportunities with the Peninsula Hotel and Merv Griffin's Beverly Hilton. Merv's hotel was right in the middle of Beverly Hills and renowned for its concierge services that brought the best of Beverly Hills to guests' hotel rooms. Merv's idea was to make these already existing posh services available to Beverly Hills residents through an exclusive BH Concierge Services annual membership. Everything from dog walking, transportation, cleaning, catered meals, salon services, etc. was just a "call away." Remember, this was in the Stone Age before apps like Uber, Fresh Direct, and Postmates. It was a creative business idea to maximize revenue from existing services and enhance the hotel's image. We developed concepts that tested well but the project was put on hold due to concerns about potential liability issues. Nevertheless, spending time with a successful innovator and entrepreneur like Merv Griffin was an education.[13] He built an empire in the entertainment and hotel industries and was always exploring what was next. Merv was one of those idea "magicians" that I was fortunate to rub against.

Windham Hill Music

In the previous chapter, I mentioned that music is an integral part of my stress relief regime. The genesis of that practice was our winning the Windham Hill Music account. Windham Hill is an adult contemporary/new age label with artists like George Winston, Will Ackerman, Janice Ian, and Jim Brickman. Marketing VP Faithe Raphael hired MELA to develop a first-ever brand campaign for the label that included TV, radio, and outdoor. The tag line for the campaign captured the brand essence nicely: "Windham Hill. The Music Inside You."

---

11. Charlton Heston https://bit.ly/CharltonHestonInfo

12. Beverly Hills Ads http://bit.ly/BeverlyHillsAds

13. Merv Griffin https://bit.ly/MervGriffinInfo

Faithe was a sharp industry executive, an expert in adult contemporary genres, and we developed a great friendship. She introduced me to this new world of music and helped curate a wonderful collection of Windham Hill CDs that still helps to keep me on an even keel. The press release announcing our campaign contained this quote from me.[14]

"Windham Hill's music really plays an important and inspirational role in the lives of their customers, and McCann is excited about the opportunity to help bring the world of Windham Hill to even more consumers."

In retrospect my words turned out to be more prophetic and personal than I realized.

McCann West: pleasure and painful regret

First the pleasure. The remaining 25% of my responsibilities initially involved oversight of the other four agencies in the McCann West region: Seattle(MES), San Diego (Phillips-Ramsey), San Francisco (MESF), and Texas (METX). Each agency had carved out a unique position in their respective markets with well-known successful creative case histories on their reels.[15] My role was advisory, assistance, and advocacy. I was supported by two terrific McCann executives in New York: my boss Don Dillon and CFO George Recine. I relied particularly on George's advice and counsel regarding financial management and operational issues.

I worked with the general managers on leveraging shared West Coast media resources, fiscal oversight coordination with McCann NY, and new business assistance as needed. Occasionally I would interface with clients if requested by the GM. The good news was that each agency's general manager was top notch and had strong management teams in place. I applied the lessons I had learned from my earlier stint at McCann overseeing the agency's allied communications agencies. I appreciated and respected each agency manager's unique strengths and management styles, and made sure each knew I was there to help and be complementary. Also, since I was in their shoes as GM of MELA, we shared experiences, challenges, and ideas that helped cultivate positive working relationships and trust.

Here's a quick snapshot. Gary Meads was GM of Philips Ramsey in San Diego with Tony Durket as his creative partner. They were young, energetic, entrepreneurial hustlers, well-respected and involved in San Diego business circles. Jim Walker was GM and creative director of McCann Seattle. He was the only creative director that also served as a GM, a special creative talent that could do it all. Jim and his team established McCann as a powerhouse in the Seattle ad community and a shining creative beacon in the McCann network.

---

14. Windham Hill http://bit.ly/WindhamHillWin

15. ME West http://bit.ly/MEWestCommercials

Soon after I arrived, Tony Pace took over as GM of the Texas agency group. He was a seasoned, savvy marketing pro who earned the respect of clients and had a great track record. Tony and I worked very well together. We stayed in touch and reunited a few years later in an interesting collaboration. San Francisco was a very competitive market with a steady stream of account shifts and volatility. MESF's general manager Ron Benza built a strong team with Dave Tutin, creative director and Penny Baldwin planning director. They did a great job under trying circumstances and kept the agency on an even keel.

Next, the regret. The seeds of my regret were planted in October 1995, when McCann purchased another San Francisco agency, Andersen & Lembke (A&L). The principals of the agency were Hans Ulmark and Steve Trygg. The agency's largest client was Microsoft, an account that McCann CEO John Dooner had been keen on adding to the agency's roster.

McCann now had two agencies in the same market and it was decided that MESF and A&L would operate separately. Coordinating which agency would solicit and pitch new accounts required artful diplomacy to avoid turf battles. I had very little involvement with A&L's management until a year after the acquisition. My boss Don Dillon asked me to work with Hans and Steve on sharing McCann resources with A&L and recruiting a new GM. But it was apparent from the beginning that my involvement was not welcome.

Hans was cordial and tolerant, Steve was hostile and negative. They planned to re-hire Mike Windsor, previously account services manager at the agency, for the new GM role. Mike was a strong experienced agency executive but management in New York was keen on placing a McCann executive in the GM position. Don Dillon, George Recine, and I felt that Lee Daley, one of McCann's best and brightest strategists, was perfect for the job. Hans and Steve agreed to hold off on a final decision until they met with him. Lee came to San Francisco and spent the day with Steve and Hans. They both felt Lee could be a good fit and agreed to continue the discussion. So far so good.

The next Monday I was back in my MELA office and was handed a copy of *Adweek*. One of the headlines hit me in the face: "Andersen & Lembke Regains Windsor as Managing Director." I couldn't believe it. While Steve and Hans were "bs-ing" me about keeping an open mind they had already signed the deal with Mike Windsor. I exploded and called Steve. When he didn't take the call, my anger boiled over and I let that Brooklyn "punch-back" attitude take over my reasoning. I took a cab to LAX, got on the first flight to SF, and went straight to A&L. I bypassed the receptionist and walked unannounced into Steve Trygg's office. I immediately got in his face and let loose a loud verbal beat-down. Steve fired back at me and we went at it. I could see that he was seething. Steve later told colleagues he was a breath away from coming from behind his desk and punching me. I was out of control—and my outburst didn't change anything. I apologized to my friend Lee Daley for wasting his time and from then on I kept my distance. Fortunately, Lee and I would collaborate on a bigger McCann stage a few years later.

I realize now that I probably deserved that punch from Steve. Their actions and behavior were dishonest and deceitful. My reactions were dumb and destructive. While I had every right to be pissed off, I overstepped my bounds. Barging into A&L's office was an egregious professional mistake and embarrassing personal behavior. I forgot lessons I learned at Geers Gross and Somerset and let other people's toxic actions take over my mindset and behavior. In business, it's important not to internalize the actions of others as personal attacks on you. In Asset-Based Thinking terms it's learning how to "trade enraged for engaged" so you can step outside the heat of the moment. My bad. This Benjamin Franklin quote nailed it for me. "Anger is never without a reason, but seldom with a good one."

Epilogue: Towards the end of 1998, A&L was faltering and Steve Trygg, Hans Ulmark, and Mike Windsor had exited the agency. Another strong McCann executive, Nick Bishop, took over as CEO.[16] Nick and I already knew each other and had an excellent relationship. Then McCann hit the mother-lode that John Dooner had been hoping for. McCann was invited by Microsoft to pitch their massive Windows account. Don Dillon skillfully coordinated a joint effort involving McCann New York, MESF, and A&L. I was involved on the periphery and worked with George Recine on developing the scope of work, staffing requirements, and fee agreement. It was by far the largest monthly fee retainer I'd ever been involved with—$3 million dollars per month.

John Dooner's "we will not be denied" persistence paid off. Microsoft became one of McCann North America's largest clients! That win set in motion the inevitable merging of MESF into A&L, which was heralded as "the first integrated online and offline agency in the McCann network."[17] Nick Bishop was named CEO of the new McCann-Erickson/A&L and Ron Benza elected to leave the agency. It was the right scenario and management move, but I was sad to see Ron close out his twenty-four-year McCann career in that way.

Extracurricular enjoyment

Another bright side of the McCann West road trip was my tenure on the American Association of Advertising Agencies western region board of directors (4AsWest). Jerry Gibbons, head of 4AsWest, invited me to join the board and I gladly accepted. Coincidentally, Jerry was friends with my friend, B&B colleague and Wilshire CC buddy, Eric von der Lieth, making that connection even more special.

This was my first major involvement with an industry association and I made the most of it. Jerry was an industry veteran with great experience and I valued his advice and expertise. Interacting with industry colleagues and being involved in the LA ad community was a good

---

16. N. Bishop article http://bit.ly/NickBishop

17. ME/A&L https://bit.ly/MESFALMerger

way to step back from my day to day routine and see the bigger picture. A wider lens that bettered my view. One 4AsWest event stands out for two reasons: honor and irony. First, the honor. The organization traditionally celebrated a leader of the year and John Fuller, CEO of The Fuller Group, and I were named co-chairs for 1997's leader of the year event.

Our committee broke precedent and selected a previous honoree, Lee Clow of TBWA/Chiat Day. And with good reason. Lee Clow is a creative legend who had a powerful impact on the industry and his agency's growth that year.[18] John and I were honored to plan and host his gala in Beverly Hills at the Regent Beverly Wilshire Hotel.

Now, the irony. Remember Bob Kuperman from last chapter, the TBWA/Chiat Day creative director who refused to have lunch with me? I received a call from Bob's secretary advising me that he was expecting a spot on the agenda to speak about his colleague Lee Clow. I guess Bob was too busy to call me himself.

My co-chair and I discussed Bob's request and decided that the agenda was already full so we could not accommodate his request. It was a wonderful event and a great time was had by all, even Bob. Also, because of my 4AsWest involvement and McCann's increased visibility on the West Coast I was called upon for commentary in trade media articles and occasional TV interviews. I enjoyed that.[19]

My 4AsWest experience was wonderful and I am grateful to Jerry Gibbons for making that possible. We collaborated on a few projects and stayed in touch until his passing in 2019. Another example of positive connections intertwining and weaving their way into my future. I appreciate and celebrate them whenever I can. Be sure to do the same.

Planting the seeds of my future

In April 1999, my son Gregg returned to New York from his successful creative supervisor job at TBWA/Chiat Day in Amsterdam. He and his art director partner, Ray Mendez, created a campaign that won a prestigious Cannes Gold Lion award. Upon arriving back at TBWA/Chiat Day New York they were told their services were no longer needed. Apparently TBWA/Chiat New York was fully staffed. Not quite the homecoming they had expected. Ray moved on to another agency and Gregg turned his situation into the best problem he'd ever had.

Gregg, his boyhood friend Will Morrison, and Griffin Stenger (remember him from Geers Gross?) decided to launch a new breed agency geared to marketing's digital future. I had a glimpse into that future with the creation of MESF/A&L and I was eager to see what they envisioned. They came to me with their business plan and asked for my advice. The name of the company was Concept Farm. They would be content creators for the next millennium's

---

18. https://bit.ly/LeeClowStory

19. *AdBiz* Interview http://bit.ly/HankAdBiz.

interactive and traditional media landscape. Their mantra was, "Fresh Ideas Harvested Daily."

I gave them a proud and enthusiastic thumbs up and decided to invest in their future. But first I looked in the mirror and saw that "cash flow" tattoo on my forehead. We calculated the start-up capital needed to provide a twelve-month revenue runway that would cover their minimum salary requirements and operational costs: $400K.[20] They incorporated, I deposited $400k in their account, and Concept Farm began operations out of Griffin's NYC apartment in July 1999. They had a year to make it work.

So there I was. Closing out a decade, heading towards my fifty-seventh birthday and looking forward to a new millennium. I was feeling pretty good about things. The first five years of my second time around with McCann were better than I expected, our family was settled and happy in Los Angeles, and I was contemplating restarting my teaching career. On top of that I was an angel investor in an innovative agency start-up with people I loved and respected. Good timing and an abundance of opportunities raised my optimism for the future sky high. Y2K here I come!

I started asking myself, is this as good as it gets? Should I settle in and make MELA the last stop on my road to retirement at age sixty-two when my benefits would be fully vested? Should I set my sights on a bigger role as regional director? The answers were not that simple.

Mad Man Wisdom

- Use your ABT sunglasses to discover hidden moments of joy in a stressful industry. Handling the blinding glare of pressure is a prerequisite for marketing management positions.
- Forget personal and petty differences. Instead, find the common ground of mutual respect.
- Cultivate your personal assets for managing difficult relationships. They won't fail you.
- Data mining = information. Data analytics = insights. Data whispering = emotional intelligence. Make sure you use all three.
- Align compensation incentives to mutually shared performance goals. Bonds are created. Both parties benefit.
- Discover the music inside you. Create your personal playlist. Listen often. Clear out clutter and unwind.

"Everything that happened to me happened by mistake. I don't believe in fate. It's luck, timing, and accident." —Merv Griffin

---

20. Concept Farm Plan http://bit.ly/CFPlan

Marketing Truisms & Tips

The Basic Brilliance of In-N-Out Burger

In-N-Out Burger is on my Mount Rushmore of companies to be admired and emulated. It's not because of their elite cadre of MBAs, data analytics, overpowering media budgets, digital media prowess, or whatever is in vogue at any particular time. In fact, In-N-Out earned its place by eschewing all of that and excelling at brand-building basics. They tuned out competitive marketing noise and listened to their inner voice.[21] It sounds a bit spiritual and it is. Here's the condensed version of how I discuss the magic of In-N-Out in my USC class using today's six Ps of marketing.

> **Product:** In-N-Out's simple credo: "Serve only the highest quality product, prepare it in a clean and sparkling environment, and serve it in a warm and friendly manner." This is not lip-service. They have a relentless focus on simplicity, quality, and living up to their motto, "Quality You can Taste." The fifteen items on the menu are a marriage of quality and affordability and largely unchanged from their inception. Buns are baked every morning, the highest quality fresh meat is ground every day and shipped directly to stores, and fries are cut on the spot. Heat lamps, microwaves, and freezers are banned. The recipes for its burgers and fries have remained essentially the same for seventy years.

> **Price:** They employ a competitive affordability and value pricing strategy. Prices are standardized and remain steady with little fluctuation so customers enjoy the same great meals at the same cost wherever they go. In-N-Out does not price promote and stands by their belief that quality and consistency cannot be discounted.

> **Place:** In-N-Out's clean white stores and signage are unmistakable and strategically placed for impact and customer convenience. Equally important, each store must be within a day's driving distance from the nearest warehouse and processing plant to insure freshness and quality. The kitchens are wide open giving customers a wide view of the process and people. The red, white, and yellow color scheme hasn't changed since the 1950s, and all employees wear the same white and

---

21. There is a wealth of wisdom in how a business created in 1948 remains so relevant today. The lessons of In-N-Out could fill a book and it has...*A Behind the Counter Look at In-N-Out Burger* https://bit.ly/InNOBook

red uniform and aprons with a big safety pin. Customers step back in time and it works because the ambiance and vibe sincerely reflect the brand's heritage.

Promotion: In-N-Out's marketing budget is relatively small and there are no promotions, sales, or happy meals. They use radio to promote the brand and outdoor directing customers to locations. Merchandising happens in store and their loyal customer base is a huge source of positive word of mouth media. Brand advocates and influencers gladly do most of the work for them. For example, over the years In-N-Out's customers discovered ways to customize their burgers and fries giving rise to In-N-Out's *secret menu* adding an array of delicious menu extensions for those in the know.

People: In-N-Out's people strategy is captured in their name. Satisfied employees on the inside beget satisfied customers on the outside. In-N-Out has always paid its employees well-above minimum wage and has one of the lowest industry turnover rates. Managers are trained at In-N-Out University to ensure the highest quality food, cleanliness, and service standards. I even attended In-N-Out U as part of my introduction to the company. The average store manager has been with In-N-Out for seventeen years, makes $163,000, and is invested in the company's success. Happy employees and avid loyal customers have always been valued as brand ambassadors enabling In-N-Out to create their own social network long before social media came along. Customers love to impress employees with their "secret menu" fluency.

Purpose: In-N-Out's purpose is rooted in its founders' vision and personal beliefs. For seventy years generations of the Snyder family have steadfastly honored Esther and Harry's company credo and Christian values. The In-N-Out foundation supports community initiatives to help abused and neglected children. In 1987, the company discretely placed bible verse references on various cups and wrappers as a way of putting that "little touch of the family's faith" on their brand. Today, thirty-eight-year old Lynsi Snyder, Guy's daughter and granddaughter of the founders, is CEO and owns 100% of the company.

She is fervently committed to keeping In-N-Out family-owned and is a staunch guardian and protector of the founders' legacy. Recently, when elements of the "cancel culture" pressured the company about the appropriateness of their use of bible verses, Lynsi stood firm and In-N-Out's customers rallied to her support. She added two more bible verses to the fries container and coffee cups.

When asked by a *Forbes* magazine journalist if she would ever "cash it in" and sell the company, Lynsi's response was quick and emphatic. "It's not about the money for us. Unless God sends a lightning bolt down and changes my heart miraculously, I would not ever sell." All of my fellow In-N-Out lovers pray that lightning bolt never comes.

Chapter 12 Footnotes

Scan QR codes for direct links to footnote content.

12.2 Jerry Maguire Scenes

12.3 MELA Winning Streak

12.4 McDonnel Douglas Article

12.5 McDonnell Douglas Commercials

12.7 Boeing Win

12.9 In-n-Out Win

12.10 In-n-Out Gear

12.12 Beverly Hills Commercial

12.14 Windam Hill Win

12.15 MEWest Commercials

12.16 Nick Bishop Article

12.19 Hank's Ad Biz Video

12.20 Concept Farm Plan

Chapter 13:

Switching From Reactive to Proactive

Acts two and three of my McCann saga unfolded in three head-spinning years at the beginning of the 2000s. I was happy and content at McCann Erickson West when change and disruption came at me in rapid succession. Opportunities pushed me in new directions and disappointments and doubt pulled me back. I re-evaluated and renovated my career twice in three years.

The first time, I was offered a new overseas position and my reactive explorer jumped at it. I hastily renovated my life and went off to London to be Executive Vice President of McCann Worldgroup and assume the global responsibility for Nestlé, McCann's second largest client. I was making the most of my new position and gaining valuable experience but was pushing myself to the limit when a confluence of circumstances, including the 9/11 terrorist attack on the World Trade Center towers, caused me to rethink where I was.

This time, my mindset was different. My initial plans lacked clarity and conviction because I was being more emotional, reactive, and introspective. Then I initiated conversations that led to a more balanced and informed purpose-built renovation of my career. The final leg of my career journey was crystal clear and I liked where it led: back to the US with another impressive McCann title and the flexibility to work with my son at his fledgling agency two days a week. It just goes to show how being proactive positions you to more clearly reevaluate and renovate your life.

When the world changed

The last five years of the 1990s set the stage for the digital deluge of the 2000s that impacted every aspect of marketing communications. At the beginning of the decade just 3% of US homes had broadband internet. By 2008, that percentage had risen to 88%. The breadth and pace of development was mind boggling. Voice over Internet Protocol (VoIP) took hold and the use of email exploded. Some of today's most popular online sites launched early in the decade: Google, Yahoo, Wikipedia, Amazon, and eBay. Internet commerce became the standard for many businesses. The popularity of mobile phones and text messaging surged in the '00s spawning the first social networking sites like Friendster, MySpace, Facebook, and Twitter. YouTube came on the scene in 2005. The 2007, introduction of the iPhone and subsequent launches of GPS and the wireless/mobile internet completely changed the game. They created a world of unparalleled peer-to-peer communication, creativity, and collaboration. The list of changes can go on for pages. By 2010, pretty much everything anyone needed to communicate and conduct business was in the palm of their hands and accessible 24/7. It was a watershed decade when technological and social changes went mainstream and permanently altered the way we live and communicate. The democratization of content creation and media had arrived.

Pundits put many labels on the 2000s: The…digital decade, disaster decade, global decade, diversion decade. My 2000 life was an amalgam of all these.

Starting Y2K with a bang

It all started with McCann management changes in October 1999, Jim Heekin was promoted to CEO of McCann. Don Dillon replaced Jim as regional director for Europe and Tony Miller replaced Don as my new boss. I was on board with all of it and particularly excited about Jim's well-earned CEO appointment. In January 2000, McCann was named *Adweek*'s 1999 global agency of the year and *Ad Age*'s business to business agency of the year for 1999. The latter was due in large part to the strong performance of MEWest. *Adweek* interviewed Jim Heekin and John Dooner in a secret location to prevent leaks. Guess where. At the office of my son's new agency Concept Farm in Chelsea! Gregg called to tell me the news. Coincidence or karma?

There was an abundance of opportunity and optimism at McCann Worldgroup as we headed into the new decade and I settled in to a satisfying and productive flow—but not for long.

At the beginning of the year I initiated low key discussions with Jim Heekin and John Dooner about how they saw my future at McCann. I assured them I was very happy at McCann and there was no urgency or issues. In February, I was attending meetings at McCann New York when Jim and John invited me to dinner. I don't remember the restaurant, but I distinctly remember standing at the bar when they unexpectedly served up an intriguing proposition.

They asked me to step into a new global role as Executive Vice President of McCann Worldgroup and assume the global responsibility for Nestlé, McCann's second largest client. Nestlé's headquarters are in Vevey, Switzerland, and I would be based in McCann's London office. McCann would supplement my compensation with an excellent expat accommodation package and there would be no need to permanently relocate. *Blimey!*

I ordered a double martini and told them I was open to the new opportunity and would discuss it with Vicki. Thinking about it on my flight back to LA, my interest and enthusiasm grew. A lucrative expat package, an exciting city, London, first-class world travel, and the chance to experience new cultures and take on different business challenges. My contented "this as good as it gets" west coast mindset started to evaporate. My penchant for taking risks and embracing the new took over.

Here we go again

When I discussed the new role with Vicki she could sense my enthusiasm. She looked at me and said, "Here we go again." But this would be our sixth business relocation and she was not thrilled about the prospect. Vicki came around when we decided to keep our home in Los Angeles so she could divide her time between London and LA to be with our grandson Lucas. We agreed she would occasionally travel with me on my business trips and we would schedule some family holidays abroad. With that settled I accepted the position and began the transition to my new role. John Dooner did not like to leave loose ends for too long so I knew things would move quickly.

Just before I started my new job more management shoes dropped. In March 2000, John was named COO of McCann's parent company IPG and was marked to replace Phil Geier as CEO after his retirement. As expected, Jim Heekin took over full control of McCann Worldgroup and his promotion was greeted with cheers and well wishes. This was the orbit in which I operated for the next three years. I was eager to get on-board, fly around the world, and make things happen.

But first I had to prepare my exit from McCann Erickson LA. As mentioned in prior chapters, having a positive impact in your position is critical, but that's not the only thing. Leaving a mark with your exit is also important. Building positive bridges to the past was an essential part of my road to success so I made it a point to play an active role in MELA's transition to new management.

I recommended the position be scaled back to encompass only MELA. The McCann West supervisory role had become an extra layer of management that was no longer needed. Next, I made a bold proposal that got people's attention. Applying my experience from the MES-F/A&L merger, I recommended IPG merge its two Los Angeles agencies, MELA and Dailey. The combined MELA/Dailey would be a powerhouse agency in Los Angeles that would enable significant economies of scale and generate increased profitability. There were very few client conflicts (Nestlé was a shared client of each agency) and, most importantly, Dailey management, Cliff Einstein and Brian Morris, were well-respected executives. I recommended installing Cliff and Brian as top management of MELA/Dailey, thereby eliminating the need to find my replacement. A win-win scenario, I thought. Alas, the recommendation was appreciated and considered but not implemented because of potential disruptive operational issues and contractual agreements with Dailey management.

We were fortunate to bring in a top manager from another IPG agency to fill the top management slot at MELA, Ian McGregor. Ian was an experienced, top-notch executive who also had an established relationship with Nestlé. Ian and I spent the month prior to the official announcement implementing the transition. All went well. No glitches or issues. I was confident that the leadership of MELA was in good hands. I had made my positive exit.

Saying goodbye to my MELA friends and colleagues was emotional. We'd been through a lot together. I was treated to a wonderful bon voyage party with laughs, tears, and memories. My going away gift was a set of black leather Coach luggage that became my constant travelling companion for the next three years. On every trip, it reminded me of my good fortune and enduring friendships from MELA. Positive connections always travel well!

Up, up, and away

Before getting to the business aspects of my new gig across the pond, here's a snapshot of our expat living arrangements. My friend and prior boss Don Dillon and his wife Fran had just completed a similar transition to London and jumped in to help. They introduced us to a listing agent who found a fantastic furnished three-bedroom flat at 45 Enismore Gardens in London's fashionable Knightsbridge. The monthly rent was around $12K US dollars. *Yikes!* Thankfully, McCann was paying for it and not me. We were one block from Hyde Park's Queen's Gate and a very short walk to Brompton Road shopping and the world famous Harrod's department store. Their food court became our local grocery store!

Vicki and I had access to a company car and driver making the excitement and joys of London and the surrounding countryside easily accessible. Our entire family even visited at Christmas for a magical holiday in London. That first year included a few months of amazing experiences we will always treasure. But there was a catch. My road warrior travel schedule turned out to be much more extensive and taxing than anticipated. In the initial eighteen months I spent just 35% of my time in London. More often than not, that beautiful flat was unoccupied.

When I arrived at McCann London in July 2000, the agency was housed in a dreary older building. Quite a different environment than the bright panoramic views of Wilshire Boulevard. Fortunately, I didn't stay there long and the agency relocated to new offices at 7-11 Herbrand street. McCann converted an art-deco ex-car park garage into a spectacular modern agency space with all the resources needed for the coming digital age. It housed the McCann London agency and Europe, Middle East, and Africa (EMEA) regional management. The Nestlé global team was assigned its own section. The new office was easily accessible from my apartment and a great environment in which to work.

The first order of business was meeting my new team and being briefed on the business by my predecessor, Jon de Kok, and the administrative assistant, Jennifer Hutcheon. Jon was gracious and helpful and it was clear that Jennifer was key to a successful transition. Jennifer knew everyone and everything about the clients, team, travel schedules. Thankfully, she stayed on as my assistant. After those briefings the breadth and complexity of my new position hit home. Yes, I was responsible for one global client headquartered in Vevey, Switzerland, but that was just the tip of the iceberg. I was about to experience a whirlwind, invaluable crash course in global brand management and marketing communications that would raise my game to new heights.

Here's my takeaway: In taking on any new position it's virtually certain to not be exactly as expected or hoped. View it as an opportunity to adapt, morph, roll with the punches, and shape it to your strengths and skills. Give yourself space to reassess and move ahead.

A master class in global brand management

The best way to explain my position and responsibilities is in the context of the Nestlé corporate management structure with which I interacted. The central communications team was headed by Frank Cella and Tom Freitgag, both of whom were smart, experienced pros. Each strategic business unit (SBU) was run by a director and support staff. My interactions were primarily with the Beverage, Nutrition, Pet Care, and Food SBUs. Nestlé segmented its global business into zones headed by a zone manager based in their respective geography. Each country's management reported to the zone manager. For example, in the United States, Nestlé USA CEO Joe Weller reported to zone manager for the Americas, Carlos Represas, who was based in Mexico. Presiding over these management teams was Nestlé's charismatic CEO, Peter Brabeck-Letmathe.

To effectively do my job I had to establish relationships with all of them. Luckily, without my asking, calls were made on my behalf to Nestlé's Vevey headquarters helping me to get off to a positive start in my new role. But relationship building at this level was not something I could do sitting behind a desk at McCann London. Success required substantial travel and honing my skills in listening, diplomacy, and the art of persuasion. My international experience at Brown-Forman, Somerset, and Capstone were assets I could tap into in this respect.

My key responsibilities leading the Nestlé global team were to ensure that the full resources of McCann Worldgroup were placed against the business, troubleshoot issues in key markets, champion initiatives to expand McCann's business unit penetration, and grow revenue. I was now responsible for managing a cost center versus running a profit center and had to shift my mindset. Ultimately, the hard metrics for the Nestlé global team's success were downstream income and revenue growth at each local agency and business unit. The softer metrics were the breadth, depth, and strength of the McCann/Nestlé relationship. I had to keep my eye on both.

McCann's regional managers covered essentially the same Nestlé zone geographies and the Nestlé global account teams lined up with the strategic business units (SBUs). One gratifying aspect of my position was that I got to work closely with three good friends and colleagues: Don Dillon, regional director for Europe, Middle East and Africa (EMEA), Marcio Moreira, global creative director, and Lee Daley, now chief strategy officer for EMEA. Being reunited with Lee had a special irony. I flashed back a few years to when I thought I had Lee lined up to take over as GM of A&L in San Francisco only to be duped by Steve Trygg and Hans Ulmark. Now I was happy he didn't get the position and cynically celebrated their duplicity. There were solid, experienced account management teams already in place and no immediate personnel issues. When account managers required special media or creative assistance the McCann London teams stepped in to help.

With everything in place I began my odyssey. In the first eighteen months, my Coach luggage and I traveled to McCann and Nestlé offices in twenty-eight countries at least once. I went to Japan and China three times and Switzerland twice per month. I visited our offices in Warsaw, the birthplace of my grandparents, and spent an emotional weekend connecting with my roots. I racked up 1.8 million frequent traveler miles on British Airways and American Airlines. Each of these visits held new business experiences and opened doors to wonderful relationships with people from different countries. I was affected in two powerful ways. It simultaneously enhanced my respect and appreciation of the rich cultural diversity of our planet and reawakened and reinforced my realization of how fortunate I was to be an American. America truly is a unique cultural melting of people co-existing and sharing a belief that anything is possible. Later in the chapter I discuss a few less pleasant downsides. My travels were filled with learning but it's not feasible to tell all those stories. However, our Nescafé experience was special and provides great insights into building and implementing a global brand plan at the beginning of the digital era.

The Nescafé story

Nestlé worked with six global agencies: Dentsu, J. Walter Thompson, Ogilvy, Lowe-Lintas. Publicis, and McCann. They assigned agencies to SBUs and were categorized as lead agencies (strategic and marketing communication planning with SBUs) and aligned agencies (brand implementation in specific geographies and markets) McCann was both an aligned and lead agency with the beverage SBU. As lead agency we had recently launched a successful, comprehensive pan-European Nesquik campaign led by account director Libby Child. Nestlé was in the process of rationalizing agency alignments and the big prize was lead global agency for the beverage SBU's biggest brand, Nescafé. Our competition was Publicis and Dentsu. Our CEO Jim Heekin made it clear he wanted McCann to come out on top and everyone on the global team rose to the occasion. Andrew Ward account director, Lee Daley, Marcio, and I spearheaded the initiative with a clear plan: consumer insights, identify the global opportunity, nail the strategy, purpose-build a power team, WIN, create, and implement.

Lee Daley and Sophie Mellet directed global research using our proprietary consumer insight tool, McCann Pulse™. We talked to thousands of young adults across the globe about their new world of coffee experiences and how they responded to marketing communications. Andrew Ward and I participated in the mainland China research.

China, notwithstanding its tea drinking culture, was a high growth potential market for coffee and Nescafé. Being on the ground in China, engaging with youth, gauging attitudes and acceptance of coffee was an eye-opening experience. We conducted one-on-one in-home interviews with young Chinese consumers in Beijing and Shanghai. They typically lived at home with their parents in cramped quarters but had internet service and connected with the global youth culture. Recently opened Starbucks stores topped their list of special places to socialize with friends when they had the yen and had saved enough yuan. We visited Starbucks locations in Shanghai and Beijing including their newly opened store in the Forbidden City. That was something to see! The vibe in those stores was not much different than a Starbucks in London or LA. McCann teams conducted similar visits in twenty cities around the world. We observed behavior and joined conversations. Two big findings jumped out. Young adults in Beijing and Milan had more in common with young adults in Los Angeles, Dubai, or any other city, than they did with older adults in their home city. They were a global tribe. Coffee was growing in popularity and caché regardless of traditional beverage consumption patterns and ready to breakout as a preferred social beverage for youth.

We presented the findings and insights to the beverage SBU headed by Olle Tegstam and recommended Nescafé step out with a focused, fully integrated global youth marketing communications effort under one powerful proposition: Nescafé is "Life's Agent Provocateur, a youthful catalyst for life's experiences." Marcio and I committed to adding dedicated creative teams and media resources to the Nescafé global team in London and embedding McCann's experiential and digital agencies. We won the lead agency assignment and Nestlé allocated $35 million dollars to support its first ever global campaign for Nescafé![1]

Marcio brought on a great creative team and we got to work on creating a big global brand idea to attract and unite a new generation of Nescafé drinkers. The organizing theme line was "One Thing Leads To Another" (OTLA), reflecting the essential truth that anything might happen over a cup of Nescafé. The campaign explored the catalytic nature of Nescafé as an active participant in the full fabric of young people's lives. We employed ironic humor to stimulate youthful imagination and show how Nescafé made life more interesting.

The centerpiece of the campaign was a series of innovative videos that dramatized stories through flashback sequences. One explained the invention of the famous "Mexican wave" at the 1986 World Cup. The video flashes back to a pair of spectators drinking Nescafé from a thermos flask. One spills his drink, rises to his feet with hands in the air, and makes history. Another execution shows a man winning big at a Las Vegas slot machine. A flashback to earlier

---

1. Nescafé press https://bit.ly/NescaféRelease

in the day shows him drinking a cup of Nescafé outside the casino doors as a glamorous woman arrives and mistaking him for a panhandler, drops the winning coin into his paper cup. A Tibetan monk kisses lipstick marks on a Nescafé mug because he saw a beautiful woman drink from it earlier. Supporting print executions showed provocative snapshots from other stories in which Nescafé was the catalyst—like a bra hanging from a ceiling lightbulb—leaving the viewer to imagine what led to its being there.[2] Enjoy the creativity.

The delivery strategy centered on the single most powerful affinity that unites and excites global youth. No, not sex…music! Campaign deployment involved a powerful combination of integrated marketing communication platforms, including global advertising, a ground-breaking global MTV sponsorship, events, web-based radio, and digital consumer relationship marketing.

The lead element of the program was a strategic alliance with MTV for its largest ever multi-million-dollar, multi-platform sponsorship deal that culminated in the first ever global sponsorship of MTV's Video Music Awards (VMAs). It cut across all the network's international channels in 260 million households in 139 territories. Ironically, the only market to be excluded from the MTV coverage was the USA where Nescafé was secondary to that other Nestlé coffee brand I worked on, Taster's Choice.

The experiential component included Nescafé hosting VMA viewing parties and sponsorship of the Ministry of Sound's deejay world tour. The web-based elements featured two innovative platforms. There was Nescafé Live, a youth focused website community enabling young people around the world to share the music that fuels their lives and Nescafé Pod, a unique web-based message sharing tool. The campaign also included investment in nascent internet radio media. In 2000 legendary radio pioneer and personality Shadoe Stevens started one of the first successful online radio/music companies, Rhythm Radio.[3] His programming premise fit nicely with Nescafé: "The sound of the world in a good mood." Nescafé signed on for year-long sponsorship that helped launch Rhythm Radio but, more importantly, it launched my wonderful, lasting friendship with Shadoe. More to come about that.

It's important to point out that all this happened in 2001—before social media, music streaming, messaging apps, and so on. The Nescafé global youth campaign was on the leading edge of marketing communications and showcased McCann at its global best. Largely because of the Nescafé success, I received the agency's H.K. McCann award for leadership—an honor I proudly accepted on behalf of the entire Nestlé global team. They earned it.

---

2. Nescafé campaign creative. Enjoy. https://bit.ly/NescaféCamp

3. About Rhythm Radio https://bit.ly/Rhythmradio

Tragedy triggers a rethink

Traveling the world was an amazing experience, but being on the road sixty-five percent of the time took its toll. Fatigue and stress made me feel progressively disconnected and anxious. I didn't want a repeat my 1995 bout of anxiety and depression so I made sure I took my meds and eased tension by heading to spas on weekends, attending music concerts, and sightseeing. On one of my trips to Japan, I signed up for Reiki sessions. Reiki is an ancient Tibetan energy channeling and healing practice rediscovered in Japan at the turn of the 20th century and is known for its calming and stress relief benefits.[4] I loved it and took level one training enabling me to practice Reiki on myself. I discovered a great Reiki master in London, Stewart Ivory, and over a few months he attuned me to Reiki levels 2 and 3. I became a Reiki master practitioner and discovered a new spirituality, serenity, and energy. I was coping with stress reasonably well until September 11, 2001.

The 9/11 attacks had a huge impact on me. How I learned of the attacks is an interesting story. Marcio Moreira and I had visited our Moscow office and on 9/11 we were at the airport getting ready to board our British Airways flight back to London. The Moscow airport was overcrowded and disorganized with a lot of cigarette smoking men giving everyone the once-over. Not a very pleasant place. While waiting on a long line to clear Russian customs Marcio received a call letting him know that a plane had hit the World Trade Center. We were shocked and like everyone else thought it was an unfortunate accident. Just as we boarded the plane he received another call letting him know about the second plane. We realized this was not an accident as the plane door closed behind us. The normally three-and-a-half-hour flight took almost six hours and we spent that entire time literally up in the air about what was unfolding. There was radio silence until we landed at Heathrow. Both of us had family living in Manhattan, and my godson Kevin worked at the World Trade Center.

The pilot told us what happened and advised us to expect heightened security as we disembarked. We weren't prepared for what awaited us. There was a massive armed military presence. Clearing customs was a nightmare and connecting with our transportation to London took hours. Marcio had a room booked at the Mandarin Oriental hotel and I returned to my apartment. We reached our families and were relieved that all was okay with family and friends. The lyrics of Joni Mitchell's 1970's anthem, "Big Yellow Taxi," played in my mind.

"Don't it always seem to go, that you don't know what you've got 'til it's gone?"

Marcio and I spent the next two days together processing the attacks and comforting each other. One evening is etched in my memory. We were having drinks at his hotel and there was

---

4. About Reiki https://bit.ly/WhatisReiki

a group of very distraught fellow Americans at the adjacent table. We chatted and discovered they were employees of Cantor Fitzgerald, a financial services firm with offices on the 101st through 105th floors of the North Tower of the World Trade Center.[5] The direct hit of one plane wiped out 658 of their colleagues, 75% of their office. Their sorrow and grief were overwhelming and the gravity of that fateful day hit hard.

Being overseas at this turbulent time was difficult, but over the next few weeks I realized I was fortunate to be in London. Wherever I went, when the Brits learned I was American they greeted me with a supportive hug and an offer to buy me a pint. Believe me, their empathy and kindness helped a lot. On September 21st, I watched the BBC broadcast of the Tribute To Heroes concert followed by the Concert For New York City on October 20th. I was overwhelmed with emotions and cried like a baby. Seeing the families of New York City cops, firemen, and first responders singing, hugging, and crying at Madison Square Garden was especially powerful. My dad, brother, and brother-in-law were NYC firefighters. My post-9/11 time in London ignited a spark of patriotism in me that grew into a flame that still burns bright today.

The world changed on 9/11 and my job perspectives changed with it. The prospect of more intense travel now hung like a grey cloud on the horizon. My sense of adventure and discovery waned and a lingering feeling of homesickness crept in. I seriously questioned whether I wanted to do this any longer. My answer crystalized at the end of October. Jim Heekin removed Don Dillon as EMEA regional director replacing him with McCann London GM Ben Langdon. Ben was a smart, results-oriented manager with a somewhat combative management style. He was one of the best at taking action and getting results but also at bringing out the worst in people and situations. When Ben told me he was planning to be more involved in the Nestlé account, I bristled. I knew our management styles would not mesh and it gave me a little extra nudge to explore ways to ease out of my position and get back to the good old USA. Sometimes it's okay to let your emotional side lead the rational you. Allowing how you feel to inform how you renovate your career requires a conscientious yin-yang thought process. It's worth it.

Stop the world, I want to get off

Act three of my McCann adventure started with some much-needed soul searching. As the global director of McCann's second largest account it was my responsibility to exit professionally and protect the business. My exit plan was to give McCann twelve months' notice so Jim Heekin had ample time to prepare and minimize disruption. I started gathering information about my contract obligations, long-term compensation plans, retirement options, and so on. I

---

5. Cantor Fitzgerald: https://bit.ly/CantFitVid

realized I was at that point in my career where the next few years would most likely be my "last hurrah" and I wanted to finish strong. Should I stay at McCann or take early retirement and play golf or maybe check out what life was like on the farm? (The Concept Farm, of course).

Jim was building his A-team at McCann and I sensed that I was not part of it. I decided to be proactive and in November sought counsel from my friend and go-to guy Kent Kroeber, IPG's HR director. As always, Kent was gracious with his time and suggested I lay all my cards on the table with Jim and see where it goes. I met with Jim the next day, bared my soul, and everything worked out better than I hoped for. First, and most importantly, Jim assured me that I was on his A-team. He wanted me to remain at McCann and John Dooner was in agreement. That meant the world to me. Then, Jim and McCann HR director Donna Borseso went above and beyond to structure a scenario just right for me.

Phase 1: In December 2001, I presented a comprehensive Nestlé business review and twelve-month plan to management that served as a road map for my successor. I would remain in my current position until May 2002, building in more LA time and working with my replacement on a smooth transition. Jim named Joop Broeren, a strong international executive, as my replacement and the transition began. Joop meshed very well with the global team and made a great impression at Nestlé in Vevey.

I scaled down my London living arrangements and in December began a month-to-month lease on a serviced apartment at the Athenaeum hotel in Mayfair (at substantially less cost than the Knightsbridge flat). I developed a new appreciation for hotel living. My apartment was in one of the hotel's adjacent Georgian era townhouses with access to all hotel amenities, daily maid service, and chocolates on my pillow each evening. The hotel's executive director, Sally Bulloch, was famous for arranging cocktail parties for celebrity guests and residents.[6] She befriended me and I was fortunate to be on Sally's invitation list. At one event I met another townhouse resident, Linda Gray, star of the *Dallas* TV series. Linda was appearing in the final run of *The Graduate* in London's West End.[7] She gave me tickets and we chatted periodically about London living, the stress of being away from home, and my Reiki experiences. Linda gave me a copy of *The Power of Now* by Eckhart Tolle—it was a precursor to my embracing Asset-Based Thinking a few years later. We kept in touch after Linda returned to California and our friendship is still going strong today. Stay tuned for more about Linda.

Phase 2 began in May 2002 and was a homerun for me. It included:

> My appointment as Vice Chairman of McCann Worldgroup and board
> member reporting to Jim Heekin.

6. About Sally Bulloch https://bit.ly/SallyBullochAthenaeum

7. Linda Gray https://bit.ly/LGrayGraduate

Being based in McCann New York with flexibility to also work out of the LA office.

A compensation package that included a NYC apartment, car services, country club dues, and a travel budget to accommodate New York/ LA travel.

Approval to work openly with Concept Farm for two days/week if I desired.

A guarantee that my position would remain in place until 2005 so at age sixty-two, I could activate retirement benefits and hopefully maximize the value of my IPG stock options.

If you start questioning your perceived value or where you stand in your job don't keep it internalized. Have proactive, frank conversations with people that matter before you draw your own conclusions. That worked big time for me.

I signed on and recommitted myself to closing out my career with McCann. But not everything was rosy back in New York. McCann's parent company IPG was having financial difficulties and CEO John Dooner was under siege. He had just completed a troubled acquisition of the True North agency when IPG announced a $181 million restatement of earnings covering the prior five years. IPG shares tanked to all-time lows. This affected McCann's executive team in two ways. First, it put even more pressure on revenue growth and profitability. Second, stock options, which were a significant portion of management compensation plans, were now under water—worthless until the stock rebounded.

Nevertheless, I was looking forward to May in the USA.

Coming back to America

In February 2002, Jim Heekin announced three McCann Worldgroup promotions: Eric Einhorn, EVP chief strategy officer; Joe Plummer, EVP director of research and insight development; and Marcio Moreira, already Vice Chairman, added worldwide director of multi-national accounts to his creative director role. My promotion to McCann Worldgroup Vice Chairman, board member, and co-director of multi-national accounts was announced in April. I was in great company and excited to start my next chapter.

I relocated to New York in May, rented a great apartment in Chelsea two blocks from Concept Farm's office, and began dividing my time between New York and LA. For the next seven months I spent the majority of my time working on McCann business so everything would be in place for me to devote two days per week to Concept Farm in 2003. In addition to Nestlé, I took on global responsibilities for Dupont, Bacardi Martini, and Johnson & Johnson. I was especially delighted about J&J since I would again be working with two good friends: Irwin Warren and Claire Roundal. Fortunately, these businesses were well-managed making my transition relatively smooth. I also worked with the management team on rolling out McCann's proprietary insight tools, pitching the agency's experiential (Momentum) and direct marketing (MRM) services to global clients and new business. In December, Nestlé appointed MRM as their aligned agency for consumer relationship management (CRM). It was a nice way to close out the year. My career renovation was progressing well and I was ready to kickstart 2003.

Meanwhile, down on the Farm...

All was well at Concept Farm's Chelsea homestead. The farmers made it through their first year without crises or cash flow issues. In just three years, the seeds planted in Griffin's apartment in the summer of 1999 had grown into a successful boutique creative agency located on a quarter-acre of loft space on West 24th Street in NYC's "Silicon Alley." The office looked and felt like a real farm complete with barn doors rescued from an actual farm, a silo fashioned into a conference room and its own cow. People loved being there.

The dotcom boom was in full bloom, domain name registering was like the Wild West, and the farmers wrangled digital start-up Register.com as a marquis client. Book4Golf.com, an online tee time website, cable media powerhouses ESPN and the History Channel, and NYC electronics retailer the Wiz also signed on as clients. The Farm was turning out bumper crops of award-winning content, developing innovative entertainment properties and its quirky, irreverent website even won a Cannes Cyber Lion.[8] At the end of 2002, there were a dozen farmhands working the fields, revenue was growing, and the balance sheet was strong. They were doing just fine without me and I was looking forward to being a part-time farmer. I just had to be careful not to get in their way.

Happy New Year...really?

Everything was falling into place nicely when an unexpected bombshell exploded. In February 2003, with IPG's financial crisis worsening and continuing stock price decline, the board decided it was time to remove John Dooner as CEO. John was replaced by another director, David Bell, and would return to his prior role as CEO of McCann Worldgroup. And so on

---

8. Concept Farm creative: https://bit.ly/CFCreative1

February 26, one of John's last official acts as IPG CEO was to fire Jim Heekin. [9] Just like that, Jim Heekin became collateral damage.

Wall Street's reaction to John's demotion was "it's about time," while the reaction at McCann was shock and disbelief. Jim was a loved and respected leader with a dedicated loyal cadre of admirers. I was one of them. I was reminded that no matter how high you climb on the ladder of success there are no certainties. Success doesn't guarantee stability and complacency is a luxury few people can afford.

Once again, I would be reporting to John Dooner. I had a lot of respect for John and we shared a long positive history so I was cautiously optimistic about the future. I'd have my answer in about three weeks!

Happy Farmer Wisdom

- Focus on attitude. The world around you changes at lightning speed. You can't control what happens, but you can control your attitude and how you deal with it.
- The only constant is change. Just when you're feeling settled and complacent is usually when the siren call of change is loudest. Whether and how you answer is up to you, so listen carefully.
- Leave an indelible mark. Make sure to stamp any exit with your personal seal of integrity and responsibility.
- Be a shapeshifter. New positions are rarely exactly "as advertised." Turn your surprise into discovery by reshaping yourself to fit the position.
- Build spirituality into your personal and business life. Find what comforts you most and call on it when needed. Breathe.
- Have a yin-yang mindset. Career decisions involve a mix of rational and emotional factors. Find the right balance for you.
- Don't let doubts fester. If concerns about your perceived value in your position creep in, don't keep it all inside. Be proactive. Open up. Have frank conversations with people that matter and reevaluate.
- Blessings are not bound by geography. Appreciate your bounty and heritage whatever your homeland.

---

9. IPGPress: https://bit.ly/DoonerIPG

Marketing Tips & Truisms

Lessons from Nescafé

"The long-term health of any brand is determined by how consumers feel
about it. We are determined that Nescafé will win a special place
in the heart of the global youth community."
—Olle Tegsatm, SVP, Coffee & Beverages Strategic Business Unit, Nestlé S.A.

In 2001, Nescafé's global youth campaign broke new ground. It was a precursor of how brands would leverage and harness the full potential of digital platforms, the mobile web, and the power of a global communications agency network. Here are some lessons from Nescafé that have stood the test of time and are relevant today.

The Good Stuff

Consumer as north star: Everything flowed from insights gathered on the ground, leading to a laser focus on a specific target: youth.

Early collaboration pays dividends: Agency, client, and media were in sync from day one.

Relevant unifying strategic idea: Coffee as catalyst resonated with youth both globally and locally.

Provocative theme: Our "One thing leads to another" line amplified the strategy and provided context for execution, opening up endless creative possibilities._

Integrated seamless content development: All agency disciplines partic-ipated and contributed from the outset. Today it's called omni-channel marketing communications.

Affinity-based media delivery strategy: Our narrow-first, broader-later focus heightened impact.

Local market creativity: Smaller markets with limited budgets are often the most fertile ground for creative applications of global campaigns. Bigger isn't always better.

The Not So Good

Mission creep: Some markets expanded the campaign to older demographics resulting in less effective deployment.

Rigid prescriptive execution requirements: Initially the use of the reverse flashback format restricted local creativity. We learned our lesson to leave room for interpretation.

"Not invented here" pushback: The NIH response was more evident on the McCann side than Nestlé. Practice in the art of persuasion helps.

Chapter 13 Footnotes
Scan QR codes for direct links to footnote content.

13.1 Nescafe Release

13.2 Nescafe Campaign Video

13.4 What is Reiki

13.5 Cantor Fitzgerald

13.7 Linda Gray Graduate

13.8 Concept Farm Creative

13.9 Dooner Exits IPG

Chapter 14:

Today's Reversal, Tomorrow's Rebirth

I confidently entered the new millennium with a crystal-clear vision of my career's final chapter. I liked how the book was going to end. But a scant two years later my vison was blurred by unforeseen, extenuating circumstances and it rapidly became opaque. The plans for my future, created with then-McCann CEO Jim Heekin were now in the hands of its former and once again CEO, John Dooner. I soon realized that my just-right graceful exit was being callously edited into a premature, unwelcome shove out the door.

It was a dramatic reversal that I ultimately overcame with a "fight for my rights" posture, a good lawyer, and a friendly intervention. Nevertheless, the experience left me with an unhealthy dose of anger and resentment. I eventually plowed through that negativity with a much healthier mix of tough (self) love and an enlightenment reboot.

Now I was ready for a new life at Concept Farm. Life on the Farm turned out to be much more than a job at an agency. It was a reawakening, a resurgence, a reinvention…my rebirth. Sure, a nasty change of plans is never welcome. But it just goes to show that with a healthy attitude and the support of others, a reversal can be the catalyst for your rebirth.

The king is dead, long live the king.

First, a quick recap. In February 2003, the board of McCann's parent company IPG decided it was time to remove John Dooner as its CEO. John stepped back into his former role CEO of McCann Worldgroup, giving Jim Heekin the boot. *Ouch.*

John wasted no time getting down to business. On Monday March 4, he convened a meeting of the McCann Worldgroup board, all twenty of us. It was an awkward, somber, and short meeting. People were still stunned and many were suspicious about the "why." Did John orchestrate this move back to McCann to save his own ass? Was Jim taking the fall for IPG's poor stock market performance?

John addressed the suddenness of the changes and explained that it was the decision of the IPG board, made in the best interest of both IPG and McCann Worldgroup. John acknowledged the skepticism and uneasiness at McCann and that some people were distraught over Jim's departure. He closed the meeting with a typically Dooner statement. He told us to take a day or two "mourning period" then get over it and get to work. And that's what we did… though the atmosphere was anything but gung ho.

The beginning of the end

There were two distinct groups at McCann at that time: the Jims (devasted over his departure) and the Johns (looking forward to his return and the old days). I had a foot firmly in both camps. I respected John and we had a great relationship. I had also enjoyed working with Jim, admired his leadership, new business talents, and was appreciative of what he did to keep me at McCann. The day after the meeting, I sent John a memo assuring him that I wanted to play hard on his team. I provided thoughts on how I could contribute and observations about the pros and cons of the current operation and staffing. I also called Jim to let him know that he would be missed. I wished him the best and we agreed to keep in touch.

On March 25, I had scheduled a meeting with John and was looking forward to having private time with him. I walked into his office thinking it would be a, "How you doin' Hank?" chat and discussion of my memo. It started out that way but then, John looked me squarely in the eye and said he thought it was time for me retire, to make room for the next generation. And there was the sonic Boomer Boom. *Where the hell did that come from?*

My reaction was shock and disbelief and I made it very clear to John that retirement was not on my list of considerations. That surprised him. John said he didn't realize I'd feel that way and suggested we get together again in about a month. I left puzzled and, the more I thought about it, the more my negative feelings towards John's out-of-the blue suggestion intensified. I was at the top of my game with forty years of experience and wisdom under my belt. I (still) had a fire in my belly and was ready to rock'n'roll with the best of them. Being told to move on and make room for the next generation hit hard. Hell, all my life I was the next generation…what happened? Savvy, experience, energy, and vision are not reasons to be put out to pasture! I was hopeful that John and I could work out a mutually beneficial solution that would keep me at McCann.

Lawyering up…lightly

I discussed the situation with my friend and McCann colleague Irwin Warren. He recommended an employment lawyer he had used in his recent McCann contract negotiations, Jonathan Sack. I hired him. The first thing Jonathan floated was threatening an aged-based wrongful dismissal suit. I ruled that out. Not my style and, hopefully, it wouldn't come to that. We agreed that going forward I wouldn't make a move without consulting with him *and* documenting every conversation.

A week later, I travelled to Mexico for a Nestlé regional meeting. While at the meeting, on April 8, I received a call from my friend and management colleague, Joe Plummer. He said that John told him I was leaving McCann and asked if I was okay. No *bueno*. I thanked Joe, hung up, and seethed. So much for our continuing conversation! I booked a meeting with John for April 22. My attorney suggested that prior to the meeting, I send John an email about Joe's call and my concerns. Here's the email I sent to John, verbatim. Yes, I saved a copy. (Words of wisdom: Always save a copy!)

John:

Glad that I'm on your calendar today it's important since I'm confused about where things stand.

When we met on March 25th you raised the issue of my considering retirement. I told you I was very surprised by that suggestion given the fact that the company talked me out of doing just that about a year ago. At that time I was asked to make a commitment to stay with McCann as vice chairman of Worldgroup. I did and completely rearranged my personal, professional, and financial lives and hunkered down here at McCann for the long haul. You said that you didn't realize that I would feel that way and wanted to regroup with me to continue our discussion and work things out.

While I was in Mexico last week I received a call from Joe Plummer in which he mentioned that in a discussion with him, you told Joe that I would be stepping down at McCann. Joe wanted to see how I was and if there was anything he could do to help. I appreciated his concern but his statements completely took me by surprise. John, I need to know what decisions have been made since we spoke and who knows what.

Thanks,
Hank

John and I had a cordial, no-nonsense meeting, where he confirmed that I was being shoved out the door into retirement. He was reshaping his management team and didn't need two Vice Chairmen. He said he had no other alternative. Marcio Moreira was in and I was out. End of discussion. In fact, John had also added an HR function to Marcio's duties.

John asked me to contact IPG's current HR director to work out the details. My friend and counselor, Kent Kroeber, had retired from IPG at the end of 2002, so I was now in the hands of his replacement, Brian Brooks, whom I'd never met. This was a one-two punch: The rug was being pulled out from under me *and* the ceiling was collapsing on top of me. Suddenly, all my carefully worked out plans were reversed and the timing could not have been worse. I was sixty and exiting McCann at that age would mean substantial financial setbacks:

worthless underwater IPG stock options, cancelling of other deferred compensation, and severely reduced retirement and medical benefits. I was now fighting for my financial future and the well-being of my family—a battle I had not been expecting. My "exit gracefully, leave a positive bridge" mindset was out, and my more aggressive self-directed stance was in. The details of the negotiations and my separation agreement are not important, but McCann's mismanagement of my swansong is a lesson in what not to do. Here's the timeline:

April 23

I met with IPG HR director Brian Brooks and recounted the entire saga, since he didn't know any of the facts. All he did was listen. Brian was obviously not prepared and said he would get back to me. Everything went downhill from there.

April 25

I was surprised to be visited by Marcio Moreira, the newly appointed HR Director. Marcio said he was the "conduit" for John and Brian and handed me a sheet of paper outlining a proposed separation agreement and release document. Just two weeks ago, Marcio was my co-Vice Chairman. Now I was negotiating my future with him. Surreal. I scanned the document and told Marcio it fell woefully short of what I was led to believe would happen, breached prior agreements, and was extremely upsetting and disappointing.

April 29

I provided McCann a formal response document that my lawyer Jonathan Sack and I had drafted. (Sidenote: It was also my oldest son's birthday. Not exactly what I wanted to be doing on that day.)

April 30

Marcio countered with a proposal, which he said he had decided on. It was a marginal improvement. So much for Marcio's being a conduit.

May 2

I met with John Dooner again, elaborated once again on my frustrations and distress and presented him with my wish list, which I also sent to Marcio. John said he would review it with IPG.

May 7

I received a slightly revised proposal from Marcio, which, as you can probably guess by now, was not in line with my requirements. I told him all future discussions would be with my attorney.

After six weeks of disappointing and frustrating conversations, I was still in limbo and without any direct follow-up from Brian Brooks. I was tired of being jerked around. Boy, did I miss Kent Kroeber. I was pissed. I was distressed about the uncertainty and frustrated at my inability to make future plans. What had transpired was reprehensible. But what happened next was remarkable.

A divine (and kind) intervention

On May 15, Vicki and I were in Los Angeles attending the wedding of Jeff Weller, son of Joe Weller, CEO of Nestlé, USA. The guests were all family and friends with one table of Joe's close business friends. Carlos Represas (Joe's boss) and his wife; Al Stefl (Nestlé SVP) and his wife Joan; Bob Bloom (CEO of Publicis USA) and his wife; and Vicki and I were all seated together. We knew each other well and enjoyed celebrating Jeff's special day. Joe, Al, and Carlos pulled me aside for a private chat and asked how things were going with my "retirement" from McCann. They were aware it wasn't my choice. How's that for a wedding surprise? I didn't go into any specifics but mentioned that it was a very bumpy road. I told them I had to hire a lawyer and was having difficulty exiting with my head held high. That's it. I mentioned it to Vicki and we both were very touched by their concern.

When I returned to McCann the next week, I received a call from Joe Weller that absolutely blew me away. Joe told me he had called John Dooner to express dismay and concern about how McCann was handling my exit. My despair turned to hope. I still get emotional recounting it all these years later. I took notes back then so I can relate in detail what Joe communicated to John:

> *Joe Weller and Carlos Represas had a follow up chat about my situation and felt compelled to call John. Joe explained to John that only four outside family people were invited to his son's wedding: me, Carlos Repressas, Al Stefl, and Bob Bloom. He, Carlos, and many others at Nestlé view me as a very close friend as well as business partner on whom they have come to rely…they value the relationship very highly. He and Carlos were quite upset that I will be leaving McCann. John told Joe that he couldn't come up with any solutions to create a new role for me. Joe said that was unfortunate since as far as they are concerned I am the go-to guy on Nestlé. Whenever they needed or need anything at McCann I was/am their man and have always delivered. They were even more upset and unhappy that I was not being treated right and fairly on the way out. John replied that he and I are friends, that he also values my contributions and thought they*

were working with me. Joe reiterated that Nestlé values people as much as they do companies and want people that work with/for them to be treated well. He told John that long after Hank leaves McCann I will remain a close friend of his, Carlos, and others and they will be very unhappy if I am not treated well. They had a long memory and would not forget how this was resolved. Joe told John I was not aware he would be calling him.

Wow! What a wonderful gesture of caring and support from my Nestlé friends. After Joe's call, I closed the door, sat completely still in my office, and reflected on what had just transpired. I was blessed to have such good friends. Joe's call reaffirmed my belief in the goodness of people and the value and joy of the human side of business. Joe gave me the shot of adrenaline I needed to reenergize and persist. Joe Weller did this for me because that's just who Joe is: a principled businessman, an amazing leader, and a good friend. A true role model.

The next day, a not-too-happy John Dooner called me. Agency CEOs don't like getting surprise calls of this nature from their second largest clients. He told me that Joe had called him and asked me why I ran complaining to Joe. I pushed back. I explained that I did not bring it up nor did I go into any details and that I was touched by how strongly they felt about my well-being. I told John that I had no choice but to give them a straight answer, that's who I am, and wished I could have said everything was just fine. I closed the conversation by telling John that McCann's approach was "how little can we get away with," that he had brushed me aside and disavowed his commitment to do the right thing. That's where we left it.

Joe's call cleared the bureaucratic log jams and negotiations progressed more swiftly and smoothly. I didn't get everything on my wish list and took a hit on stock options, but my retirement benefits would remain intact and I was comfortable enough with the separation agreement. We officially announced my retirement in July 2003 with a positive spin. In the press release, I said it was my decision to leave to be a consultant working with my son, Gregg, at Concept Farm. We received some good coverage and I particularly liked the *Adweek* headline, "Like Son. Like Father. At the Concept Farm the tree doesn't grow far from the apple."[1] I called Joe Weller to let him know how everything worked out and again expressed my deep appreciation for unswerving support. I did the same with Carlos Represas. I just can't overstate the important role that positive connections will play in your career. From small encouraging expressions of support to big gestures like Joe's, they all mean something and usually happen organically without your asking. Appreciate them as they come your way and go out of your way to do the same for others. They are priceless.

---

1. Hank Farm: https://bit.ly/HankFarm

In hindsight

Later, with the passage of time and in the cold hard light of day, I came to the realization that, given the circumstances, John made the prudent decision. Marcio had a much deeper history with McCann, making me more expendable. Marcio and I harbored no hard feelings and our friendship weathered the storm. My antipathy wasn't because I was put out to pasture before my time—that's life in business and I could deal with that. My source of anger and disappointment was IPG's cavalier disregard for prior commitments and John's arm's length dealings with me. John and I had been through a lot together, shoulder to shoulder. I deserved better and the John I knew was better than that. John's turbulent time as IPG CEO had changed him. Gladly, our friendship endured. People may change but fond memories don't.

My second time around with McCann lasted eight years—a long run in this business. While the end wasn't as I would have scripted, I overcame the reversal, and kept my positive bridge intact as I closed the book on a twelve-year relationship. I also came to grips with the fact that my traditional agency or corporate career as I knew it was over. There wasn't much demand for a sixty-year-old "mad man" in the digital frenzy that was happening in the business. I found myself standing at the edge of an uncertain and fuzzy future.

I was blessed to have the support of my family, good friends, a reservoir of new experiences waiting for me, and the opportunity to reimagine my business life down on the Farm. But before I could jump in and make the most of it all, I had to clear my head, let go of resentments and rebuild my confidence. That took some work. Luckily, I like work.

Remember this. Every career decision that is made by you or for you will cause a ripple effect in your life and those around you. You alone have the power to make sure they are positive and persistent ripples of growth.

McCann postscript: John stayed at the helm of McCann until his retirement in 2010 and was inducted into the Advertising Hall of Fame in 2019. I sent him a congratulatory note.[2] Jim continued his very successful career with a stint as CEO of Euro RSG and a stellar fourteen-year run as CEO of Grey advertising before his retirement in 2019. Jim would peek back into my life a few years later and we still keep in touch.[3]

Clearing my head to clear my path

For the first few months, my mind was racing with resentment and anger. It was a roadblock keeping me from moving on. I had to get over it and used Reiki as my release mechanism. In November, I achieved Reiki's highest level–Reiki Master Teacher–to intensify my healing

---

2. https://bit.ly/DoonerAdHallofFame

3. Heekin Retires: https://bit.ly/HeekinRetires

and energy capacity. I booked a weekend attunement and initiation session with a wonderful Reiki Master, Locopal Durham, at his upstate New York home in the Catskills. It was an intense three days with my share of out-of-body experiences. The strongest thing I drank was herbal tea. That weekend pushed me past pent-up negativity so I could focus my attention and intention on what lies ahead. It also did something else. I now viewed Reiki as a powerful "give-back" gift I had received and searched for ways to pay it forward.[4]

I read how Reiki was being utilized successfully by nurses at Sloan Kettering hospital and I was touched by accounts of its particularly wonderful effects on sick children. I contacted the head nurse at their alternative medicine group and she suggested I contact Ronald McDonald House. I called my old friend, Vivian Harris, fellow Boy Scout board member, and founder of the Ronald McDonald House in NYC, and she introduced me to the director, Ralph Vogel.

Again, my friends came through for me. I was immediately welcomed into an incredibly dedicated community of volunteers and caregivers. For three years, whenever I was in New York, I visited the House on East 73rd Street, usually two or three evenings per month. Each visit, I spent about four hours doing stress relief and centering work with the amazing families of the kids in treatment and healing work with the kids themselves. I flashed back fifteen years to meeting Ryan White, the young AIDS victim and activist, and his mom at that *People* magazine gala and thanked God our family did not have to endure such pain. The strength, courage, and faith of the children and their families was inspiring, empowering and most of all, humbling. Impossible to put into words. An editor at *Ad Age* heard about what I was doing and she told my story in the publication's *After Hours* feature. That felt spectacular.[5] Vivian was my positive bridge to the past that made it possible.

I encourage everyone to be on the lookout for your own "give-back" gift. It can be anything—a skill, time, your passion, compassion, your friendship, but it must be something that is uniquely you. You will make a difference, inspire others and yourself and it can be a powerful force in your life. As the kids at Ronald McDonald would say to me about Reiki: "May the force be with you!"

Only in New York

For the next few years I continued my bi-costal life but my McCann exit came with the loss of our subsidized NYC apartment and the need to downsize. As the planets aligned, we leased a coveted apartment at the infamous Chelsea Hotel, frequented by rock legends, artists, writers, and counter-culture misfits.[6] Leonard Cohen wrote his hit song, "Chelsea Hotel," while living there. Renting

---

4. Reiki certificates & brochure https://bit.ly/HankReiki

5. *After Hours* Article https://bit.ly/HankAftHrs

6. Chelsea Hotel: https://bit.ly/InsideChelsea

one of these apartments was as rare as finding a four-leaf clover and required screening and approval by its colorful owner and manager, Stanley Bard. Luckily, we hit a stroke of luck.

I was interviewing film maker and director Abel Ferrara in the Chelsea lobby for Concept Farm's TV show, *Cool In Your Code* (more about that later). Abel had just completed his documentary film about the hotel, *Chelsea on the Rocks*.[7] Stanley Bard was also there so I inquired about a lease. I guess he thought this former mad man would fit in with the misfits and Stanley made me an offer I couldn't refuse: a studio apartment on the top floor, room 1010, for $2000 per month (an absolute steal) and we could fix it up to our liking. For the past thirty years the prior leasee, poet and theater critic Stafan Brecht, had used it as his studio. It was in desperate need of a make-over but I had the vision.[8]

We signed the lease and, for the next few years, enjoyed a never-a-dull moment life at the Chelsea with its eclectic guests, eccentric residents, Serena's disco in the basement, and the storied El Quijote restaurant right downstairs. I was back to hotel living but it was a far cry from the Athenaeum in London. This was the quintessential, quirky, crazy, slightly seedy, uniquely New York experience. I loved it. The stories could fill another book.

Sadly, Stanley was ousted as manager of his beloved Chelsea hotel by his partners so they could prop it up for a sale. This caused a residents' revolt but we kept our lease throughout the ensuing chaos until 2010. I stayed in touch with Stanley until his passing in 2011 and am forever grateful to him for making this Chelsea memory possible.[9] The Chelsea was purchased by BD Hotels Inc. and is still under renovation. It will never be the same.

My best was up next

Being pushed from McCann's boardroom to the Farm's barnyard was the best thing that could happen to a Mad Man like me. In the post-McCann years I was blessed with more meaningful work, productivity, personal fulfillment, determination, joy, and humility than I could ever have imagined.

When I took up residence at Concept Farm homestead, the agency was in its fourth year, bountiful, and ready for its next stage of growth. But the Farm was their gig, the farmers were on a roll, and the last thing they needed was for me to be a "disruption in their force." I was almost twice their age, so we had to find the right balance. The partners had to run the business, service clients, and generate an amazing depth and breadth of creative work day in and day out. We focused on two distinctly different assets I could contribute:

---

7. *Chelsea on the Rocks* Trailer https://bit.ly/ChelRocks

8. Chelsea Life https://bit.ly/ChelLife

9. Stanley Bard: https://bit.ly/SBard

Experience: Been-there-done-that advice; new business development; and "gravitas" when they needed it.

Vision: Fueled by my passion and energy to explore, take risks, and be a "future scout."

I was the perfect "yin" to their collectively brilliant "yang." Ironically, the attributes considered of little value at a big established agency—namely, trying to be "young"—were highly valued at a young, start-up company on the cutting edge of marketing communications. There is a big lesson to learn here and is best summed by the adage: "One man's rubbish is another man's treasure." Or if you prefer the lyrical wisdom of Paul Simon: "One man's ceiling is another man's floor." Yeah, they're both a bit sexist, but they also succinctly convey a powerful message. You always have assets and talents to contribute. Always. They are not defined by your job or position. They are what makes you "you."

I eagerly embraced new challenges and roles at the Farm. But first, I had to forget my big agency "city slicker" talk, learn "farmer speak" and embrace the Farm vibe. Farm "stuff" adorned the office and farm metaphors were creatively infused in Concept Farm's communications and promotional materials. It was and still is an integral part of the Farm's brand personality. Organic thinking. Rolling up your sleeves and getting dirty with clients.

The team gave me the tile of *Wisdom Farmer* (perfect) and put me to work plowing the fields and planting seeds of the future. The rest of the decade was a whirlwind of productivity yielding bushels of bumper crops of creativity and accolades that filled five silos of farm life experiences. (See what I mean?) The stories in these silos are linked by common threads of connections and relationships—past connections that lit up my life again and serendipitous new relationships that led to unexpected adventures and new "old friends." Recounting them reminded me of the wisdom and fun of Nescafé's global youth campaign, "One Things Leads To Another." Now, rather than Nescafé being "life's agent provocateur," my youthful change catalyst was the progressive energy of Concept Farm.

So much happened in that time and it's simply not possible to squeeze it all into these pages. I'll open each silo and highlight what stands out most to me.

Agency Crops	Content Emmy Awards	Heartfelt Volunteer	Finding My Voice	Asset-Based Thinking

Silo 1: Ad agency crops

Over the remainder of the decade, the Farm dramatically expanded its A-list client roster. Income tripled and acreage increased with two additional floors. We added in-house end-to-end video production capabilities (Production Farm) and bushels of creative awards filled the shelves. But since Concept Farm did not offer media services, we needed to establish a solid relationship with an independent, like-minded media agency. Here again the solution came across one of those positive bridges to my past.

My friend Dennis Holt had left IPG's Western International Media and founded a new media agency, US International Media (USIM). I had complete confidence in Dennis and knew that he and his company could be a great media partner. I made the introduction, everything clicked, and USIM remains Concept Farm's trusted media partner to this day.

In 2004, the farmers took a big step by adding two new "pardners": Ray Mendez, Gregg's creative director partner at TBWA/Chiat Day, and Ray's colleague Blake Olson. Both had been working at DDB and they soon were able to win one of their past clients, The Bank of New York, over to Concept Farm. Blake and Ray were now equity partners in the Farm and each of the five partners gave up part of their share.[10] We were now seven partners and a staff of forty navigating a dynamic growth period and adapting our roles accordingly. Bringing in new partners was the right move at the time but, as it happens in business, seven partners eventually recalibrated back to five. More about that next chapter.

In 2008, Concept Farm was featured in *Ad Age's* 63rd annual agency report as the newest and fastest growing agency on their top 100 list. Here's how they reported it. They even used "farmer speak!"

"With a nearly seventy-one percent jump in revenue last year, The Concept Farm plowed its way up to #96 on *Advertising Age's* annual ranking of the nation's largest advertising agencies–making it the fastest growing U.S. agency."

The Farm's client roster grew bigger and better each year. Here's a list of some of the friends of the farm:

ESPN: Selected over Weiden & Kennedy and Ground Zero to create a year-long celebration of the fan for ESPN's 25th anniversary.

Windstream: The billion-dollar communications "start-up" that was formed from Nextel. The Farmers would have this client for over an

---

10. Partner portrait https://bit.ly/FarmPortrait

eight-year run.

BMW Motorcycles: The Farmer's had former automotive experience and revved up BMW Motorrad sales.

Bank of New York: Brand and retail marketing for all the retail branches. Also, the Farm was the agency that orchestrated the communications for the powerhouse merger between Bank of New York and Mellon bank, forming BNY Mellon.

James Patterson: The world's best-selling author tapped the Concept Farm to help promote his steady stream of books. Positive bridge to the past: James Patterson was also Gregg and Griffin's former boss and mentor when Jim was the President of J. Walter Thompson Advertising.

The National Women's Law Center: Concept Farm created moving and motivating content to illuminate the inequity for women in the healthcare system. Their campaign phrase, "Being A Woman Is Not A Pre-existing Condition," was used by Nancy Pelosi in her speech in Congress on the Senate floor.

TRW: One of the world's largest manufacturers of auto safety parts, Concept Farm created their brand look, feel, essence, and advertising campaigns.

Nestlé: Bested other NUSA agencies and won assignment to create a big-tent digital program to unify and enhance Nestlé's health and well-being initiatives with moms (with a little help from one Wisdom Farmer).

Healthy Monday: We had the opportunity to play a small part in the birth of a movement in which "all health breaks loose" and for me to reconnect with a beloved mad man.

It was a dynamic, bountiful period as the farmers turned out truckloads of celebrated, effective creative work.[11] For all but two of these wins, I watched from the barn, providing

---

11. Farm creative reel https://bit.ly/2I5rmo3

advice when needed while my partners did all the heavy lifting. It was exciting and gratifying to watch. I was proud. However, I did step out of the barn and strap on the good overalls to win and subsequently manage Nestlé and Healthy Monday. Both came to the Farm because of my positive bridges to the past.

The Nestlé seed blooms

My Nestlé relationship was a career gift that just kept on giving…and it still does. My friend Joe Weller retired at the end of 2005 and was replaced by long-time NUSA executive Brad Alford. Al Stefl stayed on as SVP communications to help Brad transition into his new role. In the summer of 2006, I received a call from my friend Al that turned out to be a bit more than just a catch-up chat. Al asked if Concept Farm would be interested in pitching a special corporate assignment. Nestlé had asked their current agencies for proposals but weren't satisfied with the output. That brightened this new farmer's spirits. *Yeehaw!*

We set up a follow-up briefing with the project manager, Jackie Lilley, NUSA's VP marketing communications and her number two, Mark Leavens. I knew Jackie well and was eager to collaborate with her. She had a great track record at Nestlé, was a smart, buttoned-up manager, and a tough taskmaster. The assignment was a big, challenging opportunity. Here's the essence of the brief:

> *Nestlé's global brand mantra and signature is "Good Food. Good Life." NUSA had launched a family well-being initiative directed at moms centered around the concept of "togetherness over food." The objective was to unify brand activity on the web under a synergistic, big-tent mom-centric umbrella concept. We were asked to provide recommendations for a linked web strategy for NUSA brands, a new website platform (name, architecture, etc.), content strategy, creative concepts, deployment plans, and key performance indicators (KPIs).*

This was the real deal! The farmers dug deep, stepped up big time and won the assignment. It was a powerful, comprehensive plan choreographed around purpose-built consumer-facing extranet and internal intranet portals. We created gatheround.com as the organizing resource and hub for "togetherness over food." It was conceived as a community site that was human, selfless, and dedicated to the emotional and functional needs of moms and of their families' well-being.

The Nestlé intranet component of gatheround.com was perhaps the more innovative element and was first to launch for two reasons. First, extranet deployment required much longer lead times and complex coordination with brands. Second and most importantly, an employees-first mindset was at the core of NUSA's management ethos. I knew this first-hand. NUSA fully embraced the concept of humanizing the company and its brands and committed to "living it on the inside before taking it outside." We plowed full speed ahead and launched the intranet in mid-2007 while continuing development of the extranet. Concept Farm managed the backend development, frontend content, and KPI analytics.

The internal gatheround.com was a high-involvement mini-site that lived on the company's global intranet (Nikita). It was for employees by employees—a robust, sustainable community employees perceived as their own. They enthusiastically took center stage as the face and emcees of Gatheround. The Farm created and managed weekly content calendars and produced themed content such as kid's art shows, recipe contests, and employees of the week. We created and programmed (Nestlé TV) with high-interest employee stories, entertaining short video messages, and employee created videos. Nestlé employees would be content creators, future brand ambassadors, and influencers for the consumer facing extranet.[12]

It's important to remember that this was before employee collaboration platforms such as Slack and Facebook Messenger. Gatheround was very ahead of its time and by all measures, it was a great success! It grew steadily until the mothership in Vevey, Switzerland, intervened at the end of 2008. So much for the Swiss being neutral. In an effort to better organize, consolidate, and safeguard its global intranet, Nikita, Nestlé headquarters requested that local markets cease and desist from supplemental extensions such as Gatheround. As a result, NUSA's Gatheround community was phased out and the extranet launch was cancelled. Another one of those "sh** happens" moments that happen in agency life. Disappointing, yes. Regretful, no.

Both Concept Farm and I reaped the rewards of the Nestlé partnership. It was a source of new friends of the Farm, healthy revenue, and facilitated the infusion of additional web development resources. I believe it was some of our best work and added a powerful case history to the Farm's credentials silo. Personally, it was a dramatic, big stakes, validation of my positive bridge and an immense source of pride to watch the young farmhands connect and work so well with Nestlé. It was also an opportunity for me to reconnect with many good friends and once again, roam the halls of Nestlé's Glendale, CA, offices.

During that period, Al Stefl retired from Nestlé but he and I weren't quite finished yet. Al was appointed as executive professor of marketing at Pepperdine University's Graziadio Graduate School of Business. He brought a wealth of experience to their program and invited me to be a guest lecturer in his class. I was honored and thrilled. I did that twice and it rekindled the teaching flame still smoldering in me. Thanks again, Al. Stay tuned for more on how that unfolded.

---

12. Gatheround: https://bit.ly/Ngatheround

My Monday doorway

The Healthy Monday assignment was quite different than Nestlé, but it too emanated from a special past connection. This was my party like it's 1965 moment. Remember my creative mentor from the Mad Men days at Benton & Bowles, Sid Lerner? Sid had a long creative career after B&B, authored seven books and later in his life took on a role as public health advocate and philanthropist. My kind of guy.[13] Over the years Sid and I kept in touch. We still do. Recently, when I spoke to Sid about this book he told me how he flashed back to 1968 and a-babyface-account-man (me) and an older copywriter (him) in the backyard of a Met supermarket in Flushing, Long Island, playing boxball between takes of a Mr. Whipple commercial. Sid won. Now that's a special mad man memory.

Health education and advocacy had become Sid's passion, and in 2003 he conceived and launched the *Meatless Monday* campaign—a push to encourage healthier eating by cutting out meat one day a week. The simple creative brilliance of that campaign powered by Sid's relentless evangelism created a global social movement that is now in fifty different countries! Then in 2005, Sid came back into my life in a very big way.

Building on Meatless Monday's success Sid created Healthy Monday with Monday as the rallying call for fresh healthy starts like smoking cessation, better nutrition, physical activity, and stress management. I loved Sid's line: "Monday: The Day All Health Breaks Loose." I was delighted when Sid hired the Farm for a short-term assignment to help build out the concept, brainstorm ideas, and create compelling content. Watching Sid work with and inspire our young farmers to put their creativity against this initiative was a treat for me. We developed some solid work together and the Farm was fortunate to play a small role in what is known today as the Monday Campaigns.[14]

But this re-connection was just the precursor to a much bigger impact that Sid would have on my life. Sid's advocacy and philanthropy work connected him with a number of government agencies and non-profit organizations. One day, Sid invited me to a meeting he scheduled with the American Heart Association's New York chapter to discuss Healthy Monday. I had no idea of how fateful and fruitful that meeting would be to me. More on that in the next chapter.

My big agency life was quickly fading in the rear-view mirror and I was down on the Farm filling silos with experiences and relationships. As you've read, the agency silo contained munificent crops, but they were essentially extensions of the things I had been doing throughout my career. Fantastic, yet familiar territory. The other four silos held experiences and relationships that were fresh, exhilarating and transformational as you'll read.

---

13. Sid Lerner Video https://bit.ly/sLerner

14. Monday Campaigns https://bit.ly/MondayHealth

As a wise person once said: "Don't limit your challenges. Challenge your limits."

Happy Farmer Wisdom

- Don't take it personally. Circumstances can change people and the way they see you, but not who you are.
- One man's ceiling is another man's floor. When rejection rears its head play Paul Simon's song and remember you always have something to offer.
- Support from friends and colleagues are invaluable assets. Cherish those that come your way and always pay it forward.
- Find your Reiki place. Visit it regularly to clear your head and sharpen your vision. Get grounded in you. And then...
- Occasionally check-in to your Chelsea hotel—whatever and wherever it is. Hang out with the crazy ones once in a while. Add a little pizzazz to your perspective.
- Sh*t happens. If your best work falls victim to a "sh*t happens" moment don't be dejected. Lessons learned and experiences gained will stay with you forever.
- There are always new doors to open. Don't linger outside any one doorway too long.
- Appreciate your assets every day: self, others, and situation. Watch how fast they appreciate.

Marketing Truisms & Tips

Humanizing Brands From The Inside Out

Nestlé's Gatheround intranet was, in some ways, a precursor to what is known today as the humanization of brands. I touched on elements of humanization in the Marketing Truisms and Tips sections of chapters four (Values) and five (Culture).

> "Living up to and into brand **values** differentiate power brands from the run-of-the mill. Inwardly, values create culture. Outwardly, they define your brand. Hence, the importance of living it on the inside before taking it outside."

> "**Culture** embodies how a company operates, why people want to work

there, the reasons partners enjoy doing business with them, and why customers trust and purchase from them. It must be defined and led from the top and then liberated to permeate every nook and cranny of the company."

In 2012, I was a guest speaker at my friend Jeff Pulver's Power of Now Conference at the 92nd Street Y in New York. I loved the vibe at Jeff's events…high energy, upbeat, and forward looking. The title of my talk was, "The Future of Branding: Humanization."[15] I made the point that the humanization of brands had to actually encompass what makes us human: mind, body, and soul. The soul—the "why"—was increasingly becoming the key driver, I went on. Humanization was moving more towards spiritualization—not in a religious sense but as a succinct, sincere expression of a brand's higher purpose, its reason for being. It goes much deeper than a brand rushing to embrace social causes. It requires opening up and inviting people in to experience the brand and company culture. Think of it as a personalized, one-on-one "factory tour."

I summed up humanization as a deftly choreographed mix of four things: brand purpose and values, company culture, individual employee ambassadors, and social community. That's still true today, but I've since added a fifth: *technology*.

The growing sophistication of artificial intelligence (AI), augmented reality (AR), and smarter chat bots are opening up new avenues of enhanced personalization. But, *caveat emptor*: Brands cannot overuse and abuse these tools; they should be enhancers not substitutes. Humanization starts at the top with committed leaders and requires a meticulous, adroit approach to hiring. This quote from one of my favorite CEOs captures this perfectly.

"We believe that it's really important to come up with core values that you can commit to. And by commit, we mean that you're willing to hire and fire based on them. If you're willing to do that, then you're well on your way to building a company culture that is in line with the brand you want to build." —Tony Hsieh, CEO, Zappos

---

15. Recording of my talk, "The Future of Branding: Humanization" https://bit.ly/BrandHum

Chapter 14 Footnotes
Scan QR codes for direct links to footnote content.

14.1 Hank Farm

14.3 Heekin Retires

14.4 Reiki

14.5 After Hours

14.6 Chelsea Hotel

14.7 Chelsea On Rocks

14.8 My Chelsea

14.9 Stanley Bard

14.10 Partner Portrait

14.11 TCF Reel 2

14.12 Gatheround

14.13 Sid Video

14.14 Monday Campaigns

14.15 Brand Humanization

Chapter 15:

From Know Your Limits to Test Your Limits

At the Farm, I was plowing new fields that required tapping into different skills, learning new methods, and increasing my risk tolerance. I had to quiet that "know your limits" voice in my mind. In Asset-Based Thinking it's called a deficit-based mindset. Sometimes it took the prodding and confidence of others to push it aside, and other times I rose to the occasion on my own. Regardless of how I got there, testing my limits to expand my capacity worked wonders. I surprised myself with how many projects and the types of projects I was able to take on.

It was an action-packed few years that required a pretty hectic bi-coastal lifestyle and my wife Vicki and I decided it was time to simplify and downsize. In 2004, we sold our west coast home in Hancock Park and took what we thought would be a short-term rental in one of LA's famous landmark buildings–the El Royale, an iconic old building that over the years was home to some of Hollywood's biggest names.[1] We seemed to be drawn to storied landmark buildings…the Beresford, Rutherford Place, the Chelsea, and now the El Royale. It was owned by Martha Scott, who lived in one of the two penthouses, and run by long-time manager, Sandy Griffin—they decided who could rent there. It was like LA's genteel equivalent of New York's Chelsea Hotel.

Residents were mostly an eclectic mix of Hollywood's entertainment community. When we arrived, Cameron Diaz, Sharon Lawrence, Huell Howser, and Susan Dey were residents. The studios rented apartments for talent shooting films in LA and Jack Black, Aiden Quinn, and Ellen Page popped in for extended stays. Something was always happening in the El Royale's magnificent lobby, its rooftop terrace, and even in the elevators. You never knew what to expect. John Hamburg, one of the El Royale's resident screenwriters created a sitcom caricaturing the El Royale's quirkiness called *Welcome to The Captain*.[2] It starred Fran Kranz, Jeffrey Tambor, and Raquel Welch and aired for one season on CBS. Well, at least all of us at the El Royale enjoyed it.

We loved living at the El Royale and our one-year lease turned into a wonderful eight-year stay. For the last three years we occupied the penthouse, next door to the owner Martha. It was way above what we could reasonably afford but, hey, you only live once and it was one of the best apartments in LA with spectacular views. We hosted some fantastic Fourth of July and Christmas parties that people still talk about.

---

1. About El Royale https://bit.ly/ElRarticle

2. El Royale-*Captain* Trailer https://bit.ly/RoyaleCaptain

For the last five years of the decade our bicoastal residences were the El Royale and the Chelsea Hotel. It didn't get much better, quirkier, or memorable than that. Both environments definitely helped with my "test my limits" transformation from mad man to Emmy-award winning host—yes, you read that right. It just goes to show that when you expand your boundaries and challenge your capacity you're able to accomplish much more than you ever thought possible.

Silo 2: Award-winning content

From the outset, the Farm viewed itself as more than an ad agency. We were on the leading edge of branded content marketing communications and the partners had even created a branded content and entertainment division headed by Will Morrison. This was the patch of farmland that excited me the most. I couldn't wait to get my hands dirty, dig in, and plow the fields. Here's why:

- Branded content had moved from old school advertorials to native content seamlessly integrated into media. This required bigger ideas and a deft creative touch.
- There was a rapidly growing demand for video "infotainment" and digital was democratizing video production. Family "farms" now had the same tools and equipment as the big corporate industrial ones.
- Companies increasingly recognized that "doing good" was good for business. This aligned perfectly with our desire to create purposeful content. We called it Content of Consequence.
- Most importantly, I got to work with Will, Gregg's boyhood best friend. To my wife Vicki and me, Will was our fourth son and there was an emotional connection that made it even more special.

Will is an extremely talented guy with a creative mind that is always inventing. He and his team were prolific developers of creative new programming ideas including Content of Consequence—content that informs, entertains, and makes a positive difference. It was the Farm's opportunity to make its mark *and* do good…right in my wheelhouse.

The Farm's branded content division spawned three powerful initiatives that are a great source of pride and satisfaction. Two were in-market successes: *Cool In Your Code* (*CiNYC*), which you'll read about next and *Asset-Based Thinking* (ABT), which I've saved for the next chapter. One, also discussed later, was stifled by Hollywood bureaucracy before it could make it to market: *Coolinary Kids.*

I encourage my USC students to devote at least ten percent of their creative think time to building a personal inventory of Content of Consequence ideas. They can be brought to life right away or later in their careers. Doing good never goes out of style.

Cool in Your Code (*CiNYC*)

Cool in Your Code is a tale with two stories. It is the story of an innovative content platform purpose-built to fill a market niche and that won creative accolades, strong consumer acceptance and in-market success. It is also the story a big idea that never reached its full business potential. The two stories converge into a tale of great pride, satisfaction, emotional rewards, and learning for everyone involved, especially me. Here it is.

Three emerging trends led to the creation of *CiNYC*.

- Increasing consumer-interest in local, close-to-home, personalized entertainment
- Convergence of online, off-line, and place-based broadcast delivery
- Marketers' eagerness to connect with consumers on a local level

Will and the team were working on modular short-form content about New York neighborhoods hoping to sell the concept to a local station. In June 2003, we read a *New York Times* article about New York City mayor Michael Bloomberg's plan to reinvigorate its public service offering by replacing its dry, C-span-like station, Crosswalks, with a hip and cool NYC-TV(CH25). The mayor appointed two young aides, Seth Unger and Arick Wierson, to run and program the station with NYC-centric content that would appeal to a younger, more diverse audience. They called it civic-minded TV.

It was a light-bulb opportunity for Will and me. NYC-TV owned some of the most valuable cable television airtime in the city and were hungry for new programming and fast. The Farm had bushels full of great programming concepts and was hungry for airtime. We agreed to go big and bold.

I called Arick, set up a meeting and proposed a mold-breaking revenue-sharing model. The Farm would deliver fully produced half-hour episodes of programming and NYC-TV would schedule three prime-time and three fringe-time airings per week. The Farm would be provided a minimum of three minutes of commercial time for all episode airings available for sale to sponsors. We pitched a range of programming ideas and they loved *Cool In Your Code*. We shook hands on the deal, set the necessary paperwork in motion, and NYC-TV green-lighted the production. And so, the Farm became NYC-TV's first supplier of original content.[3]

---

3. NYCTV Announcement https://bit.ly/NYCTVHan

We committed to delivering six fully produced episodes. It was a big commitment with an estimated production cost $200K and an even bigger bet—the Farm would have to eat the cost if we couldn't line up sponsors. Also, we had to operate under a PBS model, which restricted the types of sponsorships and commercials we could offer. All the partners were nervous. But we put our skin in the game, took a "build it and they will come" attitude and it worked.

So what was *Cool in Your Code*?

CiNYC was a high-energy, lifestyle infotainment show that celebrated the neighborhoods and people that make up NYC's zip codes (New Yorkers wear their zip codes with pride!). It celebrated what was cool, new, undiscovered, and different throughout New York City's 200+ zip codes. From fashion to film, celebrities and more, it was a showcase of the city from the inside out. It was a show all about New York exclusively for New Yorkers. One of our outdoor billboards summed it up beautifully: "New Yorkers Tuning In To Themselves. How New York of Them."[4]

Each show featured a range of categories (or CodeGories) with catchy titles like, *Bar Code, Cool Eats, Vocal Code, Green Code,* and *Building Code.* We covered it all. The segments were built to incorporate branded content as part of their entertainment value, which was at the heart of our PBS revenue model. Will lined up great hosts like Shirley Rumirek, Brandon Johnson, and Kenya Hunt who brought great energy to the show. Will's talented fashionista wife Sasha, a former fashion editor for *Allure* magazine and then style editor of *US Weekly* hosted *Dress Code*, giving viewers her inside access to New York's fashion scene and style tips. It was a huge hit. Will even roped me into hosting, something that pushed me far beyond my perceived limits and took me down an entirely unexpected and exciting road.

The road to the NYC Emmy's

Will made me an offer I could have refused—it was risky. The two celebrity interview segments needed a host. *Back on the Block (BOTB)* took NYC celebs back to places that shaped their lives and *Code ReAd* celebrated NYC authors. Will persuaded me to host both segments.

"You're the only one here old enough to have the *gravitas* to pull this off," he said.

I'm still not sure if that was a compliment, but it worked. I'd been involved in the production of innumerable commercials, made countless presentations, and delivered hundreds of keynote addresses, but I'd never been in front of the camera. My know-your-limits apprehension took over. But Will's confidence in me gave me the push to switch from deficit-based-thinking—*I've never done this before. I'll make a fool of myself. The cast is young and cool, I'll ruin the vibe*—to Asset-Based Thinking—*Your presentation skills are transferrable. Just be yourself and go with i*t. *Your age can add a complementary dimension.*

---

4. *CiNYC* trailer https://bit.ly/CiNYCPromo

I signed on and surprised myself. This old mad man took to it naturally. I enjoyed hosting and *loved* interviewing people. The production team called me "one-take Hank" because I usually nailed the intros on the first try. That ABT/DBT shift made all the difference. Try it when self-doubt and those know-your-limitation moments creep into your mind.

Will booked an eclectic mix of celebrities including the legendary Jerry Stiller, *Grease* star Didi "Frenchy" Conn, the Wu Tang Clan's Masta Killa, and Moby. In its first season *CiNYC* received an amazing five NYC Emmy award nominations and won two—for best graphics and, to my amazement, a best on-air host in NYC Emmy for yours truly. See, it's never too late to break into showbiz.

I can still see that "I told you so" gleam of joy in Will's eye at the Emmy gala. It was a special moment for both of us. Later, I personally thanked each *BOTB* guest for making my Emmy possible, kept in touch, and collaborated with them again. Stay tuned for that. I even wrote a thank you "rap tribute" to Masta Killa (MK) and recorded it with his mix master Quick Draw in Wu Tang's Brooklyn chamber: "*BOTB* with MK in BK."[5] It never made it to the hip-hop charts, but MK liked it. Always remember that an "attitude of gratitude" leaves a lasting positive impression. Find a unique way to express yours.

This amazing new chapter in my life was made possible by that push from Will and his "you can do this" vote of confidence. No matter how long you've been at it in your career or a particular job you still need inspiration and encouragement. It can come from anywhere, anyone, anytime. Keep your vision turned on and tuned in so you don't miss it. Take the leap.

CiNYC garnered rave reviews from critics and viewers. We had a great debut. Next, generating revenue to fund it all was the top priority.

The Farm plowed new ground with an innovative branded content model that was perfect for our newly acquired Bank of New York (BNY) client. The Bank of New York was established in 1784 by Alexander Hamilton; it was an NYC institution. We pitched the show to Len Blaifelder, BNY's advertising VP and he signed on. In an *Ad Age* article announcing BNY's sponsorship Len said, "It is such a natural fit: We are the bank for New Yorkers and have been for generations. It would be insulting if any other bank were to sponsor the show."[6] Well said, Len!

In addition to opening and closing billboards, Will and his team created entertaining ways to integrate BNY into the show. *Cash Code* featured spending sprees with BNY debit cards in different zip codes. *Caring Codes* highlighted good things BNY customers were doing in their neighborhoods. *Culture Codes* called attention to BNY's local support of the arts. BNY employees, small business clients, and customers were the stars. Win-win all around. With this first round of funding secured we confidently moved ahead with future production and

---

5. *BOTB* with MK in BK https://bit.ly/HanksEmmy

6. BNY https://bit.ly/BNYCiNYC

added additional sponsors, like Pepsi, Prudential Real Estate, and the greater New York area Pontiac dealers, the last of which came to us!

Randy Altman, media director of the Pontiac dealer group's ad agency, saw *CiNYC* on air and inquired about sponsorship possibilities. Randy championed *CiNYC* with the dealer group and they made a big commitment providing ad dollars and vehicles. We created a weekly segment, *Code Trips,* featuring unique views of zip codes from a Pontiac's eye view. Pontiac SUVs were wrapped with *CiNYC* and Pontiac branding and dubbed Codesters. They appeared in Pontiac branded segments and were also used as our production vehicles, attracting attention wherever they went. New Yorkers took pictures with Codesters and posted them to our website. The dealers ate it up.

Pepsi signed on for a test market effort launching a new niche beverage brand, Tava. We created *Local Flavor* segments showcasing New Yorkers discovering Tava's unique taste and flavor variety. For Prudential we created *Building Code* segments featuring their brokers and properties. *CiNYC* was off to a great start!

Being bolder and going bigger

Over the next few years *CiNYC* was nominated for sixteen more NY Emmy awards and won four, two for segments I hosted. One was a lively *BOTB* chat with the legendary Eli Wallach and the other for *Code ReAd* interviews with NYC authors Mark Kurlansky and S.J Rozan. The New York Emmys even invited me to be a host and presenter at the 2008 Emmy Awards gala. Opening the envelope and handing out Emmys was an honor and a lot of fun, but it didn't top winning them.

NYCT-TV promoted *CiNYC* heavily and Amy Palmer host of *New York 360,* interviewed me at the Farm for her show.[7] Billboards promoting *CiNYC* were placed in the city's huge bus shelter network. Free media! *CiNYC* also spawned a branded section in the free morning daily *Metro New York* that spotlighted the neighborhood to be profiled in that week's show.

CiNYC even made it across the Atlantic.

NewsCorp International selected *CiNYC* as a cornerstone vehicle to launch its *London Times* online platform and the Farm formed a production joint venture with the *London Times* encompassing the same proven elements of the US model. *Cool In Your Code London* was launched in April 2007 with Cisco Systems and HP as charter sponsors.[8]

It was around then that Will and I recognized that for *CiNYC* to "go big" it had to be more than a local New York show. And so we developed an innovative *CiNYC* version of *PM Magazine's* successful syndication model. *CiNYC* New York would be the anchor location from

---

7. More Emmy Videos https://bit.ly/EmmysNY360

8. *CiNYC* London Trailer https://bit.ly/CiNYCLondon

which other markets could draw content and vice-versa. Will devised a simply brilliant mechanism to transition content between markets: *Flip Code*. Flipping numbers in any zip code takes you to a different location in other cities: NYC zip code 10029 in Manhattan flips to 90210, Beverly Hills, CA. Endless possibilities. We created tailored pitch decks to syndicators and sponsors including a Los Angeles prototype show. My oldest son Brian was freelancing at the Farm and Will brought him on board to produce two prototype segments: *Cool Eats* in the Fairfax neighborhood (90036) and a *Back on the Block* segment. Working with Brian was an added bonus for me.

I asked my friend, actor Linda Gray of *Dallas* fame, to be the guest *BOTB* celebrity—a big ask since it was for spec and not guaranteed to make it to air. Linda graciously agreed to help out and Brian choreographed a great interview with Linda and me in Culver City (90064) where she grew up and went to high school. It was one of the best interviews I've done—two friends enjoying a relaxed chat about priceless coming of age moments. We had hours of great footage and edited a prototype five-minute segment.[9] It was yet another precious reminder of how friendships and positive bridges are gifts that keeps on giving.

Will and I knew that selling *CiNYC* syndication would not be easy. Well, it wasn't, and we didn't get it sold. We, and especially I, underestimated the complexity of the syndication world, the importance of inside connections, and the amount of tenacity and ass-kissing required. We were great at creating and generating interest but not great at closing the deal. It was very difficult getting traction and commitment so we had to step back and reevaluate our approach. It was a valuable lesson: Bringing innovative content ideas to market requires 360-degree planning and execution. Do everything you can to fully grasp the end game dynamics.

Our unnatural disaster

As we began working on a new strategy along came one of those unforeseen events that all farmers dread. Except it wasn't a drought, flood, or locusts; it was the Great Recession. And it triggered the perfect storm of converging factors that brought *CiNYC* to a premature end.

During the financial crisis, which began in 2007, advertising budgets were drastically reduced. Spending on "non-essential" media like *CiNYC* was hardest hit. That year, Bank of NY merged with Mellon and subsequently reduced its marketing support for retail banking. *CiNYC* didn't fit anymore. Then, the government's bailout of General Motors required the discontinuance of the Pontiac division. Bye-bye greater NY Pontiac dealers and Codesters. Oh, and with the real-estate market collapse so went Prudential's involvement with *Building Code*. Last, there was change and turmoil at NYC-TV. Arick Wierson exited to produce a documentary film and one of his lieutenants was indicted for fraudulently handling sponsor

---

9. Linda Gray *CiNYC* https://bit.ly/LIndaGrayCiNYC

funds totally unrelated to the Farm or *CiNYC*.

The Farm had no option but to halt all new production. And, as you might have guessed, syndication of *CiNYC* in this environment was a non-starter.

CiNYC was gradually phased out of the NYC-TV lineup. The last air date was July 2010. It was a colossal s**t happens moment for the Farm and big blow to Will and me. It was tough to deal with initially but we had no choice but to put it behind us, appreciate the upside of our story, and move on. *CiNYC* had an amazing, successful six-year run. We produced over forty episodes that New Yorkers loved, received twenty-one NY Emmy nominations, and won six! Powerful new credentials were added to the Farm's resumé.

Here's how I saw my personal *CiNYC* story: *Disappointment?* Absolutely. *Regrets?* None. *Lessons learned?* A few. *Expertise?* Expanded. *Confidence?* Boosted. *Progress?* Miles ahead. *Friendships?* Multiplied. *Joys?* Plentiful.

Remember that there are always two sides to the tales of your career: business and personal. They each contain pearls of wisdom. Be sure to tell yourself both—even when the business side doesn't end as well as you hoped, or, like in the case of *Coolinary Kids,* it ends before it even has a chance to really begin.

Coolinary Kids

The *Coolinary Kids* initiative was born out of the growing childhood obesity epidemic. I was particularly aware of its severity through my association with the American Heart Association. Innovative ways to make healthy eating relevant to this digital generation were desperately needed. Content had to capture the imagination of kids and also motivate parents to step into the kitchen with them.

We developed *Coolinary Kids* as an energetic, action-packed cooking show made especially for children ages six through ten, created from scratch to be destination kids programming (tv and on-line) and nutritious for the entire family. Will and his team developed content that encompassed three key components of healthy behavior change: health and nutrition knowledge, physical activity, and self-esteem building.

The show's centerpiece was an amazing "kidchen" set that was safe, kid-friendly, hands-on, and state of the art. Everything in the kidchen was reimagined from a kid's perspective; it was a "coolinary" theme park with its own language and rules. Nutrition education was embedded throughout the show—healthy eating habits, better-for-you tasty food choices, kid portion sizes, recipe math—and we empowered kids to talk to their parents about all of it. Physical activity or "kidchen calisthenics" calls to action and demonstrations were seeded throughout the show and we built "kidchen pride" by showing kids savoring the results and wowing adults with their coolinary creations.

We felt *Coolinary Kids* could be the catalyst to convene a formidable convergence of constituencies: media, NGOs, departments of health, underwriters, communities, and educators. We also recognized that to bring the concept to fruition the Farm needed a development partner that could add resources and clout. My son Brian was working with Will on the project and suggested that we pitch the idea to the Jim Henson company. He was friends with Henson's executive producer and director of development, Halle Stafford. Will and Brian sent Halle a pitch deck and she loved the concept.

In May 2006, the Henson company signed a joint venture agreement with the Farm and the fun began. We were ecstatic. Just going to meetings at the Henson offices was an adventure. The offices were housed in the landmark Charlie Chaplin studios on La Brea Boulevard in Los Angeles; it was like stepping into a Hollywood time capsule. History, energy, and creativity oozed out of the place. Watching artists, writers, and film makers collaborating and create those amazing Henson puppets was inspiring. I felt like a kid again.[10]

For the next eighteen months Will, Brian, and I worked with the Henson team refining the concept and blocking out the flow of the show. My youngest son Jason, an artist and pastry chef, contributed recipes and cool ideas on preparation and plating the dishes prepared in the kidchen. It was a family affair.

Coolinary Kids was positioned as "more than a cooking show, it's a lifestyle." It was a way to let kids feel like they're a part of something. We worked to make *Coolinary Kids* something that would capture the imaginations and appetites of kids everywhere. The Jim Henson Company commissioned writers to develop show scripts and their artists created amazing puppet hosts and helpers. We had the right recipe for success and were ready to pitch *Coolinary Kids* to distributors and media partners. The Henson company pitched the show to Disney and they optioned it. So far pretty darned good. The Concept Farm, The Jim Henson Company, and the almighty Disney...*wow!* We began working with Disney's Stage 9 development group to refine the idea. After a long time, various versions, multiple character renderings and endless meetings, Disney did a lot more than refine the concept. They ultimately decided not to go with *Coolinary Kids* and its characters and instead use it as a vehicle to promote their own characters.

The concept became *The Muppet Cooking Show* then morphed into *Fozzie's Kitchen*, an online program. As far as I know they never did actually create the show.

We pressured Disney to return the rights to Concept Farm and they did. So there we were, after twenty-six months of development and back to the barn. The harsh reality of Hollywood sunk in yet again. We were reminded that it's never a done deal until it's done. After the initial let down we used an ABT lens to push aside frustration and see the asset side. We had refined our *Coolinary Kids* concept to be better than when it started, learned a lot working with the A-teams in Hollywood, and added new friends of the Farm to our contact list. Nevertheless,

---

10. Henson Studios https://bit.ly/HensStudio

the reality of being so close and yet so far hit home.

Silo 3: Volunteering With Heart

Switching tracks, I want to tell you about some more Content of Consequence for the American Heart Association that the Farm worked on that was extremely rewarding. Here's how that amazing connection was made.

My mad man friend and Farm client Sid Lerner had arranged a meeting with the American Heart Association's (AHA) Heritage/Founders Affiliate to discuss integrating his Healthy Monday campaign into their programs. We met with Michael Weamer, affiliate EVP, and proposed an AHA/*Cool In Your Code* segment featuring their faith-based outreach, "Search Your Heart Sunday, Go Healthy Monday." We produced the segment a few months later. But that's just the beginning of the story.

Michael asked if I would be willing to attend the affiliate's regional conference, interview attendees about their roles and create a closing video. I accepted and the Farm donated the film crew and editing support. We spent the full day interviewing and filming an amazing group of volunteers, doctors, nurses, philanthropists, and staff. Then we worked all night, edited the footage, and created a powerful closing conference video. It was a big hit. After the meeting Michael thanked me for our donation. I told Michael how impressed I was by everyone's passion and commitment to the AHA and congratulated him on building such an impressive group of volunteers. Then Michael surprised me. He said, "Well if you like us that much why don't you join our board. We could use a marketing perspective." That's all it took to reignite my volunteering flame.[11] I joined the AHA Heritage/Founders Affiliate board in July 2006 for a two-year term that turned into a remarkable AHA adventure that is still going strong today. I am forever grateful to Sid for opening the AHA door and to Michael for inviting me in to join the AHA family.

I quickly learned that being on the AHA board was not a vanity position. Volunteers were expected to actively work at advancing the AHA's mission and over the past fourteen years, I have served on the national and regional AHA boards, numerous committees, and chaired the stroke and corporate relations committees. And I got as much as I gave, most notably in the form of new friends and colleagues.

While working with AHA's national communications director Matt Bannister on the communications committee, I met Jeff Hasen, CMO of a mobile marketing company, Hipcricket. Jeff gave me an early education about the potential of mobile and he has remained my go-to source for all things mobile to this day. My friend and past McCann West colleague, Tony Pace, now CMO of Subway, was also on that committee, another positive bridge to the past.

---

11. AHA BOD https://bit.ly/AHABOD

Stay tuned for more about both of these connections. A marketing campaign developed by Concept Farm was the catalyst that turned my two-year appointment into fourteen-plus years of service. It's an "only in New York" story I love telling.

Creating magnetic content

Michael invited me to a luncheon meeting with a potential major donor, John Charlsty. John was a New Yorker who had recently survived and recovered from a stroke. The physician who treated John was Dr. Ricard Hodosh, a brilliant neurosurgeon and fellow board member. John was considering a directed gift of $600,000 to fund a program educating New Yorkers about stroke signs and symptoms.

I found myself sitting at the table with an AHA mega donor and one of the world's most renowned neurosurgeons wondering what the hell I could contribute. There was that "know your limits" mindset again. John's gratitude and passion was palpable. He clearly relished the opportunity to give back to the AHA and thank Dr. Hodosh. John told us he would do anything to make sure that others don't go through what he went through. About the stroke education program, he said, "Make it New York, make it different, and have it make a difference." That was the nudge I needed to test my limits and contribute. I told John that Concept Farm would take on the assignment pro bono with the same NYC attitude and creativity as *Cool in Your Code* and donate commercial time on the show. Michael added that the Heritage/Founders affiliate would contribute $200K in funding. The deal was sealed and we left the meeting energized and eager to find ways to turn $800K into millions more in media value and in-kind contributions. I was also now in the unique position of being both agency and client.

The farmers received a briefing from the AHA team and met with stroke docs, hospital ER staff, and first responders. We learned that administering the drug TPA within a three-hour window of the onset of symptoms largely mitigates the devasting effects of stroke. We also learned that the frontline of action and treatment was NYC's 9-1-1 service, run by the city's fire department. The director, firefighter Tony Napoli, invited me to visit NYC's Metro Tech Center in Brooklyn to meet the dedicated men and women answering those 9-1-1 calls. My family's NYFD heritage—my dad, brother, and brother-in-law were NYC firefighers—made that an especially poignant experience for me.

Tony explained that NYFD's protocols placed a top priority on stroke calls. When they received a stroke call that fell within a three-hour window of symptom manifestation, that call went directly to the top of the dispatch priority ahead of everything else, including gunshot wounds. Tony and the dispatchers expressed the same frustrations as the ER docs lamenting people's lack of knowledge and fear of calling 9-1-1. Tony said he wished he could tell people, "Hey, call us. Don't be embarrassed if it's a false alarm. We won't get mad at you." That stuck with me.

Here's a layman's version of the creative brief.

> **Issue:** In the US, over 180,000 people die of stroke annually and it is the leading cause of disability. It can suddenly strike anyone.

> **Challenge:** The great majority of people are not aware of stroke signs and symptoms or what action to take. They often go ignored and people are very hesitant to call 9-1-1.

> **Opportunity:** Mobilizing emergency medical services (EMS) protocols to administer TPA and to get stroke victims to hospitals for treatment... stat!

> **Behavior Change:** Be alert to stroke signs and symptoms in yourself or others. Call 9-1-1 immediately if you notice any of them. Time is critical.

> **Tone:** Provocative, informative, accessible.

We believed that while stroke was scary, the creative didn't have to be. The campaign had to break through people's apathy and fear and draw them into the messaging. The farmers embraced John Charlsty's "I'll do anything" sentiment and began creative development with the mindset that when it comes to saving lives, nothing goes too far. That attitude spawned the campaign idea: "We'll do anything to make you aware of the signs of a stroke," and the executions that flowed from it were brilliant.

We'll do anything...even:

> Get Fordham University's cheerleading squad to create and perform a stroke cheer.

> Create an animated TV series about a stroke support group, *The Symptoms. Weaky, Blurry, Slurry, and Dizzy.* These stroke symptoms are so frustrated that people ignore them they go to group therapy. An award-winning animation company LAIKA developed the characters and produced a fully animated series at their own expense. Our *CiNYC* celebrity friends Jerry Stiller, Anne Meara, and Didi Conn "donated" their voices and talent to magically bring the symptoms to life. Move over *Simpsons!*

Run an infomercial for NYFD's 9-1-1 service spoofing the dating chat line commercials flooding the air at that time. Tony Napoli even convinced NYFD's brass to let us shoot the commercial at the call center with real NYFD dispatchers. In the commercial, a young woman provocatively identifies stroke symptoms and dispatchers interject with "call me" or "don't be shy." A bit risqué but attention grabbing. As a bonus, Carl "Apollo Creed" Weathers agreed to be the voiceover announcer for the campaign.

We produced the commercials and sent them off to AHA headquarters in Dallas for a final review. The Farm also created a robust interactive website, nostroke911.com, with micro-sites for each commercial to heighten campaign engagement.

Here's where it got a bit surreal. Michael Weamer asked me to present the campaign to the director of the Bugher Foundation, an NGO dedicated to funding stroke research. When the Bugher director walked into our meeting it became another 1965 moment. It was Dan Adams, my colleague and friend from B&B. We had worked together from 1965 to 1970 and hadn't seen each other for thirty-five years! First Sid Lerner now Dan. It was quite a B&B reunion. Dan loved the campaign and the Bugher Foundation contributed an additional $200K to the effort. We were now up to one million dollars in funding and had received pro-bono production and talent resources valued at $250K.

The Farm's media partner USIM facilitated a media alliance with Time Warner Cable (TWC) that significantly amplified paid media expenditures. For every dollar expended, TWC contributed 50% additional free commercial time, ran "we'll do anything" on-air promotions, and added an AHA programming block to their Health on Demand Channel. The New York Yankees scheduled an AHA night, showing the campaign on the Jumbotron and distributing collectible stroke symptoms magnets to fans. It was very special treat for this die-hard Yankee fan. The campaign was magnetic and attracted a diverse group of supporters and advocates. John Charlsty's $600,000 donation was about to be transformed into over 2.5 million dollars of impact. We were ready to launch! Well, almost.

Turning lemons into lemonade

I received a call from Dave Josserand, Chairman of the AHA, who was also a volunteer and, like me, a principal in an ad agency. We knew each other pretty well and he got right to the point. Dave told me that the AHA would not allow us to run the Hot Line 9-1-1 commercial or include it on the website or other AHA properties. Period. It's suggestive tone and manner were not in keeping with the AHA values. It was banned. He repeated his message a few times.

"Hank, do we understand each other?" Yeah Dave, I got the message.

I was ruffled but not shocked by the reaction. We'd pushed the envelope a bit too far. Now what? The Farm had already produced the commercial. I had to tell the farmers it was dead and at some point let Tony Napoli know that his help and assistance was for naught. The first farmer I faced was my son Gregg. He was very upset…okay, he was *really* pissed off.

"Dad, how in hell could you let them kill that great commercial?

I told Gregg that I took responsibility for what happened. I should have known better, should have used my common-sense filter, and steered the commercial in a different direction from the outset.

After Gregg and the creative team calmed down they did what great creative people do. They reinvented and turned the problem into an opportunity. The dating hotline concept was replaced with an even better one: a psychic hotline with a flamboyant psychic and her crystal ball that could sense and see stroke symptoms. I told Dave Josserand about the switch and he and I both breathed a sigh of relief. Now that we had a solution, I let Tony Napoli know about the change and we shot the new commercial two days later. Everyone was happy and even Gregg agreed that it was a better commercial. I was forgiven.

The campaign launched on schedule in September 2008 and the results were spectacular. It broke the bank in terms of consumer responses as tracked by Time Warner Cable's interactive measurements. Consumer awareness grew and stroke calls to 9-1-1 significantly increased. We submitted the campaign to the NY Emmys in the public service announcement (PSA) category and you guessed it…we won! I'm convinced the psychic commercial was a big contributing factor.[12]

It was the first ever Emmy award for the American Heart Association. They were ecstatic. I went from goat to hero in a few months. Only in New York! A year later my involvement with the AHA's stroke efforts would take an even bigger new direction. Stay tuned for that.

Another positive consequence was that my relationship with Dan Adams extended beyond the campaign. Dan and I collaborated on a few more Farm projects and continued working together advancing the Bugher Foundation /AHA alliance around stroke. Sadly, Dan passed away in June 2015 at age seventy-five.[13] Because of that serendipitous meeting at the AHA I was fortunate to enjoy six years of a wonderfully rekindled friendship. Always take time to count your blessings. Thanks again, John Charlsty.

---

12. Emmy submission/banned commercial (Statute of limitations is expired) https://bit.ly/AHAEmmy

13. AHA Tribute: https://bit.ly/AdamsAHA

Happy Farmer Wisdom

- Be bold and go big. When circumstances converge to illuminate big opportunities, seize the moment. They don't happen that often.
- Make an "attitude of gratitude" part of your personal brand. Build sincere appreciation into your relationships.
- Keep your ABT antennae turned on and tuned in. Be open to inspiration and encouragement from others at any career stage so you don't miss out.
- Make room for Content of Consequence. Higher-purpose creativity will elevate you and all those it touches. Own it proudly.
- There are two sides to every career story: business and personal. Each contain pearls of wisdom. Be sure to tell yourself both.
- Go beyond knowing your limitations to expanding your capacity. Testing your perceived edges will provide empowering answers.
- Go beyond disappointment to determination. If your great idea gets squashed, for whatever reason, there is always another way to do it. Always.
- Volunteer early and often. Calling yourself to action in service of a worthy cause adds meaning to your life.

Marketing Truisms & Tips

The Dual Lenses of Magnetic Content

For effective marketing communications in today's digitally transformed media environment you need content marketing that attracts people to your message—as opposed to intruding or enforcing it. Consequently, brands must view their role as content publishers not advertisers. Here's how I discuss it in my USC classes.

The analog communication model was linear: Attention-Interest Desire-Action (AIDA).

Today it is fluid with two new letters added **E** and **S**: Attention-Interest-Desire-*Engagement*-Action-*Sharing*. **A+IDEAS**.

The content has to be so damn good that people are compelled to consume it. Today's marketing buzzword for it is "magnetic content," content so gripping it attracts you toward it. For magnetic content, you have to bring your A-game because creativity is the differentiator.

Magnetic content is developed through the lens of its impact on the ultimate consumer, and rightly so. But there's a complementary lens that's also important. Think of your iPhone or Android with front- and rear-facing cameras. The front camera views the consumer. The rear camera views the constituencies that create, produce, and deploy the content. It's a really smart idea to use both lenses. In my class, I use Concept Farm's AHA's stroke campaign as an example.

The content was so damned good it had both front-camera (consumer) impact and rear-camera (producer) magnetism. It compelled likeminded partners to contribute at no or greatly reduced costs: LAIKA, Jerry Stiller, Anne Meara, Didi Conn, Carl Weathers, the NYFD, the Fordham cheerleaders, Time Warner Cable, and the Bugher Foundation. In ABT terms they became positive co-conspirators. Sure, the fact that the campaign was for an NGO factored into its magnetism. But the AHA had created other public service campaigns and none of them had had the dual lens power of "we'll do anything." The creative idea and execution were the differentiators. It works the same way with branded content.

Marketing guru Seth Godin describes magnetism in the context of attracting allies or accomplices. Good content attracts allies who try to help whenever they can, he says. Magnetic content attracts *accomplices* who commit fully and will risk something to put their skin in the game with you.

Create magnetism.

Chapter 15 Footnotes
Scan QR codes for direct links to footnote content.

15.2 The El Royale/Captain

15.3 NYCTV Article

15.4 CiNYC Trailer

15.5 Hank's BOTB Emmy

15.6 BNY Article

15.7 BOTB Youtube

15.7 Code Read Youtube

15.7 More Emmys & NYC 360

15.8 CiNYC London

15.9 Linda Gray CiNYC Segment

15.10 Henson Studios

15.11 AHA BOD

15.12 AHA Emmy + Hotline

Chapter 16:

Converting Assets Into Adrenaline

The Farm was adding clients, plowing new ground, planting fresh content, and reaping bushels of awards. There were forty-eight farmers working the fields creating a contagious, productive energy at the agency. I tapped into that energy to help me fill the two silos I'll open in this chapter.

Winning Emmy awards and industry accolades felt great but there were two other awards that were especially gratifying. In 2008, the Concept Farm made it on to the coveted Crain's best places to work in New York City list; it was ranked number twenty among all NYC companies and number seven on the mid-sized company list. *Nice.* That was followed by *Ad Age*'s naming Concept Farm to its top thirty Best Places to Work in Marketing and Media in the US. *Nicer.* Those recognitions made everyone at the Farm proud, especially the partners.[1]

The impetus for these recognitions went beyond the physical space, the Emmys, the wacky farm stuff, pool table, and communal kitchen. I've mentioned a few times that people are an agency's most important asset and company culture is precious currency. Then and now, the Farm culture of "fresh ideas harvested daily" fosters an environment that feeds individual creativity. Everyone feels they have something to contribute. There is a "proud farmer" vibe that makes the farmers and everyone who visits feel welcomed the moment they step into the barnyard. It just goes to show that when you appreciate the assets within you, around you, and in others they can be the adrenaline that helps you make more of "you."

Silo 4: Finding my voice

In the late '70s and throughout the '80s I was an active voice in the marketing community. I worked with the American Management Association (AMA), wrote articles for their publications, spoke at events and authored the marketing communications chapter of the AMA's official management handbook. The higher up the ladder I went, the bigger the opportunities. Airing my views on important marketing topics—and being around others who were doing the same—enriched those early years of my career. It was also reassuring that people actually wanted to hear what I had to say.

My entrepreneurial stop at Capstone and return to McCann required me to pull back from most extracurricular activities. Joining the Farm in 2003 was the shot of adrenaline I needed

---

1. Best Places Article bit.ly/CFBestPlaces

to get back on track. The unexpected restart of my career at sixty years old, *CiNYC* Emmys, American Heart Association (AHA) directorship, and the publication of the Asset-Based Thinking book series (more on that soon) opened new doors and platforms. But this time it was different. I was raising my voice in dynamic digital arenas with new audiences.

I was invited to join Technorati's Blogcritics.org, a self-proclaimed "sinister cabal of great writers," and contributed a number of articles. I offered insights about my *CiNYC* interview with Eli Wallach, I chronicled my move from McCann to Concept Farm in *From Boardroom to Barnyard*, and I provided views on making over municipal television. The largest job website, Monster.com, hired me as their marketing careers expert to write advice and opinion articles and I hosted their marketing careers message board. I was energized. And my voice was different now: less regimented and prescriptive, more open, advisory, empathetic, and conversational. More me. I liked that.[2]

My most interesting undertaking was unexpected. Out of the blue I received a call from Gil Solnin, a past colleague in the alcoholic beverage business. He was advising *Rippon Forum*, the Republican party's national magazine. I'd never heard of the publication and was registered as an independent so I'm not quite sure why he called me. Gil explained that the magazine was preparing its June/July 2006 Independence Day issue celebrating our nation's 230th birthday. The issue was titled "Branding America" and it featured Karen Hughes, President Bush's Under Secretary of State for Public Diplomacy and Public Affairs. In 2006 the world was waging its war on terror and America's image in certain parts of the world was not great. Gil asked if I could write a piece providing my "mad man" Madison Avenue take on Brand America. I said, "Hell yes"—living overseas during 9/11 had awakened my sense of patriotism and pride and this was an opportunity to share my point of view. But I told them my piece would be apolitical, accurately reflect my views, and I had to approve any edits. They agreed. I wrote a nonpartisan patriotic 1,500-word article titled, "Madison Avenue's Take on Brand America." It was published word for word, no edits.[3]

Here's the essence of the article. If any country in the world can be viewed as a brand it's America. Two hundred and thirty years ago we were the original start-up. We invented branding. So why when facing precarious times can't we leverage America's brand assets? I laid out my case in the context of America as a corporation owned by and accountable to its shareholders: American citizens. I defined America's brand essence, identified its core constituencies and evaluated its leadership's implementation. Brand America could not be captured in a snappy sentence, I wrote. Instead its essence is clearly and openly articulated in five timeless documents:

---

2. Monster Podcast https://bit.ly/HankMonster

3. Rippon Forum https://bit.ly/RipponForum

- Declaration of Independence: *Our raison d'etre*
- The Constitution: *Our rules*
- The Gettysburg Address: *Our guiding principles*
- The Inscription on the Statue of Liberty: *Our beacon*
- The Pledge of Allegiance: *Our affirmation*

I quoted the key message of each document and summed it up like this:

> *America exists to provide for, nourish, and safeguard a way of life dedicated to the freedom of all of its citizens to flourish and live rewarding lives that can be passed on to future generations. It is our duty and destiny to welcome people of like mind to come here, respect everyone's right to peacefully express their beliefs, and protect us from those that seek to undermine and destroy our way of life.*

I gave America an "A" for defining its essence but mixed grades to its leaders for failing to consistently live up to it. Then, being an ad guy, I did a creative makeover of a popular bumper sticker of that time: *America Love It or Leave It.* My update: *America Love it & Live Up To It.* The article was well-received, I got some requests for bumper stickers, and it sparked a call from Associated Press staff reporter Stephanie Hoo who interviewed me for the AP's Fourth of July feature article: "Branding America, the original startup."

Stephanie did a great job capturing my viewpoints and her article was broadly syndicated to newspapers in the US and around the world.[4] That was a first for me. The AP story led to radio interviews including a return visit to the *Aware Show* that aired on KPFK Pacifica. I'd previously appeared with the host Lisa Garr to discuss ABT and I liked her incisive interviewing style. Lisa's audience leaned towards progressive views so I was particularly eager to get their reactions to my take on Brand America. Lisa and I had a terrific lively discussion with great audience participation.[5] That was back in the days when constructive, civil exchanges of ideas were welcomed. Looking back on it now, I believe the views I expressed in 2006 are even more relevant today.

Raising and sharing my voice provided as much valuable learning and experience as any marketing skills I've acquired. Every time I write articles, do interviews, or partner with others to create content I'm energized to up my game. That is why I always encourage young leaders to expose their voices and what they stand for, to expose themselves.

Find your voice early in your career and make what you say, do, and share an integral part

---

4. AP Article: https://bit.ly/APSrticle

5. *Aware Show* https://bit.ly/AwareInterview

of your signature presence. Taking a stand doesn't necessarily mean "solve the problems of the world" sobriety. Your message can be anything from serious to satire as long as it reflects what you stand for and is delivered in a form and manner in which you're comfortable. Whatever it is, make it your own. Do it on your terms. Your audience will find you.

Start small, writing and speaking about things you know well and feel strongly about. Pick the media with which you are most comfortable. Take the time to prepare. Really prepare. There's a plethora of helpful resources available. Consider participating in writing courses, sign-up for presentation skills training, and video workshops. I also recommend one unorthodox bit of training. Join an improv class and learn the art of reacting, being thoughtfully quick on your feet, and switching from "yes but" to "yes and" responses.

Be provocative. Respectfully articulate your views, encourage debate, and value the discussion you provoke. Constructive dialogue challenges you to defend and support your work. It can strengthen your viewpoints, help hone your perspective, and, sometimes, modify and shift them. Either way you win.

Have an in-service mindset. Recognize that you are creating for your audience, not you. Then, be YOU. Wrap yourself in civility and respect, and your voice will rise above the noise.

Silo 5: Asset-Based Thinking

I first met Dr. Kathy Cramer at the Concept Farm in January 2004. I had just earned my Reiki master black belt and was emerging from my post-McCann funk. Kathy, a published author and leadership guru, was working with the Farm exploring new content avenues to broaden her already successful coaching business.

Over the previous twenty years Kathy had pioneered and developed a simply brilliant mindset management philosophy and practice she named Asset-Based Thinking (ABT). At the Cramer Institute in St. Louis, Kathy and her team developed coaching tools and practices that helped people move from negative Deficit-Based Thinking (DBT) to ABT. People emerged more confident, competent, energetic and better able to leverage both challenges and opportunities. Here's the essence of ABT.

> *Asset-Based Thinking (ABT) is an innovative way of viewing everyday life. ABT is a mental lighthouse that illuminates the best in a person, relationship, and situation. It celebrates the positive side of life's ledger and frees us of the Deficit-Based negative side. Assets fuel our passions and through Asset-Based Thinking, passions become our power. Asset-Based Thinking reveals how even the slightest shifts can lead to seismic differences enabling us to create our best future here and now. Asset-Based Thinking will change the way you see*

everything so you never look at the world the same way ever again.

Gregg and Will thought I should meet Kathy. We were close in age—me sixty and Kathy fifty-six—and as Gregg put it, "Dad, Kathy is the power of positive thinking personified and you're into all this new age enlightenment stuff so see what you can do together." And that's how I began a friendship and business partnership that profoundly impacted every aspect of the rest of my life.

So how did we get from "howdy" to a top-selling book series? Simple. Via Kathy's passionate dedication to making the world a better place through Asset-Based Thinking. This was her mighty cause. Nothing was going to get in her way. Kathy was a dynamo and I was immediately drawn to her positive energy and enthusiasm. Plus, ABT was a perfect fit for the Farm's *Content of Consequence* initiative.

Over the next few months, that midwestern Ph.D. ray of sunshine transformed this slightly skeptical Brooklyn mad man into a fully committed asset-based thinker. Then, Kathy suggested we create a book together. She already had the title: *Change the Way You See Everything (Through Asset-Based Thinking).* I loved it.

We agreed our book should live up to its title and not be the same-old-same-old business/self-help book. We wanted to change the way you saw that book genre and agreed on a development mantra: Madison Avenue meets positive psychology. It was a leap of faith for both of us. I had never written a book and Kathy was the sole author of her previous book, which conformed to traditional all-type formats. In ABT parlance we both had to turn our anxiety into anticipation. We agreed on a 50/50 partnership: work, commitment, author, and company credits, investment, revenue…everything. Kathy and I shook hands—no contracts, lawyers, or negotiation—and that's the way we always operated. This was more than a leap of faith, we required complete trust in each other. Nothing beats that feeling.

Asset-Based Creating

Kathy and I used an ABT S.O.S. *(Self Others Situations)* approach to creating and publishing the book. We focused on complementary self-strengths, drew on the assets of others, and found the upside of difficult situations. From the get-go, our goal was publishing a book that would break the mold and create an emotional reading experience that educated, inspired, and told stories. Words and concrete principles inspired visuals, visuals brought new dimension to concepts, and uplifting personal stories humanized the experience.

We began working in earnest in March, and Kathy and I settled into a productive rhythm. First we outlined the flow of the book and chapter overviews. Kathy laid down an engaging prescriptive narrative for each chapter, I edited it for "people speak," added ideas, and expanded the narrative with visual concepts that punctuated the message. John Gellos, the Farm's creative design genius, brought the book to life in an unconventional square page format. John and the Farm's art directors treated each page as a magazine ad or spread. They harnessed the power of the internet and digital technology to create an amazing visual experience that would not have been feasible just a few years earlier.

Kathy was a big believer in the power of storytelling and often used the Hero's Journey story arc in her coaching work. I learned a great deal from Kathy about storytelling, encouraging others to tell their stories, and how to listen to and learn from them. Kathy and I were fortunate that like-minded, high-profile friends gladly "gifted" their stories to inspire others. James Patterson, the world's best-selling author and a Farm client, wrote the foreword telling his childhood story about his grandfather's advice for a rewarding life. My friend actor Linda Gray shared her story and secrets to building strong relationships and a joyful life. Sonia Manzano, *Sesame Street*'s Maria, told the story of how her role on the show inspired her to encourage others to celebrate their heritage. Musician Moby talked about how his irresistible urge to be ahead of the curve led to his opening a neighborhood business and launching a line of bottled iced tea: *Teany*. Ed Mara, my dear friend and colleague from Nestlé, shared his poignant "passion to win" story about his battle with pancreatic cancer. Sadly, Ed passed away in 2008 but his inspirational story lives on in our book. Powerful reading.[6]

We made progress quickly and by November were ready to pitch the book to publishers.

Turning rejection into resolve

Kathy and I knew that getting our book published would not be easy. It was very different; the hardcover, four-color format meant higher printing costs, a relatively high shelf price ($25), and required a different editorial approach (choreographed words and visuals). Fortunately, Kathy was represented by a terrific literary agent Denise Marcel who embraced the book and guided us through the arduous getting published process.

Selling this book to a publisher required more than the traditional, formulaic pitch piece. Just reading a manuscript wouldn't cut it. We invested in printing prototypes to bring the book to life and created a pitch video. Kathy and I presented the book to ten publishers all of whom rejected it—too different and too risky. Denise and I were discouraged, but my ABT coach and partner Kathy helped us turn rejection into resolve.

Kathy urged us to push aside the naysayers, stay focused on our mighty cause, and reminded us that all we needed was one publisher to say yes. Just one. Re-energized, we pushed ahead and on the thirteenth try, Running Press, a Perseus books imprint, decided this was the book for them. A wonderful editor and development manager, Jennifer Kasius, championed the book and worked

---

6. ABT Stories https://bit.ly/ABTStories, ABT Website http://bit.ly/ABTWebsiteTCI

side-by-side with us to bring it to reality. Denise negotiated a favorable royalty arrangement and a $25,000 advance—enough to cover out-of-pocket expenditures. We wouldn't receive royalties until net income from retail book sales covered the advance, about 8000 books. No worries. Luckily, we blew past that threshold in two months. Here's how it happened.

Judging our book by its cover

Everyone felt the cover was critical and should play off the title. In the book world, the publisher usually has the final say over the title and cover but the Perseus team welcomed our cover suggestions. The Farm created an untraditional cover: lots of whitespace, no visuals, and a small title that included reverse type. It made a stark contrast to the inside of the book.

Two weeks later we met at the Farm to review the publisher's recommendations fully expecting our concept to be replaced by a traditional "safe" cover. But the Perseus designers actually used our cover as stimuli and took the design to another level.

Their cover title was in big, bold reverse type—it required a double-take to get it. And the cover material replicated burlap cloth with bright red colored borders.[7] *Wow!* We were stunned. John Gellos and I embraced it immediately. Kathy was intrigued. Denise, our agent, thought it was terrible. First the potential issues poured out. It would cause confusion on the shelf, potential readers would be put off, booksellers might think it was a misprint and send books back, and so on. Being different was good but this was much too risky. That sparked a vibrant risk-reward debate that led to agreement to go with the publisher's recommendation, no changes. Full steam ahead. The new cover also stimulated a fresh approach to subsequent development of ABT creative materials at the Farm.

This was great example of how a potential "not invented here" tension became a "reinvented better together" collaboration. There's no doubt that the confident boldness and creativity of the cover was a major reason for the book's success. It grabbed the retailer's attention, stood out on the shelf, piqued reader interest and was the perfect set up for the dramatic inside-the-book experience. It was a great lesson in how to use ABT to embrace potentially confrontational situations with a make the most of it attitude. It requires you to explore your risk-reward tolerance and the returns are well worth it.

Messaging, marketing, and magnetic windows

The Farm created an introductory communications program that included a dynamic website, ABT intro video, tip sheets, newsletters, a "Change the Way You See Everything" song CD, and ABT alphabet bookmarks that contrasted ABT and DBT words. We produced an

---

7. ABT Book Covers https://bit.ly/ABTCovers

entertaining suite of videos for on-line and on-air that ranged from ABT makeovers of NYC street signs and ABT "shift" sentences to ABT short thoughts and mindset makeovers.[8] We even had a *MySpace* page…remember them?

I created an Asset-Based Thinking in Action column on Blogcritics to support the launch. Kathy and I worked closely with the Perseus public relations team to secure placements on key review websites, interviews with bloggers and radio talk show appearances. I particularly enjoyed the interview with my friend Shadoe Stevens. Being in the studio, live and on-air with a radio legend was special. Kathy and I delivered the keynote address at the Association of Educational Publishers' (AEP) annual meeting. It was our first big duet gig. We had great chemistry on-stage and enjoyed it. But perhaps the biggest break wasn't the result of meticulous planning and polished marketing materials, but from serendipity and synchronicity.

The epicenter of our success was Barnes and Noble's two Fifth Avenue flagship stores at Rockefeller Center and 45th Street in Manhattan. The manager reached out and asked if we could meet to discuss promotion of the book in his stores. *Hell yeah!*

We met at the Rockefeller Center store and he explained that he loved the cover, was impressed with the visuals, and wanted to use them to liven up his instore merchandising. One thing led to another and he agreed to devote an entire window display and front-of-store table placement to the book for two weeks if we would provide the materials. Holy cow…window displays on Fifth Avenue for free!

The Farm created high-impact displays with oversized visuals from the book and up they went but not just for two weeks—for nine weeks! It was the power of dual lens magnetic content at work again: our magnetic content was attracting both consumers and accomplices to assist us in our efforts.

The window displays were a huge success and traffic builder. I took many strolls down 5th Avenue to observe reactions of passersby. What a feeling. That success led to similar windows at B&N's Chelsea and Upper West Side stores and instore book signing events. This spurred book promotions across the B&N network making *Change The Way You See Everything* a Barnes & Noble best seller. Success begets success and sales took off in other book stores across the country and the internet.

This chain of positive events is a great example of one my favorite ABT visualization exercises.

> *Envision a rainbow on the horizon and place yourself on the horizon's edge. From there you will see that the rainbow is a circle (really) and we only see the upper half because the horizon hides the rest. Living on the horizon's edge, you vividly see more potential, possibilities and meet other like-minded people who share the same view (like that B&N store*

---

8. ABT Videos & Song https://bit.ly/ABTVideos

manager). Be a horizon dweller.

The B&N sales success also led to an unforgettable, you-can't-make-this-up good karma experience. One week after the B&N displays went up I received a call from a woman inquiring about one of the visuals in the window. She had gotten my contact information from the B&N store manager. She asked about the "See Yourself" chapter picture we had purchased from Getty Images; it was a young boy looking in the mirror and sticking his tongue out at himself. She was visiting New York, happened to walk by the B&N store, and recognized the boy in the window. It was her now sixty-two-year-old son.[9]

Kathy just happened to be at the Farm that day and we invited her up for a visit. We had a wonderful chat and learned it was a picture of her five-year-old son taken fifty-seven years prior by her neighbor who was a professional photographer. Her family loved the picture but had lost their copy and hoped we could replace it.

Absolutely. She went home with the picture, a few signed copies of the book, a beautiful photo of the three of us at the Farm, and lots of hugs. After she left Kathy and I had one of those Casablanca movie moments: of all the store windows on all of the streets in all of New York she happened to walk by ours. Meant to be.

The sequels

Based on the book's success Running Press commissioned a sequel that Kathy and I envisioned as an empowering leadership book: *Change The Way You See Leadership*. The publisher felt the title should cast a wider net so it was changed to *Change The Way You See Yourself*. We stayed with the same hardcover format, reverse type cover (with a mirror-like finish) and dramatic, sequential inside the book visual experience. Kathy and I followed the same writing/development regimen and also included peoples' stories. One of the stories came to us from Hollywood.

Kathy and I were both fans of the movie *Akeelah and the Bee*—about a young African-American girl and her quest to win the national spelling bee—and wanted to reference its inspiring and empowering messaging in the book. Guess what? The producers of the film were Nancy and Sid Ganis—you know, "cousin" Sid, my friend and Sony client. I contacted Nancy and she gladly agreed to contribute and secure clearances for pictures. Nancy wrote about how the pursuit of her mighty cause, improving education opportunities for underprivileged youth, enabled her to get through the Hollywood maze of nay-sayers to produce this award-winning film.[10] Yet another example of past connections and positive bridges enriching today's life.

---

9. B&N Photos https://bit.ly/BNBookWindows

10. Nancy Ganis Story https://bit.ly/NGanisStory

Running Press published *Change The Way You See Yourself* in 2008. The Farm created About the Book and Meet the Authors videos for the website and four sixty-second commercials.[11] Kathy and I were the on-camera talent and we had a blast filming them. We worked as well on camera as we did on stage and writing the book. Our yin-yang chemistry was special. The blogging world was blossoming and Kathy and I also made the rounds of thought leader blogs evangelizing ABT and inviting listeners and readers to join the ABT "positive conspiracy."

While the book sold relatively well, it didn't have the force and drive of the original. Most sequels don't. Nevertheless, we covered the advance, earned some royalties, and broadened our ABT audience.

More than a third book

Kathy and I were working with Nigel Lemming at the Human Capital Institute on integrating ABT into their HR talent development programs. We received a note from his fifteen-year-old daughter Brianne telling us she had read her father's copy of our book and explained why it would be cool to have a book like this for teens. Brianne didn't realize that the seed she planted would soon grow into the third book in the series, *Change The Way You See Everything: For Teens*, and include her letter.[12]

A few months later, with Brianne's letter in hand, Kathy and I met with Kelli Chipponeri, the young adult book development editor at Running Press. We floated the possibility of the teen/tween book. She liked the idea, and we followed up with a detailed proposal, which Kelli accepted. We agreed the book would follow the same format as the prior adult book with one big difference: teens and tweens would be involved in the writing process and visual content creation. Working on this third book brought me the most joy and fulfillment.

Kathy and I spent a few months conducting interviews and work sessions with tweens and teens gathering input, insights, and ideas. It was eye-opening and fun. Creating visuals for the book was literally an extended family affair. My great nieces and nephews, grandson Lucas and his friends, Kathy's niece, and her friends' kids, our agent Denise's niece, Carol from McCann's three kids, and others contributed photos and stories. Kathy arranged a partnership with Build-A-Bear's Huggable Heroes program that recognizes outstanding teen community impact initiatives. We interviewed four of these inspirational, huggable teens and featured their stories in the book.

Over half of the visual content came from the kids. You've heard the expression "out of the mouths of babes." Well, out of the minds and cameras of teens and tweens came the most simply profound wisdom and creativity that blew us away. It was an awesome

---

11. Yourself Videos https://bit.ly/YourselfVideos

12. Brianne letter https://bit.ly/BrianneLtr

adrenaline-packed experience. We ended up co-creating a book for teens with teens and that was inspired by a teen. How good is that!

A youthful awakening

Then, a wonderful James Patterson synchronicity presented itself. The Farm was working on the launch of Jim's young adult book *Maximum Ride*, which featured Max, a fourteen-year-old girl with altered DNA that gave her wings and super powers. Jim agreed to let us include a spread with Max's ABT tips on how to deal with adversity and mad scientists. Very cool. And that's not all. Jim again wrote the foreword for the book sharing the advice he gave to his son Jack about the importance of reading books.[13]

Kathy and I greatly admired Jim's passion for instilling the love of reading books in kids through his ReadKiddoRead (RKR) outreach and we found a way to pay forward Jim's kindness. Kathy and I funded a "Mighty Cause" contest that brought together a positive convergence of people supporting librarians and their dedication to making young people readers for life: RKR, Nora Rawlinson's *Early Word,* an on-line librarian resource, and ABT. Our goal was to incite libraries and librarians across the country to start programs to encourage the love of reading among tweens and teens.

We received over fifty applications and selected ten finalists. Each finalist was given copies of our teen book for their libraries and a video camera to create a ten-minute video about their programs. The winner received a cash prize of $2,500 and a cache of books donated by Jim, Perseus books, and ABT. We received a wide range of videos highlighting the impact of reading on growing minds that is often taken for granted.

They all were impressive but one stood above the rest: South Carolina's Charleston County Public Library's (SCCPL) "A Captive Audience." It spoke to the importance of libraries and especially those librarians and teachers who look beyond the shelves to make a difference. Andria Amaral, SCPL's young adult services manager, worked with nearby Juvenile Justice Coastal Regional Evaluation Center in Ridgeville, SC, to set up a visiting library program for the teenagers incarcerated there. With each visit Andria and her staff brought new library materials to stock the facility's classroom shelves for use during in-class reading periods. She made sure there were enough to remain in the facility's cellblock pods so the residents also had reading material to fill their long periods of downtime.

There are few things more miserable than jail and Andria made it her mission to bring life and hope to these vulnerable teens. It had a huge impact on Kathy, Jim, and me. Jim created a personal video message to Andria and the teens.[14] Please watch this video.

---

13. Max, Patterson, Heroes https://bit.ly/MaxJPHeroes

14. Captive Audience: https://bit.ly/CaptiveAudienceVideo

The Farm created an interactive website (abtteen.com) with ABT superheroes, a blog and a teen version of the ABT alphabet bookmarks. My son Brian produced a video version of the ABT alphabet with his director friend Jon Sheide. They gathered a group of tweens and teens at John's house, set up a green screen, and let them do their thing. The kids helped write the script and performed wonderfully. It's a joy to watch and is filled with wisdom. I still use it in my speaking engagements.[15]

The teen book had a successful launch and both we and Running Press were pleased with its reception and sales. Promotion on the teen book stretched into the next decade and opened doors to wonderful collaborations with educators and youth advocates. Kathy and I said "howdy" in March 2004 and by the end of the decade we had published three successful ABT books, built a powerful business partnership, and developed a deep friendship. An *ABT* rifecta!

The long-tail of the teen book had a profound influence on my future outlook. It was the catalyst that brought a reinvigorated sense of purpose into focus and helped shape the direction of my next decade. I was now committed to mentor, motivate, impassion, and impact next generation leaders. I'd found my mighty cause. There I was, looking at the road ahead and knowing my destination. Now I had to select the routes I would take to get there.

Happy Farmer Wisdom

- Raise your professional voice early and confidently. Put yourself and your points of view out there. Visibility builds confidence and a stronger resumé.
- Expose who you are. Create provocations. Thoughtfully and respectfully share your expertise and insights. Then listen and be prepared to change your mind.
- Identify your personal "best places to work" criteria. Use them to select the environment in which you want to work or create when your opportunity arises.
- Pay it forward in any way you can. The "what" isn't important, the "why" is. Your intent and action will be appreciated.
- Move past not NIH (not invented here) to RBT (reinvented better together). New avenues open up when you embrace potentially confrontational situations with a make the most of it attitude.
- Join the horizon dwellers. Push yourself and your ideas to the horizon's edge and look beyond what everybody else sees.
- Test your risk/reward tolerance regularly. It's great practice for when

---

15. ABT Teen Alphabet https://bit.ly/ABTteenAlphabet

that bold, make-or-break idea presents itself.

- Turn rejection into resolve with a "you only need one" mindset. Bold new ideas are a hard sell. You really do only need one accomplice to say yes to get the ball rolling.
- Welcome to the Asset-Based Thinking positive conspiracy.

Marketing Truisms & Tips

Be the Master of Your Stories

Storytelling is integral part of human nature. We are hardwired for stories. The ABT book series leveraged the power of stories to bring ABT principles to life. In Chapter 11, I discussed the power of storytelling in marketing communications using the iconic Taster's Choice couples campaign as a best case example of episodic storytelling. Today's digital world of transmedia storytelling has exponentially increased the marketing power of stories as brand content. Just look at the popularity of Instagram and Facebook story tools. In his newsletter Seth Godin famously said, "Marketing is no longer about the stuff you make but about the stories you tell." I couldn't agree more.

The value and impact of stories, however, goes well beyond marketing communications. Heck, this book is all about telling my story. Story power can be integrated into virtually all of your communications across an array of outlets. From resumés and job interviews, PowerPoint presentations to podcasts, there are excellent storytelling tools, resources, and best practice guides available—including that improv class. Use them to help make your storytelling prowess integral to your persona.

Think of your storytelling persona as a choir of different story voices, each with their own pitch and tone and with you as the choirmaster.

Here are my five C's of stories:

> **Create:** When discussing things I've done I sometimes ask, "Do you want to hear the story behind that? Works every time. Your stories are yours alone to tell as often as you can.

> **Collaborate:** This is about the stories you develop and create with others, like Asset-Based Thinking and *CiNYC*, in my case.

> **Cultivate:** Plant your story seeds and watch them grow and share with others…my McCann story about Carol.

Coax: When people talk to me about interesting things in their life I turn the tables and ask, what's the story behind that? An empathetic connection and another story to add to my choir.

Curate: Collect and assemble stories that complement your persona and add them to your choir. Recognition of others adds another dimension.

Is that a chorus I hear?

"Stories constitute the single most powerful weapon in a leader's arsenal."
—Dr. Howard Gardner, professor Harvard University

Chapter 16 Footnotes
Scan QR codes for direct links to footnote content.

16.1 CF Best Places to Work

16.2 Monster Podcast

16.3 Ripon Forum/Bumper Sticker

16.4 AP Article

16.5 Aware Show

16.6 ABT Website

16.6 ABT Stories

16.7 CF Covers

16.7 CTWYSE Book

16.8 ABT Videos & Song CD's

16.9 B&N Photos

16.10 Nancy Ganis Story

16.11 ABT Yourself Videos

16.11 Yourself Book

16.12 Brianne Page

16.13 Max Spread & JP Forward

16.14 Captive Audience

16.14 Teen Book

16.15 ABT Tween Alphabet

Chapter 17

Answer Your Mighty Cause Call

Helping young people prepare for success has been part of my core since my mad men days teaching at Pace University: my "mini" cause. A few decades later, a convergence of factors and my Asset-Based Thinking mindset transformed "mini" into "mighty." I became dedicated to putting my experience, energy, and enthusiasm to work mentoring and motivating next generation business leaders. I answered the call of this mighty cause and it became my purpose moving forward.

The catalyst was a return to teaching after an almost fifteen-year hiatus. In 2010, I joined the University of Southern California's Marshall School of Business faculty as Adjunct Professor of Marketing. I was back! The west coast and USC became my central hub. Answering the call was easier when I recognized that it didn't necessarily have to dominate my life; rather, it would direct it. I orchestrated everything else in my life to complement my teaching and fuel my purpose. Here's how:

- Less Farm
- More American Heart Association (AHA)
- Fine-tuning My Voice
- ABT Appreciation

The pursuit of my mighty cause has made me a better person: more competent, more confident, and more content. It just goes to show…when you are patient, open yourself up, and listen you will hear your mighty cause calling. Answer that call. Then dive right in and enjoy the ripple effect you create.

The 2010s

The 2010 decade began in turmoil, with a global financial crisis and tepid economic growth in the United States. It ended with the US economy soaring and record low unemployment. There was a seismic political shift with the election of President Trump that ushered in a period of deep divisiveness in Washington, DC, and that seeped into the everyday lives of Americans.

The digital disruption that began at the end of the prior decade exploded into the digital transformation of business with marketing communications undergoing, arguably, one of the most dramatic changes. Here are some highlights. Technology opened up the information superhighway for everyone to travel at breakneck speed. Smartphones were now in everybody's hands and the internet of things became a very real thing. Cloud computing and 4G broadband completely changed the game. With the deluge of information made readily accessible, businesses pivoted to data-driven business models and shifted from an inside-out company perspective to an outside-in consumer centricity. The balance of power had shifted from the company to the customer.

The impact of social media as communication platforms surged. The Pew Research Center reported that from 2010 to 2019 global social media users rose from less than one billion to three billion and US adults using at least one social media site rose from 42% to 72%. With its acquisition of Instagram, the Facebook juggernaut ruled social media. Hashtag activism was born, influencer marketing came out of nowhere, and then along came Tik Tok. Automation, machine learning, artificial intelligence (AI), and augmented reality (AR) played significant roles in marketing's evolution. Media consumption moved dramatically to digital/mobile channels with explosive growth in streaming video and music. A mobile-first marketing strategy became the norm and expenditures and content shifted along with it. In 2019, internet media accounted for half of US ad spending up from just 15% at the beginning of the decade. Television, no longer the dominant medium, saw its 2019 share of spending fall to 27% vs 35% in 2010. Video, delivered across a multitude of channels, dominated the marketing communications landscape.

During this decade, I witnessed more substantive changes in marketing than in the forty prior years combined. The advent of TV was a watershed event in my mad men days, but the digital transformation has been an even bigger, seminal event. I'm fortunate to have been involved in both of these transformations.

Sadly for me, however, the decade began on a somber note. On December 11, 2010, (my son Gregg's forty-third birthday), my dear friend Irwin Warren passed away at age seventy-one. It was a big blow. Just three weeks earlier Irwin and I had lunch in New York making plans for his guest lecture in my USC class. He was looking forward to it. I miss Irwin and carry his memory and wisdom with me. When I review the Taster's Choice case history in my class (and this book) Irwin is there. Later in the decade another loss rocked my world.

But life goes on. It must.

Today is, without a doubt, the most dynamic, challenging, and opportunity-rich time I have ever seen in marketing. Seriously. It's because the consumer is in charge. Marketers have to connect with consumers like never before and in new and unconventional ways. Content marketing is being creatively reimagined and reenergized every day.

Am I excited about the future? You bet your bytes I am! Here's a link to a video I created for USC's 2019 incoming Master of Science in Marketing students that puts it all in perspective.[1]

---

1. Hank's Lecture: https://bit.ly/USCMSLext

Less Farm

The 2010 decade was a period of disruption, transition, and new horizons at the Farm. With *Cool in Your Code* winding down, our ABT books published, and Nestlé no longer an active client, my day-to-day involvement at the Farm lessened significantly. In 2012, Vicki and I decided to try a simpler life in the desert and moved to Palm Springs. It was close enough to Los Angeles (a two-hour drive) so we could see our son Brian and grandson Lucas regularly and I could commute to USC for the two days a week I was teaching. We're still enjoying Palm Springs life…even in the summer. It was a good move.

Now about the Farm: Disruption. As it goes in multi-partner businesses, shifts are something to be expected. By mid-decade we were back to five partners: Gregg, John, Griffin, Angel, and myself. Talented marketers, Blake Olsen, Ray Mendez, and Will Morrison had desires to try new ventures, and decided to blaze a different path forward. Angel Maldonado had been an integral part of the operations of the company since 2004 and a big contributor to the Farm's success; we all welcomed him as the newest partner. Will's exit hit me hard. In addition to my personal feelings for Will, I was disappointed that we were moving away from Farm-owned content development, but I understood and respected the decision. I learned from my DKG and Capstone experiences that business partnerships evolve over time. It's human nature and the nature of business, especially the agency business.

Next, Transition. Simultaneously the Farm went through what all agencies experience: the ebb and flow of client departures and new business wins. Our flagship client, BNY Mellon, now under new management, moved to a new agency. We gradually replaced that revenue with a mix of retainer and project work for an eclectic mix of clients:

Aruba Tourism	Empire State Building
Blueman Group	ESPNw
Bowlmor AMF	Margaritaville
Christmas Tree Promotion Board	Manhattan Mini Storage
Edison Properties	National Highway Safety Commission

The Farm continued delivering an impressive harvest of creative content during the decade and reaping top-notch creative and efficacy awards for ESPNW, Aruba Tourism, the National Highway Safety Commission "Stop the texts. Stop the wrecks," Campaign, which is still running to this day, and others.[2]

---

2. Farm Reel https://bit.ly/FarmRel

Probably, the Farm's most consequential win was Aruba Tourism in 2011. The Farm has consistently created breakthrough campaigns for Aruba that won an Effie award for effectives and bushels of travel and tourism industry awards.[3] Over the decade, the Farm became one of the most awarded agencies in that travel industry sector. They developed an impressive body of content that solidified the Farm's travel and tourism credentials and attracted other industry clients.

In 2014, *Ad Age* honored Concept Farm with its Northeast small agency of the year award. When the partners told me about it, I flashed back almost forty years to when DKG was named *Ad Age*'s 1975 agency of the year. That win was great but the Farm's award felt even better. As co-founding partner of the agency, Concept Farm's award was especially meaningful to me. It was a more personal "farm family" award that further validated the partners' founding vison and hard work. It was more emotional. That small agency of the year award was followed by the Farm being named to Enterprise.com's list of best agencies in NYC in 2017 and 2018. I was bursting with pride, admiration, and gratitude for what my partners had accomplished. Celebrating success and recognition is validating and uplifting. And over the years I've learned that it's equally meaningful and rewarding to observe and celebrate the success of those close to you. Treasure those moments.

As the Farm's credentials and client list moved toward destination brands (travel, tourism, and leisure time venues), the agency was producing acres of video content for digital and mobile platforms. We recognized that keeping content production in-house would provide more creative control, better outcomes, more efficiency for clients and additional revenue sources. The partners decided to recalibrate by focusing on this highest potential area of growth, scaling back tangential projects, and building in-house video and digital production capabilities. It was a very smart, timely plan that looked even smarter when the Farm's Silicon Alley lease came up for renewal in 2017.

New Beginnings: The Farm's landlord hit us with an exorbitantly large increase in rent, even by Chelsea standards. After fifteen years as a trailblazer in NYC's Silicon Alley, the time had come to pack up the wagons and move the homestead to smaller, greener, more affordable pastures. It was a wrenching emotional decision with big financial and workflow ramifications. We turned challenges into opportunities by seeking out affordable acreage in the up-and-coming creative hub in Long Island City, just across the East river from Manhattan. Then we made the bold decision to rent space that could be tailored to the Farm's new hybrid agency model and purpose-built for digital innovation, creativity, and "our fresh ideas harvested daily" mantra.

We leased an older building, a coat hanger factory in its prior life, and converted it to a beautifully designed open space facility that served as our office, production studio, and post-production facility. It had the same farm aesthetics and creative vibe. It was just a different

---

3. Aruba awards videos bit.ly/ArubaAwardsVid

borough...Queens! We moved in January 2018, officially launched our production facility, CF Studios, and the farmers got to work plowing new fields.[4]

By the end of the decade the Farm had transitioned to a hybrid creative content development and production company with renewed energy and a more focused business strategy. In July 2019, Concept Farm celebrated it's twentieth anniversary. It's been quite a ride since the start-up in Griffin's apartment, when there was no Facebook, Twitter, Instagram, Zoom, SnapChat, Linked In, WhatsApp, Pinterest, Reddit, YouTube, or Tik Tok.

My participation evolved into a long-distance advisory role and the other four partners are running it all with great success. I promote the Farm in my speaking engagements, media appearances, social outreach, and tap into the Farm's creative resources for my American Heart Association work and class content. It remains a successful synergy. I am one very happy farmer!

More AHA

My 2010 decade years with the American Heart Association have been a whirlwind of amazing experiences as enriching and edifying as any in my business career. The power, purpose, and magnitude of the AHA's expanded mission–*Be a relentless force for a world of longer healthier lives*–inspired me to do more. I became part of that relentless force by taking on national leadership roles, championing health initiatives, helping expand our relationship partner base, and serving on multiple committees.

So how did I get from a "banned" stroke commercial to all of this? Nancy Brown, CEO of the AHA is how. Nancy is an effective and inspirational leader right at the top of my best CEO list. She is a dynamo, capable of running any Fortune 500 company, and the AHA is fortunate to have Nancy at the helm. My attitude is simple. When Nancy asks me to take on a responsibility, I agree because I know there's a good reason behind the request and she has confidence in my ability to do it.

In 2010, Nancy and then-president Dr. Ralph Sacco asked me to take over leadership of the Stroke Association Advisory Committee that oversees the AHA's stroke outreach. Along with the chairmanship came appointment to AHA's national board of directors. The committee had traditionally been chaired by a medical professional and I would be succeeding Dr. Pierre Fayad. Honestly, I was intimidated. I asked, "Why Me?" and "Why Now?" Nancy and Ralph recognized that combatting stroke required a new holistic approach to drive awareness, education, and behavior change. They felt my knowledge of the AHA, marketing expertise, and prior NYC stroke experience made me the right choice. Again, good timing enabled opportunity. Their support and belief in me was the push I needed to be the first non-medical

---

4. Farm Pics: https://bit.ly/CFOffice   Farm Website: http://bit.ly/ConceptFarm

professional to assume this role.

My two-year appointment turned into a four-year chairmanship working with volunteer committee members and four dedicated AHA staff leaders: Meighan Girgus, Kathy Rogers, Laura Sol, and Meredith Nguyen. We built on the learning from the NYC stroke initiative to create a powerhouse national program that attracted funding from the private sector, and collaboration with EMT services, and the Ad Council. Here's a summary and some lessons learned.

Like most successful campaigns it was directed by smart strategy. We defined stroke as a continuum of three components expressed in simple, direct, and hopeful language. No gloom and doom.

Stroke is preventable, treatable, and beatable.
Together we can end stroke.[5]

We articulated the programmatic and communications context for each component. They were all connected.

Preventable: The prevention messaging for "heart" was the same for stroke so it was tweaked to encompass stroke with ancillary messaging and graphics: *Love Your Heart. Help Your Brain. Prevent stroke.*

Treatable: We simplified the symptoms message with a pneumonic device: Face Arms Speech Time.

Beatable: We aimed to improve stroke patient discharge education and advocacy for increased insurance reimbursement.

The Ad Council incorporated stroke into their public service outreach (PSA) and assigned Grey as the agency. Karma. Grey's CEO was my prior McCann boss and friend Jim Heekin. The AHA tapped into Grey's creative resources and I got to spend some quality time with Jim. Grey created a terrific multi-platform campaign around the idea of how body language can tell stroke victims and bystanders that they're having a stroke. The campaign launched in 2010 and is still running in various iterations today. I share this case history with my USC class as an example of solid strategic planning, a powerful creative brief, and inspired execution.[6]

When my chairmanship ended, the AHA team gave me a cool infographic going away card that chronicled our accomplishments. It hangs proudly in my house.[7]

Being on the national board and committees meant frequent trips to AHA headquarters in Dallas and interaction with thought leaders across the health care spectrum. It was inspiring.

---

5. ASA Video https://bit.ly/HankASAVid

6. Stroke Campaign https://bit.ly/FASTAd

7. Infographic Card https://bit.ly/HankCard

Again, serendipity intervened and reconnected me with Linda Gray. She was often in Dallas shooting the *Dallas* series reboot (2012-2014) and I introduced Linda to the AHA team. Linda came to one of our board meeting dinners and hosted an AHA contingent at the series premiere. It was a special evening and now the AHA had a new friend.[8]

Heart-healthy bridges

I worked with AHA strategic relationships officer Lyn Hughes on three projects that opened up past bridges and interesting collaborations:

Jenny Craig: A multi-million dollar program supporting Jenny's AHA-approved diet programs. It was the only company that passed AHA guidelines. Jenny was owned by Nestlé so it was also an opportunity to connect with past colleagues.

Subway: My friend and McCann colleague Tony Pace, CMO of Subway, was the driving force behind Subway's move towards heart-healthy menu items. Tony pioneered the first AHA restaurant menu food certification program. When the Go Red For Women Red Dress Fashion Gala needed a new sponsor Tony stepped in and saved the program. Tony was a CMO superstar and working with him again was a special treat. Tony left Subway in 2015 and we're still in touch.

Nintendo: Yep, Nintendo…a special convergence of volunteering, a past client, and Asset-Based Thinking. The AHA and Nintendo teamed up to introduce an AHA-branded Wii Fit gaming console as part of the AHA's active family play initiative promoting exercise and gaming. It was a comprehensive program that included consumer promotion, convening experts on how best to build activity into gaming and brand ambassador outreach. I learned a lot meeting with some of the best minds in gaming, fitness, and behavioral sciences, and played a special role in brand ambassador outreach. Nintendo launched a five-city event tour to motivate brand ambassadors to spread the AHA's healthy lifestyle message to their communities:

> Get Informed – AHA tools and resources
> Get Empowered – a motivational speaker
> Get Active – WiiFit game play

Nintendo hired me as the motivational speaker using my ABT motivational tools![9] Now that's what I call a positive convergence of serendipity and synchronicity. I also enjoyed showing the Nintendo team my Super Mario award and flashing back twenty-five years to when it all started.

---

8. *Dallas* premiere bit.ly/DalPrem

9. Nintendo Tour https://bit.ly/WIITour

Just before the end of my national board term Nancy Brown announced that I would be receiving the 2013 Gold Heart award, the AHA's highest volunteer honor.[10] *Wow.* That meant just as much as any Emmy. It also came with a bit of irony. My fellow recipient was Dave Josserand, who five years earlier had banned our stroke dating hotline commercial. We had fun telling that story at the awards dinner.

Same commitment, different coast

When my national board term ended, I joined the AHA Western States Affiliate board headed by EVP Kathy Rogers. In addition to the usual board stuff, I chair the AHA's national Corporate Relations Review Committee and am involved in two projects that line up with my youthful mighty cause: teaching gardens and teen anti-vaping initiatives.

Teaching Gardens: In 2010, the AHA teamed up with noted child-nutrition activist and philanthropist Kelly Meyer to launch the Teaching Gardens program. It's a hands-on learning experience that empowers students to become champions of change and promote healthier lifestyles to their families and school communities. Teaching Gardens is Kelly's mighty cause.

I was with Kelly and the AHA team for the launch of the first garden and again in 2012 when Kelly arranged a Teaching Gardens event in concert with Universal Picture's release of *The Lorax.* It was a star-studded event and Nancy Brown invited Linda Gray to join the AHA team attending the premiere—a big boost for the program and another nice reunion.

Since then, we've launched over 500 Teaching Gardens nationwide. In 2019, I attended the tenth anniversary celebration of Teaching Gardens at the Kelso school in Los Angeles. It was an awesome day with the kids and a tribute to the person that planted the seed: Kelly Meyer. In my spring class, I used Teaching Gardens for an in-class creative invention session and teed it up with a video I shot at the event. You gotta love the kids in the video.[11]

Teen Vaping Epidemic: This initiative drew me in immediately. The AHA was at the forefront of reducing the incidence of teen smoking from 25% in the '90s to about 7% by 2016. Then along came vaping. In the blink of an eye we were set back twenty years!

In 2018, 27% of teens were vaping. During the mad men days I saw firsthand how Big Tobacco hooked youth on cigarettes and was incensed that they were at it again. The Western States affiliate was at the forefront of California's aggressive stance on vaping and I participated with advocacy teams lobbying state legislators in Sacramento. I created a video to energize our team in this battle. In February 2019, the AHA launched a powerful, comprehensive program that exposed big tobacco's attack on our youth: #QuitLying.[12] Please get involved and help

---

10. AHA Award https://bit.ly/HankAward

11. Class Video https://bit.ly/TeachGarden, AHA website https://bit.ly/TeachGard

12. Vaping video: https://bit.ly/NoVapingVid, Quit Lying website https://quitlying.org/

win this battle.

My volunteer role with the AHA has enriched my life in many, many ways. I've certainly received more than I've given. My macro business learning is a deeper appreciation of the power of "mission." It's more than a statement about the company or brand. Mission is the guiding light for all activity and actions, the inner voice and conscience. In my class I sum it up this way: "Operate and compete like a business. Think and act like a not-for-profit." There is an AHA project, meeting, call, or event on my calendar every week. I love it and can't wait to see what the AHA has in mind for me in the next decade. Volunteer early and often and go wherever it takes you.

Fine-tuning my voice

While I continued with Asset-Based Thinking content creation and keynote speaking (more about that next) I also fine-tuned my voice courtesy of another serendipitous and synchronous ABT connection to a very special person, Erica O'Grady. It all started in June 2009, when a blog post Erica wrote about *Change the Way You See Everything* showed up in my news feed. I expressed my thanks in the comments section and we exchanged emails and phone numbers.

A few weeks later, Erica was flying to New York and sent an email inviting me to Jeff Pulver's first 140 Conference. Jeff's event was attended by a "who's who" of digital innovators and social media pioneers. At that time agencies were very skeptical about social media, concerned about its effect on their business models, and most saw it as passing fancy. Even a few of my farmer "pardners" felt that way. This was my opportunity to get an early peek behind the social media curtain.

Luckily, I was in New York, so I met up with Erica at the pre-event party and attended the conference the next day. Erica took me under her wing, guided me through the program, and introduced me to amazing people, including Zappos CEO Tony Hsieh. Erica became my social media mentor and put me on my path to reverse mentoring with some of the best: Jeff Pulver, Brian Solis, Scott Porad, Marla Schulman, Liz Strauss, Carol Roth, Chris Hueur, Mark Horvath, and others. Google them and benefit from their insights and thought leadership. Interestingly, that conference included a panel of Twitter users who built a big following by creating personas and avatars of the *Mad Men* show characters. Meeting them was the catalyst for creating my *Mad Man Confidential* series for Blogcritics. Inspiration can come from anyone…even avatars.

Hanging out with these iconoclasts and evangelists–the horizon dwellers–convinced me that social media was meaningful and would explode. I signed on to Twitter and in sixteen weeks racked up over 12,000 followers. Since then I've made it point to be an early adopter of new platforms in order to evaluate them for the Farm and be equipped to discuss and use them in my USC classes. I stay active on Facebook, Twitter, LinkedIn, and Instagram (my handle for all of of them is @hankwasiak) and occasionally drop in on Snapchat and Tik Tok. I also maintain two websites, hankwasiak.com and thewisdomguy.com with companion YouTube channels: HankWasiakTV and TheWisdomGuy. Managing my social presence requires disciplined time management to avoid getting sucked into vortexes that lead nowhere. It's been great training!

I was a guest speaker at five of Jeff's 140 conferences, attended influencer meet-ups and spoke at his SXSW (South by Southwest) conference panels.[13] There is never a dull moment with Jeff. From there one thing led to another. Here are some highlights:

- I published an article on Mashable: "How Social Media Has Radically Altered Advertising." My predictions were spot on and it generated thousands of shares.

- In 2011, I teamed up with *Ad Age* columnist Judy Shapiro to co-host a SXSW session we called "Has Facebook Jumped the Shark?" We had fun upsetting a few apple carts.

- Gail Goodwin, a positive thinking evangelist and creator of "Inspire Me Today," invited me to join her all-star team of luminaries. Using my ABT lens I created career development advice posts and podcasts.

- Jeff Hasen and I had a great discussion about branding on his podcast, "The Art of Mobile Persuasion."

- My friend Carol Roth, who is an author, TV personality, and cohost of CNBC's *Closing Bell*, interviewed me for her podcast. She titled my segment "The Modern Renaissance Man." I was flattered.

Early on I recognized the pervasive power of video and learned the basics of video content production. (It's so easy, even I can do it.) I love creating and have produced over 200 short-form "wisdom" videos for TheWisdomGuy YouTube channel. Here's the three "C" advice I give my students on how to spend their spare time: My 70/20/10 formula–70% Creating content you love, 20% Consuming content you love, and 10% Chillin'. Try it you'll like it. Links to all of the above are in the footnotes.[14]

---

13. Hank 140 Showcase https://bit.ly/Hank140Conf

14. https://bit.ly/MashSocialAdvtg https://bit.ly/FBJumpedShark https://bit.ly/HankInspiredLuminary https://bit.ly/HasenHankPodcast https://bit.ly/wisdguytv https://bit.ly/CarolRothRman

I also shared my points of view on broadcast outlets and conferences:

- Adam Shapiro invited me to be a guest on his Fox Business Channel show for a segment headlined, "What Will Happen To Madison Avenue?" Adam did a great interview and looking back on it now my commentary was largely on the money.

- Brian Solis, hosted the Pivot conferences in 2011 and 2012 and invited me to chair two panels: one with Dollar Shave Club's Michael Dubin (discussed in Chapter 13) and another, "From Impressions to Expressions," with two marketing heavyweights, Michael Donnelly Global Interactive Marketing director at Coca-Cola, and Marisa Thalberg VP Corporate Digital Marketing Worldwide at Estee Lauder. Attending the conference meant I'd be absent from my USC class so we streamed my panel discussion live to the classroom. Gotta love technology. Michael and Marissa were brilliant and the audience and my students gave them a well-deserved round of applause. I'm still in touch with both of them.

- My friend Jeff Hasen introduced me to Mario Schulzke, planning director at LA agency, WongDoody. Mario recently launched a thought leader platform, ideamensch.com and asked me to speak at his event at the agency. I titled the talk, "My Digital and New Media Rejuvenation" highlighting how ABT helped me deal with my advertising career changes. It was especially nice to be with a group of my agency peers.

Great advice and wisdom in these videos.[15]

At all these events I was THE oldest person in the room…and it felt great. I embraced my age and the more I listened and learned from my younger mentors the more they wanted to learn from me. We developed symbiotic relationships that fueled my mighty cause. Toby Keith captured how I feel and act in his song, "Don't Let the Old Man In." Great advice at any age!

"Ask yourself how old you'd be if you didn't know the day you were born."

These are just a few of the cascade of connections and capabilities that flowed from Erica's blog post. They profoundly influenced my digital renovation and intertwined with my mighty

---

15. Hank's speaking bit.ly/HankSpeaking

cause. Recently Erica described our connection as: Auspicious. Serendipitous. Divine. I added one more descriptor: Transformative.

ABT: focus, sorrow, and gratitude

My Asset-Based Thinking initiatives were focused in two areas. Keynote speaking engagements and teen outreach. Kathy encouraged me to get off my ASSets and "get out there" so I registered with All American Speakers booking agency and was hired for four speaking engagements. Kathy helped me craft an upbeat presentation that I tailored to each gig. It usually ran between thirty and forty-five minutes with slides that included visuals, graphics and video. No death by power point wordy slides from me! In addition to a nice speaking fee these keynotes were a great source of contacts and learning. I particularly enjoyed delivering the keynote at Experient's annual meeting. Experient is one of the world's leading event management companies. It was an opportunity to learn from people on the leading edge of designing and creating exceptional event experiences. The presentation was recorded for distribution on their network.[16]

Kathy and the Cramer Institute teamed up Lori Dixon, an educator and life coach, to create "Asset-Based Thinking in Action." Initially this initiative was focused on youth; we wanted to work with administrators, teachers, and students to integrate ABT into school learning programs. I embraced the cause and my son Brian and I helped Lori kickstart the program at the 2010 National Service Learning conference in San Jose, California. There were over 2,500 youth and educators exploring innovative approaches to service learning, education, youth leadership, and civic service. There was an amazing energy at the conference. Lori, Brian, and I worked our ABT in Action exhibit booth stocked with ABT Books and program materials. And there was a nice surprise: one of the Huggable Heroes featured in our teen book, Talia Hayden, was also there presenting her program, Random Kid. Meeting Talia and her mom was a special treat.

Brian and I roamed the halls asking teens to give advice to adults about service learning and videoed their responses. So much wisdom beyond their years! Lori continued with the program, worked with Kathy to broaden ABT in Action beyond youth, and made ABT an integral part of her coaching practice.[17]

In 2013, Kathy decided it was time to write the ABT leadership book she always wanted to create. In February 2014, Kathy's book, *Lead Positive: What Highly Effective Leaders See, Say and Do* was published by Jossey-Bass.[18] It received rave reviews and became another ABT power tool in Kathy's coaching practice. It's in my library and you should add it to yours.

---

16. Experient Keynote: https://bit.ly/HankExperient

17. NSL Conf https://bit.ly/HankNSLConf   ABT in Action https://bit.ly/abtinaction

18. *Lead Positive* https://amzn.to/3kboWTb

Then in early 2015, I received a gut punch call from Kathy that turned my world upside down. Kathy told me she was diagnosed with cancer. She chose to keep it private among close friends and in true Kathy style and tenacity continued working, coaching, and evangelizing ABT. Kathy and I continued with our regular catch-up calls. Kathy was making progress with her health and was her usual enthusiastic ABT self. Then on July 3rd, 2016, I received an unexpected call from Kathy's husband, John. Kathy had suddenly taken a turn for the worse and passed away. It is impossible (too emotional) for me to put my feelings into words or write her eulogy here. Kathy's family and colleagues have done that beautifully.[19] I said my final good-bye to Kathy at her funeral in St. Louis on July 18, 2016.

I lit up whenever Kathy called me. She always started our call with "Hi, Hank Wasiak. This is your pal, Kathy Cramer. What's up?" Kathy is gone but I often answer her call and hear Kathy's voice in my mind. We are still connected. I am eternally grateful for the gifts Kathy has given me and blessed to be part of Kathy's legacy.

Calling myself to action

A mighty cause is something that transcends volunteering—they can overlap but are different. Your mighty cause is a calling that's just right for you. You own it and brand it with your personal style and passion. Calling yourself to action in service of your mighty cause adds more meaning to your life. Once you commit you get an automatic boost. So, why do so many of us sell ourselves short, limit our aims, hesitate or let our cause fade or diminish?

All too often we hold ourselves back because we're intimidated by the depth and breadth of commitment required. I've experienced that pushback and it even happened over the eighteen months creating this book—which I see as a critical extension of my mighty cause to mentor and motivate next generation business leaders.

I often thought about calling it quits.

It's taking too much time.
I just can't write anymore.
Ugh, more publisher BS to go through.
Nobody will read it, so why write it?

You get the picture.

I had to channel Kathy Cramer and use my ABT lens of "self, others, situations" to focus, stay motivated and invested. And yet again, serendipity stepped in to help.

I started out creating this book with a confident you-can-do-this-on-your-own attitude.

---

19. Kathy's Eulogy https://bit.ly/RIPKathy

That didn't last too long. Soon after I began writing I realized I needed editorial guidance and assistance. Magically, I received an email from Danielle Goodman, the editor of Kathy Cramer's last book, *Lead Positive*, announcing her freelance book editing service. I'd never met Danielle but knew that Kathy held her in very high regard. Being on Kathy's A-list was all I needed to know about Danielle. She came on board and has been an invaluable resource, coach, and friend. Thanks Kathy.

My original plan was to self-publish and bypass the finding a publisher angst. Then someone I hadn't connected with for fifteen years, Jonathan Pilot, contacted me about a youth project he launched. During our conversation I mentioned this book and my plan to self-publish. Jonathan encouraged me to contact a boutique publisher he knew, JuLee Brand. I was skeptical but after a few conversations it was apparent that her company, W. Brand Publishing, was the "just one" publisher I needed and I proudly joined JuLee's cadre of authors. Along the way I've had countless chats with family, friends, past colleagues and students who urged me on. And Google was a constant companion.

Yes, you take the first step to your mighty cause, but rarely proceed alone. I certainly didn't. There's a mighty cause in you waiting to emerge and some may discover more than one over the course of their lives. Be confident there are allies and accomplices waiting to join you.

Happy Farmer Wisdom

- There is at least one mighty cause inside you. When it calls you to action, commit with confidence, jump in, and follow the ripples.
- Trust and listen to strong leaders. Their belief in you builds belief and confidence in yourself.
- Leap out of bed with your ABT vison turned on. Inspiration can come from anywhere. Be on the look-out for your Erica.
- Forget your birthday. Let what you see, say, do, and feel define your age and outlook.
- Energize the creator inside you. Give my 70/20/10 formula a try.
- When you take on big projects join Triple A: Be prepared to adapt your attitude and welcome allies and accomplices.
- Know that your voice adjusts itself with time and life experiences. Same voice, different timbre.
- The loss of friends and loved ones is always difficult, but it can also instill a lasting and profound sense of connection.

"Pursuing your mighty cause requires confidence and confidence takes courage. The confidence you wear on your face and the confidence you express through your body language, words, and actions are contagious." —Kathy Cramer

Marketing Tips & Truisms

"Operate and compete like a business. Think and act like a not-for-profit"
At the American Heart Association we're obsessed with mission. It drives everything. We recognize, however, that mission must evolve to reflect the needs of our constituencies, as you can see from our changing goals below.

1996–2006
Mission: Reduce disability and death resulting cardiovascular disease (CVD) and stroke.
Impact: Reduce coronary heart disease and stroke risk by 25% by 2006.

During that time, the majority of the outreach was directed to "fixing you when you're broken" and reducing deaths. Rapidly rising negative health and lifestyle factors such as obesity, sedentary behaviors, diabetes, and so on, in both young and old populations changed the game. And so, we pivoted our mission:

2006–2019
Mission: Build healthier lives free of cardiovascular disease (CVD) and stroke.
Impact: Improve the cardiovascular health of all Americans by 20%, while reducing deaths by 20%.

Our outreach was recalibrated to drive behavior change, promote well-being (mind, body, spirit) and touch younger constituents. We also redirected scientific research, professional outreach, programs, and fund raising in line with the new mission.

My AHA fundraising mantra is, "mission makes meaning and money." Rather than fixating on fundraising we fixate on delivering mission to market. Of course, there is a robust fund-raising apparatus behind these efforts, but they are directed and fueled by mission. The Corporate Relations Review Committee I chair evaluates corporate/sponsor relationships and the first criteria is always mission alignment. If the program is not aligned we pass on it regardless of the proposed amount.

This constituency-obsessed model and "serve not sell" mindset can be adapted and applied to any business. It opens minds and hearts to new thinking, builds value, and adds revenue.

Chapter 17 Footnotes
Scan QR codes for direct links to footnote content.

17.1 USC MS Mkt'g Lecture

17.2 TCF Reel 2010's

17.3 Aruba Awards Video

17.4 New LIC Farm

17.4 Concept Farm Website

17.5 Hank Stroke Video

17.6 FAST Campaign

17.7 ASA Infographic Card

17.8 Dallas Premiere

17.9 Nintendo Tour

17.10 Gold Heart Award

17.11 AHA Teaching Gardens

17.11 Teaching Gardens Class

17.12 Fight Teen Vaping

17.13 Hank's 140 Conf. Presentations

17.14 Mashable

17.14 Facebook

17.14 Inspired Luminary

17.14 Hasen Podcast

17.14 Wisdom Guy TV

17.14 Carol Roth

17.15 Hank's Speaking Showcase

17.16 Experient Keynote

17.17 National Service Learning Conference

17.17 ABT in Action

17.18 Lead Positive

17.19 Kathy Eulogy

Chapter 18

Leave a Legacy by Living Your Legacy

A "legacy" is passed from one generation to the next and is generally typified by gifts of money or property. I see a "personal legacy" as more multi-faceted, more than just financial assets. In the book, *Change the Way You See Yourself*, Kathy Cramer and I showed how Asset-Based Thinking can shape your personal legacy into a purposeful passing down of your chosen personal assets, like wisdom, values, skills, ideas, and so on. Consequently, what you are doing right now—today and every day—is building your personal legacy. By living your legacy you are leaving your personal legacy for those that come after you.

I've designed my living legacy around my mighty cause with teaching as the hub and driving force. Eighteen months ago, I added this book to my mighty cause plan and it's taken me in new and complementary directions. It just goes to show…when you live your legacy, life is invigorating, reassuring, and fun. You enjoy what you're doing more and you make sure that what you leave behind is much more valuable than the assets in your bank account.

Legacy catalyst

The invitation by Al Stefl to be a guest speaker in his Pepperdine graduate school class in 2009 was the catalyst that reawakened my zeal for teaching. I answered the call of my mighty cause by reaching out to the University of California Los Angeles' Anderson School of Management and the University of Southern California's Marshall School of Business. I didn't have any connections at either university so I sent a letter and resumé to each school's dean and followed up with a cold call. My cold call was met with a lukewarm response from UCLA and hot call back from Dr. Dennis Rook, marketing department chair at USC Marshall.

Dennis invited me to lunch at the USC campus and he and I connected right away. Dennis was also an ad guy turned academic (but with a Ph.D. and impressive credentials) and had worked at DDB so we had a few mutual connections. As fortune would have it, I reached Dennis at an opportune time. He was looking for an experienced adjunct professor to teach a graduate internet marketing class: MKT 556. After a great discussion, Dennis offered me the job and I said, "Hell yeah!" He connected me with the department administrator Elizabeth Mathew, and I was welcomed into the Trojan faculty family in rapid form. *Fight On!* Once again I was able to turn good timing into opportunity and optimism. I am extremely grateful to Dennis for his belief in me and opening the doors to USC.

Brave new world

Now I had to get ready to boldly step back into the classroom with a dramatically different cohort of students than those I last taught in 1995. These young minds were digital natives. I had to up my game and build curricula that reflected the new digital marketplace and classroom. I dove in head-first with a shift from threat to challenge. This was not a "have to" job but rather a "want to" joy. My guiding mantra was simple: I am privileged to be a USC faculty member and my total focus and commitment is to the students...in and out of class.

First, I approached each new class with the ABT attitude that "everyone starts with an A." Then, it's my and each individual's job to maintain it. Try adopting that mindset when beginning a new relationship. I'm willing to bet you'll like where it leads. Next, I outlined my strategic approach. The marketing core, the fundamental strategic building blocks of marketing communications, had not changed so I was very well-prepared from that angle. But the path to purchase and consumer dynamics were in constant flux, requiring me to be hyper-current and connected.

Fortunately, the Farm's digital prowess and the expertise of the horizon dwellers with whom I'd connected were assets I could tap into. I adopted new platforms, immersed myself in RSS (really simple syndication) feeds covering latest industry news and studied best practice white papers. It became glaringly obvious that marketing textbooks were outdated, heavy bricks compared to the fast-paced realities of the new marketplace. At first, I supplemented these outdated texts with real-time, ripped-from-the-headlines events and fresh guest lecturers. Eventually, I eliminated use of a textbook altogether. Instead, my students and I began creating our own each semester.

Mighty cause convergence

My USC classes are where my activities and actions converge and ultimately contribute to my mighty cause. Here's what I do in class:

- Integrate an American Heart Association project in the curriculum

- Apply relevant Asset-Based Thinking techniques into marketing practices

- Incorporate Farm case histories as best practice examples and assignments

- Bring in horizon dwellers as guest lecturers

My activities outside of the classroom are also a source of edification and gratification.

- I recently launched a *Mentor Wisdom* video series in which thought leaders create ten-minute videos sharing their personal career advice with my class: "Sage advice from today's leaders for tomorrow's stars." Highly recommended viewing![1]

- I volunteer as an advisor to student groups, participate in discussion panels, and encourage student conferences offering sane and sage career advice. Without question, these sessions make my day brighter.

- When Instagram introduced its longform video feature, IGTV, in 2018, I learned the platform and launched a documentary video series about my USC class called *Campus Chronicles*.[2] I preview my class lectures and stroll the campus interviewing students. To date, I've produced more than forty-five episodes—a "learn, live, and listen" trifecta. I learned a new platform, live, and share my class beyond the classroom, and listen as amazing students share their stories with me.

Beyond lectures

My digital native students are smart, savvy, and current. I leverage their assets by adopting a "learn together" stance. Each semester I set up a Twitter news room/hashtag (#hwusc) where students are "encouraged" to participate by posting relevant, current event material.[3] I start each lecture with a discussion of the newsroom content.[4]

One Twitter newsroom post inspired a lengthy and robust discussion around P&G's controversial "Best a Man Can Be" campaign for Gillette. I gave it thumbs down and our class debate and discussion compelled me to create and send a personal video message via LinkedIn to Marc Pritchard, P&G's Chief Brand Officer. In the video, I articulated my "ad guy" case as to why it missed the mark: #gillettefail.[5]

---

1. *Mentor Wisdom* Showcase https://bit.ly/MentorWisd

2. *CC* Trailer: https://bit.ly/CampusChronTrailer. *CC* YouTube https://bit.ly/CCChannelHank

3. By "encouraged" I mean participation factors into their grade.

4. Follow #hwusc on Twitter and join the conversation! https://twitter.com/hashtag/hwusc

5. #gillettefail video https://bit.ly/HWgillettefail

The campaign's biggest fails were its disconnect with the brand's heritage of celebrating men, offending its users (me included) by inaccurately depicting the vast majority of men as crass, ill-mannered lemmings, and its combative tone. Rather than stimulate a healthy dialogue, Gillette purposely started an argument. The students gave my ad critique a round of applause—maybe you will too. I also scheduled an invention session in which I recreated the brief and challenged students to reimagine the campaign. Some of their ideas were quite impressive. By the way, Marc didn't respond. That was disappointing.

These are the highlight marketing tips from my #gillettefail message that are especially relevant now.

- Embrace brand purpose as a sincere AWAKEning versus an opportunistic AWOKEning

- Live it on the inside before taking it outside.

- In Chapter 4, I discussed the linear path to purpose.

Meaningful Organizational Mission > Clear Brand Value Proposition > Sincere Brand Values Articulation > Purpose-Built Content Platform

This critical framework helps instill the "living it on the inside before taking it outside" culture essential for brand success. And I strongly recommend one last check before brands venture down the path to purpose. The people running the brand should do a long and hard "look yourself in the mirror" test. You must be absolutely sure you're not fooling yourself. If you're not convinced, hit pause, because consumers will smell it a mile away.

Fight On Family

My first class in 2010 has led to ten consecutive years of teaching in Marshall's graduate, undergraduate, and Executive MBA (EMBA) programs. I've taught eighteen separate classes and nearly 1000 next-gen students have passed through and enriched my life. One of my USC faculty role models is Dr. Diane Badame. In 2015, Diane was asked to head-up a new specialized masters graduate program, Masters of Science in Marketing. Diane asked me to contribute ideas for the program and invited me to join her and Dr. Dennis Schor on the admissions committee. This was a first for me. I was part of the genesis of the program and able to watch it grow and prosper, literally, student by student. In 2019, the program admitted fifty-two students from fourteen countries. In just five short years, the Marshall's MS in marketing is ranked in the top 20 by World University Ranking. Congrats and thanks to Diane.[6]

The family descriptor is often overused but it accurately captures my view of USC Marshall. I've been privileged to work with some of the University's best minds and talent under the dedicated leadership of Dean Jim Ellis. And perhaps the most gratifying part of the faculty family is the laser focus on our collective North Star: the students. That's our family bond.

Happy mentor wisdom

Each year, Diane Badame hosts a ceremony for the MS in Marketing graduates attended by the graduates, their families, and select faculty. I attend them and Diane asks me to provide words of advice to the students. I never pass up an opportunity to speak with students and addressing the graduates of this program is a special treat. In May 2019, I spoke to fifty-three program graduates. When I first met this class they were words on an application and a resumé. Now, I was looking out at them seeing the joy and excitement in their eyes. I focused my talk on the last word in their degree: "marketing." I included a top ten marketing check-point check list, parts of which have appeared in prior chapters. Separately, I created a video of the talk to share with other students.[7]

Here were the highlights:

"If you can dream it, you can achieve it."

This quote from Walt Disney is more than magical, motivational encouragement, in marketing today, it is reality. Along with that reality comes the responsibility to harness that potential wisely.

Here are my top ten tips to help you along the way:

1. The consumer is your North Star. Marketing is serving and selling.

2. Your first filter should be, "Is it right for the consumer?" Then make sure it's right for your brand or business.

3. Values-driven businesses and purpose-driven brands connect deeply with consumers...but only if they are genuine and sincere. You can't fake it.

---

6. MS in Marketing https://bit.ly/MSScienceMktg

7. bit.ly/MSCareerAdvice

4. Run and operate like a hard-nosed business but think and act like a not-for-profit.

5. Always choose positivity over negativity. Create positive provocations…What if _____? Fill in the blank with something specific and positive.

6. Forget perfection and pursue progress. Embrace risk. Be a prolific juggler. Fail fast, learn faster, iterate, and keep on moving.

7. Be a 5-to-1 Opportunity Advocate. Seize five opportunities for every one big problem solved.

8. Mentors matter…find yours and be one to others

9. Volunteer early and often…and be humble.

10. Never underestimate the power of a creative idea. It is the most important differentiating factor in marketing.

My overarching message is that your career should be focused on what is now! Make the most of every day. Pursue "want to" work rather than "have to" jobs and be amazed at how many paths unfold…no matter what life stage you're in!

I'll leave you by closing with this quote from a mentor of mine, DDB founder and visionary Bill Bernbach. It bears repeating.

"An idea can turn to dust or magic depending upon the talent that rubs against it."

Go out and be the magicians that people want to have around them. Surround yourself with other magnificent magicians. Make magic happen.

The last word

My Brooklyn "tree of life" mentioned at the beginning of the first chapter has strong roots and its four sturdy branches are blossoming. Most importantly, my family is doing well. Vicki and I are immensely proud of our sons and grandson and we're enjoying life. My career, albeit quite different from the Mad Men days, is still active as a happy Farmer "pardner" and advisor.

Kathy's legacy of ABT remains a vibrant part of my life. What started as my second career at Pace College in 1970 is now my first priority at USC. I'm living my legacy every time I step into that classroom, post on IGTV, or have a student conference. I can't wait for the start of my 2020 USC classes and to meet new next-gen stars.

Publishing this book is a big milestone for me and I'm looking forward to where the journey leads. I hope you will get as much value and satisfaction from reading this book as I did in creating it…fifty-five years of sane, sage advice from a Mad Man marketing guru still crazy about the ad biz.

So there it is. I am blessed to be living my legacy by design and pursuing my mighty cause with vigor and purpose. Bring on the 2020s. I'm looking forward to writing the next decade's chapter in 2030. The End…until then.

WAIT…stop the presses!

Okay, so this is how I originally planned to end the book, closing out the decade.

Then, 2020 happened. *Holy cow!* In farmer terms, 2020 simultaneously ushered in a drought, a plague of locusts, flash floods, tornados, and twisters. At the last minute, I decided to sow some ABT seeds of wisdom about how to make the 2020s the best problem you ever had. That's next.

Chapter 18 Footnotes

Scan QR codes for direct links to footnote content.

18.1 Mentor Wisdom Showcase

18.2 Campus Chronicles Trailer

18.2 Campus Chronicles Youtube

18.5 #gillettefail

18.7 MS Career Advice

Epilogue: Hindsight + Insight = Foresight

So, my original plan was to publish this book on July 5, 2020, a significant date for me because it was my seventy-seventh birthday. But the party pooper of the century COVID-19 pushed the pub date to January 2021. In the big scheme of things, it's a miniscule inconvenience.

To make the publication date, my final manuscript needed to be completed by October 31, 2020 (Halloween!). Here are my thoughts as of that date. Some of them scary, most of them not.

This pandemic is the real deal, a big deal. Unprecedented, tragic, and devastating are words we've heard and used to describe it, and they're all apt descriptors. The world turned upside down and there's likely not a human on earth that hasn't been impacted. Uncertainty is clouding pretty much everything, particularly the economic and business outlook. After the initial shock, I used my Asset-Based Thinking lens to see this problem (albeit a really, really big one) as a pause…a recalibration to make it the best problem I ever had. By no means am I trying to minimize what all of us are going through. Rather, I'm using my ABT sunglasses to focus, reflect and provide my perspective on how the current reality relates to what I've written in previous chapters. I've drawn on those insights to look ahead with positivity and purpose. If there ever was time that cries out for—hell, *demands*—Asset-Based Thinking, it's now. Especially in marketing communications. I am taking on the challenge of making this unprecedented uncertainty an ally not an enemy.

I've categorized and organized my thoughts in three buckets:

> **Now**–reflecting on the current environment and the effect on my mighty cause.
> **Next**–looking at macro factors impacting the future of marketing.
> **New**–using Asset-Based Thinking to create your future.

Now: Rising up to meet the challenge

Most business have already passed through and processed these following mindset changes and challenges:

> Denial: It may not be that bad…we'll be fine.
> Anger: My business model is being dismantled and destroyed!

Despair: This is just too overwhelming. Will it ever end?

Acceptance: It is what it is. We must adapt to survive.

The good news is that "these trying times" have helped strengthen the one business asset essential for future success: adaptability. Individuals and organizations have proven to be amazingly resilient, tenacious, and creative in ensuring their survival—more so than anyone thought possible. Here's a snapshot of that adaptability in action in each branch of my mighty cause tree.

Family

We are blessed that everyone is safe, feeling well, and adapting. We're also putting Zoom through its paces with regularly scheduled get-togethers and celebrations. You know what? They're a lot of fun and will likely remain a part of our family time. That said, like everyone else, we long for the day we all can get together for a well-deserved big hug. Personally, I can't wait to actually see other peoples' faces again. I really miss the smiles behind the masks.

Business: Concept Farm

COVID is having a significant dampening effect on the Farm's tourism and destination-focused business model as you might imagine. This vibrant, thriving, high-potential business sector that drove many of our strategic decisions in 2018 is now "on hold" and still struggling to get back on track. Fortunately the Farm's largest client, the Aruba Tourism Authority, has continued their partnership and the agency is creating a steady stream of content as Aruba smartly re-opens its borders to visitors. Other clients initially curtailed the marketing programs but some are slowly reactivating their plans.

We've weathered the initial storm by doing what virtually all small businesses have done: transition to remote work, make temporary compensation adjustments, and tap into government support programs. We're now back to a productive hybrid on-site/remote work regimen (which most likely will be permanent), closely managing expenses, and doing all we can to maintain the creative energy at the Farm. We also enhanced CF Studios with the addition of a COVID-compliant virtual studio. It incorporates Take2Production Technology which utilizes enterprise-level solutions enabling us to capture broadcast-quality content in real time, remotely, and safely from anywhere in the world.

The biggest challenge is that the prospect for near-term new business growth in the travel tourism sector is not bright. Our planning for 2021 and beyond will require a re-evaluation of core strategies, a renovation of business plans, and a re-assessment of personal priorities by each partner. The farmers have embraced big challenges before and I'm confident we'll make the right decisions.

Volunteering: American Heart Association

Virtually every aspect of the AHA's operations have been impacted by COVID-19—from research to healthcare outreach to advocacy and fundraising. AHA's leadership responded quickly and confidently to ensure that critical programs would be maintained while recalibrating operations to address a sharp decrease in fundraising. People with underlying cardiovascular issues are a high-risk population for COVID-19 and we've mobilized outreach and support to medical and healthcare professional cohorts on the front lines and scientists and researchers studying the virus.

Healthcare is one of the areas in which the trend of digital tools and resources (i.e., telehealth) has accelerated dramatically during the pandemic. The AHA convened industry leaders to make sure we stay at the forefront of these developments. When doctor and hospital visits precipitously declined due to COVID-19 fears, we initiated a public educational outreach, "Don't Die of Doubt," informing people about the importance of vigilance and action.[1]

A significant portion of AHA funding is garnered at live, participatory events: Heart Walks, Go Red For Women lunches, Heart Ball galas, and so on. The pandemic required an almost overnight pivot to virtual versions of these events, and the AHA stepped up in a big way. I've been involved in a few of these pivots and could not be prouder and more impressed by how the AHA staff and volunteers saved the day. These past few months have served as a constant reminder of the importance of devotion to mission, the awesome power of people rising to the occasion and "where there's a will there's a way" conviction.

Teaching: USC

My spring 2020 class started out strong and the campus was as vibrant as ever. Then COVID-19 decided to enroll and the campus locked down in March right after spring break. The entire university mobilized to make the transition to remote learning as smooth as possible.

It was my first time teaching online so I had a lot to learn fast. Fortunately, I had a great teaching assistant by my side guiding me every step of the way. Yongyu Tang was a lifesaver. The Marshall IT staff was also amazing, my students were supportive and helpful, and that now all too familiar phrase, "we're all in this together," became our new reality.

Here are two ways I made the campus closure the best problem I ever had.

---

1. https://bit.ly/AHADoubt

1. Flipping the class format. Since students were back home and spread across time zones from Seoul to NYC, my classes were now asynchronous; students had the option to attend class live or view Zoom recordings on their own time. To compensate for the challenges of serving these two audiences and to build deeper student engagement, I converted many of my sessions to a "flipped class" format. I sent students lecture material in advance so we could dive right into discussions about the content on Zoom. Less me, more them, better engagement. I will continue using this format when USC returns to on-campus classes. I'm also using this time as an opportunity to further hone my video creation skills to make my pre-recorded content more robust, interesting, and personal.

Another Zoom feature that I put to good use is break-out rooms in which students can collaborate on in-class projects and I can schedule impromptu group discussions. Zoom has proven to be, in some ways, better than a traditional classroom.

On October 12, 2020, I was notified that my Spring 2021 class will be online. There were forty-eight available "seats" and they were all filled up just two days after registration opened! I'm excited and ready to Zoom back to class on January 15, 2021.

2. Adopt A (Virtual) Intern. I also found one other way to bring my "mighty cause" to life. The pandemic basically wiped out the summer internships that a majority of USC students rely on, especially juniors. So, I created my personal Adopt a Virtual Intern program and sponsored three paid internships: two for of my students, Izzy Singer and Kaitlin Morris and one for my grandson, Lucas, who graduated from Sonoma State in February. These young, digital dynamos committed to working twenty-five hours per week for eight weeks and I set up Paypal accounts to compensate them for their valuable contributions. I placed Kaitlin in the creative department at Concept Farm, and Izzy and Lucas at the American Heart Association. They all performed exceptionally well, and I checked in with each of them every week for mentoring sessions. This was win-win-win for everyone, and I plan on continuing the program next year.

Next: Pause…then go to the edge

Now, businesses must look beyond merely coping and surviving in order to transform their business models accordingly. The businesses that don't will simply wither away. Here's my Happy Farmer approach:

1. Put yesterday in the rear-view mirror.

2. Assess and tactfully respond to the "must dos" directly on the road in front of you.

3. Make regular visits and glances to the horizon, where a safer, calmer, COVID-free world awaits. It will happen!

The view from the horizon's edge is a much clearer and energizing place from which to envision the future. But notice I didn't say "the new normal," which seems to be the meme of the moment. I'm not a fan of that perspective. "New normal" is a limiting static mindset; it implies settling into a dressed-up, new routine. But even before the pandemic, digital was transforming "normal" into a constantly in-flux reality. Playbooks were—and are—being updated or recreated every day. Post-pandemic, that in-flux reality will advance much faster so my advice is don't settle into any one mode of being too comfortable.

What's changed: a helluva lot and not very much

All businesses, from global behemoths to mom and pop local retailers, have been impacted by the pandemic. The disruption has affected ways of working, supply chains, revenue generation, value propositions, and, most importantly, serving customers. So, in the current "surviving" context a helluva lot has changed and, for the most part, organizations have adapted and risen to the challenge. But I believe that in terms of the key business drivers of a "thriving" future, not very much has changed.

Success will be continue to be driven by an acceleration and intensification of the best practices, adjustments, and trends that are already in play and discussed in this book. In many business categories, these trends have been turbo-boosted by three or more years (in healthcare, as much as five years). Post-pandemic success will test business leaders in different and, arguably, more complicated and layered ways. As such, moving forward cannot be a pivot backward to polished-up past practices. Leaders must think through multiple possibility scenarios specific to their business, develop adaptable strategic plans, and execute with alacrity.

I call it "anticipatory agility." There are some ABT tips on creating this future at the end. Here are the top ten accelerating trends on which to focus:

Consumer-centricity is even more essential. The consumer North Star is shining brighter than ever. A "humans at the center" mantra must guide all business activity. Humanity and togetherness will come back strong.

Renewed data-driven consumer insights are critical. Traditional consumer behavior has shifted rapidly during the pandemic and it is essential that marketers continually vet and update their data for both current and future accuracy. Data from just a month ago may no longer be actionable.

Personal "segments of one" targeting. Data about consumer behavior, values, and passion points are getting deeper, more granular, and are being sliced in an increasingly dizzying number of ways. Data whisperers who are experts at uncovering the insights that enable hyper-personalization will be what the Coca-Cola company has dubbed the "new messiahs."

Mission and purpose have never mattered more. Staying true to your core remains paramount. Your brand's values and how they are articulated both internally and outward-facing to the consumer, should be revisited, reaffirmed, and refined as needed.

Culture currency has increased in value. The challenge will be maintaining the important human connection among employees while adapting to a more prevalent, flexible, hybrid workplace. The transition "back" will require more finesse, adjustability, and a deft personal touch.

Streamlined omni-channel business models. The move to e-commerce and direct-to-consumer business models (DTC) continues across an even broader array of categories. Seamless channel hand-offs are critical.

Brand humanization. Empathetic, personalized messaging and connection are a must. But, it must move past the brand comfort of "we're all in this together" to the brand conviction of "here's how we are serving you."

Digital/mobile-first delivery. Boosted by the power of 5G, the digital-first migration has shifted into hyper-drive and expanded into every aspect of business. Companies must smartly and aggressively realign their priorities accordingly and be adept at turning "high-tech" into "high-touch" in quick manner.

24/7 creative content delivery. The democratization of content creation and delivery has opened the opportunity floodgates for marketers. Barriers to creating steady streams of quality video content have been torn down. Companies that encourage and empower employees as responsible creative assets will reap the rewards.

Big idea ninjas and creative magicians will take the spotlight.

New: ABT the way you see the future

In *Change the Way You See Yourself,* Kathy Cramer and I challenged the conventional wisdom of seeing the future with Asset-Based Thinking. What we wrote back then is especially relevant now.

Conventional Wisdom	Asset-Based Thinking
The future...	
Is tomorrow	Is today
Is uncertain and daunting	Is expansive and inviting
Should be planned	Should be rehearsed
Can be predicted	Can be created

Our conventional way of thinking is to divide our imaging and planning into three categories: past, present, and future. Then, we structure our thinking and actions relative to each time zone: We remember the past, attend to the present, and envision the future. Asset-Based Thinking collapses these boundaries allowing you to focus on all of them simultaneously through the narrative power of storytelling and the visual impact of storyboarding.[2] Here's how it works in two short steps.

1. Tap into what is going on with yourself, the others around you, and the situation you find yourself in. (Self, Others, and Situations)

2. Create and tell yourself specific stories about the future you most desire as if it all has already happened. That story becomes a memory and a vision all at once. Dig deep, see yourself as an adventurer, and be the author and producer of the future you most want so you can "live it" right now. Have a dress rehearsal of your adventure story by following the techniques of great storytellers and using the visioning tools of moviemakers.

That's it! It's invigorating, fun, and surprisingly easy to do. To help, I've included a link in the footnotes to specific ABT methods detailed in our book.[3] Give it a try.

Yep, these are trying times, but they are not immutable times. The future may seem like a blurry dot in the distance, but it's actually beginning right now—just a split second away. I'll close my journey of this book with wonderful advice from one of the last century's great humorists and salutations from one of the future's most profound thinkers.

"I look to the future because that's where I'm going to spend the rest of my life."
—George Burns (said at age eighty-seven…he passed away in 1996 at age 100!)

"Live long and prosper."
—Spock (1st officer and senior science officer, Starship Enterprise)

---

2. A storyboard is a graphic representation of how the narrative of a video unfolds, scene by scene.

3. ABT Storyboarding tips https://bit.ly/FutureStoryBoard

Epilogue Footnotes

Scan QR codes for direct links to footnote content.

Epilogue 3 Future Storyboard

Acknowledgements

Writing this book has been a cathartic eighteen-month journey with occasional detours of apprehension and the constant fuel of appreciation. To push aside apprehension and stay on-track I constantly reminded myself that I wasn't writing this book for me; it is a "live my legacy" gift to next-generation leaders.

A persistent stream of remembering, reliving and revival, my appreciation for the love and support from family, friends, colleagues, and students grew while creating this book. As you can imagine, over a career of fifty-five years there are many, many people that influenced my life and I've mentioned a number of them in this book. I'll use these acknowledgement pages to pay some special recognition. No surprise, I've approached it through an Asset-Based Thinking lens to create my personal G.A.P. analysis.

> Gratitude for peoples' love, support, influence, and inspiration
> Appreciation for the bounty and blessings life and living have to offer
> Perspective for which values and priorities are most important

So, here goes.

Appreciation, admiration, and profound love to my wonderful family for always being there for me. Always! To my wife Vicki, our family's loving rock, nourishment, and *consigliere*. To Brian for his strength, resilience, optimism, and our grandson Lucas. To Gregg for his steadfast, steady perspective, big heart, and omni-present wit and humor. To Jason for being the rebel, pioneer, and creative explorer who pushes our boundaries. To Lucas, our family's joy and love, who inherited our collective best qualities. Lucas's positive "always up" demeanor and wisdom beyond his years inspires us and impresses everyone he meets. Our future is bright! When Lucas says, "Grampy, I love you very much," my heart skips a beat.

Gratitude, love, and respect to the first family I knew: my dad Henry, my mom Josephina, older brother Ken, and younger sister Ginny. Mom and dad set each of us on the right path to our respective futures and we truly are beneficiaries of our "greatest generation's" values and sacrifices. I look on in admiration at how both Ken and Ginny prospered and raised their own great families. Our family tree, planted in Brooklyn, stands proud, sturdy, and tall.

I am forever grateful to my Concept Farm "pardners" for creating an amazing company and providing the fertile fields that spawned my second time around. Thanks Will Morrison, Griffin Stenger, John Gellos, Angel Maldenado, and Gregg Wasiak for twenty years of rebirth, rejuvenation, and rewards. You are the cream of the crop.

Eternal gratitude to my dear friend and positivity co-conspirator, Kathy Cramer, for her life-changing gift of Asset-Based Thinking. Her spirit and infectious enthusiasm live on in everything I do.

Heart-felt appreciation to Nancy Brown and my American Heart Association friends and colleagues for opening their hearts, inspiring me with their passionate mission, and providing the platform for me to add more purpose and meaning to my life.

"Fight On" gratitude to my USC colleagues and friends for welcoming me into the Trojan family and providing the opportunity to continue with my second career. Special thanks to four great marketing department chairs—Dennis Rook, Gary Frazier, Joe Nunes, and Anthony Dukes—and the support of department administrator Elizabeth Mathew.

A+ grades of gratitude to all my students—past, present, and future—for being a source of inspiration as I aspire to be my very best in the classroom. Their inquisitive minds, zest for life, and passionate pursuits keep me focused on the future and rejuvenate my youthful spirit. It is an honor and privilege to live my legacy with them.

Appreciation and admiration to my horizon-dweller friends and mentors for teaching an old Mad Man new tricks. Special thanks to Erica O'Grady, Jeff Pulver, Brian Solis, Chris Brogan, and Jeff Hasen.

Daily gratitude to all those wonderful nurturing Mad Men mentors, like Sid Lerner, Tom Griffin, Roy Bostock, Derrick O'Dea, Irwin Warren, Shep Kurnit, and Neil Calet. They imparted their wisdom and guided me on the path to a rich, adventure-filled career. The cascade of invaluable business experiences, connections with inspiring leaders, and amazing creative talent that flowed from those beginnings could fill a book. And they did!

Special appreciation and gratitude to the talented people who helped bring this to book to life:

> Danielle Goodman, my developmental editor, was Kathy Cramer's special gift. Danielle has been by my side every step of the way coaching, encouraging, and keeping me on track. She has a special ability to stimulate better writing and make my words count and come alive. Danielle's positivity, lessons taught, and friendship are enduring assets that will continue to enrich my life.

Caroline Teagle Johnson, an imaginative designer, for creating a special cover that captures the essence of my story and for crafting the book's pages into a beautifully simple and inviting format.

Kerin Smith, a resourceful and talented web designer, who created the companion website that brings this book to life as a rich and engaging digital experience.

Yongyu Tang, my invaluable teaching assistant, who managed my ever-changing footnote references, created all the QR codes, and spruced up my word documents.

JuLee Brand, W. Brand Publishing, for her belief in this book and bringing it to fruition. JuLee provided encouragement and a hassle-free hybrid publishing platform purpose-built for this book.

Finally, my respectful gratitude to the good ole "US of A" for making it possible for me to live my American dream for seventy-seven years.

HANK WASIAK is a communications industry leader with an impressive resumé of experience working with the corporate elite of global business. He is co-founder of Concept Farm, an award-winning digital agency, an author, Emmy-award winner, keynote speaker, university professor, and a Reiki master. Hank's professional journey began in the Mad Men era at Benton & Bowles and took him to and through the corporate boardrooms of the ad world's biggest names. He learned from the best in the business to become the best in the business.

Hank retired as Vice Chairman of McCann WorldGroup and served on that company's board playing an integral role in the management of McCann's global clients. Hank was president of Geers Gross Advertising and Ketchum Communications. He also had a stellar career on the client side as President of Brown-Forman's Jos. Garneau Division, COO of Somerset Importers, and EVP of Charles of the Ritz. Hank currently serves on multiple boards of the American Heart Association.

Hank teamed up with Dr. Kathryn D. Cramer, Ph.D., to create an innovative business and self-help book series published by Running Press: *Change The Way You See Everything*, *Change The Way You See Yourself*, and *Change The Way You See Everything – For Teens*. Hank was executive producer and host of Concept Farm's Emmy award-winning TV show, *Cool In Your Code* and won three New York Emmys for his on-camera performances.

Hank has had extensive experience teaching marketing at a number of prestigious universities including Pace University, Eckerd College, University of South Florida, and the University of Louisville. He is currently an adjunct professor at the University of Southern California's Marshall School of Business.

Hank earned a bachelor's degree in advertising from Pace University and an MBA in marketing from the Lubin School of Business of Baruch College. He resides in Palm Springs, California.

www.hankwasiak.com,
www.thewisdomguy.com

nformation can be obtained
ICGtesting.com
in the USA
062119120621
97LV00016B/375

9 781950 385485